CONSTITUTIONS IN AUTHORITARIAN REGIMES

Constitutions in authoritarian regimes are often denigrated as meaningless exercises in political theater. Yet the burgeoning literature on authoritarian regimes more broadly has produced a wealth of insights into particular institutions such as legislatures, courts, and elections; into regime practices such as co-optation and repression; and into non-democratic sources of accountability. In this vein, this volume explores the form and function of constitutions in countries without the fully articulated institutions of limited government. The chapters utilize a wide range of methods and focus on a broad set of cases representing many different types of authoritarian regimes. The book offers an exploration into the constitutions of authoritarian regimes, generating broader insights into the study of constitutions and their functions more generally.

Tom Ginsburg is the Leo Spitz Professor of International Law at the University of Chicago, where he also holds an appointment in the political science department. He is also a member of the American Academy of Arts and Sciences and a research professor at the American Bar Foundation. He holds B.A., J.D., and Ph.D. degrees from the University of California at Berkeley. He currently codirects the Comparative Constitutions Project, an NSF-funded data set cataloging the world's constitutions since 1789. His recent coauthored book, *The Endurance of National Constitutions* (2009), won the best book award from the Comparative Democratization Section of the American Political Science Association. His other books include *Judicial Review in New Democracies* (2003), *Administrative Law and Governance in Asia* (2008), *Rule by Law: The Politics of Courts in Authoritarian Regimes* (with Tamir Moustafa, 2008), and *Comparative Constitutional Law* (with Rosalind Dixon, 2011). Before entering law teaching, he served as a legal advisor at the Iran-U.S. Claims Tribunal, The Hague, The Netherlands, and he has consulted with numerous international development agencies and governments on legal and constitutional reform.

Alberto Simpser is Assistant Professor of Political Science at the University of Chicago. His research focuses on the topics of electoral manipulation, election monitoring, mechanisms of authoritarian political control, redistributive spending, subnational governance, and corruption. His book, *Why Parties and Governments Manipulate Elections: Theory, Practice, and Implications* (2013), is a comparative study of the incentives underpinning electoral manipulation, with broad regional focus. Professor Simpser has been Research Fellow at the Center for Globalization and Governance at Princeton University and National Fellow at the Hoover Institution at Stanford University. He holds a B.Sc. from Harvard College and a Ph.D. in political science and an M.A. in economics from Stanford University. He is a native of Mexico City.

COMPARATIVE CONSTITUTIONAL LAW AND POLICY

Series Editors:

Tom Ginsburg
University of Chicago

Zachary Elkins
University of Texas at Austin

Ran Hirschl
University of Toronto

Comparative constitutional law is an intellectually vibrant field that encompasses an increasingly broad array of approaches and methodologies. This series collects analytically innovative and empirically grounded work from scholars of comparative constitutionalism across academic disciplines. Books in the series include theoretically informed studies of single constitutional jurisdictions, comparative studies of constitutional law and institutions, and edited collections of original essays that respond to challenging theoretical and empirical questions in the field.

Volumes in the Series:

Comparative Constitutional Design edited by Tom Ginsburg (2012)

Consequential Courts: Judicial Roles in Global Perspective edited by Diana Kapiszewski, Gordon Silverstein, and Robert A. Kagan (2013)

Constitutions in Authoritarian Regimes edited by Tom Ginsburg and Alberto Simpser (2014)

Constitutions in Authoritarian Regimes

Edited by
TOM GINSBURG
University of Chicago
ALBERTO SIMPSER
University of Chicago

CAMBRIDGE
UNIVERSITY PRESS

CAMBRIDGE
UNIVERSITY PRESS

University Printing House, Cambridge CB2 8BS, United Kingdom

Cambridge University Press is part of the University of Cambridge.

It furthers the University's mission by disseminating knowledge in the pursuit of education, learning and research at the highest international levels of excellence.

www.cambridge.org
Information on this title: www.cambridge.org/9781107663947

First published 2014
Reprinted 2014

A catalogue record for this publication is available from the British Library

Library of Congress Cataloguing in Publication data
Constitutions in authoritarian regimes / Tom Ginsburg, University of Chicago; Alberto Simpser, University of Chicago.
pages cm. – (Comparative constitutional law and policy)
Includes bibliographical references and index.
ISBN 978-1-107-04766-2 (hardback)
1. Constitutional law. 2. Authoritarianism. I. Ginsburg, Tom, editor of compilation. II. Simpser, Alberto, 1971– editor of compilation.
K3165.C63 2013
342–dc23 2013030082

ISBN 978-1-107-04766-2 Hardback
ISBN 978-1-107-66394-7 Paperback

Contents

List of Contributors

Michael Albertus is Assistant Professor of Political Science, University of Chicago.

Zachary Elkins is Associate Professor of Government, University of Texas at Austin.

Jennifer Gandhi is Professor of Political Science, Emory University.

Tom Ginsburg is the Leo Spitz Professor of International Law and Ludwig and Hilda Wolf Research Scholar, University of Chicago Law School; Research Professor, the American Bar Foundation; and Professor of Political Science, University of Chicago.

Henry E. Hale is Professor of Political Science, George Washington University.

David S. Law is Professor of Law, Washington University in St. Louis.

James Melton is Postdoctoral Fellow, IMT Institute for Advanced Studies, Italy.

Victor Menaldo is Assistant Professor of Political Science, University of Washington, Seattle.

Gabriel L. Negretto is Associate Professor, Division of Political Studies, CIDE.

Adam Przeworski is Carroll and Milton Petrie Professor of European Studies and Professor of Politics and Economics, New York University.

Alberto Simpser is Assistant Professor of Political Science, University of Chicago.

Kristen Stilt is Professor of Law and Professor of History, Northwestern University.

Mark Tushnet is William Nelson Cromwell Professor of Law, Harvard Law School.

Mila Versteeg is Assistant Professor of Law, University of Virginia.

Xin He is Professor, School of Law, City University of Hong Kong.

1

Introduction

Constitutions in Authoritarian Regimes

Tom Ginsburg and Alberto Simpser

An old Soviet joke has it that a man goes into a restaurant and surveys the menu. "I'll have the chicken," he says, only to be told by the waiter that the restaurant is out of chicken. He asks for the beef, only to be told the same thing. Working his way through the menu, he is repeatedly told that the restaurant is out of the selected dish, until he gets upset and says, "I thought this was a menu, not a constitution." The joke captures the usual perception of dictatorial constitutions as meaningless pieces of paper, without any function other than to give the illusion of legitimacy to the regime.

But this view raises a puzzle. Formal written constitutions are ubiquitous features of modern nation-states and are found as often in autocracies as in democracies. Furthermore, they are costly to adopt, consuming significant political energy and time. Stalin, along with many Soviet elites, played a direct role in drafting the 1936 Constitution and took the process quite seriously (Getty 1991: 22). The seventeen years required to draft the recent constitution of Myanmar may have been exceptional, but there is no doubt that some authoritarians spend political effort on constitution making. Why would they bother to do so if the documents are meaningless? The standard answer that the constitution is a legitimating device begs the question: How can an obvious sham document generate any legitimacy?

This volume of essays begins to attack this puzzle. Authoritarian regimes have been the subject of a burgeoning literature in recent years, as scholars have recognized that dictatorship is an internally heterogeneous category (Levitsky and Way 2002; Schedler 2006). This work has produced a wealth of insights into particular institutions, such as legislatures, courts, and elections; into regime practices such as co-optation and repression; and into nondemocratic sources of accountability. Yet there has, to date, been relatively little work on authoritarian constitutions per se outside of individual country case studies (e.g., Barros 2002). We have very little understanding of the logics and dynamics of constitutional design and practice in countries that have "constitutions without constitutionalism" (Murphy 1993;

Okoth-Okendo 1993). Such countries have the form of a constitution, but without fully articulated institutions of limited government. It is our hope that an exploration into constitutions in these countries can not only provide insights into the regime practices of authoritarians but also generate broader insights into the study of constitutions and their functions more generally. The chapters here, which utilize a wide range of methods and focus on a broad set of cases representing many different types of authoritarian regimes, provide a good deal of material for this inquiry.

This introductory chapter advances and unpacks the idea that authoritarian constitutions cannot be dismissed – that they matter. With this goal in mind, we consider three overlapping questions: What do authoritarian constitutions do? How do they work? And why are they adopted in the first place? Consider the first question: What are the functions of authoritarian constitutions? In other words, what problems do such constitutions solve? Generic problems of governing seem to be paramount. We devote a section of this introduction to the role of authoritarian constitutions in mitigating such problems, and in incentivizing different parties to do what authoritarian rulers wish them to do.

Three important subcategories of problems include the challenges of coordinating multiple actors, controlling subordinates, and eliciting cooperation from subjects. As the literature has suggested, constitutions can help authoritarian rulers meet these challenges, in some cases by increasing the ruler's control and in others by tying the ruler's hands. Somewhat more generally, as the contributions in this volume suggest, authoritarian constitutions perform a variety of functions that can be grouped into four categories that we designate as operating manual, billboard, blueprint, and window dressing. We devote a section of this chapter to elaborating on these functions.

The claim that authoritarian constitutions matter raises the question of why they are efficacious, and this is the second question we consider in this introduction: If authoritarian rulers are above the law, why and how can constitutions make a difference? We explore several mechanisms. First, authoritarian constitutions can help oligarchic actors to work together by establishing focal points, procedures, and institutions, thereby addressing problems of coordination and problems of commitment. Second, constitutions may have normative properties that confer upon them a certain independent force, even in the context of authoritarian rule. Constitutions may function as "hallowed vessels," meaning that their contents, by virtue of being part of a document called the "constitution," enjoy special public visibility and a privileged normative status. Such status, we argue, becomes especially important during moments of intra-elite conflict or of regime crisis. Authoritarian constitutions also influence the contours of permissible and impermissible discourse. Finally, as Albert Hirschman (1986) suggested about the law in general, constitutions can influence the values of citizens over time.

But understanding the functions of authoritarian constitutions and the mechanisms underpinning them does not suffice to explain why such constitutions are written or changed, or to account for the specific provisions that are adopted. Even when constitutional framers are strategic, they are not omniscient. Moreover, even authoritarian constitutions often reflect processes of collective choice among elites with divergent interests. Therefore, despite the fact that authoritarian rulers enjoy more discretion than their democratic counterparts in deciding when and how to draft a constitution, it may be incorrect to assume that authoritarian constitutions reflect optimizing behavior on the part of a unitary ruler. Thus, it is necessary to entertain the possibility that the reasons that constitutions are adopted may frequently differ from the roles that constitutions play, especially over the long run. Why, then, are authoritarian constitutions written? A variety of motivations exist. In some cases, the process of constitution making may be valued in itself, independent of any short-term or long-term consequences that specific constitutional provisions may have. We return to these issues in the penultimate subsection of this chapter. We end the chapter with a brief discussion of the lessons about authoritarian constitutions that derive from the chapters of this volume and of directions for further research.

CONSTITUTIONS AS SOLUTIONS TO PROBLEMS OF GOVERNING

Constitutions have a wide array of functions, and some of these functions are likely to be shared across both authoritarian and democratic regimes. A very central function of formal rules including constitutions is simple coordination. All regimes need institutions and need to coordinate on what institutions will play what role. Laying out the structures of government facilitates their operation because it prevents continuous renegotiation. A written constitutional text can thus minimize conflict over basic institutions for any regime. Furthermore, we know that certain institutions can facilitate coordination within the core of the governing elite itself. Robert Barros's (2002) study of the Chilean constitution under Augusto Pinochet documents how the constitution, especially the Constitutional Tribunal, facilitated coordination among the various military branches that composed the junta. Coordination, then, is a ubiquitous need of government that can be facilitated by formal written constitutions, facilitating elite cohesion.

Authoritarian constitutions also can facilitate coordination by *democrats* at crucial moments of transition. When Zine el Abidine Ben-Ali of Tunisia fled his country in the Arab Spring of 2011, his prime minister briefly took over as president in defiance of the constitution. After several hours, it was decided that the formal provisions of constitutional succession should be followed, leading to the president of the Chamber of Deputies, Fouad Mebazza, taking office as a caretaker before elections could be organized. This simple coordination function can become extremely important at the end of authoritarian regimes, preventing conflict from spiraling out of control over basic institutions.

Other "standard" constitutional functions may also operate in both dictatorships and democracies. We know, for example, that constitutions help address problems of intertemporal credibility by making commitments endure across time. While authoritarians and democrats may differ in the precise character of the commitments they wish to undertake, the basic modality of entrenching certain policies to enhance credibility may be useful to all leaders. Military authoritarians, in particular, may use the opportunity of a constitution to set a timeline for a return to civilian rule, as well as the terms under which such a return may take place. Announcing such a project will raise the costs of violating the text of the constitution and may also facilitate a period of "legitimate" authoritarian rule.

Constitutions may also be useful to set up institutions to control lower-level agents. All regimes need mechanisms to control agents, and the problem of gathering information on the activities of agents is an enduring one. There are many standard solutions to the problem: hiring a second agent to monitor the first (or otherwise improving detection and increasing punishment), selecting agents for loyalty and affinity, structuring systems of hierarchical appeal to higher-level agents, and creating a powerful ideology that is internalized by the agents themselves so that they self-monitor. Historical examples of government solutions to the agency problem include the imperial Chinese institution of the censorate, a separate branch of government to monitor the bureaucracy. This solution, however, creates the standard problem of "who guards the guardians?" Imperial China was also an early pioneer in the hierarchical approach to the agency problem, utilizing what eventually became known as a Weberian bureaucracy with higher levels supervising those lower down. Max Weber celebrated it as the most technically efficient of government structures, but it is costly and creates its own problems of information flow. It also requires careful ex ante screening of potential agents to ensure loyalty. Ideology is another tool to enhance loyalty, and it is favored by some mass political parties and religious institutions such as the Catholic Church. It is difficult to sustain, though very effective when it is in high operation.

Jean Bodin, in *The Six Books of the Republic* (1576), was one of the first to explore how constitutions can help to resolve principal-agent problems via institutional design. Bodin noted that the French king adopted a solution of parliamentary immunity to help generate information about lower-level agents. The parliamentary representatives had an absolute right to bring complaints about provincial agents of the king without fear of punishment. This was central to generating important information to provide more effective monarchical governance, a kind of early version of the "fire alarm" model of administrative law (McNollGast 1989; Root 1989).

Constitutional solutions to the agency problems also include institutions whereby a ruler ties his own hands. Doing so can be a means for enabling the powerful to enter into credible commitments (e.g., Root 1989). Roger Myerson's work is also important in understanding the emergence of constitutionalism generally and the utility of constitutional logic to authoritarians. In his study of the foundations of the constitutional state, Myerson provides a model in which, in equilibrium, it is in the autocrat's interest to create a court of notables with the ability to remove him from power. "Without such an institutionalized check on the leader," Myerson writes, "he could not credibly raise the support he needs to compete for power" (2008a: 130). In a related model, Myerson (2008b) focuses on the agency problem facing powerful rulers. In the model, a prince faces the possibility that his agents, the governors, could be corrupt or rebel against him. To prevent this, the prince must credibly assure governors that he will not unfairly cheat them. Myerson suggests that the prince can attain this goal by punishing a governor only after a trial and by inviting other governors to observe all trials. Under this arrangement, should the prince cheat a governor, the others would lose faith in the prince (Myerson 2008b: 18). As Myerson observes, the early kings of England needed mechanisms to ensure that taxes were collected and that agents were properly motivated to do so. But agents would not be thus motivated unless they could trust that the king would refrain from arbitrary punishment. The Court of the Exchequer, in Myerson's account, provides a constitutional solution to the problem. In the Exchequer, a panel of leading figures of the realm witnessed legal and financial transactions between the king's Treasurer and the sheriffs who governed the provinces of England in the king's name. Thus the Exchequer established common knowledge among the agents of the king about any question of whether a provincial sheriff might deserve punishment. Common knowledge and the constitutional commitment by the king to punish only those agents whose malfeasance was publicly verified helped to assure appropriate incentives for the king's principal agents and thus made government more effective. This simple constitutional setup solved agency and commitment problems on the part of the monarch.

James Fearon's (2011) work points to another way in which constitutions might be beneficial to autocrats. Autocrats face the problem that the public cannot trust them to refrain from shirking or stealing, and therefore will periodically choose to rebel against the ruler. One way to address this problem is to adopt a constitution that provides for fair elections to be held regularly. Because the results of such elections aggregate and make public the citizens' private information about the ruler's performance, they make it possible for the ruler to be rewarded by the citizenry for governing well.[1] This model again elaborates the common need for regimes – both democratic and autocratic – to facilitate information flows.

OPERATING MANUALS, BILLBOARDS, BLUEPRINTS, AND WINDOW DRESSING

Coordination, precommitment, and agency control are all essential governmental functions that can be played by various institutions, but constitutions are particularly good solutions that have become standard in the modern era. When a written

[1] Simpser (2013) points to a different, more perverse side of information flows associated with electoral institutions, whereby a ruler utilizes electoral manipulation in order to appear powerful to the public and enhance his control over allies and rivals.

constitution describes actual political practice, it is serving as what Adam Przeworski in his essay here (see Chapter 2) characterizes as an *operating manual*. The constitutional text describes how government is to function, allowing various players to cooperate by following its instructions. Przeworski's particular puzzle is why the 1952 Polish constitution, framed at the apex of Communist power in Poland, accorded de jure authority to the government and not to the Communist Party. Przeworski shows that, in so doing, the Communist Party framers chose to "rule against rules," creating unnecessary difficulties for themselves. Przeworski's discussion suggests that, in their role as operating manuals, constitutions provide some genuine constraints on leaders. Consistent with this, Jennifer Gandhi's essay (Chapter 9) argues that authoritarian constitutions influence possibilities, in electoral authoritarian regimes, for opposition parties to join efforts in order to beat an autocrat at the polls. Opposition parties, she argues, will enter into a coalition with each other insofar as they can trust that, should their coalition win the election, whichever party is installed in the presidency will honor its promises to the other coalition partners. Gandhi's key point is that constitutions determine the degree and kind of power associated with control of the presidency. The greater the power of the presidency as set out in the constitution, the less credible it is, ex ante, that promises to coalition partners who do not control the presidency will be fulfilled in the future.

Beyond serving as operating manuals, constitutions can play several other roles that we characterize as *billboards, blueprints*, and *window dressing*.[2] The *billboard* role is common to both dictatorships and democracies.[3] Constitutions are advertisements; they seek to provide information to potential and actual users of their provisions. As authoritative statements of policy, constitutions can also play a role in signaling the intentions of leaders within the regime to those outside of it. These audiences might be international – from the very beginning, written constitutions have been adopted in part to signal capacity to engage on the international plane (Golove and Hulsebosch 2010). Or the audiences may be domestic, consisting of the population that will be subject to the constitution.

Consider as an example the contemporary constitution of the People's Republic of China, discussed by Xin He in this volume (see Chapter 11). Since 1979, the People's Republic of China has pursued a program based in part on the promise of socialist legality, which is contrasted with the disorder and lawlessness of the Cultural Revolution. The adoption of the 1982 constitution, with its references to legality, was part of this program.

The 1982 constitution is not itself judicially enforceable, and judges who attempted to introduce it as a binding source of legal norms during the 2000s were unsuccessful.

[2] Thanks to Dan Slater for helping us to crystalize this framework.

[3] With apologies to Adrienne Rich, whose acceptance speech for the 2006 Medal For Distinguished Contribution To American Letters noted that poetry is neither a "blueprint, nor an instruction manual, nor a billboard." See http://www.nationalbook.org/nba2006_dcal_arich.html#.T3fc4qvCWf4. Andras Sajo, however, has noted that the operation of constitutions has poetic qualities (Sajo 2011).

As Donald Clarke (2003) once said, the constitution may be the least important document in the Chinese legal system, but this does not imply that it has no political importance. Since 1982, the Chinese Communist Party has amended the document four times, each time to provide signals of ideological legitimacy to particular voices within the party. For example, in 2004, the constitution was modified to include the "Three Represents" theory of Jiang Zemin, including explicit mention of the "advanced productive forces" in society, a euphemism for capitalists. The party of the people now represents the rich too. Such symbolic changes may simply confirm policy developments that have already taken place, but their elevation to the level of the constitution signals their authoritative victory within the ideological debates of the party. The meaning for international audiences is that China is open for business; for domestic audiences, it signals that getting rich is not only glorious, as Deng Xiaoping said, but politically acceptable as well.

Sometimes, of course, the promises in constitutions are not accurate signals of policy, but pure fictions. This *window dressing* role of constitutions, aptly captured in the Soviet-era joke at the beginning of the chapter, is one in which the text is designed to obfuscate actual political practice. To use another Chinese example, the constitution promises its citizens freedom of speech and demonstration (Art. 35), freedom of religion (Art. 36), and the right to criticize the government (Art. 41). But these things are routinely violated in practice. North Korea's constitution may be seen as a pure sham for guaranteeing its citizens "democratic rights and liberties" (Art. 64), though its list of rights is actually relatively limited compared to many other communist texts (see Law and Versteeg, Chapter 8, this volume). The point is that the extensive list of rights found in many totalitarian constitutions is hardly meant to provide for meaningful constraint on the state, or to signal government intents, but is instead a kind of "cheap talk" that adopts the mere language of rights without any corresponding institutions. This may respond to a sense that the constitution needs to *look* complete and to fit in the global scripts that define the basic formal elements, but without risk of costly constraints. Cheap talk is window dressing.[4]

The term "window dressing" might be taken to imply hiding actual practices from external scrutiny. At the margin, it might be that gullible outsiders believe that the practice is actually implemented. But this is unlikely to be effective as a general matter, as Przeworski points out in Chapter 2. Why then do authoritarians put up window dressing? One possibility is that the goal might be not so much to keep outsiders from seeing in, but to keep those inside the country from seeing out. When Stalin included his list of rights in the 1936 constitutional text, he was debasing the very currency of rights and suggesting to his information-starved citizenry that

[4] Our usage of the term "cheap talk" differs from its use in game theory. In game theory, cheap talk refers to information that does not directly affect payoffs. Game theoretic cheap talk may nevertheless affect payoffs indirectly – for example, by contributing to coordination.

rights *everywhere* were meaningless promises.[5] Constitutional window dressing has this two-faced quality.

Dictators may also use the gap between promise and reality to demoralize internal opponents: the false promise is a costly signal of one's intent to crush opponents. We draw here from an idea developed by Hollyer and Rosendorff (2011) in the context of the Convention Against Torture, in which accession to the convention is accompanied by an *increase* in the level of torture, at least for certain countries. Hollyer and Rosendorff note that the accession serves as a costly signal of the intention to repress: the dictator is asserting that he can abuse human rights *even with increased costs* (Hollyer and Rosendorff 2011). One might imagine that this was part of the intention behind Stalin's famous constitution, which inspired jokes like the one at the outset of this chapter. Another way in which authoritarian rulers routinely abuse the gap between constitutional promises and actual practice in order to demoralize would-be opponents is by holding elections but manipulating them excessively and blatantly, even when victory is assured (Simpser 2013). The mere fact, however, that rights are not observed in practice does not mean that the constitution is playing a window-dressing function. Gaps between promises and their actual observance are ubiquitous in law, even in countries that might be considered to be fully operational constitutionalist regimes (see Law and Versteeg, Chapter 8, this volume). This is in part because constitutions also operate as a kind of *blueprint,* describing things not as they are but as they might be. Constitutions are aspirational documents that can serve to motivate people to build a future society.

Indeed, looking at the long history of rights, one observes that authoritarian regimes may be particularly likely to treat constitutions as blueprints. Mexico's 1917 constitution was particularly innovative with regard to economic and social rights, promising land, education, and labor to the citizenry. These provisions might not have been mere window dressing for a totalitarian party, as might be said of equivalent promises in Stalin's constitution of 1936, but instead could be understood as aspirations. The land reform promises articulated in the Mexican constitution might be understood as a blueprint that influenced land policy over the decades that followed, during which a large proportion of farmland was redistributed. In short, we see that the same type of provision can be a blueprint in one regime and window dressing in another. This highlights that the particular mix of roles – *operating manual, billboard, blueprint,* or *window dressing* – will vary across time and space, and even across different provisions of the same constitution.

Individual provisions within constitutions can play multiple roles. Kristen Stilt's description of constitutional amendments in Egypt (Chapter 6 in this volume) provides a nice example. When Hosni Mubarak was confronted with external pressure to liberalize the Egyptian political system in 2005, he modified the article of the constitution dealing with presidential elections. The new scheme was detailed and

[5] Thanks to Scott Gehlbach for this point.

complex, providing that nominees could come only from political parties that had been in existence for five years and had 5 percent of the seats in each house of parliament. Only Mubarak's party met the threshold, but other legal parties (which did not include the Muslim Brotherhood) were allowed to nominate candidates for the first election. The provision served as a complex operating manual, laying out a scheme that could be followed to the letter while maintaining Mubarak's rule. But it also served as window dressing, providing just enough democratic veneer to forestall further U.S. pressure.

More generally, the literature on competitive or electoral authoritarian regimes – those that hold regular, multiparty elections but on a notoriously uneven playing field – has noted that their democratic-like constitutions may in fact help extend regime survival (Gandhi 2008; Levitsky and Way 2002). Albertus and Menaldo's study in this volume (Chapter 4) argues that constitutions contribute to regime endurance by facilitating the consolidation of political power and the internal coordination of the governing coalition. Constitutional commitments can also facilitate investment and growth, which in turn may extend the lives of regimes. Drawing on large-N data on Latin American dictatorships from 1950 to 2002, they find empirical support for the proposition that authoritarian constitutions significantly extend the life expectancy of dictatorships and enhance investment and economic growth.

The categories of operating manuals, billboards, blueprints, and window dressing cover a great deal of terrain, but they do not exhaust the functions of constitutions. The provisions of authoritarian constitutions, for example, can provide resources for the regime's endgame. A paradigmatic example, well documented by Barros (2002), is the Chilean transition, which was laid out in a constitutional document enacted by the military junta in 1988. This called for a plebiscite in 1988, in which General Augusto Pinochet ran alone and lost. But under the terms of the constitution, he remained commander in chief for another ten years, and the military was able to appoint a certain number of "institutional" senators. The constitutional framework remained basically intact even after the transition to democracy, lasting until a comprehensive reform in 2005. A contemporary example is provided by ongoing events in Myanmar: while most observers thought that the product of the seventeen-year effort of writing the constitution was a mere fig leaf for continued authoritarian rule, it has provided a modest opening for the return to politics of the National League of Democracy and its charismatic leader Aung San Suu Kyi. The text provides a coordinated and orderly process of inclusion, with the potential to lead to true transformation down the road.

Henry Hale's contribution in this volume (Chapter 10) shows how constitutions matter for politics in hybrid regimes, not simply because of formal institutions, but through their effect on informal political arrangements. He shows how presidentialist constitutions encourage clientelism around a single power structure, whereas semipresidentialist constitutions promote more elite competition. He highlights the downstream effects of these institutional choices in his study of the

Ukrainian, Kyrgyz, and Moldovan democratic episodes in the early twenty-first century.

FUNDAMENTAL PROBLEMS OF AUTHORITARIAN CONSTITUTIONS: MECHANISMS OF EFFICACY

The study of constitutions in authoritarian regimes must contend with a set of fundamental questions that do not plague democratic constitutions (or do not plague them to the same degree). Our second question is: How do authoritarian constitutions work? More specifically, what is the source of an authoritarian constitution's force when the authoritarian ruler is above the law and there is no third-party enforcer? When a judicial enforcement apparatus is in place, constitutional provisions evidently make a difference. Because they will be enforced, they raise the costs of certain activities and lower the costs of others. Not so under authoritarian regimes, where enforcement tends to be at the pleasure of the ruler. Therefore, if one is to argue that authoritarian constitutions matter, it is imperative to delve into the basic mechanisms that grant such constitutions force. Mark Tushnet's contribution to this volume (Chapter 3) wrestles with this issue elegantly, concluding that authoritarian constitutionalism is indeed possible.

We have already suggested various mechanisms underpinning the possibility for authoritarian constitutionalism. One important mechanism is the role of constitutions in *coordination*, which is closely associated with their function as operating manuals. Coordination is a powerful source of constitutional force. Once a self-enforcing system is in place, deviations are costly to any party, even without a formal apparatus of judicial enforcement. Weingast (1997), for example, argues that the cost for a ruler of transgressing the constitution (off the path of play) is popular rebellion. The prior discussion of billboards and window dressing points to a second mechanism behind the force of authoritarian constitutions, namely their *information-related properties*. The role of information in making it possible for authoritarian rulers to credibly commit to future courses of action is well illustrated by Myerson's and Fearon's arguments discussed earlier: by establishing procedures to divulge information that could potentially be used against them, rulers make themselves vulnerable and, in consequence, enhance their credibility. In other cases, authoritarian constitutions may serve to obscure information about the true intentions of a ruler or about the actual practices of a regime, as discussed earlier in this chapter. And, as argued previously, constitutions can enable certain kinds of costly signaling that rulers can harness in order to discipline opponents, subordinates, and allies.

Another reason authoritarian constitutions have force is that they can, and often do, function as *hallowed vessels*. The document called "constitution" often enjoys a privileged normative status in the minds of the public, independent of the content of such document. Whether or not judicial enforcement is available, the very idea that a particular proposition is enshrined in the constitution carries normative force in arguments and in behavior. Striking examples of the power of constitutions as hallowed vessels can be found in contemporary dictatorships such as Vietnam and China. Authoritarian constitutions generally call our attention away from the U.S. fetish with judicial enforcement. As Balme and Dowdle (2009: 2) point out, "even in the most effective constitutional system, significant aspects of constitutional structure are invariably nonjusticiable." In countries such as Vietnam and China, a vigorous constitutional debate has emerged without a constitutional adjudication system.

In Vietnam, this involves frequent invocation of the constitution by legislative and executive bodies to overturn policies and on the basis of the constitutional rights. For example, in 2003, the Hanoi People's Council tried to limit traffic congestion by issuing a directive limiting people to owning a single motorbike, and the policy was subsequently adopted by the national Ministry of Public Security (Bui 2011). But responding to public pressure, the Law Committee of the National People's Assembly argued that the law violated property rights protected by Art. 58 of the constitution. The national prohibition was withdrawn by the Public Security Ministry. Since then, the Ministry of Justice has repeatedly invoked the constitution to oppose policies of other ministries. Constitutional reform is, at this writing, a major issue in Vietnamese politics.

The famous 2003 Sun Zhigang case in China, discussed by Xin He in Chapter 11 in this volume, presents a similar story. Sun was a student in Wuhan who was arrested in Guangzhou for failure to have his registration documents. He was brought into custody in a system known euphemistically as "shelter and repatriation," in which those found outside their location of residency are internally deported back home. Sun, as an educated young man, may have protested his treatment, and he was killed in custody. This led to a national outcry among intellectuals, who argued that the shelter-and-repatriation detention system should be abolished. Legal scholars called it unconstitutional and called for the standing committee of the National People's Congress (which is the only institution with the power of constitutional review in China) to reform the system. These efforts were mooted when the State Council, China's highest executive authority, repealed the system. As in Vietnam, this example evidences a vigorous constitutional politics that occasionally operates in a way that enhances liberty.[6]

Looking at these stories through the lens of legal enforcement would miss the point. In neither the Vietnamese or Chinese case was a government agency formally required to repeal its policies because they were illegal or unconstitutional. But in

[6] In other cases, constitutional politics may be harnessed for the purpose of silencing rivals without subverting formal institutional channels. The intense constitutional politics in contemporary Iran provide a number of examples: The constitutional order features a Guardian Council that uses constitutional power to check candidates for the elected offices in the system, a Supreme Leader with power to control the judiciary, media, and military, and a political system that is often subject to tinkering. Indeed, there is occasional discussion of switching to a parliamentary system to enhance the power of the Supreme Leader.

both cases, the outcome was the same. The mechanism for constitutional protection was political, although the language was legal, and the constitution served as a basis for mobilization within inter-elite politics.

A final reason authoritarian constitutions have force is that they can shape social norms and public preferences. As Albert Hirschman put it, "a principal purpose of publically proclaimed laws and regulations is to stigmatize antisocial behavior and thereby to influence citizens' values" (1986: 146; see also Sunstein 1993). A monarchical constitution, for example, could potentially buttress the social acceptability of kingly rule, while a constitution that protects free speech might, over time, foster an attitude or norm of tolerance for diversity of opinion. Of course, this need not always be the case: as the idea of constitutions as window dressing suggests, constitutions can also ring hollow to the public, especially when regime practices are sharply at odds with them.

WHY WRITE? PRODUCT AND PROCESS

The final fundamental question with which the study of authoritarian constitutions must grapple is: Why are constitutions written? Several of the arguments that we have offered thus far are excellent explanations of the *functions* of constitutions understood as sets of rules but are silent about the reasons such rules might be collected in a written document. To underline this point, note that Myerson (2008a) refers to such sets of rules among notables as "personal constitutions," suggesting a distinction from written constitutions. Self-enforcing elite pacts can be informal. Mexican presidents, for example, were for decades chosen by the informal practice of *dedazo*, whereby the outgoing president would handpick his successor. At the same time, presidential term limits were formally coded in the law. Both term limits and the *dedazo* were recognized by the Mexican public as the prevailing modus operandi (Langston 2006), and both institutions were uniformly and stably applied over a period of time longer than the lifetime of many constitutions in other countries (Elkins, Ginsburg, and Melton 2009). Nevertheless, term limits were formalized while the *dedazo* was not.

Why then do authoritarian rulers write or retain a constitution? In addressing this question, it is necessary to draw a distinction between the choice to write a constitution (or to retain a preexisting one), on the one hand, and the constitution's function, on the other. We have described a range of possible functions or roles played by constitutions. But can we infer the reasons for the adoption of a constitution on the basis of the constitution's functions? We must at least entertain the possibility that framers might have had as much of a difficult time as contemporary scholars at predicting the downstream effects of adopting a constitution and of particular provisions within it. For one thing, laws, regulations, and formal institutions are known to elicit offsetting behavior (Peltzman 1975). Negretto's study of constitution-making by Latin American militaries illustrates the point (see Chapter 5). He argues that militaries choose to write constitutions to facilitate their long-term objectives of political, social, and economic transformation and to enhance their influence over post-transition democratic governments. But crucially, militaries are not always successful in these endeavors, and Negretto argues that the key variable is whether they can mobilize partisan support for their institutional innovations. The point is that dictators, like democrats, do not have perfect foresight as institutional designers.

Another possibility is that sometimes the *process* of writing the constitution serves a political purpose. It allows the regime to be seen as engaged in an important project. This seems consistent with the idea that authoritarians, as compared with leaders in democracies, may be more insulated from social forces in choosing the timing and process of constitution making. In the Maldives, for example, the constitution allowed the creation of a special *majlis*, composed of a mix of elected and appointed persons, to undertake the process of constitutional reform. President Maumoon Gayoom, who held office from 1978 to 2008, set up a special *majlis* soon after taking office. The constitution-making project took some seventeen years, leading to a new document that quite clearly enshrined presidential rule in 1998. The process of constitution making was itself a discrete political project with its own logic: it allowed Gayoom a set of governmental positions that facilitated patronage as well as an ability to gain information on new political talent through the electoral process. The point of the process was not necessarily the final product, which could have been produced much more quickly.

The processes of authoritarian constitution making are often hidden to us, and, as Przeworski notes here, this prevents us from understanding the internal conflicts and motives of drafters (see also Barros 2012). No doubt there is more than meets the eye. For example, recent archival research into the drafting and early implementation of the 1936 Soviet constitution has revealed that party officials were organizing contested elections within the constitutional framework, only to reverse themselves in favor of single-party elections just before the 1937 elections (Getty 1991: 29). We can only speculate about the internal decision making, but it seems plausible that the drafters intended that some of the provisions be more than window dressing.

It also appears that there was an important component of information-gathering in the process, as Moscow demanded that local and party officials initiate broad discussions of the document. Soviet citizens contributed many thousands of comments (as did their Polish counterparts in 1952 in Przeworski's account). Many of the Soviet comments complained about the constitutional guarantee of free social benefits to workers but not peasants (Getty 1991: 24–7). The regime was thus able to gauge what issues were important to the public, even if it chose to ignore them in the final analysis.

We have been implicitly assuming through much of the discussion that the interests of authoritarians are the dominant motives at play. Interests are easy enough to identify through the kind of ex post reconstruction we have been conducting on the basis of the final texts. In some circumstances, however, it seems plausible that authoritarian constitution making will involve a mixture of "reason, passions and interests," as do democratic constitution-making exercises (Elster 1995). While the proportions among these factors may be different across regime type, we should not discount the role of reason and passion (Brown 2008).

Reason is analogous to public-regarding constitutional design. We observe it in the examples in which the leader constrains herself, for example, through institutions to protect property rights (in which case there may be a confluence of reason and interest). Passion is also apparent, particularly in constitutional preambles. North Korea's Great leader Comrade Kim Il Sung, for example, is "the sun of the nation and the lodestar of the reunification of the fatherland." Constitutional production with such exhortatory language shows also that constitutional production can also be a "consumption activity" for rulers.

BEYOND SHAMS: THE LESSONS OF AUTHORITARIAN CONSTITUTIONS

We conclude this introduction with some thoughts on the lessons of authoritarian constitutions as well as some open questions that beg further inquiry. The lessons can be divided into those for the study of authoritarian regimes and those for the study of constitutions generally.

The first lesson is that rules matter, even when there is a lot of discretion at the top. No single person rules absolutely, and therefore there is a need for intra-elite coordination, as well as for devices to control subordinates. In some circumstances, constitutions serve to meet these functional needs. Furthermore, *some* authoritarians seek to commit themselves to limit particular courses of action. Tushnet's essay on the normative possibilities of authoritarian constitutionalism (Chapter 3) seems to suggest that this is not only possible but also desirable.

Authoritarian constitutions – and the processes of making them – also provide important clues into regime practices. They structure authoritative discourse and provide a political idiom, whether it be of a "socialist market economy" or blessing the family and civil society (as did Chile's 1980 constitution). By setting the terms of political discourse, constitutions can define what are acceptable as opposed to unacceptable speech acts, legitimating one set and delegitimizing another.

Still, there are many outstanding questions that remain. The large-N studies here by Law and Versteeg as well as Elkins, Ginsburg, and Melton begin the project of unpacking the constitutional practices of different subtypes of authoritarians. Law and Versteeg (Chapter 8) examine the different categories drawn from the literature in terms of their "sham" quality or deviation from practice. Elkins, Ginsburg, and Melton (Chapter 7) identify a subcategory of authoritarian constitutions that seem closer to democratic ones in form and that lead to democratic rule. Further case-study exploration will be needed to confirm this finding and to see whether it maps onto the conventional categories in the literature of different types of authoritarian regimes. There is at least the possibility that we might use the constitutional forms to typologize authoritarian regimes and predict which are more favorable toward their citizenry in terms of providing public goods. This project would connect nicely with Tushnet's normative suggestion that certain forms of helpful authoritarian constitutionalism are possible.

Our framework of considering the roles of constitutional provisions as *operating manuals*, *billboards*, *blueprints*, and *window dressing* may generalize beyond authoritarian regimes. After all, no constitution is perfectly implemented, and each contains elements of advertising, aspiration, and even obfuscation. Comparing the balances among these functions across regime types may provide further insights and help generate new typologies.

Finally, there is great utility in longitudinal analysis of constitutional sequences in individual countries. As the highest normative act of the state, constitutions mark an exercise of power and create a historical legacy. We observe that constitutions in dictatorships are often replaced or amended by new leaders who come to power. To understand these documents, one needs to read them in light of the predecessor documents, as the sequence of documents will provide clues over the particular leaders' political concerns and predilections. Constitutions have an "afterlife" (Ginsburg 2009). The legacies – of democratic constitutions on authoritarian rulers and of authoritarian constitutions on democratic ones – may shape behavior and idiom long after those who promulgate formal documents are gone.

Our thanks to the three programs at the University of Chicago that sponsored the conference around which this volume is based: the Law School, the Center for Latin American Studies, and the Initiative on Regime Practices. Ginsburg would like to thank the Russell Baker Scholars Fund for support as well. Leslie Goldstein and Kristen Stilt provided terrific comments on this introduction, and Dan Slater was an early and supportive intellectual collaborator in this venture. We gratefully acknowledge *World Politics* for allowing Hale to contribute a revised version of his article "Formal Constitutions in Informal Politics: Institutions and Democratization in Eurasia," which had appeared in volume 63 and to the Hong Kong Law Journal, which published an earlier version of the chapter by Xin He. Special thanks to our commentators at the conference: Nathan Brown, Jose Cheibub, Jordan Gans-Morse, Scott Gehlbach, Nicholas Howson, Steven Levitsky, Eric Posner, Milan Svolik, and Dali Yang. Randall Peerenboom and Edward Malesky also made helpful contributions. Research assistance was provided by Sonali Maulik and Sean McClelland. The errors, needless to say, are ours, but the merits of the volume are the product of a collective effort.

REFERENCES

Balme, Stéphanie and Michael W. Dowdle. 2009. "Introduction: Searching for Constitutionalism in 21st Century China." In *Building Constitutionalism in China*, edited by Stephanie

Balme and Michael Dowdle. New York: Palgrave Macmillan. New York: Palgrave Macmillan.
Barros, Robert. 2002. *The Constitution of Dictatorship*. New York: Cambridge University Press.
Barros, Robert. 2012. "On the Outside Looking In: Secrecy and the Study of Authoritarian Regimes," manuscript, Argentina, Universidad de San Andrés.
Bodin, Jean. 1576 [1992]. *On Sovereignty*. Ed. Julian Franklin. New York: Cambridge University Press.
Brown, Nathan. 2011. "Reason, Interest, Rationality, and Passion in Constitution Drafting." *PS: Political Science & Politics* 6(4): 675–89.
Bui, Ngoc Son. 2011. "Constitutional Developments in Vietnam." Paper presented for Fourth Asian Constitutional Law Forum, Hong Kong University.
Clarke, Donald. 2003. Puzzling Observations in Chinese Law: When is a Riddle Just a Mistake? In *Understanding China's Legal System: Essays in Honor of Jerome Cohen*, edited by C. Stephen Hsu. New York: New York University Press.
Elkins, Zachary, Tom Ginsburg, and James Melton. 2009. *The Endurance of National Constitutions*. New York: Cambridge University Press.
Elster, Jon. 1995. "Forces and Mechanisms in the Constitution-Making Process." *Duke Law Journal* 45: 364–408.
Fearon, James. 2011. "Self-Enforcing Democracy." *Quarterly Journal of Economics* 126(4): 1661–1708.
Gandhi, Jennifer. 2008. *Political Institutions Under Dictatorship*. New York: Cambridge University Press.
Gehlbach, Scott and Alberto Simpser. 2012. "Electoral Manipulation as Bureaucratic Control," unpublished manuscript, University of Wisconsin, Madison, and University of Chicago.
Getty, J. Arch. 1991. "State and Society under Stalin: Constitutions and Elections in the 1930s." *Slavic Review* 50: 18–35.
Ginsburg, Tom. 2009. "Constitutional Afterlife: The Continuing Impact of Thailand's Post-Political Constitution." *International Journal of Constitutional Law* 7: 83–105.
Golove, David and Daniel Hulsebosch. 2010. "A Civilized Nation: The Early American Constitution, the Law Of Nations, and the Pursuit of International Recognition." *New York University Law Review* 85: 932–1066.
Hirschman, Albert O. 1986. *Rival Views of Market Society and Other Recent Essays*. New York: Viking.
Hollyer, James R. and B. Peter Rosendorff. 2011. "Why Do Authoritarian Regimes Sign the Convention Against Torture? Signaling, Domestic Politics and Non-Compliance." *Quarterly Journal of Political Science* 6(3–4): 275–327.
Langston, Joy. 2006. "The Birth and Transformation of the Dedazo in Mexico," pp. 143–159 in Gretchen Helmke and Steven Levitsky, eds., *Informal Institutions and Democracy: Lessons from Latin America*. Baltimore, MD: Johns Hopkins University Press.
Levitsky, Steven and Lucan A. Way. 2002. "Elections Without Democracy: The Rise of Competitive Democracy." *Journal of Democracy* 13(2): 52.
Levitsky, Steven and Lucan A. Way. 2010. *Competitive Authoritarianism: Hybrid Regimes After the Cold War*. New York: Cambridge University Press.
McNollGast. 1989. "Structure and Process, Politics and Policy: Administrative arrangements and the political control of agencies." *Virginia Law Review*, 75: 431–482.
Murphy, Walter. 2006. *Constitutional Democracy*. Baltimore, MD: Johns Hopkins University Press.

Murphy, Walter. 1993. "Constitutions, Constitutionalism and Democracy," pp. 3–7 in Douglas Greenberg, S. N. Katz, B. Oliviero, and S. C. Wheatley, eds., *Constitutionalism and Democracy: Transitions in the Contemporary World*. New York: Oxford University Press.
Myerson, Roger B. 2008a. "The Autocrat's Credibility Problem and Foundations of the Constitutional State." *American Political Science Review* 102: 125–3.
Myerson, Roger B. 2008b. "Leadership, Trust, and Power: Dynamic Moral Hazard in High Office," mimeo, University of Chicago, October.
Okoth-Okendo, H. W. O. 1993. "Constitutions Without Constitutionalism: An African Political Paradox," pp. 65–84 in Douglas Greenberg, S. N. Katz, B. Oliviero, and S. C. Wheatley, eds., *Constitutionalism and Democracy: Transitions in the Contemporary World*. New York: Oxford University Press.
Peltzman, Samuel. 1975. "The Effects of Automobile Safety Regulation." *Journal of Political Economy* 83(4): 677–726.
Root, Hilton T. 1989. "Tying the King's Hands: Credible Commitments and Royal Fiscal Policy During the Old Regime." *Rationality and Society* 1(2): 240–58.
Sajo, Andras. 2011. *Constitutional Sentiments*. New Haven, CT: Yale University Press.
Schedler, Andreas. 2006. *Electoral Authoritarianism: The Dynamics of Unfree Competition*. Boulder, CO, and London: Lynne Rienner Publishers.
Simpser, Alberto. 2013. *Why Governments and Parties Manipulate Elections: Theory, Practice, and Implications*. New York: Cambridge University Press.
Sunstein, Cass R. 1993. *After the Rights Revolution: Reconceiving the Regulatory State*. Cambridge, MA: Harvard University Press.
Weingast, Barry. 1997. "The Political Foundations of Democracy and the Rule of Law." *American Political Science Review* 91(2): 245–63.

PART I

The Category

2

Ruling against Rules*

Adam Przeworski

The Polish Constitution of 1952 appears in all substantive aspects to be a constitution of democracy. Most importantly, it does not contain the clause giving the communist party "the leading role in the state," a clause standard in communist constitutions, beginning with the Soviet one of 1936. This fact is puzzling because Communist Party had a *de facto* monopoly of power, and exercising *de facto* power against written rules creates unnecessary difficulties. Indeed, it may not be accidental that the communist rule in Poland was most vulnerable to political crises, including the first breakdown of communist regimes.

A CONSTITUTION

Here are some articles from a constitution:

Article 15.

§1. The highest organ of State power is the Parliament.
§3. The Parliament adopts laws and executes control of activities of other organs of power and public administration.

Article 16.

§3. A deputy to the Parliament cannot be prosecuted or arrested without the consent of the Parliament or, during periods when the Parliament is not in session, of the Council of State.

Article 28a.

§1. The Highest Control Chamber oversees economic, financial, and organizational organs of public administration.

* I appreciate comments by Jennifer Gandhi, Andrea Pozas-Loyo, Robert Barros, and Alberto Simpser.

Article 29.
§1. The Parliament constitutes and revokes the Government, the Council of Ministers and its members.

Article 30.
§1. The Council of Ministers is the highest executive and administrative organ of state power.
§2. The Council of Ministers accounts and reports its activities to the Parliament and when the Parliament is not in session to the Council of State.

Article 46.
§1. The administration of justice is executed by the Supreme Courts as well as by regional, district, and special courts.

Article 49. Judges are independent and subject only to laws.

Article 70. The [Country] guarantees citizens the freedom of conscience and religion. . . .

Article 71.
§1. The [Country] guarantees citizens the freedom of speech, print, meetings and demonstrations, marches and manifestations.

Article 72.
§1. The [Country] guarantees citizens the right of association.

Article 74.
§1. The [Country] guarantees citizens physical inviolability. Deprivation of freedom can occur only in cases regulated by law. An arrested person must be freed if not charged within 48 hours.
§2. Laws protect inviolability of residences and secrecy of correspondence.

Article 80. Elections to the Parliament are universal, equal, direct, and secret.

Article 91. The Constitution can be modified only by law adopted by a two-thirds majority of the Parliament in the presence of at least one-half of the deputies.

THE PUZZLE

These are, albeit tendentiously selected, excerpts from the 1952 Constitution of the People's Republic of Poland. Now, 1952 was the peak year of communist power in Poland. All rival groups had been repressed or safely tucked under communist control. Repression was rampant. Communists controlled the government, the courts, all the media, all voluntary organizations, and trade unions. With the support of the Soviet Army, they could have done what they wanted.

Among things they wanted was a new constitution that would replace the provisional one, promulgated in 1947. The new constitution was unanimously adopted by the Parliament on July 22, 1952. The operative parts of the constitution could have passed for a constitution of democracy. While the Preamble and some other declaratory parts were imbued with communist jargon, the organization of government, the system of elections, and the judiciary, as well as rights and freedoms, were the ordinary stuff of democratic constitutions. When in 1976 a group of dissidents held a press conference to protest repression of striking workers, they embarrassed the regime by claiming they were just exercising their constitutional rights. And they were.

Why would a regime that has total political control adopt a constitution that has no relation with the political reality and that it obviously does not intend to implement and respect?

RULING AGAINST RULES

The puzzle is profound because ruling without having some kind of a manual is difficult and exercising *de facto* power against written rules even more so. The situation the 1952 constitution created in Poland was one in which power rested with the Political Bureau of the Polish United Workers (PUWP, Communist) Party but authority rested with the Government responsible to the Sejm (the parliament), "the highest organ of State power" according to Article 15, §1. The distinction between "power" and "authority" may appear artificial, but the language is of the protagonists, not mine. The phrase "authority of power" (*autorytet władzy*) was common in Poland. And by the early 1970s, the political program of the Party became to "strengthen the authority of power."

The havoc created by situations in which power diverges from authority is illustrated by the story of the visit of French President Valery Giscard d'Estaing to Warsaw in June 1975. Giscard arrived on a rainy June afternoon, and as he left the plane, he was greeted on the tarmac by a long list of officials. The first person with whom he shook hands was the president of the Council of State, Professor Jabłoński, who was a nobody, at best number 100 in a real hierarchy of power. As a biting rain inundated the officialdom, next came the Prime Minister, who was about number five, the Minister of Foreign Affairs, about number twenty, and so on. The real ruler of the country, the First Secretary of the Party, Edward Gierek, who did not occupy any government position, was far down the line. Mr. Power was low on the hierarchy of authority.

While this is just an anecdote, the divergence between power and authority was a source of difficulties that were structural. As Machiavelli observed, whenever power is shared, some rules are necessary to allocate authority.[1] The Constitution did assign

[1] Barros (2002) provides a wonderful account of the emergence of the legal system under the military rule in post–1973 Chile. One of his examples is that during the first moments after the coup, it was not clear who had the authority to regulate curfews, so that one general imposed it at 8 PM while another at 10.

specific prerogatives to the formally constituted state organs: the elected Parliament, the government responsible to the Parliament, the Council of State (elected by the Parliament, with decree power when the Parliament was not in session), the courts, and an Oversight Organ (*Najwyższa Izba Kontroli*). But it was silent about the role of the Communist Party, while in fact all the power in the state (with a caveat concerning the security apparatus, discussed in the following section) was exercised by the Political Bureau of the Party, whose membership hovered around fifteen. Moreover, the power of the Political Bureau was not contingent on elections[2] but rested on physical force, the Soviet Army.[3]

Ruling against rules is a source of two difficulties. Because rules are silent about real power, it is unclear who is competent to make final decisions. Because rules do not specify the prerogatives of the effective bearers of power, authority and responsibility are diffuse.

AUTHORITY VERSUS POWER

Formally, territorial administration was vertically organized in successive levels of government. The central government regulated the functioning of the largest territorial units, the "voievodships," which in turn supervised the lower level, "poviats," and these oversaw the activities of the lowest units, "gminy." The same was true of the administration of the economy, the functional administration. The government (before 1955, in fact, the Central Planning Commission) regulated the functioning of economic ministries, which directed the conglomerates (*zjednoczenia*), which in turn supervised particular productive enterprises. Yet there was another hierarchical organization, the Party. The structure of the Party mimicked both the administrative and functional organizations: there were Party units, each with a secretary in charge, at each level of government and in all functional entities (factories as well as offices). Hence command flowed vertically through two pairs of hierarchies: administrative and political, functional and political. But horizontally, at each level, real power rested again with the Party, the local or factory Party secretary.

One can easily guess the consequences. Consider the situation of a mayor of a poviat. He receives instructions from the administrative hierarchy, but to undertake any action, he must get consent of the poviat Party secretary, who receives directives through the party apparatus. The town is the site of biweekly agricultural markets,

[2] Ehrlich (1956: 49) argued that it is only natural that the Party directs the Parliament, which is true in every parliamentary system. He conveniently ignored the fact that the Communist Party was not competitively elected.

[3] When in October 1956 the Central Committe of the Party decided to replace the then first secretary, Edward Ochab, with Władysław Gomułka, the Soviets moved two army divisions toward Warsaw, top Russian leaders suddenly arrived in the capital, and the change took place only after it was approved by the Russians. The same occurred in 1981.

which leave every hidden corner replete with excrements. The mayor is formally responsible for the sanitary level of the population, so he decides to build a public toilet. The secretary, however, is instructed in the Party line against private sale of agricultural products. Moreover, the mayor and the secretary hate each other's guts: the mayor resents having to kowtow to the secretary; the secretary considers the mayor disobedient.

Here is another anecdote. An engineer in a large tractor factory, not known for his political activism, holds a fiery speech at a meeting commemorating an anniversary of the Great Soviet Revolution, promising that the factory will honor its political commitment to the realization of the targets of the plan for the year. What he is in fact doing is pressuring the plant Party secretary to intervene with the Party leadership to intervene with the respective ministry to assure the supply of parts without which the factory is at the present paralyzed, meaning that it will not fulfill the plan and will not get bonuses. But note that if the tractor factory was not getting the necessary parts, it was because the available parts were going to another plant, so that if the intervention would be successful, some other factory would become paralyzed.

Because of the chaos and often paralysis it engendered, the organization of these multiple hierarchies and regulation of relations among them was the subject of endless reforms. I cannot even begin to list them: reforms of territorial structure, functional administration, and the relation between them and the Party were part of everyday life of the socialist society. And they were repeatedly futile, until the coup d'état of 1981, when the Army threw the Party out of day-to-day administrative activities.

Diffuse Power

The second source of difficulty of ruling against the rules is that power not regulated by rules tends to be diffuse. Yet another story goes as follows. A high-level Party bureaucrat was spending a vacation in a village that was scheduled to be inundated to construct a dam, build a lake, and divert peasants from agriculture to tourism. When the peasants discovered that the vacationer was a man of power, they asked him to reverse this decision. The official's competence within the Party apparatus had nothing to do with dams, or for that matter economic issues. But for the peasants, any man of power had power.

While the peasants had been to some extent mistaken – the Party bureaucracy was divided into functionally defined departments – they were not wrong in thinking that the prerogatives of particular holders of power were not sharply defined. Those of the formal institutions were regulated by the constitution but those within the Party and between the Party and the state only by rules adopted by the Party itself. This ambiguity was tragically revealed by the massacre of shipyard workers in Gdynia on December 17, 1970. Until today, it remains unclear who gave the order to shoot at workers with live ammunition: the Vice-Minister of Defense, the Vice-Minister of

Interior, the local Party Secretary, or a particular member of the Political Bureau. The responsibility was subject to investigation by two intraparty commissions, neither of which arrived at conclusions. Twelve persons are still being prosecuted today, and the prospects that those responsible will be identified are dim. If responsibility cannot be established, it is because no one knows even today who had the authority to give this order. Indeed, three independent groups were charged with maintaining order when the strike erupted: one led by the Vice-Minister of Defense, another led by the Vice-Minister of Interior, and one by two members of the Political Bureau. Workers were shot at when they were returning to work in the morning, responding to an appeal by the Vice-Premier, who claimed that he was not aware that the army would open fire. Everyone had the power to issue orders, and as a consequence, no one had the authority.

A particularly thorny issue was the relation between the Party and its presumed agents of repression, the secret police. In a situation in which power exists only *de facto*, everyone who has power can exercise it, and the secret police had power. The Ministry of Public Security was, to a large extent, independent from the Party until the death of Stalin in March 1953, controlling all aspects of social, political, cultural, and economic life. The Ministry had units at all levels of territorial administration and in all large enterprises. The armed forces had their own intelligence unit. Both institutions had direct ties with the corresponding Soviet institutions. Several tens of Russians, headed by a general, were installed in the Warsaw headquarters of the Ministry. They had their own communication networks, own spy networks, and own prisons. Even members of the Political Bureau (the top organ of the Party) were subject to scrutiny by the secret police: Department X of the Ministry was in charge of the "security of the party" with the mission of preventing "hostile elements" from penetrating it. These institutions thus constituted a "state within the state" (Czubiński 1992: 266). A somewhat attenuated version of the same situation emerged in the late 1960s when a contender for party leadership, Mieczysław Moczar, became the Minister of Interior. Who, then, was to decide whether a high Party leader was betraying the interests of the regime: the Party itself or the secret police?

THE "LEADING ROLE"

Ruling against rules has its costs. They were finally recognized by the Party leadership when Edward Gierek became the General Secretary in the aftermath of the Gdynia events. The Party decided to legitimize its rule, to "render authority to power." The instrument was to be a clause that became known as "the Brezhnev Amendment": a clause that would grant the Communist Party "the leading role in society and the State."

Because it is the absence of this clause in the original text of the 1952 constitution that is most puzzling, its history merits recounting. A version of this clause was first introduced in the 1936 Soviet constitution, albeit somewhat camouflaged in Article 126, which guaranteed freedom of political activities and continued to assert that "the All-Union Communist Party (Bolshevik) is the vanguard of the working people . . . and the leading core of all labor organization, both public and private." The crucial importance of Article 126 was caught immediately in 1938 by a Polish legal scholar, W. Komarnicki (1938), who saw in it the evidence that "The essence of the Soviet system is the dictatorship of the Communist Party" and went on to comment that all the democratic principles of this constitution were just "Bolshevik phraseology," while the truth was revealed by this article.

The clause about the leading role of the Party in the state was absent from communist constitutions that were adopted before Communists consolidated their power: the Soviet constitutions of 1919 and 1924 and those promulgated in Albania in 1946, Bulgaria in 1947, Yugoslavia in 1946, and North Korea in 1948. It was not incorporated into the Czechoslovak constitution of 1948, but President Edward Beneš refused to sign it anyway and resigned. The Hungarian constitution of 1949 (Article 56, §2) awarded the status of the leading force to the "working class" but not to the Party, while the Chinese constitution of 1954 mentioned in the preamble the Communist Party as the directive force of the Popular-Democratic Front but not of the state. The first communist constitution to copy the Soviet 1936 one was the Romanian Constitution of 1952, again submerging it in an article (86) concerning the right to associate, "The Romanian Workers Party is the leading force of the working of all organizations and state bodies and institutions." When the Communist rule became secure, the formula appeared in the 1960 Czechoslovak constitution as a separate article (4), which awarded Communists the "leading role in society and the State." The same phrase appeared in the preamble to the Mongolian constitution of 1960 and as a separate article in the Yugoslav constitution of 1963. It was also brought to the fore as a separate article in the Romanian constitution of 1965 and in the Bulgarian constitution of 1971. Finally, the 1977 Brezhnev constitution of the USSR (Article 6) granted the Communist Party of the Soviet Union (CPSU) the status of "the leading and guiding force of the Soviet society and the nucleus of its political system, of all state and public organizations." This is why this clause became known in Poland as the "Brezhnev amendment."

The original project of the amendment in Poland also referred to the "leading force of the society and the State." One argument in favor of this proposal (Łopatka 1963) was that constitutionalizing the leading role of the Party in the state would have prevented the abuses committed by the security apparatus under Stalinism. The proposal was met, however, with open protest, and on February 10, 1976, the Party adopted a compromise, which consisted of declaring that Poland is a socialist country and that "the leading political force in the construction of socialism is the Polish United Workers' Party." Hence, the Party for the first time appeared in the constitution, but it failed to authorize its exercise of power over the state. The intensity of the conflicts – the insistence by the Party leadership, a rare public letter of dissenting intellectuals – is the best evidence that something was at stake, that the clause mattered.

In fact, Communist parties always claimed the mantle of the "leading force." This role was first usurped by the 1919 Statutes of the Bolshevik Party, and it was claimed in the 1959 as well as the 1971 Statutes of the Polish United Workers Party. Weaving in endless citations from Lenin, a party ideologue, Adam Łopatka, proclaimed in 1963 that the directive role of the Party is a "necessary condition of socialist democracy." He attacked a renowned sociologist with roots in the Polish Socialist Party (PPS), Julian Hochfeld,[4] who maintained in 1956 that the leading role of the Party and the constitutional principle that the Parliament is the highest organ of the state are incompatible. According to Łopatka (1963: 91), the leading role of the Party and the superior authority of the Parliament are complementary: the Party "inspires all the activities of all the organs of the State and the Parliament follows the political inspirations of the Party in executing its legislative and control functions." The crowning argument, in the typical communist style, was a quotation from a speech by the Party leader, Władysław Gomułka, who announced that "The Parliament is an important institution. But the Parliament is not and cannot be the blacksmith of the fate of the working class, which is the working class itself. The Parliament can only aid it in this task, but can never replace it."

In the end, then, the puzzle is why, at the moment their effective power reached the zenith, Communists shied away from recognizing it formally. While the Polish version of Wikipedia refers to the 1952 constitution as "Stalinist," it was not quite that. True, Stalin's constitution of 1936 was copied quite faithfully in the Polish one of 1952, as it was in all other communist constitutions. But the crucial phrase was absent from the Polish one. The Communist Party had power; the elected Parliament had authority.

EXPLANATIONS

Rozmaryn (1961: 36ff) claims that intentions of constitution makers can be identified only from their product, that is, the constitution itself, rather than from any "subjective" analysis. That the constitution incorporates some topics but not others is sufficient evidence of what constitution makers considered important. This methodological principle leads him to assert (Rozmaryn 1961: 53), in what must have been a camouflaged polemic, that "Only constitutional institutions are basic institutions."[5] Yet his analysis, repeatedly emphasizing the superiority of the constitution as the

[4] Hochfeld was a teacher of mine. He was marginalized politically in 1962 by being sent to work in UNESCO and died in Paris in 1966.

[5] The allusion is even more explicit in the passage where Rozamaryn (1961: 121) considers the relation between customary law and the constitution: "[A]ll customary legal norms, even if they considered institutions particularly important from the social-political point of view, could not be considered as constitutional norms. . . . "

exclusive source of normativity, ends with a positive account of the role of the Party:

> It would be a serious error to limit the issue of constitutional guarantees to the existence or absence of legal institutions and to abstract away from the factor of highest social-political importance, namely, the role of the Party of the working class. Law does not act by itself. Law is created and applied by people. In a society, in which the directive force is the working class, the leading role in all aspects of political and social life belongs to the Party of this class. . . . [The Party] holds the position that without a strict obedience to the law of the People's Poland there is no rule of law. This position of the Party is fundamental for the realization of constitutional norms in everyday systematic activities of the organs of people's State. (Rozmaryn 1961: 213)

Hence, the constitution is an equilibrium because the Party wants to implement it. But then why not recognize this role of the Party formally?

Rozamaryn's (1961) normative posture deprives us of a crucial source of information because he was a prominent participant in the entire constitutional process, having compiled several drafts and having served as the secretary of the committee that prepared the final draft. He knew who wanted what and why, what was controversial, and who was decisive. Yet he refuses to comment on the motivations, pretending that they can be read from the letter of the document. We have one and only one account of the process, reconstructed in long-delayed retrospect by a participant, Marian Rybicki (1990).

It bears emphasis that the constitution was carefully prepared and every detail was subject to repeated discussions. The constitutional process began in June 1949, and the law regulating the preparation of the constitution was adopted in May 1951. The committee charged with preparing the text included 103 members, of whom 61 were parliamentary deputies. The membership was composed of representatives of political parties belonging to the Front of National Unity, of local authorities, trade union federation, various official associations, scientists, and cultural personalities. The chair of the committee was the First Secretary of the PUWP and the President of Poland, Bolesław Bierut. Several committees and subcommittees met several times, and the penultimate draft was scrutinized by the Political Bureau, and edited by hand by Stalin[6] as well as Bierut. The final project of the constitution was subjected to a national discussion in which, according to official sources, took part 11 million people in more than 200,000 meetings. Still according to the official sources, this

[6] The extent of Stalin's corrections was controversial: according to one eminent leader of the Party, Jakub Berman, Stalin made only insignificant changes to the Preamble, but other sources report that he made fifty corrections and still others report eighty-two substantive changes that changed "the sense of the Constitution" (Czubiński 1992: 252). A copy of the Russian text of the constitution with Stalin's handmade corrections is now available from Google. The Russian translation contained several grammatical mistakes, which Stalin faithfully corrected. Most of his corrections were stylistic and most concerned declaratory parts of the text. Some, however, were substantive.

campaign generated 2,822 suggestions for substantive modifications. This draft was discussed during four days by the Parliament, with the participation of thirty-two deputies, without any further modifications.

Hence, the omission of the "leading force" clause could not have been inadvertent. That the issue was a subject of attention is manifested by the sequential editing of the relevant part of the Preamble. The draft submitted to Stalin read, "The basis of national power is the alliance of working class and working peasantry." Stalin inserted "*nachelniei*" (superior) before "national" and added "in Poland." Bierut, however, did not follow Stalin, inserting nebulous "*obecnej*" (current) in its place, while retaining the reference to Poland. Something was going on.

Unfortunately, it is impossible to tell what. According to Rybicki (1990), from its first meeting on June 21, 1949, the dominant view in the Constitutional Committee was that the role of the Party is a constitutional matter that should be included, as in the Soviet 1936 constitution, in the article concerning the right of association. The first draft of the constitution contained a clause (Article 69, §3) that said, "Polish United Workers Party . . . constitutes the directive force in the state and all organizations of working people." No doubts concerning this article were raised at the second meeting of the committee on October 20, 1950. Indeed, some members wanted to move this clause to the front or to formulate it as a separate article. This draft was reviewed at a meeting of the Political Bureau of the Party in November 1950. In its aftermath, the committee received comments that included an instruction by one of the Bureau's members, Jakub Berman, "Drop Article 69, §3." No explanation was given and that was that.

Without direct evidence about intentions, we can only speculate. The benchmark explanation must be that the framers of the constitution believed that it would be operational, that is, that they intended it to be observed. The story would go as follows. Except for isolated groups, an overwhelming part of the "working people," as the constituency was defined, support the regime and the Party. All the opposition had been already destroyed by repression, intimidation, and forced political unification under the leadership of the Communist Party. Hence, even if people were to exercise all the freedoms guaranteed by the Constitution, the result would be continued political hegemony of the Communists. The Constitution would be self-implementing.

True, some doubts must have lingered, and just in case the Constitution contains escape clauses, were not cited above. Article 70, §3 warned that "Abuse of the freedom of conscience and religion against interests of the Polish People's Republic is punishable."[7] Article 72, §3 made it explicit that "Organization of and participation in associations whose goals or activities are directed against the political and social

7 This paragraph was subject to attentive editing. The original draft submitted to Stalin read "forbidden," which Stalin changed to "punishable and forbidden." Bierut, in turn, crossed out "forbidden" and inserted "legislatively" before "punishable." The final version says only "punishable." This entire article was eliminated in the constitutional revision of 1976.

system or the legal order of the Polish People's Republic is prohibited." But these are legal, not political, clauses: the law prohibited activities directed against the political order, but the sanctions were to be administered by the legal system, not by political instances.

The explanation that the façade of democracy was maintained as "window dressing" for the outside world is not plausible. "Socialist democracy" was true democracy, as the 1977 Soviet constitution would explicitly assert, superior to the Western ones, which were just a formal shell for the dictatorship of the bourgeoisie. The single party was the instrument of the unity between the rulers and the ruled and the commonality of interests of all "working people." Hence, there was no reason to hide its role. Moreover, the Polish Party claimed its superiority over the state in its Statutes (1959, 1971): it was not hiding anything.

The explanation that the 1952 constitution was intended as window dressing for the Poles is also hard to believe. By 1952, repression was rampant: everyone knew that the constitution was just parchment. The Party and the secret police did what they wanted, without even a veneer of legality.

In the end, I am not wiser. It remains quite plausible that at least some framers of the Polish constitution believed that it would be observed, at least in some future. The Communist Party would govern with general support, so that its leading role in the state would spontaneously emerge from the society without being guaranteed by the constitution. After all, there are many countries in which the same party or a coalition repeatedly won fully democratic elections during very long periods of time: in Luxembourg from 1831 until 1974, but also for a long period in postwar Japan and Italy. Clearly, the Polish framers did not envision having to face an electoral opposition, but there is nothing in the constitution they wrote that would preclude it. All the evidence shows that the lawyers and politicians who participated in the making of the constitution took their task most seriously and responsibly. At one moment, they even hired two prominent novelists to polish the language of the constitution.

And yet I find this interpretation hard to believe. The Constitutional Committee was writing all kinds of clauses protecting physical integrity, freedom from arbitrary imprisonment, and freedom of religion, speech, and association as its own members were being arbitrarily dismissed from their employment, placed under house arrest, and in a couple of cases imprisoned without a trial. How could they have thought that the words they were writing would have any effect?

Even more puzzling is that the framers of the constitution were inclined to imitate the Soviets, while the order to drop the "leading rule" clause came from the leadership of the Party, specifically from Man No. 2 within the regime, the person in charge of the security apparatus.[8] In contrast to his loquacious colleagues, he left

[8] A daring hypothesis is that Berman was protecting the security apparatus from control by the Party, but the question still remains as to why the other members of the Political Bureau would consent. Berman was expelled from the Party in 1956 for "insufficient oversight" over the security apparatus.

no memoirs, and to my best knowledge no one else cast light on this decision. Stalin seems not to have blinked an eye at the absence of the clause, or at least he made no corrections to this effect. This is all we know.

CONCLUSION

Constitutions organize ruling. They constitute government and regulate its relation with the people. Constitutions are operating manuals. They specify how rulers are to be selected, who is competent to make which decisions, who is responsible to whom, for what, and how. It may be also true, as Holmes (2011; also Poulantzas 1973) argues, that in order to rule others, the institutional rulers must restrain themselves. To paraphrase Holmes (1995), at least some "disabling is enabling."[9] The constitution studied here did both, and it did it well enough to satisfy most exacting constitutional lawyers.

Constitutions are not just *ex post* descriptions of an existing political order; they are intended to create an order. As Tom Paine (1989: 89) knew, "[a] constitution is a thing antecedent to a government. The constitution of a country is not the act of its government, but of the people constituting its government." Framers are not scribes; they are engineers. But to create a political order is to specify rules each will want to follow if others are following them. The new order materializes only if the constitution induces everyone, the rulers and the ruled, to follow the rules specified on the piece of paper, only if it generates an equilibrium.

To generate such an equilibrium, constitutions cannot deviate too far from the *de facto* relations of power. As Holmes (1995: 160) put it, "To influence a situation, an actual power-wielder must adapt himself to preexistent patterns of force and unevenly distributed possibilities for change. . . . " Every influencer must be influenced. This is a central axiom of any realistic theory of power. When preinstitutional power is monopolized, constitutions are designed to minimize the possibility that the actual rulers would lose institutional power. Gargarella (2000 152) comments about two constitutions, promulgated by successive rulers of Ecuador, that they appeared as little more than means designed to fortify their own power against the opposition. When power is balanced and the future uncertain, constitutions tend to minimize the cost of losing institutional power, but even constitutions intended to be democratic sometimes merely codify a temporary partisan advantage.[10] Constitutions designed to prevent someone powerful from becoming the ruler are just

9 The claim that the first role of constitutions is to constrain the rulers, made prominent by Elster (1984, 2000) is logically incoherent: unless the government is constituted first, there is nothing to constrain. This is true of Elster's (1984) original version in which rulers constrain themselves as well as in the revised version (2000) in which they are constrained by others.

10 Here is Brenan's (1943: 261–2) description of the Spanish Republican Constitution of 1931: "Everything that could be thought of was thought of – except that the people for whom it was designed might not want it. . . . It had all the faults, all the inevitable make-believes and hypocrisies of new attempts to lay down by one party what shall be done by all parties in the future."

futile: the 1919 "Little Constitution" of Poland was aimed at Marshall Piłsudski,[11] who made a coup seven years later, while the 1946 French constitution was directed at General de Gaulle, who came to power twelve years later.

The communist parties came to power by force, revolutionary in the Soviet Union and external in Eastern Europe. They monopolized power by massive repression. By 1924 in the Soviet Union and the late 1940s in Eastern Europe, communist parties had an effective monopoly of power, even if an incomplete control over the repressive forces through which they exercised this monopoly. The issue facing communist framers was whether to grant constitutional, legal power to this monopoly – to transform it into "authority" – or to just design a legal system in which they could exercise this monopoly *de facto*. Whether the leading role should be enshrined in the constitution was a subject of disagreements in the debate about the project of the Soviet Constitution of 1924. Proponents of including this clause seem to have anticipated the consequences of divergence between power and authority. M. A. Reisner (quoted in Łopatka 1963: 109) argued that "Everything that is a fact should be written in the Constitution. . . . Why would we leave our great party in the situation of a fact not confirmed by the constitution?" This view prevailed in the Yugoslav debate about the constitution of 1963: "We do not consider the role of the League of Communists primarily as a theoretical question, but as matter of our social and political practice and the reality of our life; and the Constitution is bound to reflect that reality" (Vlahović 1963: 50). Opponents in the Soviet debate, however, maintained that the leading role should not be a legal attribute. Although the clause was present in the 1919 Statutes of the Bolshevik Party, Lenin did not want it included in the 1919 Soviet constitution and it was not included in the 1924 one. The reason may have been that including it would have given credence to Trotsky's accusation that the dictatorship of the proletariat was being transformed into the dictatorship of the party. Yet beginning from 1936, wherever and whenever communists consolidated their de facto power, they also gave it legal authority. Except for Poland.

One could think that although the Polish communists could not organize their rule according to the document they wrote, they could rule effectively because an informal set of rules would emerge spontaneously to guide everyone's actions. A Polish saying of the period says, "Law is like a telegraph pole: one cannot go through it but one can go around it." In this theory, the constitution coordinates law-avoiding activities. Hence, even if the equilibrium is not the one described by the constitution, it is still an equilibrium: everyone knows what everyone else will do. The problem with this theory is that law-avoiding activities are not a monopoly of the principals but also of their agents: if the formal rules are not operative, everyone

[11] The fact that the leader of the State was Józef Piłsudski, a man who was an eminent personality and at the same time a political adversary of the Endecja [nationalist political party] which was strong in the *Sejm* . . . weighted on the decisions of the Little Constitution. It introduced a parliamentary system in an extreme version (Krukowski 1990: 13).

can invent ways of getting around them. The incessant tinkering with the formal rules – the never-ceasing reforms of practically everything – shows that the system did not work to the satisfaction of rulers, that law-avoiding activities were constantly escaping the control of the Party. The dynamic of such a system was that the agents were escaping the control of the principals; the principals sought to control the activities of the agents by writing new rules; the agents found ways of going around the new telegraph poles; the principals wrote new rules; and so on, until there so many, often contradictory, rules that the safest strategy was inaction.[12] There was no informal equilibrium.

What the Polish Communists did in 1952 was to write an operating manual, but not for the car they were to drive. As long as the car functioned, powered by the force of the Soviet Army, no manual was needed. But when it started breaking down, no one knew how to fix it. And things broke down often: in the 1956 riots of Poznań, the 1968 student demonstrations in Warsaw, the 1970 strike in Gdynia, and the 1976 general strike. By the time it occurred to the rulers to constitutionalize their rule, it was too late. And after the military coup of 1981, the Party lost its *de facto* leading role. One cannot help but wonder whether Poland was not particularly prone to these breakdowns, including the final one in 1989, precisely because it was the only country within the communist bloc in which power never had the authority to rule. Perhaps constitutions that do not reflect real political conditions render regimes unstable.

REFERENCES

Barros, Robert. 2002. *Constitutionalism and Dictatorship*. New York: Cambridge University Press.

Brenan, Gerald. 1943. *The Spanish Labyrinth: The Social and Political Background of the Spanish Civil War*. Cambridge: Cambridge University Press.

Czubiński, Antoni. 1992. *Dzieje Najnowsze Polski, 1944–1989*. Poznań: Wielkopolska Agencja Wydawnicza.

Ehrlich, Stanisław. 1956. *Praworzdność, Sejm*. Warszawa.

Elster, Jon. 1984. *Ulysses and the Sirens: Studies in Rationality and Irrationality*. New York: Cambridge University Press.

Elster, Jon. 2000. *Ulysses Unbound: Studies in Rationality, Precommitment, and Constraints*. New York: Cambridge University Press.

Gargarella, Roberto. 2000. *Los fundamentos legales de la desigualidad: El constitucionalismo en América (1776–1860)*. Madrid: Siglo XXI.

[12] The mayor who wanted to build the public toilet gave up on his project. According to the rules of the Ministry of the Communal Economy, the toilet should have been placed 2.6 meters below the street level; according to the instructions issued by the Voievodship (the administrative level above) authorities, it should have been 1.9 meters; and according to the town architect, it should have been 2.3 meters. "If I build it 1.9 meters below and the roof will collapse," he reasoned, "I will end in jail for endangering public safety; if I build it 2.6 meters, the Party Secretary will accuse of wasting public resources. Hence, I will not build it."

Holmes, Stephen. 1995. *Passions and Constraint: On the Theory of Liberal Democracy*. Chicago: University of Chicago Press.
Holmes, Stephen. 2011. *Constitutions and Constitutionalism*. Ms. Law School, New York University.
Komarnicki, W. 1938. *Nowy ustrój państwowy Zwizku Sowietów*. Wilno.
Krukowski, Stanislaw. 1990. "Mala Konstytucja z 1919 r," in *Konstytucje Polski: Studja monograficzne z dziejów polskiego konstytucjonalizmu* vol. 2. Warszawa: Państwowe Wydawnictwo Naukowe, pp. 7–18.
Łopatka, Adam. 1963. *Kierownicza Rola Partii Komunistycznej w Stosunku do Państwa Socjalistycznego*. Poznań: Wydawnictwo Poznańskie.
Paine, Thomas. 1989 [1971]. *The Rights of Man*, in *Paine: Political Writings*, Cambridge: Cambridge University Press.
Poulantzas, Nicos. 1973. *Political Power and Social Classes*. London: New Left Books.
Rozmaryn, Stefan. 1961. *Konstytucja Jako Ustawa Zasadnicza PRL*. Warszawa: PWN.
Rybicki, Marian. 1990. "Konstytucja Polskiej Rzeczypospolitej Ludowej z 1952r," in Marian Kallas, ed., *Konstytucje Polski*, vol. 2. Warszawa: PWN, pp. 311–43.
Vlahović, Veljko. 1963. "Role of the Leading Factors of the Social Consciousness. Beograd." *Review of International Affairs* 1: 49–53.

3

Authoritarian Constitutionalism

Some Conceptual Issues

*Mark Tushnet**

Legal scholars and political theorists interested in constitutionalism as a normative concept tend to dichotomize the subject. There is liberal constitutionalism of the sort familiar in the modern West, with core commitments to human rights and self-governance implemented by means of varying institutional devices, and there is authoritarianism, rejecting human rights entirely and governed by unconstrained power holders. Charles McIlwain's often-quoted words exemplify the dichotomization: "[C]onstitutionalism has one essential quality; it is a legal limitation on government; it is the antithesis of arbitrary rule; its opposite is despotic government, the government of will instead of law," and "[a]ll constitutional government is by definition limited government" (1947: 20–1).

This chapter explores the possibility, perhaps implicit in a restrained understanding of McIlwain's formulation, of forms of constitutionalism other than liberal constitutionalism. After describing two possibilities – absolutist constitutionalism and "mere" rule-of-law constitutionalism – the chapter examines in more detail what I call authoritarian constitutionalism. That discussion is connected to recent literature in political science on hybrid regimes that have been labeled variously electoral authoritarianism (Schedler 2006) and competitive authoritarianism (Levitsky and Way 2010). The literature in political science is more concerned with the conditions for the emergence and stability of hybrid regimes than with normative issues, but some parts of the literature shed light on normative issues, as does the related literature on the functions of constitutions and courts in truly authoritarian regimes. Drawing on these literatures, this chapter

* This chapter is a preliminary version of the introduction to a longer work in progress on Singaporean constitutionalism as an example of authoritarian constitutionalism. Geoffrey Curfman, now a research intern in the Middle East Program at the Center for Strategic and International Studies, provided important research assistance at an earlier stage of the project.

outlines some characteristics of authoritarian constitutionalism understood normatively.[1]

The reason for such an exploration parallels that for the analysis of hybrid regimes. For a period, those regimes were described as transitional on the assumption that they were an intermediate point on a trajectory from authoritarianism to liberal democracy.[2] Scholars have come to understand that we are better off seeing these regimes as a distinct type (or as several distinct types), as stable as many democracies. In short, they have pluralized the category of regime types. Similarly, I suggest, pluralizing the category of constitutionalism will enhance understanding by allowing us to draw distinctions between regimes that should be normatively distinguished. Consider one "list of... electoral authoritarian regimes (as of 2006)... [:] Armenia, Azerbaijan, Kazakhstan, Kyrgyzstan, Russia, and Tajikistan;... Algeria, Egypt, Tunisia, and Yemen;... Burkina Faso, Cameroon, Chad, Ethiopia, Gabon, Gambia, Guinea, Mauritania, Tanzania, Togo, and Zambia;... Cambodia, Malaysia, and Singapore" (Schedler 2006: 3). Whatever the utility for political scientists of treating these nations as a single group, for a normative constitutionalist there are obvious distinctions to be drawn: from a constitutionalist's point of view, even as of 2006, Russia was different from Singapore and Malaysia. Describing a category of authoritarian constitutionalism – and, more generally, pluralizing our understanding of constitutionalism – may contribute to analytic clarity in law as it did in political science.

ABSOLUTIST AND MERE RULE-OF-LAW CONSTITUTIONALISM

Consider first the possibility of absolutist constitutionalism: imagine an absolute monarchy in which the monarch's decisions are authoritative.[3] The monarch makes decisions after receiving advice from a group of advisers s/he has personally chosen. The monarch chooses the advisers after consulting widely in the nation, by holding discussion sessions with the nation's citizens.[4] The monarch makes it clear that the advisers provide only advice and that s/he will make the final decision. There are no mechanisms for formally challenging a decision once taken. But the monarch allows widespread discussion of policy options before decisions are taken and criticism of

[1] This chapter is an exploration of a conceptual possibility that has some connection to empirical reality, but I do not claim that any existing system fits my concept of "authoritarian constitutionalism" precisely. For similar explorations, see Baogang He and Mark E. Warren, "Authoritarian Deliberation: The Deliberative Turn in Chinese Political Development" (2011); John Rawls, *The Law of Peoples* (1999) (discussing the conceptual possibility of a "decent hierarchical society").

[2] See Steven Levitsky and Lucan Way, *Competitive Authoritarianism: Hybrid Regimes after the Cold War*, pp. 3–4 (referring to a "democratizing bias" and the "assumption that hybrid regimes are... moving in a democratic direction" in the relevant literature).

[3] The example is drawn from Bhutan's recent history, but I emphasize that it is stylized, not historically accurate.

[4] Or, today, by inviting widespread participation in some sort of Internet forum.

her/his choices afterward. Sometimes such criticisms lead the monarch to modify the chosen policy, but not always. The monarch's decisions are typically motivated by a combination of concerns – that the decision not undermine and perhaps actually enhance the monarchy's stability (defined as the continuation of governance by the monarch and her/his designated successors) and that the decision promote the welfare of the nation's citizens as the monarch understands their welfare. Finally, the monarch does her/his best to imbue potential successors – children, members of the more extended royal family – with the values that animate the monarch's own choices.

This is an absolute monarchy, not a constitutional monarchy on the model of Great Britain or Denmark, but a monarchy that should satisfy the most minimal requirements of normative constitutionalism and probably quite a bit more than that. The example suggests that McIlwain's dichotomization between will and law misses something: the absolute monarch exercises her/his will, but not despotically (even in the long run), and does not engage in arbitrary rule even though the monarch is not limited by law. If that is correct, the example suggests that normative constitutionalism may require a substantial degree of freedom of expression and some informal mechanisms for determining what a nation's citizens believe to be in their interests but not, importantly, a full-fledged system of democratic representation and accountability.

Mere rule-of-law constitutionalism is another variant. Mere rule-of-law constitutionalism is a system that satisfies such core rule-of-law requirements as publicity, prospectivity, and generality.[5] Consider a stylized example of a system that satisfies those requirements but is not fully normatively constitutionalist.[6] The government arrests a critic, charging him with violating a statute prohibiting the public distribution of statements likely to cause racial disharmony by publishing a newspaper editorial criticizing the government's policies on affirmative action. The judge before whom the prosecution is brought dismisses the prosecution on the ground that the editorial did not violate the statute because it was unlikely to cause racial disharmony. The judge orders the critic released. As the police are completing the paperwork to accomplish the release and putting the critic in a taxicab to take him home, the government passes a new statute making it a crime to criticize government policies on affirmative action. The statute defines "criticizing" to include the failure to

[5] The list is, of course, taken from Lon Fuller, *The Morality of Law*. Fuller includes eight items in his list of the rule of law's characteristics, and I limit my example to those in the text solely for expository reasons. Fuller appears to believe that legal systems that conform to the rule of law are highly likely (or even certain) to conform as well to full normative constitutionalism understood more thickly, incidentally though not definitionally or deductively. This chapter is not the place to develop my view that this is mistaken, although the very enterprise of describing mere rule-of-law and authoritarian constitutionalism rests on that view.

[6] The example is loosely based on an incident in Singapore's constitutional history, modified to bring out "mere rule-of-law" features. The case on which it draws is *Chng Suan Tze v. Minister of Home Affairs* (1989).

withdraw from public access statements made before the statute's enactment. When the critic steps out of the taxicab at his house, the police arrest him for violating the new statute.[7] Holding the critic liable is, I believe, consistent with the minimal requirements of the rule of law: the new statute is public, general, prospective, and capable of being complied with.[8] But I think it clear that the government's action is inconsistent with full normative constitutionalism.[9]

Now generalize the government's behavior so that the example is not a simple one of a violation occurring within a normatively constitutionalist system but is rather a typical example: the government is alert to challenges, does its best to anticipate them, alters the laws in place whenever it discovers a problem but does so consistent with the requirements of publicity, generality, prospectivity, and the like. We then have mere rule-of-law constitutionalism.[10] As with absolutist constitutionalism, mere rule-of-law constitutionalism conforms to some of McIlwain's criteria but not others: the government is limited by law and, to the extent that it responds to challenges only after the event, perhaps we ought not to describe it as completely despotic, and yet the government seems not truly limited or nonarbitrary at least in potential.

Neither the absolutist but benevolent monarch nor the regime in a rule-of-law system acts arbitrarily, which implies that they are constitutionalist systems under McIlwain's definition. Yet, both fall short of the requirements of a thicker normative constitutionalism. These possibilities suggest that pluralizing the idea of constitutionalism might be analytically helpful.

CONSTITUTIONS, COURTS, AND ELECTIONS *IN* AUTHORITARIAN SOCIETIES

Most of the scholarship by political scientists on constitutions in authoritarian regimes is analytically descriptive rather than normative, although it is written against a normative backdrop: if constitutionalism entails limitations on government, and authoritarian regimes are ones in which government is unlimited, why do such regimes even have constitutions? Of course, every regime has a *descriptive* constitution, some reasonably regular processes for policy development and conflict

[7] Assume that the critic has a cell phone with him in the taxicab, so that he could receive notice of the new statute's adoption and direct supporters to withdraw the editorial from public availability.

[8] Fuller's list requires some degree of stability in law. A single modification provoked by a newly perceived problem would not, I think, be inconsistent with that requirement.

[9] Note that the stylized account I have given includes action by a judge, who we can assume is independent of the regime but enforces its positive law. Even if we add "independent judges" to the list of requirements of the rule of law, we will not guarantee compliance with anything more than the regime's positive law (unless we make quite strong assumptions about how independent judges inevitably act).

[10] In my judgment, Gordon Silverstein, in "Singapore: The Exception That Proves Rules Matter" (2008, in Tom Ginsburg and Tamir Moustafa's *Rule by Law: The Politics of Courts in Authoritarian Regimes*), ascribes rule-of-law constitutionalism, not authoritarian constitutionalism, to Singapore.

resolution.[11] Yet the literature on hybrid regimes seems animated by an interest in understanding why such regimes have constitutions that appear to go beyond merely mapping out power relations within the government and yet are not mere shams.[12] For present purposes, even if this account of some motivations for this literature is inaccurate, analytic descriptions of constitutions in hybrid regimes illuminate some features of authoritarian constitutionalism.

Ginsburg and Moustafa (2008) provide a helpful catalogue of the "functions of courts in authoritarian states."

> Courts are used to (1) establish social control and sideline political opponents, (2) bolster a regime's claim to "legal" legitimacy, (3) strengthen administrative compliance within the state's own bureaucratic machinery and solve coordination problems among competing factions within the regime, (4) facilitate trade and investment, and (5) implement controversial policies so as to allow political distance from core elements of the regime. (Ginsburg and Moustafa 2008: 4)

Though the subject is outside Moustafa and Ginsburg's immediate concern, I note that constitutions as a whole, not only courts, serve some of these functions as well.

Functional or instrumentalist accounts of law, courts, and constitutions are subject to important instabilities, which are especially acute in connection with authoritarian regimes. The general point is simple: such regimes will use law, courts, and constitutions to achieve these goals only so long as doing so serves the regime's interests. And, because the regime is authoritarian, it faces no constraints on abandoning law, courts, and constitutionalism when doing what would serve the regime's interests – or, perhaps more interestingly, when law, courts, and constitutionalism appear to be interfering with the regime's (other) goals.

The point can be seen most clearly in the account of courts as institutions "to facilitate trade and investment." The basic story is straightforward: authoritarian regimes have the power to expropriate property at will. Knowing that investors will be reluctant to invest in the nation. The regime can provide investors with the assurance that their investments will not be expropriated by embedding a guarantee against the relevant kinds of expropriation in the constitution and then by establishing courts to enforce that guarantee: "[B]y establishing a neutral institution to monitor and punish violations of property rights, the state can make credible its promise to keep its hands off" (Ginsburg and Moustafa 2008: 8).

The difficulty, which arises in different forms with respect to each component of the functionalist or instrumentalist account, lies in explaining why the promise

[11] For a discussion of the term "constitution" in a descriptive sense, see Mark Tushnet, "Constitutions," in Michel Rosenfeld and Andras Sajo (eds.), *The Oxford Handbook of Comparative Constitutional Law*.

[12] On the idea of constitutions as maps of power, see Okoth-Okendo, 1993. The 1936 Constitution of the Soviet Union is the usual example of a sham constitution, but there are many additional examples in recent years.

is a credible one. The neutral institution – the combination of a constitution and a court enforcing the constitution – is said to make the promise credible. But, just as an authoritarian regime can revoke its promise when its rulers believe that doing so would be to their advantage, so can it eliminate the neutral institution at the same time. If the regime finds the institution useful for other purposes, it can manipulate the court's jurisdiction and personnel,[13] or modify the constitution in a targeted way, to allow the institution to serve – at least momentarily – those other purposes. Yet at this point, we can see a classic problem of "unraveling." Investors learn that the promise was not credible when the regime eliminates the institution's neutrality to allow expropriation. Observing that development, all those targeted by the other functions, such as securing legitimation or delegating controversial reforms, should anticipate similar responses whenever the constitution or the courts impede rather than promote the regime's goals. Knowing that, the targets should not give any special weight to the constitution and courts even when the regime does not interfere with them. Manipulating the constitution or the courts' jurisdiction with respect to investment and expropriation reveals "the man behind the curtain" with respect to delegating controversial reforms as well.

One important constraint on the unraveling of constitutions in authoritarian regimes leads in the direction of understanding authoritarian constitutionalism in some electoral or competitive authoritarian regimes.[14] Andreas Schedler defines electoral authoritarianism: "[E]lections are broadly inclusive . . . as well as minimally pluralistic . . . , minimally competitive . . . , and minimally open" (Schedler 2009: 382). For Beatriz Magaloni, "hegemonic-party systems allow opposition parties to challenge the incumbent party through multiparty elections" (2006: 32). I will return to how authoritarian constitutionalism deals with elections, but the key point here is that electoral authoritarian or hegemonic-party regimes are assured of victory in these elections. But, Magaloni emphasizes, not just victory – so is the dominant party in a dominant-party regime – but landslide yet minimally manipulated victories: "[H]egemonic-party systems are far more overpowering than predominant-party systems, usually controlling more than 65 percent of the legislative seats – so that they can *change the constitution unilaterally*, without the need to forge coalitions

13 See Steven Levitsky and Lucan Way, "The Rise of Competitive Authoritarianism" (2002), listing impeachment, bribery, extortion, and cooptation as techniques for manipulating the judiciary. I would add manipulation of jurisdiction to their list.

14 Levitsky and Way note a temporal constraint in their discussion of regimes that "subsequently punish judges who rule against them" (2002: 57). Authoritarian rulers can misjudge the need to interfere with the institutions' neutrality. Delayed intervention can signal the possibility that the institution's neutrality will be sustained long enough for regime opponents to take advantage of opportunities for opposition, which may in turn last long enough to undermine the regime more generally. In my view, this is the account offered in Tamir Moustafa, *The Struggle for Constitutional Power: Law, Politics, and Development in Egypt* (2007). As I interpret Moustafa's account, the Mubarak regime manipulated the neutral institution by changing its jurisdiction and personnel after it discovered that neutrality was undermining the regime and did so in time to limit the courts' effects on the regime's stability.

with opposition parties. This implies that there is no binding set of constitutional rules . . . " (2006: 32, emphasis added).[15]

The risk of unraveling occurs precisely because there is no such set. And yet, the existence of more-or-less real elections indicates that these regimes are not fully authoritarian. Again, political scientists can offer functional accounts for conducting elections, but such accounts have the same vulnerabilities as functionalist accounts of other neutral institutions. So, for example, Magaloni identifies these functions: elections "are designed to establish a regularized method to share power among ruling party politicians[,] . . . to disseminate public information about the regime's strength that would serve to discourage potential divisions within the ruling party[,] . . . to provide information about supporters and opponents of the regime[,] . . . [and] to trap the opposition, so that it invests in the existing autocratic institutions rather than challenging them by violent means" (2006: 9–10). It should be clear that these functions could be served by other institutional mechanisms, as, for example, occurs in the authoritarian People's Republic of China. With autocratic control, more-or-less real elections will occur when, but only when, they produce the kinds of massive victories that give the regime control over the processes for modifying the constitution.

The main contribution of the scholarly literature on competitive or electoral authoritarianism to an inquiry into authoritarian constitutionalism is its focus on elections that are open, competitive, and pluralistic, though minimally so, according to Schedler. They must be only minimally so lest the authoritarian regime become simply a liberal democracy with a dominant party. All the accounts make electoral manipulation a feature of these regimes. Yet, as Schedler and Magaloni note, while it is easy to distinguish "mere" manipulation from gross fraud and intimidation, it is much more difficult to distinguish it from the ordinary practices of politicians in liberal democracies.[16] Schedler (2009) enumerates "the enactment of discriminatory election laws, the repression of protest marches, [and] the exclusion of candidates from the ballot by administrative fiat" as mechanisms to ensure massive victories. But, he continues, because "people may differ in their concrete definitions of democratic minimum standards, . . . the frontier between electoral democracy and electoral authoritarianism represents essentially contested terrain" (Schedler 2009: 385). Similarly, Magaloni observes that "the ruling party can commit electoral fraud or threaten to repress its opponents," but criticizes Schedler for treating as "manipulations" behavior that "can also take place in systems that we normally regard as democratic," such as " 'self-serving rules of representation granting themselves a decisive edge when votes are translated into seats' " (2006: 19, 33–4).[17]

15 See also Magaloni (2006: 259–61) (describing how hegemonic-party control in Mexico produced "the [e]ndogeneity of the Constitution").

16 A good account of electoral manipulations in the United States is Samuel Issacharoff and Richard Pildes, "Politics as Markets: Partisan Lockups of the Democratic Process" (1998).

17 Quoting Schedler, "Elections Without Democracy: The Menu of Manipulation." *Journal of Democracy* 13: 36–50, 45 (2002).

Consider several examples. Singapore's government has been controlled by the People's Action Party (PAP) since the nation's founding in 1965, and the PAP has won elections by wide margins, until 2011 by winning more than 80 percent of the votes cast.[18] Its constitution bars from the Parliament anyone who "is an undischarged bankrupt" (Constitution of Singapore, Article 45 (1)(b)). This provision can readily be defended on good-government grounds: it keeps out of office a class of people who might use the power of office for personal advantage, that is, to get enough money to emerge from bankruptcy. The PAP intimidates the opposition not by arresting opponents for political offenses or on fake charges but by suing them for libel. Using what Levitsky and Way (2002: 58) describe as "colonial-era" libel laws,[19] the PAP's leaders obtained substantial judgments based on publications fairly treated under the libel laws as libelous statements about the crass motivations of politicians promoting the PAP's policies. Notably, J. B. Jeyaretnam, a prominent opposition leader, twice lost his seat in Parliament, once after being convicted of a financial offense in connection with his party's funds and once for failing to pay damages to PAP leaders for libeling them (Mydans 2008). The libel laws Singapore's leaders use to intimidate the opposition are indeed old fashioned and almost certainly not in tune with standards that prevail even outside the United States, with its especially severe restrictions on libel law as applied to public figures. Yet certainly taken on their own, and probably even in connection with Singapore's wider system of regulating expression, Singapore's libel laws seem within the bounds of liberal constitutionalism – as might be suggested by the fact that other common-law nations used quite similar rules until relatively recently and were at those times rather clearly liberal constitutional states anyway.

Another example of electoral manipulation well short of fraud is Singapore's "group-representation constituencies"[20] (GRCs). These constituencies are multi-member districts. Parties present lists of candidates for each GRC, and (simplifying for expository ease) at least one member of the list must be non-Chinese. Voters cast their ballots for party lists, not individual candidates. Again, this design has an obvious good-government rationale, that of ensuring representation of Singapore's minorities. The dominant Chinese population might win every parliamentary seat. Were all districts to be a single member, and even if minorities dominated in a few districts, their representatives would be swamped in the parliament as a whole. But the GRCs also serve to impede opposition electoral success. A charismatic or otherwise extremely popular opposition candidate might win in a single-member district but might find it more difficult to carry the whole list to victory in a GRC:

[18] The 2011 election resulted in a vote margin of 60%, which political observers, including the PAP's leadership, regarded as a massive repudiation of the party.

[19] See also Levitsky and Way (2010: 9), describing "the widespread . . . use of libel or defamation laws against journalists, editors, and media outlets."

[20] "Group Representation Constituency," on *Wikipedia*, provides a good overview of the GRC system.

one charismatic candidate and two dull ones might lose to a PAP slate of three solid but unexciting candidates.[21]

Finally, William Case (2006) argues that the leaders of the Malaysian electorally authoritarian regime engage in vote buying by providing supporters with valuable benefits such as "on-the-spot 'development grants' for new clinics, paved roads, or mosques." Similarly, "Singapore's government has threatened to cut off state funding for public housing upgrades in those districts where opposition candidates win" (Case 2006: 103–4).[22] Magaloni puts the point more generally: "[T]he ruling party monopolizes the state's resources and employs them to reward voter loyalty and to punish voter defection" (2006: 19). From another perspective, though, these are examples of ordinary pork-barrel politics or credit claiming by elected politicians in liberal democracies (Mayhew 1974).

These examples illustrate the difficulty in distinguishing electoral manipulations in hybrid regimes from ordinary politics in liberal constitutional ones.[23] After several pages seeking to distinguish competitive authoritarianism from pure authoritarianism and democracy, Levitsky and Way find themselves offering a summary of the "level of uncertainty" associated with competitive authoritarian elections: the level is "[l]ower than democracy but higher than full authoritarianism" (2010: 13). At some point, of course, matters of degree become matters of kind, and the cumulative effects of several types of manipulation might exceed even a rather extensive exercise of an individual type in a liberal democratic regime. But perhaps we should consider some hybrid regimes as falling within the domain of normative constitutionalism.

AUTHORITARIAN CONSTITUTIONALISM

How can authoritarian constitutionalism be distinguished from (mere) authoritarianism and rule-of-law constitutionalism? For present purposes, constitutionalism is normatively weighted, not necessarily applicable to all states that have written constitutions, even written constitutions setting out institutional arrangements and individual rights. The 1936 Constitution of the Soviet Union was such a constitution, but the Soviet Union was fully authoritarian. I take as a rough definition of authoritarianism that all decisions can potentially be made by a single decision

21 In 2011, an opposition list won a GRC for the first time.

22 Note that Case (2006) refers to denying upgrades, not withdrawal of existing subsidies.

23 I note my sense that some of the work on hybrid regimes trades on failing to distinguish sharply enough between electoral fraud and electoral manipulation, evoking images of fraud to motivate analyses that describe systems that are of particular interest because only manipulation occurs. For examples, see Magaloni (2006: 18) ("A third instrument hegemonic parties employ to deter party splits is raising the costs of entry to potential challengers by . . . threatening to commit electoral fraud against them and to use the army to enforce such fraud.") and Levitsky and Way (2002: 52–3) ("Incumbents violate . . . rules so often and to such an extent . . . that the regime fails to meet conventional minimum standards for democracy . . . . Members of the opposition may be jailed, exiled, or – less frequently – even assaulted or murdered."). In contrast, see Magaloni (2006: 21) (Figure 1.1, identifying a category in which there is "[n]o need for electoral fraud").

maker[24] whose decisions are both formally and practically unregulated by law, though as students of authoritarian constitutions have emphasized, they might be regulated by conflicts of power,[25] even rather structured and predictable conflicts.[26] Constitutionalists differ on the content of normative constitutionalism, and I do not intend to take a position on anything other than what its broad boundaries are.

Here are some of the characteristics of authoritarian constitutional regimes.

(1) The regime, which for expository convenience I will assume is controlled by a dominant party, makes all relevant public policy decisions, and there is no basis in law for challenging whatever choices the regime makes. This is what makes the regime authoritarian.

(2) The regime does not arrest political opponents arbitrarily, although it may impose a variety of sanctions on them, such as the risk of bankruptcy from libel judgments in Singapore.

(3) Even as it employs such sanctions, the regime allows reasonably open discussion and criticism of its policies. The PAP's "defeat" in the 2011 elections may have resulted from the increased use of social media, and, notably, a government-sponsored study published in 2008 encouraged the government to allow wider use of social media than it had done before.[27] The regime's critics find themselves able to disseminate their criticisms even after they have been sanctioned. The Singaporean libel judgments impoverish the government's critics, but they still have access to resources through friends and family who are not themselves active critics of the government (and therefore cannot be sanctioned because of the limitations rule-of-law constitutionalism places on the regime).[28]

(4) The regime operates reasonably free and fair elections, with close attention to such matters as the drawing of election districts and the creation of party lists to ensure as best it can that it will prevail – and by a substantial margin – in such elections. Fraud and physical intimidation occur, if at all, only sporadically and unsystematically. As Carlos Casteneda put it, referring to Mexico, the dominant party was "no 'tea party'" but "'[r]epression was

[24] Which might be a collective body, such as the Central Committee of the Chinese Communist Party. He and Warren use the term "command authoritarianism" (Baogang and Warren 2011: 273).

[25] This definition implies that political constitutionalism, as discussed in the British literature, must describe politics as more than a mere power struggle, the precipitate of which yields normative constitutionalism, but as implicating in politics itself arguments about law.

[26] It is probably worth noting that an authoritarian regime might choose to implement normative constitutionalism on the condition that it remain free to replace it at any time. I think it is an interesting question whether the adoption of normative constitutionalism has a ratchet-like effect, such that once adopted it cannot be repudiated. I am inclined to think that it does not.

[27] See *Report by the Advisory Council on the Impact of New Media on Society, Engaging New Media: Challenging Old Assumptions* (2008).

[28] For a description of how Jeyaretnam conducted his life after bankruptcy, see "Joshua B. Jeyaretnam: Singapore Opposition Leader," Oct. 1, 2008 (obituary).

truly a last resort' " (Magaloni 2006: 10–11). Levitsky and Way (2010) describe competitive authoritarianism as combining both occasional "high-intensity coercion" and more routine "low-intensity coercion." The latter includes "surveillance . . . low-profile physical harassment . . . , denial of employment, scholarships, or university entrance to opposition activists; denial of public service . . . to individuals and communities with ties to the opposition; and use of tax, regulatory, or other state agencies to investigate and prosecute opposition politicians, entrepreneurs, and media owners" (Levitsky and Way 2010: 58). Authoritarian constitutional regimes lower the intensity of coercion even more, as with Case's example of denying upgrades in services, not the services themselves, to districts in which the opposition is strong.

(5) The dominant party is sensitive to public opinion and alters its policies at least on occasion in response to what it perceives to be public views. Its motivation for responsiveness may be mixed, although a desire to remain in power dominates other motivations such as judgments about what is in the nation's best interests.

(6) It may develop mechanisms to ensure that the amount of dissent does not exceed the level it regards as desirable. Magaloni focuses on the hegemonic party's efforts to keep whatever dissent occurs within its ranks by holding out the prospect of rewards not only to party loyalists but also to party activists who challenge the party from within. "Co-optation is better than exclusion" because it allows the hegemonic party to achieve the massive victories it requires (Magaloni 2006: 16). The PAP leadership in Singapore institutionalized co-optation by creating positions for opposition party members and elites outside the PAP. "Non-constituency members of Parliament" (NCMPs) are members of political parties outside the government (Constitution of Singapore, Article 39 (1)(b)). They are appointed to Parliament to provide some voice within it to an opposition that, by design, cannot win parliamentary seats.[29] NCMPs are the best (but losing) vote getters from major opposition parties. In addition, the government can appoint "nominated members of Parliament" (NMPs), drawn from universities and other sectors of civil society (Constitution of Singapore, Article 39 (a)(c)). NCMPs and NMPs can vote on nearly all substantive legislation, although not on the budget and related issues, and, notably, on proposed constitutional amendments. These mechanisms of co-optation may have the collateral effect of increasing the regime's responsiveness to public opinion and criticism.

With these characteristics, I believe, authoritarian constitutionalism is at least as normatively constitutionalist as the absolute monarchy I described. And, though

[29] As amended in 2010, the Constitution provides that "up to" nine NCMPs can be named, and the exact number selected can depend on whether opposition candidates have won elections on their own.

what I have described is something like an ideal type, Singapore provides some indication that authoritarian constitutionalism is also empirically possible. The primary question about authoritarian constitutionalism is whether it describes a regime that is reasonably stable over a reasonably long period.[30] Other than Singapore, there are few examples of actual systems that appear to fit the description of authoritarian constitutionalism, and some candidates that might have done so at some points have not persisted long.[31] The PAP's leadership provides a good example of what Case (2006) describes as the importance of "skill" in designing institutions that sustain authoritarian constitutionalism. The co-optation mechanisms there are quite cleverly designed.[32]

Instability can be resolved in two directions. An authoritarian constitutionalist regime could lose its authoritarian character and become fully constitutionalist,[33] or it could lose its constitutionalism and become purely authoritarian.[34] (a) The first path might involve something like learning: toleration of some dissent increases so that more dissent emerges and the mechanisms of co-optation expand to encompass more people but weaken the commitment the co-opted have to the regime's authoritarianism. At some point, members of the regime itself see little personal threat in abandoning the regime's authoritarian characteristics at least in part because the emerging leaders of the nascent fully constitutionalist regime understand that providing such assurances is essential to the transition after which they hope to be the new regime's leaders.[35]

30 The qualifications are necessary because one cannot demand "permanent" stability of any regime, and because I am willing to concede that fully democratic constitutionalist regimes may persist for longer periods than other constitutionalist ones, but not willing to concede that such regimes provide the definition of stability we should use. See also Thomas Christiano, "An Instrumental Argument for a Human Right to Democracy" (2011), which argues that a "consultation hierarchy," a regime similar to the monarchy I have described, "is not impossible; it is just very unlikely" because its stability depends on sustained choices by the monarch and his/her successors, which cannot be assured. I put aside as relevant to a different sort of analysis the question of the social and economic preconditions to authoritarian constitutionalism, but the point is almost inevitably made in discussions of Singapore that the nation's economic success under the PAP regime has an important role in sustaining the regime.

31 For example, the Islamic Republic of Iran prior to the 2009 elections might have qualified as an authoritarian constitutionalist regime, but that year's fraudulent presidential election either transformed it into a fully authoritarian regime or confirmed that it was already such a regime.

32 Singapore's system for compensating high civil servants is another example of design skill (coupled with the nation's economic success). High civil servants receive salaries "pegged to economic performance and the salaries of the top echelons of a group of key professional classes" (Kumar and Siddique 2010: 15).

33 For a discussion of this possibility, see Baogang and Warren (2011). Levitsky and Way (2010) argue that competitive authoritarian nations with strong links to the West – a description that fits Singapore – are more likely than other such regimes to democratize.

34 Cf. Levitsky and Way (2010: 25–6) (describing the possibility that competitive authoritarianism will become stable authoritarianism).

35 I include the regime members' inheritable wealth within the items they might be concerned about. So they do not anticipate confiscation of that wealth either directly or when passed on to their heirs.

(b) The transformation to authoritarianism (or mere rule-of-law constitutionalism) might itself have several variants. For example, (i) the regime's leaders might be unable to transmit a normative commitment to consultation and responsiveness to their successors.[36] The successors become increasingly less responsive and deal with increasing dissatisfaction through repression and violence. Or (ii) the regime's leaders face increasing public dissatisfaction but cannot obtain assurances that they would not suffer severe losses were they to leave office. To avoid those losses, they repress dissent.[37]

CONCLUSION

There may well be additional forms of normatively constitutionalist systems that are not fully constitutionalist. I hope that these observations will contribute to a more sustained consideration both of additional conceptual possibilities and, in my view more important, of cases in which we can observe something other than authoritarianism and full normative constitutionalism. I believe that there are such cases and that examining them would shed light not only on questions of institutional design within a normatively constitutionalist framework but also on normative constitutionalism itself.

REFERENCES

Advisory Council on the Impact of New Media on Society, The. 2008. *Engaging New Media: Challenging Old Assumptions* (report).

Baogang, He and Mark E. Warren. 2011. "Authoritarian Deliberation: The Deliberative Turn in Chinese Political Development." *Perspectives on Politics* 9: 269.

Case, William. "Manipulative Skills: How Do Rulers Control the Electoral Arena?" in Andreas Schedler, ed., *Electoral Authoritarianism: The Dynamics of Unfree Competition*. Boulder, CO: Lynne Rienner Publishers, 2006.

Chng Suan Tze v. Minister of Home Affairs. 1989. MLJ 1: 69 (Singapore Court of Appeal).

Christiano, Thomas. 2011. "An Instrumental Argument for a Human Right to Democracy." *Philosophy & Public Affairs* 39: 142.

Constitution of Singapore.

Fuller, Lon. 1964. *The Morality of Law*. New Haven, CT: Yale University Press.

Ginsburg, Tom and Tamir Moustafa (eds.). 2008. *Rule by Law: The Politics of Courts in Authoritarian Regimes*. New York: Cambridge University Press.

[36] One question about the Singaporean example is the extent to which it is parasitic on the special intellectual and charismatic characteristics of Lee Kuan Yew, the nation's leader since independence (a leadership that was formal for many years and now is informal, with Lee Kuan Yew serving in the nonstatutory post of Minister Mentor). Notably, the current Prime Minister is Lee Kuan Yew's son, who is generally regarded as less charismatic than his father but almost as intellectually able. Or, put in more general terms, Lee Kuan Yew's overwhelming role has meant that the PAP has not had to face severe problems of leadership succession and the possibility of intra-elite competition for leadership.

[37] Again, I put to one side other origins of a transformation into authoritarianism such as defeat in a foreign adventure or severe economic stress, whether caused by regime missteps or exogenously.

Issacharoff, Samuel and Richard Pildes. 1998. "Politics as Markets: Partisan Lockups of the Democratic Process." *Stanford Law Review* 50: 643.

Kumar, Sree and Sharon Siddique. 2010. *The Singapore Success Story: Public–Private Alliance for Investment Attraction, Innovation and Export Development* 15. New York: United Nations.

Levitsky, Steven and Lucan A. Way. 2002. "The Rise of Competitive Authoritarianism." *Journal of Democracy* 13: 51.

Levitsky, Steven and Lucan A. Way. 2010. *Competitive Authoritarianism: Hybrid Regimes After the Cold War*. New York: Cambridge University Press.

Magaloni, Beatriz. 2006. *Voting for Autocracy: Hegemonic Party Survival and Its Demise in Mexico*. New York: Cambridge University Press.

Mayhew, David. 1974. *Congress: The Electoral Connection*. New Haven, CT: Yale University Press.

McIlwain, Charles. 1947. *Constitutionalism: Ancient and Modern*. Ithaca, NY: Cornell University Press.

Moustafa, Tamir. 2007. *The Struggle for Constitutional Power: Law, Politics, and Development in Egypt*. New York: Cambridge University Press.

Mydans, Seth. 2008. "J. B. Jeyaretnam, Persistent Opposition Figure in Singapore, Is Dead at 82." *The New York Times* (5 October 2008), 43.

Obituary. "Joshua B. Jeyaretnam: Singapore Opposition Leader." *The Times Online* (1 October 2008). Available at http://www.timesonline.co.uk/tol/comment/obituaries/article4855720.ece (visited 28 September 2011).

Okoth-Okendo, H. W. O. 1993. "Constitutions without Constitutionalism: An African Political paradox," in Douglas Greenberg, S. N. Katz, B. Oliviero, and S. C. Wheatley, eds., *Constitutionalism and Democracy: Transitions in the Contemporary World*. New York: Oxford University Press, pp. 65–80.

Rawls, John. 1999. *The Law of Peoples*. Cambridge, MA: Harvard University Press.

Schedler, Andreas (ed.). 2006. *Electoral Authoritarianism: The Dynamics of Unfree Competition*. Boulder, CO: Lynne Rienner Publishers.

Schedler, Andreas. 2009. "Electoral Authoritarianism," in Todd Landman and Neil Robinson, eds., *The Sage Handbook of Comparative Politics*. Los Angeles: Sage, pp. 381–94.

Silverstein, Gordon. 2008. "Singapore: The Exception that Proves Rules Matter," in Tom Ginsburg and Tamir Moustafa, eds., *Rule by Law: The Politics of Courts in Authoritarian Regimes*. New York: Cambridge University Press, pp. 73–101.

Tushnet, Mark. 2012. "Constitutions," in Michel Rosenfeld and Andras Sajo, eds., *The Oxford Handbook of Comparative Constitutional Law*. New York: Oxford University Press, pp. 217–32.

Wikipedia. Group Representation Constituency. Available at http://en.wikipedia.org/wiki/Group_Representation_Constituency.

PART II

Constitutional Design in Authoritarian Regimes

4

The Political Economy of Autocratic Constitutions

Michael Albertus and Victor Menaldo

Austria adopted a new constitution in 1934, as did Portugal in 1933, Poland in 1935, Turkey in 1924, and Brazil in 1937 and again in 1967. Besides the fact that these are constitutions adopted in countries characterized by colorful political histories marked by periods of both drastic change and hard-fought stability, what do their constitutions share in common? They were adopted under dictatorship. Although all of these countries eventually transitioned to democracy, these constitutions were not designed to bring about democracy – although some of them served, decades after being adopted, as vehicles for introducing elections and checks on executive authority.

Why do autocrats adopt constitutions? This chapter argues that the fundamental reason is that constitutions can help dictators consolidate power, increase investment, and boost economic development – all while generating a steady flow of rents for themselves and their cronies without empowering challengers that might undermine their authority. This claim may come as a surprise to most readers. It certainly challenges the status-quo, minimalist view that an autocratic constitution is merely window dressing that provides lip service to the rule of law and rights without the sincere intention to enforce them (see Posner and Young 2007, and Chapter 1 of this volume). It also challenges the view that in a dictatorship, a constitution is a formality and afterthought that merely announces that the dictator's authority is supreme and formally and publicly announces his political agenda (Brown 2002).

In arguing and demonstrating that constitutions under dictatorship matter, we draw on a strain of research that views constitutions as part of a package of institutions that foster self-enforcing stability in autocratic regimes (Albertus and Menaldo 2012a; Albertus and Menaldo 2012b; Barros 2002; Elkins et al. 2009; Elkins 2010; Menaldo 2012; Myerson 2008; Negretto 2013; Ordeshook 1992; Weingast 1997). Several chapters in this volume, such as those by Ghandi, Negretto, and Przeworski, also advance this general idea. In the introduction, Ginsberg and Simpser refer to this role as the "operating manual" model of constitutional politics under autocracy.

Like these authors and this volume in general, our contribution therefore helps reconcile this debate between comparative political economists regarding the role played by constitutions in autocratic regimes. Autocratic constitutions play a crucial role in consolidating the inner ranks of the autocratic regime by fostering loyalty and trust between the dictator and his launching organization (LO) – those individuals who helped him grab power – early in the regime, when uncertainty about the dictator's intentions is considerable and the LO's de facto power is at its height (Albertus and Menaldo 2012a).

One key function of autocratic constitutions is to consolidate a new distribution of power. To accomplish this, autocratic constitutions may outline limits on executive authority, codify individual rights and political obligations, and, given the right conditions, impose constraints on executive authority. Autocratic constitutions can then serve as coordinating devices for the elites who helped the dictator gain power. This insight draws from an established body of work on how constitutions can enable political actors to establish mutual expectations and impose self-enforcing limits on executive authority (see, e.g., Carey 2000; Hardin 1989; Myerson 2008; Weingast 1997).

We test this theoretical framework on a panel data set of Latin American dictators between 1950 and 2002. We find that the creation of a constitution under dictatorship can enable an autocratic coalition to co-opt threats to their rule and last longer in office, a finding that holds even after controlling for other possible indirect institutional pathways and after instrumenting autocratic constitutions with constituent assembly elections held prior to constitutional promulgation. Autocratic constitutions also serve to provide clearer definitions of property rights to the organization that supports a dictator's rule in office and are therefore associated with stronger property rights protection, higher rates of private investment, and economic growth. Because of the possibility of selection bias, whereby some unobserved factor jointly determines both constitutional adoption and leader consolidation, the analyses control for other determinants of autocratic consolidation and country fixed effects.

It is important to note that constitutions do not *only* serve to legitimate and strengthen a dictator's rule, nor are they are a panacea for dictators. Dictators can avail other strategies to consolidate political power as well, including repression and personal patronage networks that cultivate loyalty and dependence among a set of powerful elite supporters (Bueno de Mesquita et al. 2003; Haber 2006). Of course, autocratic constitutions can serve other functions besides consolidating political authority and protecting elite property rights, as highlighted by several chapters in this volume and by Ginsberg and Simpser in the introduction. Moreover, constitutional adoption does not always occur at the start of an autocratic coalition's tenure. Yet, a sufficient number of constitutions do serve to consolidate the dictator's rule vis-a-vis his launching organization, explaining why the central tendency in the data shows a positive association between constitutions and autocratic coalition survival, stronger property rights protection, and higher investment and economic growth after holding other factors constant.

The chapter continues as follows. In the first section, we review the literature on the political economy of dictatorship, focusing on accountability mechanisms under autocratic rule. The second section provides a theoretical foundation for understanding why autocrats adopt constitutions, arguing that these constitutions aid in formalizing a new distribution of power and consolidating executive rule. This section provides a series of empirically testable implications regarding the effects of autocratic constitutions on coalition survival and property rights regimes. The third section systematically explores these empirical implications. Multivariate statistical analyses investigate the effect of constitutions on autocratic coalition survival, property rights protection, private investment, and economic growth.

INSTITUTIONS AND POWER SHARING UNDER DICTATORSHIP

Although the prototypical autocrat may divide and conquer potential challengers or terrorize opponents into submission through the threat of torture or death (Acemoglu et al. 2004; Haber 2006), successful dictators often relegate coercion to a last resort. They instead rely primarily on institutions that help them generate trust and create a stable distributional arrangement. This distributional arrangement pertains to the political elites that launch a new dictator into office rather than the majority of citizens. Credibly committing to protect the property rights of the members of the launching organization is therefore one key to autocratic success.

The burgeoning literature on the political economy of autocratic regimes has established that not all dictators are predatory and advanced our understanding of why this is the case. Although collegial military juntas, legislative assemblies, and political parties can help dictators co-opt challengers and cooperate with allies (Gandhi and Przeworski 2006), elites may also use these institutions to impel dictators to curb their discretion (Barros 2002; Haber et al. 2003; Magaloni 2008; Myerson 2008; North and Weingast 1989). So why then would dictators tolerate these institutions? Our argument draws on Myerson's (2008) explanation for the endogeneity of autocratic institutions. By introducing or sustaining institutions that make him vulnerable to overthrow, a dictator cultivates his supporters' trust and legitimizes his rule. Our main concern here is to outline the foundations of autocratic accountability: when it is most likely to arise, to whom it is likely to be directed, how long such an equilibrium is likely to last, and what are its most important effects.

Magaloni (2008) details how elections enable credible power sharing between the dictator and his ruling coalition, with the result that electoral one-party regimes are considerably more durable than single-party regimes that do not hold elections. She argues that regular elections enable single-party regimes to credibly commit to their rank-and-file supporters. The political leverage of these core supporters increases because they can threaten to defect from the ruling party and join an opposition party. A nominally communist one-party state continues safely in power in China and has overseen three decades of spectacular growth. Saddam Hussein's *Baath* Party survived in office for almost the same amount of time. Iraq not only experienced high economic growth rates; Hussein was also able to cling to power for more than a decade following the 1991 Gulf War despite a severe economic crisis and punishing sanctions. But hegemonic parties of this sort are only one of several possible institutional strategies adopted by a dictator to curry favor with his key supporters and protract his rule.

Self-enforcing limits on executive authority strategically adopted by nondemocratic rulers also have implications for economic development. North and Weingast (1989) show how the emergence of constitutional limits on the power of the crown in seventeenth-century England lowered borrowing costs and spurred the development of capital markets. Similarly, Summerhill (2007) argues that during Brazil's parliamentary monarchy in the nineteenth century, sovereigns were able to develop a credible commitment for the same reason and with similar results. Other researchers have identified a plethora of unorthodox mechanisms relied on by dictators to extend a credible commitment to elites in order to boost investment and economic growth (Besley and Kudamatsu 2007; Gehlbach and Keefer 2011; Haber et al. 2003; Wright 2008).

THEORY

Following the literature on the political economy of autocratic rule, we assume that the most serious threat faced by dictators emanates from *within* their support coalition (Geddes 2003; Haber 2006), a claim Svolik (2012) demonstrates empirically. To understand how and why dictators are able to consolidate their authority by currying the favor of this group, it is helpful to distinguish between two stages of autocratic rule. The first is a resolution of uncertainty over the dictator's loyalty soon after the transition itself. The second is the institutionalization of a system that establishes how the spoils of office will be distributed. That there are many ways *ex ante* to divide the pie (i.e., multiple equilibria) makes the resolution of this second challenge particularly important.

Bueno de Mesquita et al. (2003: 100) elegantly summarize the first stage of autocratic rule: "[I]nitially an autocrat's coalition is relatively unstable since members fear exclusion. However, as the learning process continues . . . their fear of exclusion diminishes and the loyalty norm strengthens." This begs the question, however, of how the dictator's launching organization learns to trust him, especially if the dictator took power by overthrowing and thus betraying the previous leader. We follow Albertus and Menaldo (2012a) and affirm that the act of expropriating the preexisting elite (PE), the individuals privileged under the previous regime, is one powerful way for a dictator to signal his willingness to reassign property rights to favor those individuals who helped him grab power, the launching organization (LO). The LO can be composed of key members of the military, a political party, or even a religious sect (see Albertus and Menaldo, forthcoming). What these individuals share in common, across different organizational affiliations, is that they were able to solve their collective action problem to help put the dictator into power.

But what comes next after the dictator has broadcast his loyalty to the LO through destroying or taming the PE? How does the dictator go about ruling – establishing and enforcing LO property rights so that they remain loyal over the long run and generate revenues that allow both the dictator and the LO members to continue to enjoy the benefits of political power? All of these requirements call for some set of rules and a structure of political authority beyond the *de facto* power possessed by the LO.

Constitutions are one important mechanism by which political groups and organizations other than the dictator can codify their rights and interests. Because uncertainty about the dictator's rule is at its height at the outset of his rule and the LO remains well organized, the LO will usually push for a constitution at the beginning of a new regime's tenure. If this window of opportunity passes, it will be more difficult for the LO and other political groups and organizations to use conventional, nonconstitutional instruments to influence the politics of the regime.

How are autocratic constitutions different from other autocratic institutions such as parties, legislatures, and elections? Autocratic constitutions play a critical role in consolidating the inner ranks of the autocratic regime by fostering loyalty and trust between the dictator and his launching organization. The key difference between constitutions and other autocratic institutions is that while constitutions codify and protect the rights and interests of insiders at the dawn of a new regime, elections, legislatures, and political parties often address emerging threats and challenges and are usually sanctioned by both the dictator and LO acting in concert to forestall challenges to their authority. It is the constitution that ensures that LO members will have a hand in crafting the rules that structure these subsequent political institutions, making it more likely that they will occupy key posts in a party or legislature. These other autocratic institutions, therefore, are often derivative to the constitution.

The Content and Operation of Autocratic Constitutions

The cornerstone to creating a stable distributional arrangement within an autocratic regime is to enshrine and enforce LO property rights, giving them an incentive to remain loyal over the long term. A constitution aids this process through several steps. First, constitutions can establish clear rules about who qualifies as a member of the ruling group. The constitution can make the boundaries of the ruling group less fluid by identifying regime insiders and making their rights explicit. This may require the destruction of a group of preexisting elites. Second, constitutions can establish norms regulating access to rents and codify institutions that distribute the spoils of office. Third, constitutions can create institutions that monitor the ruler's actions to enforce these norms.

By weakening or destroying alternative sources of political and economic power, a constitution can enable the rise of a new autocratic coalition. This complicates the ability of a dictator to betray the LO because it eliminates an alternative potential option for support. For instance, the Bolivian dictator Colonel Rene Barrientos used a new constitution in 1967 to dismantle the mine workers' union, suppress strikes, exile union leaders (using Articles 112 and 138), and grant private investors preferential treatment (Articles 141 and 145). These policies severely weakened the political coalition that had supported his predecessor, Paz Estenssoro, whom he had toppled in a coup. They also bolstered his reliance on his LO, composed of rural oligarchs, urban business moguls, and military generals. A similar situation occurred in Mexico under the *Partido Revolucionario Institucional* (PRI). The first few dictators to rule under the 1917 constitution used its provisions (e.g., Articles 27 and 123) to fight against a group of powerful economic actors who were holdovers from the previous regime, eventually enabling the members of the LO to vanquish the old guard and coordinate to enforce their rights for decades under the PRI.

One common example of how autocratic constitutions can incorporate the LO into a dictator's political coalition is by granting the military a special role in politics, enabling it to maintain leverage after any individual dictator loses power. For example, Article 213 of Peru's 1933 constitution states that "The purpose of the armed forces is to secure the rights of the Republic, the fulfillment of the Constitution and the laws, and the preservation of public order." Ensuing interventions were justified by the Peruvian armed forces on the grounds that they were upholding Article 213. The military annulled election results in 1936 and deemed several parties ineligible to compete in the upcoming elections in 1939. Article 213 was also used by the military to justify the coups of 1948, 1962, and 1968. Similarly, in the Honduran constitution of 1957, Articles 318 through 330 stipulate that the Chief of the Armed Forces would be selected by the military, that his command over the military would supersede the president's, and that he could deny presidential oversight of the military budget.

Beyond the initial function of destroying the preexisting elite from a former regime and empowering a new autocratic coalition, autocratic constitutions also typically stipulate how power will be exercised and rotated under the new order by defining the institutions that will be created and function under the new regime. Defining the terms of political office and rules of reelection can aid in stabilizing the expectations of those empowered in the regime and provide a focal point to coordinate to sanction a dictator who violates his promises. It can also enable elites to make long-term plans and reduce potential conflict among them.

The institutions that distribute power can vary from a clear separation of powers, which many of Latin America's autocratic constitutions have codified, to the concentration of power, as in Panama's 1972 constitution. The institutions for executive selection can also vary; while many autocratic constitutions call for direct presidential elections that are subsequently rigged to ensure reelection by incumbents, others have used indirect elections, such as Brazil's 1964 constitution and Honduras's 1956 constitution. Some have codified electoral formulas and practices that disproportionally favor incumbents, such as Guatemala's 1956 and 1965 constitutions.

Autocratic constitutions also regulate the allocation of property rights, the distribution of rents, and the granting of status and opportunities for upward mobility. There are myriad ways to divide the pie within any political regime. In democracies, institutions that define agenda control, gatekeeping power, and veto power mitigate this complexity (Shepsle and Weingast 1981). The same is less often true in autocracies. The destruction of the old system of property rights and spoils enables a new arrangement to be established. For example, Barros (2002) shows how an institutionalized system of divided political authority in Chile's 1980 constitution allowed the various branches of the armed forces to check General Pinochet's power by establishing a unanimity rule over major decision making and obedience to a constitutional tribunal, even though its members were appointed by the Military Junta. These measures served to bolster the power and budgets of each branch of the armed forces, guaranteeing a stable distribution of rents for the military generals that constituted Pinochet's LO.

Enforcement and the Threat of Free Riding

Once the ruling group has been established and the institutional structure of the regime created, the elites should gain the *ability* to enforce the constitution by monitoring the executive's actions and meting out agreed-on sanctions in retaliation against any transgression of the elites' property rights. But does every member of the ruling group also have the *desire* to join her fellow elites? How are autocratic constitutions actually enforced?

De Figueiredo and Weingast (1997) shed light on this question. They argue that an individual's support for a coup increases when an executive's behavior threatens his core "rights." Even when the odds that the leader violates any one individual's rights are quite low, it makes sense to withdraw support from a predatory executive because the rights are so dear that they are worth safeguarding at any cost. Therefore, even if a ruler transgresses against a member's rights, and even if this only slightly increases the odds that the ruler will victimize a different member tomorrow, the expected benefits of contributing to the coup outweighs the costs. Shirking one's duty to punish the ruler today reduces the probability of reaching the critical mass needed to unseat him and, therefore, increases the odds of future predation. With normal discount rates and the capacity to enforce the constitution, elites should therefore choose to join a collective punishment against a norm-violating ruler.[1]

Theoretical Predictions

An autocratic constitution can help ameliorate the uncertainty endemic in the initial stages of a new autocratic regime by establishing rules that define the rights and privileges of elites and regulate these interests in the future, as the power balance between a dictator and his launching organization may shift. A constitution solidifies expectations between LO elites and gives them a greater stake in the regime. This argument yields several empirical implications. First, autocratic constitutions should be adopted at the outset of a new autocratic coalition seizing power. Second, an autocratic coalition that adopts a constitution will be more likely to survive longer than one that does not.

Constitutions can also have other consequences beyond the survival of an autocratic coalition. Because a constitution enables elites to coordinate to enforce their rights and interests, property rights should be stronger following constitutional adoption than in its absence, when a dictator faces fewer self-enforcing constraints on his authority. By extension, autocratic constitutions can impact economic investment and growth by establishing clearly favored policies and limits to the dictator's discretion. This will incentivize the members of the LO to engage in productive activities that contribute to economic growth.

The investment rate will increase because the new elites' property rights are secure. This should translate into capital accumulation because the ruler and elites will have settled on a self-enforcing distributional arrangement and foreclosed open-ended rent seeking. Finally, both the dictator and the LO elites will protract their planning horizons by virtue of longer tenures and an institutionalized succession mechanism. This will motivate both the elite and regular citizens to make the type of irreversible investments in assets that raise productivity. Dictators who inherit previous constitutions and operate under them can also benefit because the constitution means that the executive's credible commitment is not a function of his personality or idiosyncrasies but of the standardization of expectations among elites and their ability to coordinate to enforce their rights.[2]

[1] Although the willingness of elites to defend an autocratic incumbent may be conditioned by their outside option, their leverage is largely a function of their ability to coordinate on the regime's norms. Because elites cannot easily coordinate in a political vacuum on an alternative focal point, they are more likely to abide by extant norms that have been codified, usually constitutionally.

[2] Indeed, an ordinal measure of "constitutionalism" that captures no constitution, constitutional inheritence, constitutional inheritance with amendments, or the creation of a new constitution (in ascending order of constitutionalism) yields similar results to those presented in the tables, although the results for private investment are weaker.

RESEARCH DESIGN

This section empirically examines the theoretical implications outlined previously. We use a panel data set of Latin American dictators from 1950 to 2002 to show that autocratic coalitions that adopt constitutions survive in office longer, have better property rights protection, and experience higher rates of private investment and economic growth. These results are robust to how we code autocratic constitutions, the use of country fixed effects, and potential endogeneity. We focus on Latin America, given the region's long history of dictatorship, with significant variation in the type of dictators who have exercised power, as well as both the dependent and independent variables of interest.

Unit of Analysis and Autocratic Coalitions

We operationalize the concept of an autocratic regime as an autocratic coalition. Autocratic coalitions tend to outlast individual dictators, as in Mexico under the single-party dictatorship of the PRI, which lasted seventy-one years and was composed of a sequence of dictators who held power in six-year intervals. At the same time, a single spell of autocracy may contain several different autocratic coalitions (e.g., Svolik 2012; Wright 2008). In Honduras after World War II, for example, there were several key changes in the identity, ideology, and policy orientation of the groups that held power under a single autocratic period. Even if a single spell of autocracy is presided over by an uninterrupted chain of military generals, coups and countercoups that replace one general with another often bring to power dramatically different autocratic coalitions. This challenges the notion that such an autocratic spell is constituted by a single, coherent autocratic coalition.[3]

We define an autocratic coalition as a set of chronologically contiguous autocrats that are not interrupted by an irregular transfer of power. Using the Archigos data set (Goemens et al. 2009), we code leaders as belonging to the same coalition when there is no interruption caused by a coup, assassination, popular revolt, or democratic transition. We do not consider an incumbent assassinated by an unsupported individual as an interruption. We also do not consider as interruptions an incumbent who dies in an accident or natural death, is removed in an internal power struggle short of a coup, or is replaced through an election.

Using this definition of autocratic coalitions, we constructed a panel data set of Latin American dictators from 1950 through 2002. The unit of observation is the leader-year, because there can be changes in the autocratic coalition that holds power within a given year and changes in the dictator chosen to head the coalition. We code leader years as autocratic according to Cheibub and Gandhi (2004), adjusting their coding to the leader-year level. To avoid potential bias arising from left-censored data (Box-Steffensmeier and Jones 1997), we adjust the tenure and independent variables

[3] The results for autocratic coalition survival are nonetheless robust to using regimes.

for autocratic coalitions that seized power before 1950 and were still ongoing in this year. The data set contains 572 observations for seventy-one autocratic coalitions. Nested within these coalitions are 135 individual rulers.

Dependent Variables

Autocratic Coalition Exits

We code Autocratic Coalition Exit as a "1" in the leader-years in which an autocrat coalition exits power. This variable depends on how one dictator replaces another. As detailed previously, a coalition ends when the incumbent is removed irregularly. We therefore code this variable as a "1" during years when the executive who heads the autocratic coalition is (1) ousted in a coup through the threat or use of force; (2) assassinated; or (3) removed in a popular revolt. Autocratic Coalition Exit is also coded "1" when there is a transition to democracy.

Autocratic Coalition Exit is coded as a "0" in leader-years in which the autocratic coalition remains in power. We also code this variable as "0" when the executive that heads the coalition (1) dies from natural causes; (2) dies in an accident; (3) is ousted by a foreign invasion; (4) is assassinated by an unsupported individual (as with Somoza in 1956); (5) is removed in an internal power struggle short of a coup and the institutional features such as a military council or junta persist; or (6) is replaced through peaceful elections.

There is significant variation in autocratic coalition exits. An exit is observed in 67 of the 572 observations in the data set (11.7 percent). The average autocratic coalition duration is 11.8 years, with a standard deviation of 12.3 years. In three cases – Mexico during the PRI regime, Paraguay under Stroessner, and Cuba under Castro – long-lived coalitions endured thirty or more years.

Political Economy Outcomes

Property rights protection is coded using a measure of contract-intensive money (CIM) (see, e.g., Clague et al. 1996, 1999). CIM is a metric of property rights in so far as it captures citizens' decisions regarding the form in which they choose to hold their financial assets. When there is institutional stability in banks and when the government protects property rights and enforces contracts, citizens can be more confident that banks or the government will not confiscate their deposits. As Clague et al. (1996, 254) summarize, "Those forms of money, such as currency, that rely least on the fulfillment of contractual obligations by others will be preferred when property and contractual rights are insecure, whereas other forms of money are more advantageous for most purposes in environments with secure contract-enforcement and property rights." Data on the CIM ratio, as in Ahlquist and Prakash (2008), are here measured as (M2–M1)/M2, where M2 is "money and quasimoney" and M1 is money outside the banking system. The measure therefore captures the proportion of the money supply held in the banking system. Data are taken from the World Bank's World Development Indicators. The CIM ratio varies between 2.6 percent and 86.6 percent with a mean of 46.2 percent and a standard deviation of 20.8 percent.[4]

If autocratic constitutions can successfully encourage greater property rights protection, then leaders who create these constitutions should exhibit higher private investment rates. Private Investment is measured as a percentage of GDP from the Global Development Network Growth Database (GDNGD). Private Investment ranges from 3.1 percent to 40.6 percent of GDP and has a mean of 14.8 percent with a standard deviation of 4.3 percent. An institutional arrangement that protects property rights and provides incentives for private investment also likely has an impact on economic growth. Autocratic constitutions should thus be associated with higher growth. Economic Growth is the logarithmic rate of growth of Per Capita Income and varies from –0.43 to 0.13 with a mean of 0.014 and a standard deviation of 0.048.

Key Independent Variable: Autocratic Constitutions

We distinguish constitutions from either amendments or other rules or laws. Following Elkins et. al. (2010), constitutions are coded as documents that are (1) explicitly identified as the constitution or fundamental law of a country; (2) contain explicit provisions that establish it as highest law; and (3) change the basic pattern of authority by establishing or suspending an executive or legislative branch of government.

Data on constitutions are taken from the Comparative Constitutions Project, which codes the formal characteristics of written constitutions for nearly all independent states since 1789 (see Elkins et al. 2010). Because these data are coded at the country-year level, we used a host of country-specific sources to recode them by leader-year for years in which more than one leader was in office. We code a constitution as a "1" both the year in which it is adopted by an autocratic coalition and every subsequent year for the duration of the autocratic coalition's tenure.

A total of thirty-four constitutions were created under dictatorship during the period. Most countries experienced constitutional reformation under dictatorship (see Albertus and Menaldo, forthcoming, on the political and economic effects of autocratic constitutional engineering post-democratization). Table 4.1 provides an overview of these cases. In a total of seven cases, constitutions were created under dictatorship not to elongate an autocratic coalition's tenure but rather to transition to a new ruling arrangement. These cases include Argentina in 1972 under Lanusse;

[4] Our theory suggests that secure property rights will only obtain for a portion of the population – the LO. Therefore, an aggregate indicator of property rights (such as CIM) may not capture the fact that property rights are selective and targeted to perhaps just a minority of the population, not the whole society. Although this is true, it is not a concern from the perspective of bias: it should be harder to find an association between constitutions and property rights because such an aggregate will underreport the degree to which the LO's property rights are secure.

TABLE 4.1. *Cases of autocratic constitution adoption in Latin America, 1950–2002*

Country	Dictator	Constitution year	Type of constitution
Argentina	Lanusse	1972	Democratization
Bolivia	Paz Estenssoro	1961	Autocratic
Bolivia	Barrientos	1964	Autocratic
Bolivia	Barrientos	1967	Autocratic
Brazil	Castello Branco	1967	Autocratic
Chile	Pinochet	1980	Autocratic
Cuba	Batista	1952	Autocratic
Cuba	Batista	1953	Autocratic
Cuba	Castro	1959	Autocratic
Cuba	Castro	1976	Autocratic
Dominican Republic	Trujillo	1955	Autocratic
Dominican Republic	Balaguer	1961	Autocratic
Dominican Republic	Filiberto Bonnelly	1962	Autocratic
Dominican Republic	Bosch	1963	Autocratic
Ecuador	Arosemena	1967	Autocratic
Ecuador	Rodríguez Lara	1972	Autocratic
Ecuador	Poveda Burbano	1976	Autocratic
Ecuador	Poveda Burbano	1978	Autocratic
El Salvador	Osorio	1950	Autocratic
El Salvador	Portillo	1962	Autocratic
El Salvador	Magaña Borjo	1983	Democratization
Guatemala	Castillo Armas	1956	Autocratic
Guatemala	Peralta Azurdia	1965	Democratization
Guatemala	Mejía Victores	1985	Democratization
Honduras	López Arellano	1965	Autocratic
Honduras	Paz García	1982	Democratization
Nicaragua	Somoza García	1950	Autocratic
Nicaragua	Somoza Debayle	1974	Autocratic
Panama	Torrijos	1972	Autocratic
Paraguay	Stroessner	1967	Autocratic
Peru	Morales Bermúdez	1979	Democratization
Peru	Fujimori	1993	Autocratic
Uruguay	Álvarez Armalino	1985	Democratization
Venezuela	Pérez Jiménez	1953	Autocratic

Notes: The table includes all cases of autocratic constitutions adopted from 1950 through 2002 as coded by Elkins et al. (2010) and adjusted to leader-years by the authors. There were also five cases of constitutional adoption prior to 1950 for which the autocratic coalition that adopted the constitution continued in power through 1950: Mexico, Bolivia, Honduras, Nicaragua, and Venezuela. Types of constitutions are as follows. Autocratic: Created by a dictator whose coalition then operates under the constitution; Democratization: Created under dictatorship in order to transition to democracy.

El Salvador in 1983 under Borjo; Guatemala in 1965 under Azurdia and in 1985 under Victores; Honduras in 1982 under Garcia; Peru in 1979 under Bermudez; and Uruguay in 1985 under Armalino. Although we do not consider these as autocratic constitutions in most model specifications, we report and discuss results below that are robust to recoding these as autocratic constitutions.

There are six cases of multiple adoption after 1950, five cases of countries that enter the sample with a constitution adopted previous to 1950, and one case (Nicaragua) that fits into both of these categories. The six cases of subsequent constitutional adoptions by the same autocratic coalition after the first constitution were Bolivia in 1967, Cuba in 1953, Cuba in 1976, the Dominican Republic in 1963, Ecuador in 1978, and Nicaragua in 1950 and 1974. The five cases of autocratic coalitions in our data that adopted constitutions prior to 1950 and continued in power through this year were Mexico, Bolivia, Venezuela, Honduras, and Nicaragua.

Accounting for these adjustments, there were twenty-five unique autocratic coalitions operating under a constitution in our data set. These represent 35 percent of the seventy-one autocratic coalitions observed in the sample. In terms of leader-years, there were 328 leader-years (57.3 percent) observed with an autocratic constitution using the narrow coding criteria that excludes the "democratic transition constitutions" and 244 leader years without one (42.6 percent).

The Timing of Constitutional Adoption

Because constitutions help weaken preexisting elites and empower a new coalition, constitutions are typically adopted at the outset of a new autocratic coalition's rule. Figure 4.1 displays a bar plot of the time it takes an autocratic coalition to adopt a new constitution. The *y*-axis depicts the count of the constitutions adopted by autocratic coalitions. The *x*-axis depicts the year in office at the time that the coalition adopted the constitution. Most constitutions are adopted early in a coalition's rule. Indeed, adoption drops nearly monotonically with coalition tenure, and only three constitutions were passed after six years of a coalition's rule. None were passed after fifteen years in office. That the adoption trend in Figure 4.1 declines with time also suggests that these constitutions may help autocratic coalitions survive in office rather than the possibility that it is the coalitions that are able to survive in office that subsequently adopt constitutions.

EMPIRICAL ANALYSIS: THE EFFECTS OF AUTOCRATIC CONSTITUTIONS

Autocratic Coalition Exits

What effect does an autocratic coalition's adoption of a constitution have on its survival in office? The estimation of autocratic coalition exits here centers on panel

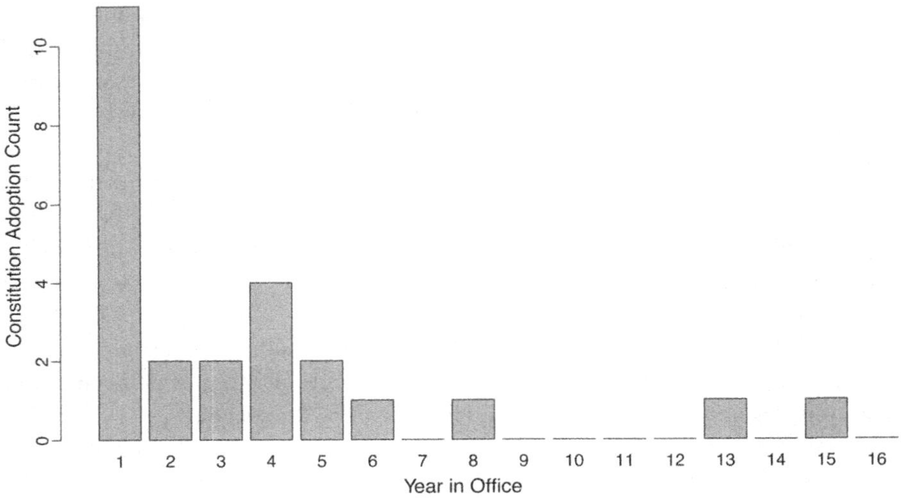

FIGURE 4.1. Timing of Constitutional Adoption by Dictators in Latin America, 1950–2002. *Note*: The *y*-axis depicts the count of the constitutions adopted by Latin American autocratic coalitions. The *x*-axis depicts the year in power at the time that the coalition adopted the constitution.

probit models. Robust standard errors are clustered by country to address the correlation between the observations of several variables within the same country.[5] This technique also makes the standard errors consistent in the presence of heteroskedasticity. Following Carter and Signorino (2010), we include Autocratic Coalition Tenure polynomials to account for temporal dependence. We orthogonalize these variables to eliminate multicollinearity. In most of the specifications, we control for country fixed effects, which allows the models to implicitly control for any country-specific time-invariant unobserved factors that may influence both the likelihood of an autocratic coalition adopting a constitution as well as its survival in office. We also avail a two-stage estimation strategy in several models, instrumenting autocratic constitutions with constituent assembly elections, to address the possibility of reverse causation. Finally, we also tackle additional concerns about robustness and potential misspecification by measuring constitutional adoption in different ways.

Column 1 of Table 4.2 is a pooled, baseline model that includes several basic control variables. Following Londregan and Poole (1990), we control for Log (Per Capita Income) and the Economic Growth Rate (of Per Capita Income percentage). We expect a negative sign for both. We also control for ongoing Civil War because leader tenure may be reduced by violent revolutions that can generate political instability. As per Smith (2004), we control for Total Resources Income Per Capita and expect a negative sign. Lastly, we control for the coup trap hypothesis – the idea that the incidence of a coup in the near past fosters the reoccurrence of a coup

5 The results hold if we instead cluster the standard errors by year or include year dummies.

TABLE 4.2. *Autocratic constitutions and autocratic coalition survival in Latin America, 1950–2002*

	Probit						IV Probit	
Model specification:	Exclude DTC					Include DTC	Excl. DTC	Incl. DTC
Coding of const. variable	Model 1	Model 2	Model 3	Model 4	Model 5	Model 6	Model 7	Model 8
Autocratic Constitution	−0.567***	−0.546***	−0.552*	−0.990***	−1.001***	−0.577**	−2.996***	−2.491***
	(0.187)	(0.189)	(0.283)	(0.367)	(0.363)	(0.271)	(0.727)	(0.505)
log (GDP Per Capita)	−0.207	−0.243	−0.375	1.072	0.863	0.898	1.679**	1.524*
	(0.170)	(0.181)	(0.261)	(0.926)	(0.981)	(0.860)	(0.850)	(0.786)
Growth Rate	0.012	0.011	0.013	−0.004	−0.003	−0.007	0.008	0.004
	(0.015)	(0.015)	(0.019)	(0.020)	(0.020)	(0.020)	(0.020)	(0.019)
Civil War	0.329	0.334	0.358	0.219	0.211	0.301	−0.115	−0.029
	(0.235)	(0.243)	(0.277)	(0.422)	(0.419)	(0.420)	(0.448)	(0.416)
Resources Income Per Capita	0.451***	0.472***	0.690***	1.208	1.287	1.118	0.727	0.599
	(0.160)	(0.177)	(0.173)	(0.898)	(0.925)	(0.985)	(0.899)	(1.109)
Coup Count	0.030*	0.029*	0.008	−0.195**	−0.189*	−0.163*	−0.258***	−0.194**
	(0.017)	(0.017)	(0.023)	(0.099)	(0.100)	(0.086)	(0.084)	(0.080)
Military Regime		0.080	0.138	0.308	0.316	0.413	−0.220	−0.039
		(0.193)	(0.230)	(0.240)	(0.241)	(0.252)	(0.458)	(0.479)

(continued)

TABLE 4.2 (*continued*)

	Probit						IV Probit	
Model specification:	Exclude DTC					Include DTC	Excl. DTC	Incl. DTC
Coding of const. variable	Model 1	Model 2	Model 3	Model 4	Model 5	Model 6	Model 7	Model 8
Single-Party Regime			−1.142***	−1.990***	−2.000***	−1.782***	−2.309***	−2.061***
			(0.430)	(0.484)	(0.471)	(0.451)	(0.423)	(0.407)
Multiple Parties			0.124	0.657**	0.627**	0.599**	0.876***	0.834***
			(0.253)	(0.268)	(0.267)	(0.273)	(0.272)	(0.273)
Legislature			−0.371***	−0.372***	−0.369**	−0.411***	−0.269	−0.311
			(0.138)	(0.144)	(0.147)	(0.144)	(0.234)	(0.196)
Election Previously Held			1.144***	1.460***	1.450***	1.450***	1.341***	1.447***
			(0.355)	(0.458)	(0.459)	(0.459)	(0.482)	(0.462)
Stage 1 IV:								
Constituent Assembly Election							0.365***	0.354***
							(0.139)	(0.129)
Temporal Duration Controls	YES	YES	YES	YES	YES	YES	YES	YES
Country Fixed Effects	NO	NO	NO	YES	YES	YES	YES	YES
Observations	543	543	519	519	461	519	519	519

* $p < 0.10$; ** $p < 0.05$; *** $p < 0.01$ (two-tailed)
Standard errors clustered by country in parentheses. DTC = Democratic Transition Constitution. Model 5 Excludes Mexico. All independent variables lagged except Constitutions, Military Regime, Single-Party Regime, Multiple Parties, Legislature, and Elections. Constant estimated but not reported. Tenure count polynomials estimated to control for temporal duration but not reported. Country dummies estimated but not reported in FE models.

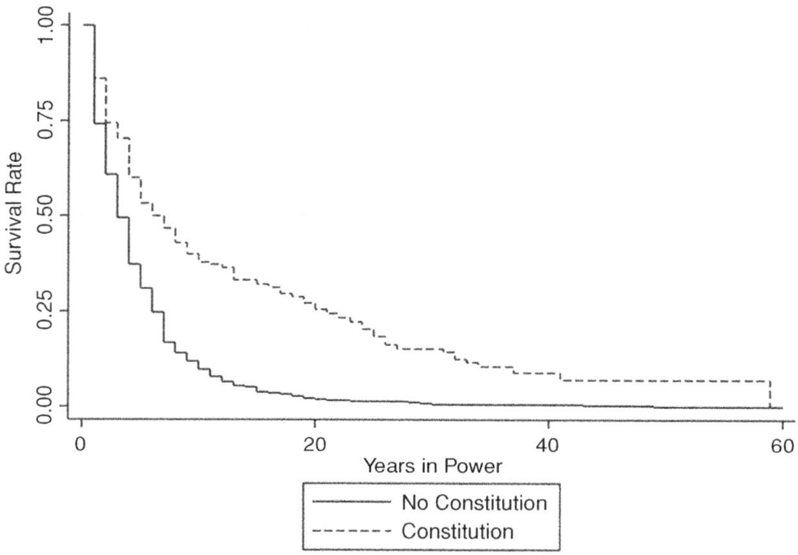

FIGURE 4.2. Survival Rates for Latin American Autocratic Coalitions by Autocratic Constitution. *Note*: Survival rates calculated after adjusting for log(GDP Per Capita), Economic Growth Rate, Civil War, Resources Income Per Capita, and Coup Count. The Figure is similar even excluding constitutioned autocratic coalitions with extraordinarily long tenures such as that supporting Castro, Stroessner, the PRI in Mexico, or Pinochet (or all of these simultaneously).

(Londregan and Poole 1990). We code a running count of the number of coups based on the Archigos data set, starting from the earliest available date (1875) or the date of independence.

Consistent with the theory detailed previously, an autocratic coalition that operates under a constitution is less likely to exit power. This coefficient on Autocratic Coalition is positive and highly statistically significant ($p < .01$). Holding continuous covariates at their means and setting civil war to 0, the probability of an exit is reduced by 10 percent for coalitions that have constitutions.

Figure 4.2 displays survival estimates for autocratic coalitions that adopt constitutions versus those that do not adopt constitutions. The Figure 4.2 estimates fix the control variables from Column 1 at their averages. The cumulative survival rate of autocratic coalitions that have adopted an autocratic constitution drops below 50 percent in roughly eight years. By contrast, dictators who do not adopt a constitution reach the 50 percent survival threshold in three years, less than half the time. In addition, the survival curve demonstrates a growing difference in survival rates over time between autocratic coalitions that have adopted constitutions and those that have not. The results are not driven by autocratic coalitions with extraordinarily long tenures such as the coalition supporting Pinochet in Chile, Castro in Cuba, the PRI in Mexico, and Stroessner in Paraguay. The Figure 4.2 findings hold even excluding these long-term autocratic coalitions with constitutions.

Could the omission of a variable measuring military regimes account for the results in Column 1 of Table 4.2? Several scholars have found that military regimes exit more rapidly than other types of leaders (Geddes 2003; Wright 2008). Military regimes are also less likely to adopt constitutions. In Column 2, we therefore control for whether the dictator heads a Military Regime, with data taken from Wright (2008) and recoded it at the leader-year level. Military Regime has the expected positive sign but is not statistically significant. The substantive effect of autocratic constitutions on exit remains almost identical: the marginal effect is now a reduction in the probability of exit by 9.8 percent. The results do not materially change if we instead employ a more inclusive coding of Military Regime that includes military hybrids: any blend of military, personalist, and single-party components.

There are several other alternative explanations for an autocratic regime's survival that, if not accounted for, may confound the Table 4.2 results. Some researchers argue that single-party regimes endure longer than other autocracies (Geddes 2003; Wright 2008). Others argue that what matters is the presence of multiple parties (Schedler 2002), legislatures (see Boix and Svolik 2008; Gandhi and Przeworski 2007; Wright 2008), or regular elections (Gandhi and Przeworski 2007; Magaloni 2008). We capture these hypotheses by adding several variables to the regression. The first is Wright's (2008) Single-Party Regime variable, recoded at the leader-year level. The second is Multiple Parties, taken from Cheibub and Gandhi (2004), which indicates whether the autocratic coalition allows other political parties to compete for power. The third is Legislature, also from Cheibub and Gandhi (2004). Legislature is an ordinal variable coded "1" when the autocratic coalition has a legislature that is appointed, "2" when the legislature is elected, and "0" otherwise. The fourth is Election Previously Held, which we generate using information from the Nelda elections data set (Hyde and Marinov 2012).[6] This variable captures whether a presidential or legislative election was held at any point during the coalition's tenure.

The results of this regression are reported in Column 3 of Table 4.2. As expected, single-party regimes are more durable than other types of autocracies. Legislatures also protract autocratic survival. The presence of multiple parties has no measureable impact on autocratic survival. Finally, elections make it *more* likely that an autocratic coalition will lose power. The results for autocratic constitutions are somewhat weakened with the addition of these other institutional variables. Constitutions are nonetheless still negatively associated with the odds that an autocratic coalition will exit ($p = .05$). After setting Civil War and the new controls to 0 and the other covariates at their means, autocratic coalitions that operate under constitutions are an estimated 7 percent less likely to terminate.[7] One potential conclusion to draw from

[6] We also coded a measure for the presence of independent courts but did not include this measure because of the little variation exhibited in our sample (results were nonetheless robust to its inclusion).

[7] The reduction in the significance of Autocratic Constitutions in Column 3 is partly attributable to the fact that twenty-four observations are dropped from the regression because of missing data for the

Column 3 is that although a constitution may indirectly affect autocratic coalition survival by operating through ruling parties and legislatures, it also has a direct effect not captured by the typical autocratic institutions and practices identified in the literature.

Column 4 of Table 4.2 adds country fixed effects to the Column 3 specification to account for the possibility that some unobserved, time-invariant factor may jointly determine both autocratic constitutions and autocratic longevity. The estimated effect of an autocratic constitution on the duration of an autocratic coalition increases both substantively and in statistical significance ($p = .007$). Multiple Parties now gains statistical significance at conventional levels and is associated *positively* with autocratic exit.

Is it possible that the previous Table 4.2 model results are driven by the case of Mexico? Mexico's 1917 constitution was the linchpin of the country's long-lived single party, making it perhaps the quintessential case of an autocratic coalition that operates under a constitution. That the Mexican regime is also the longest-lived regime in our data set – lasting a total of seventy-one years and observed from 1950 to 2000 in the data set – suggests that it could disproportionately influence the correlation between constitutions and autocratic survival. We test this by removing Mexico from the Column 5 model. Although the number of observations is reduced to 461, the statistical and substantive significance of Autocratic Constitution slightly increases.

How would the results be affected if we recoded "democratic constitutions" adopted by dictators as autocratic constitutions? Table 4.1 lists the constitutions that were explicitly adopted to usher in a democratic transition. As stipulated by the constitution, each of these cases was followed by free and fair elections shortly after constitutional adoption. And in each case, a democratic transition occurred within one or two years of adoption, with transitions coded according to Cheibub and Gandhi (2004). Until now we have coded these as "0" for Autocratic Constitution. Column 6 includes a version of autocratic constitutions that is recoded as a "1" for these democratic constitutions during dictator-years in which they are present. Although the autocratic constitutions coefficient is reduced by almost half, it is still statistically significant at the .03 level. The decision to treat these constitutions differently is not driving the Table 4.2 results.

Robustness to Endogeneity in Constitutional Adoption

Could it be the case that it is the autocratic coalitions with greater political stability that can afford to adopt a constitution and operate by it, leading to reverse causation? To address this concern, Columns 7 and 8 of Table 4.2 use an instrumental variable (IV) approach designed to capture the exogenous variation in constitutions. A valid

Multiple Parties variable. We also note that including separate terms for presidential and legislative elections does not change the basic results.

instrumental variable must satisfy the exclusion restriction: its effect on the dependent variable of interest should work exclusively through the potentially endogenous right-hand side variable. In this case, the instrument must be correlated with the dependent variable in a first-stage regression, Autocratic Constitution, but not correlated with the error term of a second-stage regression, where Autocratic Coalition Exit is the dependent variable.

One good candidate for an instrument that satisfies these requirements is whether the dictator at the helm of an autocratic coalition holds elections for a constituent assembly. This is a good instrument because there is no guarantee that such an election will actually yield a new constitution, let alone a constitution that persists across the duration of the autocratic coalition. Indeed, several examples from Latin America evidence that the success of constitutional assemblies convoked by dictators does not necessarily usher in constitutions (Negretto 2013).[8]

Data on constituent assembly elections after 1945 are taken from the Nelda data set (Hyde and Marinov 2012). To identify constituent elections before 1945, we use primary and secondary sources. We code a dichotomous variable indicating whether an autocratic coalition holds an election for a constituent assembly intended to draft a constitution. This variable is coded "1" in years in which an election was held during the autocratic coalition's tenure and subsequent years until the termination of the autocratic coalition. Consistent with the logic above, this coding does *not* depend on if constituent assembly elections are followed by an actual constitution. As with the variable Elections Previously Held, we adjust this variable from the country-year to the leader-year level using Archigos.

To mirror the logic of the previous Table 4.2 regressions, we generated two different instruments. The first version of constituent assembly elections excludes elections convoked explicitly to set up a timetable for a democratic transition. The second, more inclusive version includes these constituent assembly elections. The first version codes a total of ten constituent assembly elections. This yields 121 leader-year observations (21.1 percent) in which an autocratic coalition is observed as having had a constituent assembly election. The second version codes a total of fifteen constituent assembly elections, comprising 137 leader-years (23.9 percent).

Columns 7 and 8 report the second-stage results of a series of IV probit models.[9] We also report the first-stage coefficient on the instrument of constituent assembly elections. Following convention, we include all of the controls used in the previous Table 4.2 models, including country dummies. The instrument used in Column 7

[8] Elsewhere, we have provided several examples of this phenomenon in Latin America to support the claim that constitutional conventions satisfy the exclusion restriction (Albertus and Menaldo 2012b).

[9] Because there is no IV estimator for a dichotomous dependent variable in the first stage (in this case, Autocratic Constitution) when the error term is heteroskedastic, we estimate the first-stage models via OLS even though the dependent variable is a binary variable. We therefore estimate linear probability models with robust standard errors clustered by country that provide consistent estimates. The implication is that the first-stage parameter estimates cannot be interpreted in terms of log odds.

is the version of constituent assembly elections that excludes "democratic" constituent assemblies. As theorized, Constituent Assembly Election is positively and statistically significantly associated with autocratic constitutions. The second-stage results reported in Column 7 confirm our previous, non–IV results: holding all else equal, autocratic coalitions protract the survival of autocratic coalitions. The results are highly statistically significant ($p < .001$).

In Column 8, the dependent variable in the first-stage regression is the more inclusive autocratic constitution measure, which includes the seven constitutions intended to usher in democracy. The instrumental variable of interest is therefore the more inclusive version of constituent assembly elections that includes constituent assemblies convoked to bring about democracy. Constituent Assembly Election is again strong positively associated with autocratic constitution. As in Column 7, Column 8 indicates that autocratic constitutions extend the survival of autocratic coalitions ($p < .001$).

Property Rights Protection

Table 4.2 provides strong evidence that autocratic constitutions extend autocratic coalition survival. However, we have not yet provided evidence in support of the claim that the mechanism linking autocratic constitutions to survival is the dictator's ability to reassign property rights to his closest supporters and to create clear limitations on his ability to readjust those property rights. This section analyzes whether autocratic constitutions stabilize property rights as measured by contract-intensive money (CIM). Because the outcome variable is continuous, we employ Ordinary Least Squares (OLS) models with country fixed effects. Robust standard errors clustered by country address serial correlation and heteroskedasticity.

As with the regressions for autocratic coalition exit, a number of potentially confounding variables are controlled for in the property rights regressions. Following Clague et al. (1996), we control for Log(Per Capita Income) and expect a positive sign. We also control for Economic Growth Rate (of Per Capita Income, in percent), which can yield more attractive institutional arrangements associated with property rights protection (Glaeser et al. 2004). Because civil war may result in political instability that undermines property rights, we include Civil War as in the Table 4.2 models. Because autocratic coalitions that are dependent on investment of the productive domestic economy have incentives to establish constraining institutions that can protect property rights whereas those that are not may avail resource rents (Wright 2008), we include a measure of Total Resources Income Per Capita and also expect a negative sign. Because previous coups can foster political instability and additional coups (Londregan and Poole 1990), which are inimical to the establishment of a stable order of property rights, we include Coup Count as in the Table 4.2 models. We control for whether the dictator in power is the head of a Military Regime, because these regimes tend to rely on small coalitions to support their rule

TABLE 4.3. *Autocratic constitutions and property rights protection in Latin America, 1950–2002 (Dependent variable: contract intensive money)*

	Model 1	Model 2	Model 3	Model 4
Autocratic Constitution	10.339*	6.908**	5.476*	4.952*
	(4.876)	(3.161)	(2.763)	(2.811)
log(GDP Per Capita)	21.621**	−5.137	−1.332	−1.392
	(9.682)	(14.213)	(13.739)	(13.587)
Growth Rate	−0.123	0.197	0.222	0.232
	(0.166)	(0.173)	(0.170)	(0.166)
Civil War	6.441	−0.522	−1.197	−0.925
	(7.672)	(5.918)	(5.586)	(5.575)
Resources Income Per Capita	1.694	−2.393	−2.520	−2.272
	(6.837)	(7.327)	(7.148)	(7.236)
Coup Count	4.650***	2.224**	2.647***	2.675***
	(0.797)	(0.838)	(0.869)	(0.889)
Military Regime			−8.007	−7.854
			(4.625)	(4.616)
Legislature				0.719
				(0.775)
Year Effects	NO	YES	YES	YES
Country Fixed Effects	YES	YES	YES	YES
Observations	386	386	386	386
R-Squared	0.820	0.881	0.888	0.888

* $p < 0.10$; ** $p < 0.05$; *** $p < 0.01$ (two-tailed)
All independent variables lagged except Constitutions, Military Regime, and Legislature. Robust standard errors clustered by country in parentheses. Constants estimated but not reported.

and are less likely to extend property rights more broadly (Bueno de Mesquita et al. 2003). Their more rapid exits from power also leave less time to create a stable property rights regime (see, e.g., Geddes 2003). Finally, we control for the presence of a legislature, which may function as a credible constraint on a regime's confiscatory behavior, enhancing property rights protection (Wright 2008).

Another potential control variable is ideology, because it is possible that the presence of right-wing dictators in Latin America that are more likely to commit to liberal economic institutions is also more likely to deliver high growth rates. Although it may also be useful to account for a leader's ideology, it is difficult to do so empirically for two reasons. First, data on ideology for dictators (e.g., from the Database of Political Institutions) during the period are sparse. Second, including ideology could introduce concerns with reverse causality, in that a dictator who delivers strong growth is more likely to be considered right wing *ex post*.

Table 4.3 presents the results. Autocratic constitutions are linked with increased property rights ($p < .10$) in Model 1. An autocratic constitution is associated with a roughly 10 percent increase in the CIM ratio of the proportion of the money supply held in the banking system. Log(Per Capita Income) is also positive and strongly associated with a higher CIM ratio. Finally, Coup Count is positive and highly statistically significant. This may be a proxy for a strong military willing to intervene when a populist or leftist government takes power and threatens property rights, or, because the sample is limited to autocratic leader-years, it could be indicative of more transitions to democracy and therefore greater experience with institutions of limited government. The sample size in Model 1 is smaller than that in Table 4.2 because data for the CIM ratio are only available after 1960.

Model 2 is specified similarly to Model 1 but includes year fixed effects to account for secular trends and exogenous shocks in the CIM ratio. The coefficient for Autocratic Constitution declines in magnitude but increases in statistical significance. Log(Per Capita Income) loses significance. Model 3 introduces a dummy variable for military regimes. These regimes are associated with roughly 8 percent lower CIM ratios than nonmilitary regimes, although the coefficient is just short of statistical significance at conventional levels. Model 4 introduces an additional variable for autocratic legislatures. The coefficient is positive but statistically insignificant. The other results, including those for autocratic constitutions, are largely similar to those in Model 2.

Could it be the case that it is the autocratic coalitions that successfully foster property rights that subsequently adopt a constitution to reflect those *de facto* rights, leading to reverse causation? To test this possibility, we ran a Hausman Test for endogeneity that evaluates the hypothesis that the coefficient on Autocratic Constitution from the OLS model represented in Column 4 is the same as a coefficient obtained on Autocratic Constitution from the second stage of an IV regression. The Hausman Test could not reject the hypothesis that the OLS coefficient and the IV coefficient are essentially the same, suggesting that there is no evidence of reverse causation running from the CIM ratio to Autocratic Constitution and that the OLS regressions are preferred to avoid the considerable loss of efficiency implied by an IV approach in the absence of endogeneity.[10]

Private Investment

We argue that the creation of a constitution under dictatorship can enable a dictator to co-opt threats to his rule and create stronger property rights protection for his array of supporters. Tables 4.2 and 4.3 provide empirical evidence in support of these claims. This section examines an additional implication of the theory – namely, that autocratic constitutions should be linked to higher private investment rates. As in Tables 4.2 and 4.3, the Table 4.4 models include country fixed effects, and robust standard errors are clustered by country.

[10] The chi-squared statistic was 6.15 with p-value > 0.99.

TABLE 4.4. *Autocratic constitutions and private investment (percentage of GDP) in Latin America, 1950–2002*

	Model 1	Model 2	Model 3	Model 4	Model 5
Autocratic Constitution	2.369***	2.322***	2.749**	3.066**	2.883*
	(0.742)	(0.748)	(0.998)	(1.359)	(1.477)
Resources Income Per Capita	0.155	0.173	−0.333	−0.677	−0.701
	(2.953)	(3.032)	(2.937)	(2.931)	(2.964)
Coup Count	−1.089	−1.146*	−1.122*	−1.227*	−1.264*
	(0.672)	(0.621)	(0.582)	(0.573)	(0.596)
Civil War	−3.496***	−3.630***	−3.927***	−3.977***	−3.842***
	(0.693)	(0.863)	(0.895)	(0.802)	(0.845)
log(GDP Per Capita)		−0.820	0.480	−1.745	−1.913
		(3.705)	(3.576)	(4.587)	(4.602)
Inflation			0.524	0.683	0.659
			(0.532)	(0.539)	(0.571)
Military Regime				2.169	2.329
				(2.146)	(1.937)
Legislature					0.257
					(0.733)
Year Effects	YES	YES	YES	YES	YES
Country Fixed Effects	YES	YES	YES	YES	YES
Observations	220	220	204	204	204
R-Squared	0.552	0.552	0.570	0.577	0.577

* $p < 0.10$; ** $p < 0.05$; *** $p < 0.01$ (two-tailed)
All independent variables lagged except Constitutions, Military Regime, and Legislature. Robust standard errors clustered by country in parentheses. Constants estimated but not reported.

The regressions include a series of control variables that may also affect private investment. The first is Total Resources Income Per Capita, because autocrats that can generate resource revenues to sustain their rule may be less likely to cultivate domestic private investment (Wright 2008). Because a history of coups can foster political instability (Londregan and Poole 1990), destroying wealth stocks and threatening investment, we include the measure of Coup Count as in Tables 4.2 and 4.3. Similarly, we control for Civil War given the negative impact that conflict may have on investment. We also control for Log(Per Capita Income), because a higher level of development may be linked to stronger contract rights that can encourage investment (Clague et al. 1996). We include a control for Inflation (log of change in consumer price index) because high inflation rates can discourage investment. We also control for Military Regime, because these regimes are less stable and less likely to provide the broader property rights security important for private investment (Bueno de Mesquita et al. 2003). Finally, we control for the presence of a legislature, which when binding may enhance investment (Wright 2008).

Table 4.4 presents the results. The number of observations in the Table 4.4 models is reduced relative to the full sample of leader-years of dictatorship given that private investment data are only available after 1970 for this sample of states and have sparser country-level coverage. Despite the relatively small sample and country and year fixed effects, autocratic constitutions are strongly linked to higher rates of private investment. The coefficient for Autocratic Constitution is positive and statistically significant ($p < .01$) in Model 1, and its substantive effect is large. Autocratic constitutions lead to an estimated 2.4 percent increase in private investment as a share of GDP in Model 1. Civil War is negative and highly significant, indicating that civil conflict substantially decreases private investment.

The statistical and substantive significance of autocratic constitutions holds in Model 2 when Log(Per Capita Income) is added. Coup Count is negative and significant in Model 2, as in the rest of the Table 4.4 models, indicating that a history of more coups decreases private investment. The coefficient on Autocratic Constitution remains positive and significant in Models 3 through 5 as Inflation, Military Regime, and Legislature are sequentially added to the specification. In sum, autocratic constitutions are linked to higher rates of private investment.[11]

Economic Growth

If autocratic constitutions can successfully encourage property rights protection and private investment, as indicated in Tables 4.3 and 4.4, then leaders who create these constitutions should be linked to higher economic growth rates as well. This section examines this additional empirical implication. As in Tables 4.3 and 4.4, the Table 4.5 models include country fixed effects, and robust standard errors are clustered by country.

The Table 4.5 models control for a number of variables that are also hypothesized to affect economic growth. The first is Resources Income Per Capita. Whereas many scholars have found a negative association between resource wealth and economic growth (e.g., Sachs and Warner 1995), others have found a positive relationship (e.g., Brunnschweiler 2008). We include Coup Count because coup history may affect the growth rate, although some find no effect (e.g., Londregan and Poole 1990). We include a dummy for Military Regime because these regimes may be both associated with greater instability (Geddes 2003) as well as more likely to seize power when economic performance is poor (Londregan and Poole 1990). We also add a variable for the presence of an autocratic legislature, which if it constrains a regime's confiscatory behavior may encourage economic growth (Wright 2008). We include private Investment (percentage of GDP), which may spur economic growth (Wright 2008). Indeed, Table 4.4 indicates that constitutions are

[11] As with Table 4.3, we investigated the possibility of endogeneity using a Hausman test. The results suggested that there was no evidence of reverse causation, although the small number of observations in the sample precluded the estimation of a positive definite variance-covariance matrix.

TABLE 4.5. *Autocratic constitutions and economic growth in Latin America, 1950–2002*

	Model 1	Model 2	Model 3	Model 4	Model 5	Model 6
Autocratic Constitution	0.015**	0.017**	0.017**	0.017**	0.011	0.007
	(0.007)	(0.007)	(0.006)	(0.007)	(0.011)	(0.017)
Resources Income Per Capita	−0.036***	−0.011	−0.012	−0.012	−0.020	−0.020
	(0.008)	(0.017)	(0.017)	(0.018)	(0.029)	(0.035)
Coup Count	−0.002	0.001	0.001	0.001	0.004	0.002
	(0.002)	(0.002)	(0.002)	(0.002)	(0.007)	(0.009)
Military Regime			0.002	0.002	−0.014	−0.019
			(0.012)	(0.012)	(0.011)	(0.015)
Legislature				−0.000	−0.002	−0.001
				(0.004)	(0.005)	(0.006)
Investment (% GDP)					0.005*	0.005*
					(0.003)	(0.003)
Inflation						−0.004
						(0.010)
Year Effects	NO	YES	YES	YES	YES	YES
Country Fixed Effects	YES	YES	YES	YES	YES	YES
Observations	425	425	425	425	181	166
R-Squared	0.084	0.281	0.281	0.281	0.514	0.502

* $p < 0.10$; ** $p < 0.05$; *** $p < 0.01$ (two-tailed)
All independent variables lagged except Constitutions, Military Regime, and Legislature. Robust standard errors clustered by country in parentheses. Constants estimated but not reported.

strongly linked to increased investment. If private investment is the causal mechanism linking autocratic constitutions to growth by limiting the dictator's discretion and providing a more predictable environment for investment, the coefficient on autocratic constitutions should decline and lose significance when private investment is added to the regressions. Indeed, Table 4.4 indicates that constitutions are strongly linked to increased investment. Finally, we include a measure of inflation (log of change in consumer price index), which may impact either growth or private investment.

Other country-specific, relatively time-invariant factors cited as important to growth, such as ethnolinguistic fractionalization, legal origin, and religious makeup, are implicitly controlled for by using country fixed effects. We also tried controlling for Government Share of GDP (in percentage terms from the Penn World Tables) following Barro (1998), who argues that higher spending on government outlays not related to education should lower economic growth because it crowds out private investment. We do not include those results here because this variable was statistically insignificant and did not affect the Autocratic Constitution coefficient.

Table 4.5 presents the empirical results. Autocratic constitutions are positive and statistically significantly associated with higher economic growth rates in Model 1.

Model 2 introduces year fixed effects to address secular trends and shocks in growth rates. The Autocratic Constitution coefficient retains its statistical and substantive significance. Model 3 introduces Military Regime, and Model 4 adds Legislature. Neither of these variables has statistically significant coefficients. Autocratic Constitution, however, remains positive and significant. Model 5 adds Investment (percent of GDP) to the Model 4 specification. Because of more limited coverage for this variable, the sample size is now reduced to 181. Investment is positively related to economic growth, and Autocratic Constitution loses its statistical significance and declines in magnitude, suggesting that the mechanism whereby autocratic constitutions increase economic growth is through their positive impact on private investment. The results for these variables remain similar when inflation enters the specification in Model 6. In short, autocratic constitutions are linked to higher rates of economic growth, and this effect operates through increasing private investment.[12]

In sum, Tables 4.2 through 4.5 demonstrate that a constitution under dictatorship can have a strong impact both on an autocratic coalition's tenure in office and for a number of dimensions of the domestic economy. Autocratic constitutions are linked to longer tenure in office. They also result in greater property rights protection, increased private investment, and higher rates of economic growth.

CONCLUSION

We advance a theory of how dictators who destroy some elites upon coming to power can simultaneously credibly commit to not destroying others. When the organization that launches a new dictator into power is uncertain about whether he will remain loyal to them, a dictator's decision to destroy the preexisting elite (e.g., through expropriation) may contribute to political stability by signaling his exclusive reliance on this group. Yet once a dictator survives past the first stage of his rule marked by uncertainty about his intentions, he has to ameliorate his launching organization's concerns that they too could have their interests abrogated. As a result, the dictator may find it useful to complement informal norms and institutions by codifying rules of the game and institutions in which he can help forge a self-enforcing stake in the regime. An autocratic constitution can complement preexisting norms by outlining who qualifies as a member of the new autocratic coalition and align expectations and norms among this group. It can help coordinate behavior and credibly threaten sanctions for those who deviate.

Using new data compiled on constitutions instituted under autocracy in Latin America from 1950 to 2002, we demonstrate that the creation of a constitution under dictatorship can enable an autocratic coalition to survive in office longer. Autocratic

[12] As in Tables 4.3 and 4.4, we investigated the potential reverse causality, using a Hausman test. The results indicated that there was no evidence of endogeneity.

constitutions also contribute to greater property rights protection, private investment, and economic growth.

These results have important implications for the burgeoning literature on the political economy of dictatorship. That autocratic regimes tend to adopt many of the institutional trappings of democratic regimes has puzzled researchers who study authoritarianism. Because dictators tend to violate many of the "aspirations" outlined in their constitutions or seem to unilaterally modify these documents when it is convenient for them, researchers often view these documents as simple window dressing or lip service to democratic values. Perhaps these norms have become universal and therefore must be acknowledged – even by dictators who are intent on disregarding them. We argue that while autocratic constitutions do not typically set limits on executive authority in a direct way as they do in a democracy, they nonetheless help accomplish this function in an indirect way: by allowing a new set of elites to coordinate to discipline the dictator. This is true even in situations in which, ironically, the new dictator consolidated his authority by expropriating the preexisting elite.[13]

REFERENCES

Acemoglu, Daron, James Robinson, and Thierry Verdier. 2004. "Kleptocracy and Divide-and-Rule." *Journal of the European Economic Association Papers and Proceedings* 2: 162–92.

Albertus, Michael and Victor Menaldo. 2012a. "If You're With Them You're Against Us: The Effect of Expropriation on Autocratic Survival." *Comparative Political Studies* 45(8): 973–1003.

Albertus, Michael and Victor Menaldo. 2012b. "Dictators as Founding Fathers? The Role of Constitutions Under Autocracy." *Economics & Politics* 24(3): 279–306.

Albertus, Michael and Victor Menaldo. Forthcoming. "Gaming Democracy: Elite Dominance During Transition and the Prospects for Redistribution." *British Journal of Political Science*.

Ahlquist, John and Aseem Prakash. 2008. "The Influence of Foreign Direct Investment on Contracting Confidence in Developing Countries." *Regulation & Governance* 2: 316–39.

Barro, Robert. 1998. *Determinants of Economic Growth*. Cambridge, MA: MIT Press.

Barros, Robert. 2002. *Constitutionalism and Dictatorship*. Cambridge: Cambridge University Press.

Besley, Timothy and Masayuki Kudamatsu. 2007. "Making Autocracy Work." Unpublished manuscript.

Boix, Carles and Milan Svolik. 2008. "The Foundations of Limited Authoritarian Government: Institutions and Power-Sharing in Dictatorships." Unpublished manuscript.

Box-Steffensmeier, Janet and Bradford Jones. 1997. "Time Is of the Essence: Event History Models in Political Science." *American Journal of Political Science* 41(4): 1414–61.

Brown, Nathan. 2002. *Constitutions in a Nonconstitutional World: Arab Basic Laws and the Prospects for Accountable Government*. Albany, NY: SUNY Press.

Brunnschweiler, Christa. 2008. "Cursing the Blessings? Natural Resource Abundance, Institutions, and Economic Growth." *World Development* 36(3): 399–419.

[13] For systematic evidence supporting this claim see Albertus and Menaldo (2012a).

Bueno de Mesquita, Bruce, Alastair Smith, Randolph Siverson, and James Morrow. 2003. *The Logic of Political Survival*. Boston: MIT Press.

Carey, John. 2000. "Parchment, Equilibria, and Institutions." *Comparative Political Studies* 33(6): 735–61.

Carter, David and Curtis Signorino. 2010. "Back to the Future: Modeling Time Dependence in Binary Data." *Political Analysis* 18: 271–92.

Cheibub, Jose-Antonio and Jennifer Gandhi. 2004. "Classifying Political Regimes: A Six-Fold Classification of Democracies and Dictatorships." Unpublished manuscript.

Clague, Christopher, Philip Keefer, Stephen Knack, and Mancur Olson. 1996. "Property and Contract Rights in Autocracies and Democracies." *Journal of Economic Growth* 1: 243–76.

Clague, Christopher, Philip Keefer, Stephen Knack, and Mancur Olson. 1999. "Contract-Intensive Money." *Journal of Economic Growth* 4: 185–211.

Elkins, Zachary. 2010. "Diffusion and the Constitutionalization of Europe." *Comparative Political Studies* 43: 969–99.

Elkins, Zachary, Tom Ginsburg, and James Melton. 2009. *The Endurance of National Constitutions*. Cambridge: Cambridge University Press.

Elkins, Zachary, Tom Ginsburg, and James Melton. 2010. *The Comparative Constitutions Project*. Available at http://comparativeconstitutionsproject.org.

de Figueiredo, Rui and Barry Weingast. 1997. "Rationality of Fear: Political Opportunism and Ethnic Conflict," in Jack Snyder and Barbara Walter, eds., *Military Intervention in Civil Wars*. New York: Columbia University Press, pp. 262–3.

Gandhi, Jennifer. 2008. *Political Institutions under Dictatorship*. Cambridge: Cambridge University Press.

Gandhi, Jennifer and Adam Przeworski. 2006. "Cooperation, Cooptation and Rebellion Under Dictatorship." *Economics and Politics* 18(1): 1–26.

Geddes, Barbara. 2003. *Paradigms and Sand Castles*. Ann Arbor: University of Michigan Press.

Gehlbach, Scott and Philip Keefer. 2011. "Investment without Democracy: Ruling-Party Institutionalization and Credible Commitment in Autocracies." *Journal of Comparative Economics* 39(2): 123–39.

Glaeser, Edward L., Rafael La Porta, Florencio Lopez-de-Silanes, and Andrei Shleifer. 2004. "Do Institutions Cause Growth?" *Journal of Economic Growth* 9(3): 271–303.

Goemens, Henk, Kristian Skrede Gleditsch, and Giacomo Chiozza. 2009. "Introducing Archigos: A Dataset of Political Leaders." *Journal of Peace Research* 46: 269–83.

Haber, Stephen. 2006. "Authoritarian Government," in Barry Weingast and Donald Wittman, eds., *The Oxford Handbook of Political Economy*. New York: Oxford University Press, pp. 693–707.

Haber, Stephen, Armando Razo, and Noel Mauerer. 2003. *The Politics of Property Rights*. New York: Cambridge University Press.

Hardin, Russell. 1989. "Why a Constitution," in Bernard Grofman and Donald Wittman, eds., *The Federalist Papers and the New Institutionalism*. New York: Agathon, pp. 100–20.

Hyde, Susan, and Nikolay Marinov. 2012. "Which Elections Can Be Lost?" *Political Analysis* 20(2): 191–210.

Londregan, John, and Keith Poole. 1990. "Poverty, the Coup Trap, and the Seizure of Executive Power." *World Politics* 42: 151–83.

Lust-Okar, Ellen. 2006. "Elections under Authoritarianism: Preliminary Lessons from Jordan." *Democratization* 13: 456–71.

Magaloni, Beatriz. 2008. "Credible Power-Sharing and the Longevity of Authoritarian Rule." *Comparative Political Studies* 41(4/5): 715–41.

Menaldo, Victor. 2012. "The Middle East and North Africa's Resilient Monarchs." *Journal of Politics* 74(3): 707–22.

Myerson, Roger. 2008. "The Autocrat's Credibility Problem and Foundations of the Constitutional State." *American Political Science Review* 102: 125–39.

Negretto, Gabriel. 2013. *Making Constitutions: Presidents, Parties, and Institutional Choice in Latin America*. Cambridge: Cambridge University Press.

North, Douglass and Barry Weingast. 1989. "Constitutions and Commitment." *Journal of Economic History* 49: 803–32.

Ordeshook, Peter. 1992. "Constitutional Stability." *Constitutional Political Economy* 3: 137–75.

Posner, Daniel and Daniel Young. 2007. "The Institutionalization of Political Power in Africa." *Journal of Democracy* 18: 126–40.

Sachs, Jeffrey and Andrew Warner. 1995. *Natural Resource Abundance and Economic Growth*. NBER Working Paper No. 5398.

Schedler, Andreas. 2002. "Elections Without Democracy: The Menu of Manipulation." *Journal of Democracy* 13: 36–50.

Shepsle, Kenneth and Barry Weingast. 1981. "Structure-Induced Equilibrium and Legislative Choice." *Public Choice* 37: 503–19.

Smith, Benjamin. 2004. "Oil Wealth and Regime Survival in the Developing World, 1960–1999." *American Journal of Political Science* 48: 232–46.

Summerhill, William. 2007. "Sovereign Credibility with Financial Underdevelopment: The Case of Nineteenth-Century Brazil." Unpublished manuscript.

Svolik, Milan. 2012. *The Politics of Authoritarian Rule*. Cambridge: Cambridge University Press.

Weingast, Barry. 1997. "The Political Foundations of Democracy and the Rule of Law." *American Political Science Review* 91(2): 245–63.

Wright, Joseph. 2008. "Do Authoritarian Institutions Constrain? How Legislatures Affect Economic Growth and Investment." *American Journal of Political Science* 52(2): 322–43.

5

Authoritarian Constitution Making

The Role of the Military in Latin America[*]

Gabriel L. Negretto

Latin America is a region characterized by a high level of constitutional instability. Since independence, constitutions have been drafted and redrafted following successive changes between governments with different partisan interests and programmatic goals. During the twentieth century, military dictatorships contributed to this pattern by replacing a large number of constitutions enacted during both authoritarian and democratic periods. This proliferation of constitutions under military rule is somewhat paradoxical given that military regimes are provisional in nature and usually justified by the need to restore constitutional order under a civilian government. Why would military rulers invest time and resources in drafting constitutions?

This chapter argues that military leaders want to adopt new constitutions when their intervention in politics seeks broad transformations in the political, social, and economic order. Given these objectives, a constitution makes possible the adoption of effective and enduring reforms by providing the regime with a more solid legal basis and involving a plurality of institutional actors in the decision-making process. Constitutions also facilitate imposing constraints on the functioning of the future democratic regime, something military rulers typically intend to do to preserve their reforms and protect their personal and corporate interests after leaving power. Yet the capacity of military rulers to achieve these goals through constitution making is always limited. In order to adopt and maintain their constitutions, military dictators must be able to mobilize popular and partisan support for the authoritarian regime. Because this condition is rarely met, military rulers often fail to perpetuate their institutional legacy.

The chapter starts with a discussion of the extent of authoritarian constitution making in Latin America from 1900 to 2008. The second section proposes a series

[*] I would like to thank Allyson Benton, Jose Antonio Cheibub, Julio Rios-Figueroa, Marcelo Bergman, and participants at the conference Constitutions in Authoritarian Regimes for their helpful comments and suggestions on a previous version of this chapter.

of hypotheses about the incentives and capacities of military rulers to engage in successful constitution making. The third section provides preliminary support for these hypotheses using cross-national data and a qualitative analysis of the 1966 to 1972, 1972 to 1978, and 1964 to 1984 military governments in Argentina, Ecuador, and Brazil, respectively. A brief conclusion follows.

AUTHORITARIAN CONSTITUTION MAKING IN LATIN AMERICA

Authoritarian rule, both civil and military, prevailed in Latin America before the expansion of electoral democracy in the region in the early 1980s. From 1900 to 2008, Latin American countries were under authoritarian rule for an average of 65.2 years. While all authoritarian governments were established by coups or noncompetitive elections, they often decided to institutionalize their rule by means of a new constitution. In fact, most constitutions enacted in Latin America during the twentieth century were created by or under the influence of authoritarian rulers.

In order to analyze the extent of authoritarian constitution making in Latin America, I have created a database that codes all constitutions enacted in the region between 1900 and 2008 as either democratic or authoritarian.[1] If authoritarian, constitutions are further classified as military or civilian. A constitution is considered to be democratic if it was adopted in a democratic year or enacted during a transition to democracy by a constituent body made up of civilian parties selected in a competitive election.[2] A constitution is considered to be authoritarian if it was enacted during an authoritarian year and the constituent body was not elected in a competitive election. Authoritarian constitutions are classified as military or civilian depending on whether the head of the government at the time of enactment was a member of the regular armed forces.

Table 5.1 summarizes the number of constitutions per country in each category. According to this classification, the vast majority (70 percent) of the total number of constitutions enacted in Latin America between 1900 and 2008 are authoritarian. Within authoritarian constitutions, most (67 percent), in turn, have been made by or under the influence of military governments.

As is well known, military dictatorships have been a pervasive phenomenon in Latin America. Yet the fact that more authoritarian constitutions were enacted during periods of military government does not reflect that Latin American countries spent more years under military rule or that military dictatorships were more enduring

[1] For more general information about my database on constitutional change in Latin America and the sources used in building it, see Negretto (2013) and the website: http://www.la-constitutionalchange.cide.edu/.

[2] The classification of democratic and authoritarian years follows Smith (2005) up to 1950 and Przeworski and colleagues (2000) subsequently. A constitution enacted during the last year of an authoritarian regime is considered to be democratic if it was adopted by a constituent assembly whose representatives were selected in an election in which more than one independent party competed. The 1979 Peruvian constitution or the 1983 Salvadorian constitution belongs to this category.

TABLE 5.1. *Constitutions enacted in Latin America by government, 1900–2008*

Country	Constitutions 1900–2008*	Authoritarian civilian	Authoritarian military	Democratic
Argentina	2	0	0	2
Bolivia	5	2	3	0
Brazil	5	2	1	2
Chile	2	1	1	0
Colombia	1	0	0	1
Costa Rica	2	0	1	1
Dom. Rep.	3	0	1	2
Ecuador	8	4	2	2
El Salvador	5	0	4	1
Guatemala	4	0	2	2
Honduras	6	0	4	2
Mexico	1	1	0	0
Nicaragua	7	1	5	1
Panama	4	3	1	0
Paraguay	3	0	2	1
Peru	4	2	1	1
Uruguay	5	2	0	3
Venezuela	15	1	11	3
TOTAL	**82**	**19 (.23)**	**39 (.48)**	**24 (.29)**

* Reinstated constitutions not counted as new constitutions.
Source: Latin American Constitutional Change Database (http://la-constitutionalchange.cide.edu/data) for constitutions per country; Bethell (1990, 1998), Nohlen (2005), Przeworski and colleagues (2000), and Smith (2005) for coding constitutions as democratic or authoritarian.

than civilian ones. It is related rather to the relatively larger number of military over civilian authoritarian regimes and the larger proportion of the former that engaged in constitution making. Table 5.2 shows these comparative data.

Whereas the accumulated years of military rule represent about half of the total number of country-years that Latin American countries lived under authoritarian

TABLE 5.2. *Authoritarian regimes and constitutions in Latin America, 1900–2008*

Type	Regimes	Years	Mean duration	Regimes adopting constitutions	Constitutions	Mean duration
Military	75	588	7.8	25	39	14.9
Civilian	62	586	9.5	15	19	18.6
TOTAL	**137**	**1174**	**8.6**	**40**	**58**	**16.7**

Source: Same as Table 5.1 for constitutions; Smith (2005) for authoritarian years before 1950 and Przeworski and colleagues (2000) for authoritarian years after that date.

rule, the average duration of an authoritarian military regime was 7.8 years, compared to 9.5 years of its civilian counterpart.[3] Whether military or civilian, comparatively few authoritarian regimes enacted new constitutions. Yet from a total of seventy-five military regimes, twenty-five of them (33 percent) adopted one or more constitutions, compared to fifteen out of sixty-two (24 percent) of the civilian authoritarian regimes that engaged in constitution making. Although larger in number, constitutions enacted under a military regime were less resilient than those of their civilian counterparts. The average duration of constitutions enacted under military rule was 14.9 years, compared to 18.6 years for those adopted during civilian dictatorships.[4]

There are spatial and temporal variations within the total set of military dictatorships and constitutions. Before 1950, military dictatorships that lasted ten or more years were found only in countries in which military interventions had been pervasive since the early decades of the twentieth century.[5] During the 1960s and 1970s, however, the number of countries experiencing enduring military dictatorships increased regardless of their history of military rule.[6] As a consequence, whereas the average duration of the last military dictatorship established before 1959 was 8.3 years, the average duration of the last military dictatorship established before 1989 was 13.8 years. Interestingly, however, the proportion of military regimes adopting new constitutions did not increase over time. Whereas 64 percent of the military dictatorships established between 1930 and 1959 enacted new constitutions, only 50 percent of those established between 1960 and 1989 did so.

Military constitutions have been drafted by different procedures, among which predominate executive commissions and constituent congresses or assemblies. Constitutions designed by executive commissions may be imposed or subject to ratification in a referendum, as was the case of the 1978 Ecuadorean constitution and the 1980 Chilean constitution. Drafting the constitution by a constituent congress or assembly dominated by military rulers is the most common procedure. These bodies are made up of delegates directly appointed by military rulers or elected under their supervision. Examples are the 1967 constitutions of Bolivia and Brazil and most constitutions enacted in Honduras, Guatemala, and El Salvador during military governments. In most cases, constituent congresses and assemblies were responsible not only for adopting a new constitution but also for inaugurating a new period of government through the indirect election of the president.

Constitutions created under the influence of military rulers have had different life histories. One can observe, however, two basic types. The first corresponds to

3 Regimes are counted by continuous years of military or civilian authoritarian rule.

4 Both, however, are below the mean duration of democratic constitutions enacted between 1900 and 2008, which was 19.9 years.

5 These countries were Bolivia, Dominican Republic, El Salvador, Guatemala, Honduras, Nicaragua, Paraguay, and Venezuela.

6 For instance, countries such as Panama and Uruguay, which did not have a previous history of military rule, were subject to enduring military dictatorships in the 1960s and 1970s.

constitutions created during a military regime and in force only for the time the regime is in place; the second corresponds to constitutions created or amended during the military regime that are in force during a subsequent democratic period for the whole or a substantial portion of their lives. The 1967 constitutions of Brazil and Paraguay illustrate the former type, and the 1967 constitution of Bolivia, the 1980 constitution of Chile, the 1972 constitution of Panama, or the 1978 constitution of Ecuador are examples of the second type. The largest number of authoritarian constitutions created under the influence of the military (thirty-one out of thirty-nine) belongs to the first type. Table 5.3 shows the number of constitutions by country corresponding to each type.

The reason for the predominance of constitutions in force only during years of military rule is obvious. Most democratic regimes either reinstate the preauthoritarian constitution (with or without amendments) or create a new one. Maintaining an authoritarian constitution is usually not an option unless it was ratified by popular vote (as was the case of the Ecuadorian constitution of 1978) or the military regime was strong enough (as in the case of Chile or Panama) to impose legal constraints on the new democracy. Democratic regimes, particularly after long years of authoritarian rule, need to recreate a new form of legality by means of a constitution drafted in a freely elected constituent assembly (Geddes 1990).

This analysis shows that although most authoritarian constitutions in Latin America have been adopted during military dictatorships, not all military rulers have been able to do so. Moreover, when they did adopt a constitution, it did not necessarily outlive the duration of the military dictatorship. This brings to the fore the question about the goals that military rulers pursue when they adopt a constitution and the varying capacities they have to engage in successful constitution making. I turn to this question in the following section.

MILITARY RULERS AS CONSTITUTION MAKERS

There is something seemingly counterintuitive in the idea of a constitution adopted by military rulers. The enactment of a new constitution signals the intention of a dictatorship to institutionalize its rule. However, the mission of a professional military is to defend the constitution, not to exercise constituent power. It is precisely for this reason that military interventions, even in the interpretation of their own leaders, are temporary by nature. Regardless of the actual circumstances that prompted the intervention, it is nearly always justified in the need to restore the abolished democratic order. As Alain Rouquie has argued, a permanent system of military rule is almost a contradiction in terms "because it is precisely the subsequent government, the successor regime, that legitimates the prior military usurpation" (Rouquie 1986: 111).

The routinization of military rule by means of a constitution may also work against the preservation of the military as an institution. The maintenance of internal unity

TABLE 5.3. *Military constitutions by periods of enforcement, 1900–2008*

Country	Military constitutions	In force during authoritarian years	In force during democratic years
Argentina	0	–	–
Bolivia	1938	Yes	No
	1945	Yes	No
	1967	Yes	Yes
Brazil	1967	Yes	No
Chile	1980	Yes	Yes
Colombia	0	–	–
Costa Rica	1917	Yes	No
Dom. Rep.	1924	Yes	No
Ecuador	1906	Yes	No
	1978	No	Yes
El Salvador	1939	Yes	No
	1945	Yes	No
	1950	Yes	No
	1962	Yes	No
Guatemala	1956	No	Yes
	1965	No	Yes
Honduras	1906	Yes	No
	1924	Yes	No
	1936	Yes	No
	1965	Yes	Yes
Mexico	0	–	–
Nicaragua	1905	Yes	No
	1911	Yes	No
	1939	Yes	No
	1950	Yes	No
	1974	Yes	No
Panama	1972	Yes	Yes
Paraguay	1940	Yes	No
	1967	Yes	No
Peru	1933	Yes	Yes
Uruguay	0	–	–
	1901	Yes	No
	1904	Yes	No
	1909	Yes	No
	1914	Yes	No
	1922	Yes	No
Venezuela	1925	Yes	No
	1928	Yes	No
	1931	Yes	No
	1936	Yes	No
	1945	Yes	No
	1953	Yes	No
TOTAL	39	31*	8

* Number of constitutions in force only during authoritarian years.
Source: Same as Tables 5.1 and 5.2.

is key for the survival of the armed forces as an institution that claims to protect state sovereignty and the permanent interests of the nation. Factionalism, however, is inevitable the more frequent and deeper is the involvement of the military in politics. The longer the military stay in power, the more likely it is that conflicts between different military leaders and factions will arise about policy making or alternation in power. In the face of internal divisions, it becomes increasingly probable that the existing military government either be terminated by another coup or voluntarily leave power.[7]

The apparent paradox of constitution making under military regimes is somewhat dispelled if one thinks of members of the military as actors with goals that go beyond a narrow interpretation of their institutional and professional mission. This has been the case in most of the countries of Latin America in which the professional military that emerged in the early decades of the twentieth century soon became involved in internal defense functions, economic development strategies, and the resolution of internal political conflicts. This type of intervention was already visible in the 1930s and 1940s, when military officers took power in several countries not simply to overcome a temporary crisis situation but also to implement social reforms, industrialization policies, internal security plans, and political reforms (Rouquie and Suffern 1998: 149–54). The nature and scope of military regimes, however, has varied both across countries and over time.

There is a group of countries that since the 1930s (or even earlier) experienced increasingly expansive and enduring military regimes. Those countries were Paraguay in the Southern Cone, Bolivia and Venezuela in the Andean region, El Salvador, Guatemala, Honduras, and Nicaragua in Central America, and the Dominican Republic in the Caribbean. Particularly in Central America, military dictatorships such as those of generals Hernandez Martinez (1931–1944) in El Salvador and Ubico (1931–1944) in Guatemala were among the first to be established to pursue long-term goals. They aimed at eradicating internal enemies – usually leftists and reformists – controlling social organizations, shifting economic policy choices, and penetrating political groups. In most countries, however, the scope of military interventions tended to increase over time, especially after World War II.

Until the 1950s, the typical military intervention in Latin America conformed to what Alfred Stepan called the *moderator* model, in which the military would step in to govern for a relatively brief period to depose a government that adopted decisions against their interests or to prevent access to power to a political group unacceptable to them (Stepan 1973: 51). Although the military would take the opportunity to promote some policies while in power, the essential goal was to arbitrate in institutional

[7] It is for this reason that military dictatorships are usually less enduring than their civilian or personalistic counterparts. According to Geddes, while military dictatorships last for an average of nine years, personalistic and single-party dictatorships have endured an average of fifteen and twenty-three years, respectively (Geddes 2003: 126).

and partisan conflicts by creating a provisional *de facto* government until democratic order was restored. By the 1960s and 1970s, however, military interventions were being undertaken for grander and less specific political objectives than in the past. In a context of international and domestic radicalization of political conflicts, the proponents of military interventions unveiled ambitious plans to restructure the political system, the economy, and society at large, to an extent that had never been attempted before.

Seen from this perspective, it seems clear how constitution making could become an important part of the military intervention in politics. The loftier the objectives that military rulers pursue, the longer they may need to remain in power and the more important it becomes to put their decisions on a relatively solid legal basis. A constitution enables an authoritarian regime to demand obedience in the name of the law, to win legal recognition from the international community, and to regulate access to power within the authoritarian elite.[8] In addition, if the constitution imposes some limits to the arbitrary power of the executive and involves a plurality of institutional actors in the decision-making process, it may also secure more effective support for government decisions from ordinary citizens and organized political forces.

When a military intervention has a limited objective – say, to make possible the transfer of executive power in an exceptional crisis situation – it may be sufficient to suspend the existing constitution and rule by provisional executive acts.[9] Such a temporary suspension of the existing constitutional order has the advantage of being consistent with the justification of the military intervention as a necessary evil to protect constitutional order. Yet a military government that rules by means of provisional executive acts is condemned to remain as a *de facto* government whose decisions are bound to lapse once political normality is restored. This is clearly inconvenient if military rulers seek more permanent goals, such as promoting a particular model of economic development, eradicating certain political options, or transforming the nature of political competition in the country.

In other words, any military government that seeks to introduce fundamental and lasting changes in the social and political order is likely to prefer to have its own constitution. Moreover, because the military must eventually withdraw from power, the constitution can also be used to create advantages for their political allies, preserve their reforms, and protect their personal and institutional interests after the inauguration of democracy. One may doubt whether military rulers want a constitution to bind themselves, but it is clear that they would like to use the

8 Regulating interactions within the authoritarian elite, in particular terms in office and reelection rules, is considered to be the typical function of authoritarian constitutions, both military and civilian. See Fitzgibbon (1940) and Hartlyn and Valenzuela (1998: 13–14).

9 These executive acts receive various names (*estatutos, actas, actos institucionales*), but they typically subordinate the application of the constitution to their own provisions regulating the rights of citizens, government powers, and decision-making processes.

constitution to bind others.[10] Most military regimes, however, are likely to find that it is extremely difficult to implement a successful strategy of constitution making.

To imitate the forms of a constitutional government, military rulers need to demilitarize the nature of their system of domination.[11] This implies first of all adopting the constitution in a seemingly representative manner. The constitution should thus be approved in a popular referendum or in a constituent body that is formally independent from the executive. The difficulty, of course, is that because military rulers want to design the constitution to fit their needs, they also need to keep control over the outcome of the constitution-making process. If the constitution is designed by or under the control of the military, a referendum may be effective because it relies on direct popular consent. This is risky, however, because it requires either having strong popular support or else manipulating the results to the point that the referendum might not be credible.[12] Passing the constitution in a formally independent constituent body may be safer as long as this body remains under the influence of the military. This influence requires that either the military government appoint the members of the constituent body or a party supportive of military interests obtain majority control over it after some form of election.

To be sure, if the reason for adopting a new constitution is to strengthen the legal foundations of the military regime and make it more inclusive, having a party or coalition supportive of military interests in a constituent body should be preferable to having the government appoint delegates directly. In addition, even a partial or noncompetitive election of the constituent body may be closer to the formalities of democratic constitution making than its direct control by the government. The civilian partner of military rulers could be either a preexisting political party co-opted by the military, as was the case of the PNH in Honduras and the ANR in Paraguay, or a party directly created under the sponsorship of the military, as was ARENA in Brazil, the PRUD and PCN in El Salvador, the PID in Guatemala, and the PRD in Panama.[13]

The existence of a civilian party that articulates the interests of the military also lends credibility to the civilianization of military rule. Since the presence of military officers in key government positions contradicts the basic tenets of a representative government, military rulers usually need a large contingent of civilian partners willing to represent the regime. Some of these partners, particularly those who occupy

10 On the use of constitutions to bind others, see Elster (2000: 92–4).

11 On the various forms a demilitarization process can take, see Rouquie (1986).

12 This is what happened with the referendum used to approve the 1980 constitution in Chile. On this issue, see Barros (2002: 172–3).

13 PNH: Partido Nacional de Honduras (National Party of Honduras); ANR: Asociación Nacional Republicana (Republican National Association); ARENA: Aliança Renovadora Nacional (National Renewing Alliance); PRUD: Partido Revolucionario de Unificación Democrática (Revolutionary Party of Democratic Unification); PCN: Partido de Conciliación Nacional (National Reconciliation Party); PID: Partido Institucional Democrático (Democratic Institutional Party); PRD: Partido Revolucionario Democrático (Democratic Revolutionary Party).

high positions in the administration, may be nonpartisan public officials. However, if military rulers are willing to tolerate the existence of a legislative body in which limited participation of opposition forces is possible, it is clearly convenient to have a pro-government party organization to interact with the opposition in policy negotiation.[14]

Finally, military rulers would benefit from the support of a civilian party to make the survival of their institutional legacy after a transition to democracy possible. This is perhaps the single most difficult issue that military regimes must confront. Expansive military interventions may not set a fixed date for withdrawal from the beginning. But because a transition to democracy is at some point inevitable, military rulers are always forced to plan this event ahead of time to preserve the reforms made during their government and protect their institutional and personal interests in the postauthoritarian order. Constitution making is a key component in this strategy.

Although military rulers may want a constitution to provide the regime with a more solid legal foundation or make their decisions more acceptable to citizens and organized political forces, they also want to determine policy outcomes. This implies that a constitution adopted by military rulers would inevitably have some power-concentrating and centralizing features, such as limited or conditional constitutional guarantees, restrictive or no methods of election, presidential powers greater than those of Congress or the judiciary, and a national government that stands above local powers. As they prepare a transition to democracy, however, military rulers need new institutions that disperse and decentralize power along with institutions that create restrictions on the decisions of the future democratic regime.

This means that if military rulers managed to enact a constitution during their period in power, at the end of their terms they would attempt to introduce amendments that strengthen some civil and political freedoms and at the same time impose constraints on the new democratic order. For instance, military rulers would like to select electoral rules that benefit their political allies, proscribe certain political parties or individuals, preserve areas of military influence, or prevent their future prosecution for crimes committed while they were in power.[15] If they were unable to create their own constitution, toward the end of the regime military rulers might nevertheless attempt to influence future electoral and policy outcomes by means of amendments to the preauthoritarian constitution or by adopting a new constitution before the transition takes place.

In either case, military rulers are only likely to be successful in imposing constitutional constraints on a democratic regime if they find a party or parties willing to

[14] On the adoption of representative political institutions by authoritarian regimes to co-opt the opposition, see Gandhi (2008).

[15] Although these strategic objectives usually predominate in the institutions designed by military rulers, the latter may also attempt to pursue some "efficiency" goals. For instance, depending on the perceived root of political evils in the country, the military may seek electoral reforms that reduce the number of parties when the party system has been traditionally fragmented or reduce the advantage of majority parties when strong popular parties were able to win large majorities in the past.

support them. Moreover, unless the military regime is itself strong enough to be able to impose conditions on democratic forces, its partisan allies should have a relatively significant following among voters. Because democratic parties would frequently attempt to signal the birth of a new democratic era by convening a constituent assembly, the only way to preserve a constitution drafted under the influence of the military is if a party close to the outgoing regime wins the first democratic election or obtains sufficient political and institutional representation to veto the initiative.

The vexing problem for military rulers, however, is that they may not be able to find or organize a party that is inclined to collaborate with the regime and at the same time is capable of preserving its institutional legacy in the postauthoritarian period. The influence of the military in politics may be pervasive and yet civilian partners may not be available to form such a party. Military rulers have often intervened to save the country from a "corrupt" party system, in which case they typically banish all existing parties. As a consequence, these parties tend to form a homogenous bloc of opponents to military rule. Military leaders have also deposed strongly popular parties from power, which reduces the incentives of other parties to support, at least openly, their rule. Any party associated with the military government under these conditions would compromise its future performance in democratic elections.

The level of institutionalization of civilian parties during years of competitive elections is probably the most crucial determinant of the capacity of military leaders to co-opt or create an ally party.[16] Existing parties are more vulnerable to penetration by military interests, and civilian groups are more likely to join a party sponsored by military rulers when the country has had limited or no experience with competitive elections or when party organizations are unstable. In this context, existing parties have not yet developed strong ties of allegiance between voters and have less to lose by supporting a military government. Opportunistic politicians, in turn, may also find the formation of a new party to support the military regime attractive as an instrument to benefit from the spoils of office. For this reason, it is perhaps no accident that in countries with long-standing democracies and stable party systems, such as Argentina, Colombia, and Uruguay, military regimes have been unable to mobilize partisan support.

Yet even if the military regime manages to co-opt or create an ally party, this party may not be willing or able to control the transition and preserve the constitutional structure designed by the military. Parties that were co-opted by the military may decide to detach themselves from the regime in order to prove their democratic credentials before the transition to democracy. On the other hand, parties sponsored by military rulers may agree to represent the regime in the postauthoritarian era but have insufficient electoral support to influence decisions at the inauguration of democracy. Even in cases in which the military retained considerable popular

[16] The institutionalization of party systems has several components, but the most important are the age of parties and the stability of voting patterns across elections. See Mainwaring and Scully (1995: 4–6).

support at the time of leaving office, the parties directly sponsored by them, such as the PCN in El Salvador and the PID in Guatemala, tended to perform poorly in competitive elections.

To sum up, expansive military interventions are likely to provide military rulers with an incentive to engage in constitution making to make more effective transformations during their rule and have influence over the functioning of democracy after they have left power. Their capacity to achieve these goals, however, depends on relatively stringent political conditions, such as the availability of partisan partners that are willing and able to institutionalize a military regime and preserve its legacy. This explains why not all military rulers are capable of adopting their own constitution and why even fewer manage to have their constitution maintained following the inauguration of democracy.

CROSS-NATIONAL EVIDENCE AND CASE STUDIES

The main hypothesis that can be derived from the previous discussion is that although the scope of military intervention determines the incentives of military rulers to adopt a constitution, their capacity to engage in successful constitution making depends on the availability of a party supportive of military interests. Partisan support for a military regime, in turn, may depend on the level of institutionalization of competitive parties in the country. In order to explore the plausibility of these arguments, I have collected aggregate data on various political and institutional features of the years spent under military rule in all countries of Latin America from 1900 to 1990. I have also relied on more detailed case studies in which we can trace the objectives of military rulers, their interaction with organized parties, and the role of constitution making both during their rule and at the beginning of the transition to democracy.

Cross-National Evidence

It is not apparent that we can isolate a single factor determining variation in the scope of military interventions in politics. As I have argued, some countries experienced expansive military interventions since the early decades of the twentieth century, others only after World War II. Moreover, some countries have been relatively immune to comprehensive military interventions. Yet one variable that may affect both the scope of military interventions and the incentives of military rulers to adopt a constitution is the accumulated years of military involvement in national politics.

The accumulation of years of military government in a country signals that either new conflicts emerged over time or the underlying problems that triggered previous interventions remained unsolved. In either case, it is plausible to think that as the total number of years of military rule increases in a country, military leaders may become more ambitious in their plans of political transformation. In addition, the longer the military intervenes in national politics, the more likely it is that military interventions

TABLE 5.4. *Constitutions and years of military intervention, 1900–1990*

Country	Years of military intervention	Constitutions
Argentina	23	0
Bolivia	46	3
Brazil	26	1
Chile	23	1
Colombia	16	0
Costa Rica	3	1
Dom. Rep.	51	1
Ecuador	32	2
El Salvador	59	4
Guatemala	34	2
Honduras	53	4
Mexico	13	0
Nicaragua	49	5
Panama	16	1
Paraguay	58	2
Peru	30	1
Uruguay	9	0
Venezuela	47	11
TOTAL	588	39

Source: Same as Tables 5.1 and 5.2.

become a norm of ordinary politics and that military and civilian political actors develop relationships of mutual dependence and influence. Both loftier objectives and the blurring of boundaries between exceptional and ordinary rule may induce military leaders to "institutionalize" their rule by means of a constitution.

As shown in Table 5.4, aggregate comparative data suggest a relationship between accumulated years of military intervention in a country and the number of constitutions enacted during periods of military rule. Except for the Dominican Republic, all countries in the region with more than forty accumulated years of military rule from 1900 to 1990 are the same countries that have the largest number of military constitutions. The bivariate correlation between accumulated years of military rule in a country and the number of constitutions adopted by military regimes is positive and highly significant ($p < .001$).

On closer examination, however, the accumulated years of military rule are not likely to provide a sufficient explanation for important differences in outcomes across countries. For most of the twentieth century, Argentina and Brazil had similar patterns of military intervention in politics. Yet while military governments in Argentina were never able to constitutionalize their rule, the military in Brazil adopted in 1967 a constitution that was in force for twenty years. Uruguay and Panama did not experience continued years of military rule until the early 1970s and late 1960s, respectively. But whereas the military in Uruguay tried but failed to legitimize their rule by means of a constitutional amendment in 1980, their counterparts in Panama enacted an entire new constitution in 1972 that remains in force – with adaptations, of course – until this day. The obvious reason for these different outcomes is that not all military rulers have the same capacity to deepen and extend their domination by mimicking the workings of a constitutional government.

As I have argued, whenever they attempt to institutionalize their rule, military leaders face the challenge of adopting a constitution in a way that resembles a representative process while keeping control over the outcome. This means that military rulers need not only an appropriate institutional setting but also a set of reliable actors who can be trusted with the task. Legislatures and constituent assemblies may provide the institutional setting to discuss proposals of constitutional change, pass constitutional amendments, and create new constitutions. But since the appointment of members of the constituent body by the government is a visible imposition, military rulers are likely to need partisan support to make the constitution-making process both seemingly representative and predictable.

As shown in Table 5.5, military regimes often permit a legislature to exist. A legislative assembly functioned – at least part of the time – in fifty-four of seventy-five military regimes in Latin America. Because a functioning legislature is frequently – though not always – associated with the popular election of its members, the existence of a legislative assembly may signal the intention of the military regime to adopt the formalities of a regular constitutional government. Yet it is not clear that having a legislature is associated with the adoption of a constitution. The correlation between years in which a legislature exists and years in which a constitution adopted by military rulers is in force is positive but not statistically significant.

Less common than a functioning legislature is the existence of a civilian party supporting the military regime. As shown in Table 5.5, there have been promilitary parties in only twenty-two of seventy-five military regimes in the region. Yet the existence of a party supportive of military interests often coincides with the enactment of at least one new constitution by the military regime. At the same time, military regimes tend not to adopt constitutions in the absence of partisan support. With the exception of the military dictatorship established in Chile in 1973, military rulers without a party base usually opt for suspending the preexisting constitution and ruling by means of temporary institutional acts. In a bivariate correlation, the association between years in which a party supportive of military interests exists and years in which a military constitution is adopted and in force is positive and statistically significant ($p < .001$).

I used a cross-sectional time-series logistic regression to perform a preliminary test of the determinants of constitution making by military rulers. The dependent variable is the adoption and maintenance of a new constitution during years of military rule. It is a dummy variable that takes a value of 1 in the year a new constitution is adopted

TABLE 5.5. *Military regimes, legislatures, and partisan support, 1900–1990*

Country	Military regimes (1)	With legislature (2)	With partisan support (3)	Enacting new constitutions (4)
Argentina	6	0	0	0
Bolivia	7	5	1	2
Brazil	2	2	1	1
Chile	3	1	0	1
Colombia	3	3	0	0
Costa Rica	1	1	1	1
Dom. Rep.	7	5	2	1
Ecuador	6	5	1	2
El Salvador	3	3	1	1
Guatemala	4	4	4	2
Honduras	7	5	2	4
Mexico	2	2	0	0
Nicaragua	8	8	3	4
Panama	1	0	1	1
Paraguay	5	4	1	1
Peru	5	2	2	1
Uruguay	1	0	0	0
Venezuela	4	4	2	3
TOTAL	75	54 (.72)	22 (.29)	25 (.33)

(1) Number of military regimes, defined as continuous years of military government.
(2) Number of military regimes with a functioning legislature.
(3) Number of military regimes in which a party supportive of the military existed.
(4) Number of military regimes that adopted new constitutions.

and during each successive year up to the year the constitution is replaced or the military regime ends, and 0 in all other years. The main independent variables are the accumulated years of military rule in a country, the existence of partisan support for the military regime, and the degree of institutionalization of competitive parties. The regression first uses observations from 1900 to 1990 and then a more restricted sample from 1945 to 1990, for which data on all the relevant variables were available. The latter is also the period in which expansive military interventions took place in most countries in Latin America.

The first independent variable (YEARSMILITARY) is a numerical variable measuring the number of accumulated years of military rule in the country. An authoritarian year counts as a year of military rule if the head of government came to power as a result of a coup or a noncompetitive election and is a member of the regular armed forces.[17] The second variable (PARTYSUPPORT) is a dummy variable that takes a value of 1 for all the years a military regime has support from a party or

[17] Data for coding this variable were obtained from Bethell (1990, 1998), Nohlen (2005), and Smith (2005).

coalition and 0 otherwise. A party or coalition is identified as supportive of military interests when it competes in presidential, congressional, or constituent assembly elections as a representative of the military regime.[18] Both of these variables are expected to have a positive effect on the probability that a military regime adopts a new constitution and maintains it in force.

The final relevant variable (DEMOPARTYINST) captures the institutionalization of competitive parties during years of congressional elections.[19] Because military rulers are less likely to obtain partisan support when the main parties in the country have been able to develop ties of allegiance among voters, the degree of institutionalization of competitive parties should have a negative effect on the adoption and maintenance of a constitution. This variable consists of an index created by Perez-Liñan and Mainwaring (2013) that reflects the average age of the parties in Congress, weighted by their seat share in the lower or single chamber and by their experience with democracy since 1900. Unlike other measures of party institutionalization, this index counts only the years in the life of a party that elapsed under a competitive regime.[20] Given the expected negative correlation between the institutionalization of democratic parties and the existence of parties supportive of military interests, these variables will be used in separate models.

As control variables, I have used the number of constitutions replaced in the country since 1900 and the average rate of gross domestic product per-capita growth in five-year blocks. The first variable (CONSTABILITY) captures the impact of previous constitutional instability, and the second (GROWTH) measures the effect of economic growth. Both variables are expected to have a positive effect on the probability that military rulers enact new constitutions.[21] Preexisting patterns of constitutional instability should lower the costs of constitutional replacement, thus making military rulers more inclined to adopt a new constitution after taking power.[22] Economic growth, on the other hand, should strengthen the position of military rulers, making it more likely that they decide to institutionalize their rule by means of a new constitution. Table 5.6 shows the results.

The first model uses the complete sample and includes partisan support for the military regime as the main independent variable. It shows that only the accumulated years of military rule and the existence of a party supportive of military interests are statistically significant explanatory variables. Both are positively associated with the

18 Data for coding this variable was based on Bethell (1990, 1998), Nohlen (2005), and various country sources.

19 If congressional elections do not take place during the military regime, the level of democratic party institutionalization takes the score of the last congressional election before the installation of the regime.

20 The formula for the index is described in Perez-Liñan and Mainwaring (2013: 15).

21 Data for constitutional instability and economic growth obtained from Negretto (2013) and the Oxford Latin American Economic History Database (http://oxlad.qeh.ox.ac.uk/), respectively.

22 On the impact of legacies of constitutional instability on the probability of constitutional replacements, see Elkins, Ginsburg, and Melton (2009: 120).

TABLE 5.6. *Determinants of constitution making under military regimes, 1900–1990*†

	Dependent variable = new constitution		
Independent variables	1900–1990	1945–1990	1945–1990
YEARSMILITARY	.057**	.012	.036
	(.026)	(.056)	(.066)
PARTYSUPPORT	1.601***	2.254***	–
	(.344)	(.634)	
DEMOPARTYINST	–	–	−3.517***
			(.798)
CONSTABILITY	−.129	.601	1.212**
	(.151)	(.439)	(.547)
GROWTH	.068	.223**	.274**
	(.046)	(.098)	(.117)
N	424	169	165

† Fixed-effects logistic regression. Standard errors in parentheses.
*** $p < 0.01$; ** $p < 0.05$; * $p < 0.1$

adoption and maintenance of a new constitution by a military regime. The second model retains the same variables but uses the restricted sample from 1945 to 1990. This model shows similar results in the effect of partisan support for the military regime. However, the accumulated years of military rule no longer have a statistically significant effect. Economic growth, in turn, turns out to be positively and statistically significantly correlated with the creation of a constitution by a military regime.

The third model maintains the restricted sample but replaces partisan support for the military regime by the degree of institutionalization of competitive parties. Both variables are inversely correlated with a high degree of significance (.74; $p < .001$), which supports using them in separate models and is consistent with the idea that military rulers are more able to create or co-opt parties that support their government when the level of institutionalization of parties in competitive elections is low. This last analysis shows, as expected, that the higher the degree of institutionalization of competitive parties in the country, the lower the probability that military rulers would adopt and maintain a constitution. Both previous patterns of constitutional instability and economic growth have a positive and statistically significant effect in this model.

To be sure, the above analysis is not intended to sustain any strong causality claim about the factors that determine the adoption and maintenance of constitutions by a military regime. But it suggests the plausibility of the association between the constitution-making activity of military regimes and their ability to mobilize partisan support. This association is consistent with the idea that the adoption of a new constitution is part of a broader strategy for civilianizing the system of military domination by imitating the forms of a representative government. The statistical analysis does not, however, capture the link between the scope of military intervention and constitution making and the impact of the interaction between military regimes and party organizations on the influence of a military constitution after the inauguration of democracy. To these purposes, I have relied on selected case studies.

Case Studies

I have selected three cases that illustrate the logic of constitution making by military rulers: Argentina 1966 to 1972, Ecuador 1972 to 1978, and Brazil 1964 to 1984. The military regimes under analysis are not only close in time – all established in the 1960s and 1970s – but also similar in scope. All these regimes were inaugurated by a so-called revolutionary coup with lofty ambitions to bring about a political, economic, and social transformation. Consistent with these objectives, none of the military interventions established a fixed date for a return to civilian rule. In spite of these similarities, however, each case shows a marked difference in the explanatory variables of interest and the outcome of constitution making. Military rulers in both Argentina and Ecuador lacked partisan support to enact a constitution after they took power, but in the latter case the military were able to attract civilian parties to help them impose some constitutional constraints on the subsequent democratic regime at the end of their term. In contrast, the military in Brazil had the support of a promilitary party to enact a constitution a few years after taking power. This constitution lasted twenty years but did not survive the military regime. It was replaced after the military and their partisan allies lost control of the transition to democracy in the mid-1980s.

Argentina, 1966 to 1972

In 1966 in Argentina, a military coup prematurely terminated a civilian government for the fifth time since 1930. The main leader of the coup and the first *de facto* president, General Onganía, declared that this time the military government would have no fixed expiry date. This intention became explicit in the main legal instrument of the dictatorship, the Argentine Revolution Act (Estatuto de la Revolución Argentina), which regulated the functioning of the new government. According to this act, the *de facto* executive would be called "president" rather than "provisional president" – as in previous military governments – and there would be no time limit to the president's term in office. In addition, executive orders would now have the same legal status as ordinary laws enacted by Congress. However, although the Revolution Act was supposed to be part of the existing constitution, no new constitutional order was enacted. The main legal basis of successive governments until 1972 was the 1853 constitution in all those parts that were not suspended by the institutional act of the military government.

In a way, this outcome resembled previous episodes. There had been attempts to create a new constitutional order in 1930 and 1955, but in the end military rulers governed by means of provisional executive decisions. One of the main reasons for this failure was the lack of support for the project among existing political parties. It has been rightly argued that there was close interaction between political parties and the military in Argentina (Rouquie 1987: 275). Yet no important political party in the country officially supported a military government or offered to work as a vehicle for the electoral ambitions of military officers. The Radical Party (UCR) was the main beneficiary of military interventions since 1955. This party was, however, a relatively well-institutionalized democratic party that could not compromise its future by explicitly associating itself with a military government. For the same reason, the UCR usually joined with the Peronist Party (PP) in repudiating military leaders' attempts to produce constitutional transformations during their rule.

Military leaders did not, however, relinquish the ambition to produce constitutional changes that would take effect after the inauguration of democracy. In 1957, after deposing Perón and abrogating the 1949 constitution, the military restored the 1853 constitution and convened a constituent assembly to adopt a series of ambitious reforms before the 1958 democratic elections.[23] Once party delegates were elected, however, the assembly became deeply divided over the legality of the constituent assembly convened by the military. In the end, the convention only formalized the restoration of the 1853 constitution with a new provision including a short list of social rights.

In 1971, at the end of the military cycle initiated in 1966, General Lanusse proposed a new constitutional reform to be implemented after a democratic government was elected in 1973. At the beginning of the process, the option most favored by the military was to adopt the reforms as part of a preelection agreement in which political parties would support a military candidate as the first elected president. No political party, however, agreed with this proposal (Potash 1994: 286). Approval of the reform in a popular referendum was briefly considered (Lanusse 1977: 280). But a referendum was not an attractive option, given the low popularity of the military government at the time.

The military managed to force the parties to accept the reform as a precondition for scheduling democratic elections. The final draft of the amendment was based on a proposal by a political commission led by the Ministry of the Interior and the recommendations of an expert commission appointed by the government. Although at various points in the process the military government renewed its attempt to include parties in the negotiation of some reforms, in the end no political party participated in the process or gave support to any of the amendments.

[23] The military government proposed the strengthening of federalism, judicial independence, and congressional powers; the absolute proscription of presidential reelection; and restrictions on the appointment powers of the executive. The military also adopted for the first time in the country a system of proportional representation to secure pluralism in the convention. See Padilla (1986: 583).

Imposing constraints on the newly elected government was one of the important objectives of the constitutional reform. Although General Lanusse lifted the proscription on the Peronist Party (by then renamed Partido Justicialista or PJ), he maintained it against Peron by increasing the number of years of residence in the country necessary for a candidate to compete in the presidential election. This had the effect of excluding Perón from the presidential election, because he had been in exile since 1955. In addition, the military tinkered with electoral rules to prevent the election of a Peronist president. The Peronist party was assumed to be the plurality winner in competitive elections, but the military expected that a candidate from this party would fall short of an absolute majority in the presidential election (Potash 1994: 407). For this reason, the reformers replaced the existing electoral college system, which allowed a candidate to be elected with just a plurality of popular vote, with a majority runoff formula for electing the president (Negretto 2004). With this system, military leaders hoped that an alliance of centrist forces could elect a non-Peronist candidate in the second round. In addition, in order to reduce the advantage of the majority party, the military also enacted an electoral law adopting a PR system for the election of deputies. This law also increased the minimum number of deputies elected per district from two to three to benefit voters from smaller provinces.

Contrary to the military's expectations, the coalition that supported the Peronist candidate managed to win the presidential election as well as a majority in both chambers of Congress. According to the text of the constitutional reform imposed by the military, the new elected government would have three years to accept or reject the reforms for the future. However, even before a new military coup terminated the democratic government in 1976, it was clear that none of the established parties in the country accepted the constitutional amendment imposed by the military. As a result, the reform was abandoned and never restored.

Ecuador, 1972 to 1978

In 1972, the fourth military coup in Ecuador's history deposed populist president Velasco Ibarra. As in Argentina, the government installed after the coup proclaimed itself as revolutionary and declared that it would not be an interim government but rather a long-term venture. In spite of these aspirations, and similar to the Argentine case, military leaders in Ecuador did not create a new constitutional order during their rule. They did succeed, however, in adopting a new constitution that would be in force at the inauguration of democracy in 1979. The particular interaction between the military and political parties in Ecuador was crucial to an explanation of this outcome.

Thanks to its program of radical social reform, the military government of Rodriguez Lara gained the sympathy of some small leftist parties. Yet none of the main existing parties provided the new government with active support. Center and center-right parties, such as the traditional Liberal and Conservative parties and the more recently created Social Christian Party (PSC), were neither in favor of the new government's economic program nor did they have close ties with the military. The populist Concentración de Fuerzas Populares (CFP) and Velasquistas were natural political opponents of the military because they were the immediate victims of the military coup. In this context, Congress remained closed and political parties were banned. The government formally restored the 1945 constitution, but it remained *de facto* suspended.[24]

In spite of Rodriguez Lara's intention to remain in power for a long time, an internal coup in 1976 terminated his government in the midst of an economic crisis and mounting political and social opposition. This time, the new military government announced its intention to be a caretaker government committed to the restoration of democracy. As was the case in Argentina, however, the military did not want to give up power without introducing constitutional changes that would shape the working of the future democratic regime. Accordingly, the government proposed the adoption of a new constitution by a referendum scheduled before presidential and congressional elections.

The Ecuadorian military was more successful than their Argentinian counterparts in the attempt to negotiate constitutional changes with political forces. Although traditional political groups (Velasquistas, liberals, and conservatives) rejected the proposal, several others, in particular the most recently created parties, such as Izquierda Democrática (ID), Democracia Cristiana (DC), and Frente Radical Alfarista (FRA), agreed to participate in the adoption of new constitutional rules (Mejia Acosta 2002; Mills 1984). In addition, although the military government had institutional preferences in several areas of design, it organized the referendum not as a yes-or-no vote to a single proposal but as a choice between two alternatives.

The government appointed three committees to prepare the proposals for reform. These committees were made up of experts, party delegates, and representatives from civil-society organizations. The first committee was in charge of revising the 1945 constitution, the second of proposing a new constitution, and the third of drafting a new law of elections, referenda, and political parties. The proposals submitted to popular vote were a revised version of the 1945 constitution and an entirely new constitution, the alternative most favored by the military. In the referendum held in January 1978, a majority of voters opted for the new constitution.

Although the military did not formally participate in the committees, the ruling junta had the final word on approval of the proposals and they did favor specific provisions, particularly regarding the electoral system. The military desired electoral rules that would promote party pluralism while preventing the rise of populist leaders. As in the case of Argentina in 1972, military leaders in Ecuador favored replacing

[24] An executive act suspended constitutional guarantees for four years.

plurality by majority runoff presidential elections.[25] This reform was meant to frustrate the election of populist leader Assad Bucaram, who was expected to win a plurality but not a majority of popular votes in the 1978 presidential election (see *Latin American Weekly Report*, April 22, 1977). With majority runoff, the CFP candidate might have to compete in the second round against a more centrist candidate supported by the rest of the political parties (see *Latin American Weekly Report*, December 16, 1977).[26] Further measures included in the reform also intended to prevent populist politics, were reducing the term of the president in office, introducing absolute proscription of presidential reelection, and adopting an inclusive electoral system for congressional elections.

Although the military did not have a specific party supporting their interests either during their rule or in the postauthoritarian period, they managed, before leaving power, to obtain the agreement of several parties to negotiate reforms. The support of these parties was crucial for mobilizing voters in favor of adoption of the new constitution in the referendum. This constitution, which incorporated several provisions conforming to the military rulers' ideas about the proper functioning of democracy, remained in force for twenty years, until its replacement in 1998.

Brazil, 1964 to 1984

Following the 1964 coup, military rulers in Brazil perceived this intervention as a true revolution and made clear their commitment to transform the country's political institutions. They fulfilled this promise, at least in terms of legal change. From 1964 to 1984, military presidents in Brazil enacted seventeen Institutional Acts that suspended or introduced temporary modifications to provisions of the existing constitution.[27] More importantly, however, they had a new constitution enacted in 1967. This constitution contained the first three institutional acts and substantive reforms to the 1946 constitution. It was subject to several suspensions and modifications until 1981 but remained in force until 1988. What explains this use of constituent power by the military?

Two important factors were the low level of institutionalization of democratic parties in Brazil and the ability of the military to co-opt some of these parties to support their regime. From 1946 to 1963, Brazilians experienced the first period of democratic elections in their history. The main parties competing in these elections,

[25] On the role of the military in introducing majority runoff elections in Latin America, see Negretto (2006). See also Rouquie (1987: 382).

[26] In the end, the military resorted to a more direct strategy to prevent Assad Bucaram from winning the coming presidential election. On January 20, 1978 (after the new constitutional text won majority support in the referendum), the Minister of the Interior announced that candidates for the presidency must have Ecuadorian parents. This excluded Bucaram, whose family was Lebanese.

[27] They also enacted more than 100 Complementary Acts, which spelled out the specific interpretation of the rules contained in Institutional Acts.

the Partido Social Democrático (PSD), União Democrática Nacional (UDN), and Partido Trabalhista Brasileiro (PTB), were founded in 1945. Some of these parties, in particular the center-right PSD and the conservative UDN, had ties with the military since their creation. In the presidential elections of 1945, for instance, the candidates for these two parties were drawn from the high ranks of the military.[28] UDN was, however, the party that remained closest to the military and usually advocated military intervention as a mechanism for arbitrating political conflicts (Bethell 2008: 95).

Unlike Argentina, where the military deposed both the UCR and the PP, the two largest political forces in the country, from power, the military in Brazil usually intervened to overthrow governments (both authoritarian and democratic) with low or declining popular support. In 1964, the Brazilian military toppled president Goulart, a politician from the PTB, which obtained only 20 percent of the popular vote in the 1962 congressional elections. Goulart, who became president after the resignation of Janio Quadros, was opposed by the military from the beginning and was allowed to take power with the provisional support of the PSD and UDN, which together achieved a majority in Congress.[29] By 1963, in the midst of a critical economic situation, Goulart threatened to pass radical social reforms without congressional support. This led to an immediate reaction from the military: they deposed the president with the explicit support of the UDN and important sectors of the PSD.

After the coup, the military decided to maintain representative institutions while limiting their functions. Congress was allowed to meet but with limited autonomy to legislate. Elections for president and Congress would also take place but only through mechanisms that granted government control over the outcome. In particular, president and senators would be elected indirectly. The system to elect deputies remained nominally a PR system, but its working was altered by the limited number of electoral options. A 1965 electoral reform allowed only two parties to compete: a government party (ARENA) and an opposition party (MDB). The large majority of members of the government party came from UDN, followed by the PSD (Bethell and Castro 2008: 179). Once this basic institutional framework was established, congressional elections took place in November 1966, with the government party winning a large majority of seats. With this majority, the government asked Congress to approve a new constitution in January 1967.

While the constitution created an institutional configuration that opposition forces could use to their advantage, it also constrained their capacity to influence political outcomes. The new constitution established a restrictive system of indirect elections and a distribution of powers that clearly favored the executive over any other

[28] The candidates were General Dutra (PSD) and General Gómez (UDN).

[29] These parties would control the new presidency by means of a constitutional reform adopted before Goulart took office. According to this reform, which the military accepted as a precondition for letting Goulart be president, he would share power with a Council of Ministers presided over by a Prime Minister appointed by and accountable to Congress. See Bethell (2008: 139).

institution. The president had unilateral power to appoint governors,[30] members of the judiciary, and high officials of the administration. He also had extraordinary powers to legislate and limit individual rights in crisis situations. The constitution was subject to successive reforms, all of which exacerbated these features until the late 1970s. The term of the president was extended from four to five years in 1969 and from five to six in 1977. In 1968, the president was invested (Institutional Act No. 5) with the power to dissolve Congress and legislate by decree, intervene in local governments, and suspend political rights. Successive reforms were also aimed at manipulating the composition and jurisdiction of the Supreme Court.

As the possibility of initiating a democratic transition emerged with the presidency of Ernesto Geisel in the mid-1970s, military leaders intended to adapt the existing constitutional framework to more competitive conditions. To this purpose, they eliminated some authoritarian features of the constitution while introducing new rules that would allow military rulers and the government party to control the transition. Some of these reforms altered the distribution of powers between branches of government. For instance, a constitutional amendment of 1978 abrogated the power of the president to dissolve Congress and suspend political rights. As expected, however, the most important reforms made in preparation for the transition to democracy affected the electoral system.

In 1977, a constitutional amendment passed by executive decree established that one third of senators would be directly appointed by the state electoral colleges that had elected governors since 1970. Because the government party controlled all but one of these colleges, the new senators would effectively increase the government party's dominance in the upper chamber. At the same time, the amendment increased the size of the Chamber of Deputies while imposing a minimum of six deputies per state. The reform was intended to overrepresent the less-developed states of the north and northeast, where the government party had an advantage (Bethell and Castro 2008: 211). In 1979, the government authorized free formation of parties as a strategy to fragment the opposition while maintaining unity within progovernment forces. The government party simply changed its name (from ARENA to PDS), but the opposition broke up into four parties that competed among themselves. To complement this strategy, the government prohibited alliances between parties and constrained voters to vote for candidates of a single party for all elective positions.

As a result of these reforms, in the 1982 elections the government party managed to maintain a majority in the Senate and reach a majority of votes in the Electoral College that would elect a new president in 1985. It also remained the largest party in the Chamber of Deputies. Under these conditions, the military government and its partisan allies initially intended to preserve the 1967 constitution by means of a series of negotiated amendments that would further adapt the constitution to new political conditions. The project failed, however.

30 Since 1970, however, state assemblies were allowed to elect state governors.

In April 1983, the Partido do Movimiento Democrático Brasileiro (PMDB) sponsored an increasingly popular amendment to allow direct presidential elections. The government succeeded in opposing and defeating this amendment in Congress, but at a great political cost (Skidmore 1988: 244).[31] The popularity of the amendment galvanized the political opposition and civil society in support of a radical transformation of the authoritarian constitutional structure.[32] It also caused defections and divisions within the government party that ultimately led to the defeat of the official candidate in the 1985 presidential elections and the severe defeat of the government in the 1986 congressional elections. Without partisan or popular support, the military left power, and a democratically elected constituent assembly replaced the 1967 constitution in 1988.

CONCLUSIONS

Military rulers have been the most active constitution makers in Latin America during the twentieth century. At first glance, this enthusiasm for writing constitutions seems quite intriguing given that military rule is provisional in nature and only justified by the need to restore constitutional order. Yet having a constitution is important when military regimes pursue broad long-term objectives of political, social, and economic transformation. Given these objectives, constitutions facilitate the adoption of more effective and enduring reforms. They also make it possible for the military to exert influence over future governments as they prepare a transition to democracy.

I have argued that whether military rulers are successful in using constitutions for these purposes depends on their capacity to mobilize partisan support. Having partisan support is crucial for demilitarizing the system of domination and imitating the formalities of a constitutional government. It helps the adoption of a new constitution in a seemingly representative manner and its maintenance after the military leave power. The problem is that partisan allies are not always available, and when they are, they may fail to support the military regime until the end.

Whenever long-standing democratic political parties exist, they are unlikely to support the institutionalization of a military regime, because this may imply

[31] On April 1984, a few days before the vote on the opposition-sponsored amendment, President Figueiredo proposed an alternative reform of 138 articles of the constitution, including restoration of direct presidential elections in 1988. The government withdrew the proposal, however, fearing that negotiating these amendments might complicate its most important objective, which was to frustrate the adoption of direct presidential elections in 1985. On this process, see Cachapuz de Medeiros (1985).

[32] As late as 1982, the PMDB remained deeply divided as to whether the party should recognize or reject the 1967 constitution as the basic institutional framework for the transition to democracy. It was the popularity of the amendment for direct presidential elections and its defeat that unified the PMDB in alliance with other opposition parties to replace the authoritarian constitution by means of a constituent assembly. See Martinez Lara (1996: 35–8).

perpetuation of military rule and the indefinite postponement of elections. In the absence of strong democratic parties, military rulers are more likely to co-opt some of the existing political organizations or create one of their own. But although these party organizations may favor the initial adoption of a constitution, they may not be willing or able to sustain it after the military withdraw from power. Promilitary parties may want to detach themselves from the regime before competitive elections are held, or they may not have sufficient institutional strength to prevent replacement of the authoritarian constitution at the inauguration of democracy.

Military rulers can only preserve their institutional legacy if the regime, its partisan allies, or both have relatively strong popular support at the installation of democracy. Pinochet in Chile was able to enact a constitution in 1980 and keep it later to impose institutional constraints on the subsequent democratic regime thanks to the popular support that the regime retained in 1989. The military regime established in Panama in 1968 was also able to enact its own constitution in 1972 and preserve it after the transition to democracy. Key to this success was the ability of the PRD, the promilitary party sponsored by Omar Torrijos in 1978, to emerge as one of the main political parties in the country after the transition to democracy was initiated in the early 1980s. These are, however, extremely exceptional cases.

Since the 1990s, Latin American countries have not been subject to military dictatorships. Democracy is well entrenched, and most constitutions today have been drafted by freely elected constituent assemblies. Yet the legacy of constitution making by military rulers is quite significant for understanding patterns of constitutional instability in the region. Military rulers have been the most active constitution makers during the twentieth century, but they typically failed to use constitutions to preserve their institutional legacy. This chapter is an attempt to explain why this was the case.

REFERENCES

Barros, Robert. 2002. *Constitutionalism and Dictatorship: Pinochet, the Junta, and the 1980 Constitution*. New York: Cambridge University Press.

Bethell, Leslie (ed.). 1990. *The Cambridge History of Latin America*, Volume VII. New York: Cambridge University Press.

Bethell, Leslie (ed.). 1998. *Latin American Politics and Society Since 1930*. New York: Cambridge University Press.

Bethell, Leslie. 2008. "Politics in Brazil under the Liberal Republic, 1945–1964," in Leslie Bethell, ed., *Brazil Since 1930*. New York: Cambridge University Press, pp. 87–164.

Bethell, Leslie and Celso Castro. 2008. Politics in Brazil under the Military Rule, 1964–1985," in Leslie Bethell, ed., *Brazil Since 1930*. New York: Cambridge University Press, pp. 165–230.

Cachapuz de Medeiros, Antonio. 1985. "Constituentes e Constitucioes do Brasil," in *Advogado*, April–June 1985: 19.

Constituciones Hispanoamericanas, http://www.cervantesvirtual.com/portal/constituciones (accessed November 2010).

Elkins, Zachary, Tom Ginsburg, and James Melton. 2009. *The Endurance of National Constitutions.* New York: Cambridge University Press.
Elster, Jon. 2000. *Ulysses Unbound.* New York: Cambridge University Press.
Fitzgibbon, Russell H. 1940. "Continuismo in Central America and the Caribbean." *Inter-American Quarterly* II (July 1940): 56–74.
Gandhi, Jennifer. 2008. *Political Institutions Under Dictatorship.* New York: Cambridge University Press
Geddes, Barbara. 1990. *Democratic Institutions as a Bargain among Self-Interested Politicians.* Paper presented at the 1990 meeting of American Political Science Association, San Francisco, CA.
Geddes, Barbara. 2003. Paradigms and Sand Castles: Theory Building and Research Design in Comparative Politics. Ann Arbor: University of Michigan Press.
Harltyn, Jonathan and Arturo Valenzuela. 1998. "Democracy in Latin America Since 1930," in Leslie Bethell, ed., *Latin America. Politics and Society Since 1930.* New York: Cambridge University Press, pp. 3–66.
Lanusse, Alejandro Agustín. 1977. *Mi Testimonio.* Buenos Aires: Lasserrere.
Latin American Constitutional Change Database, http://la-constitutionalchange.cide.edu (accessed December 2012).
Latin American Weekly Report, "Ecuador: Exit Blocked," 22 April 1977, p. 118.
Latin American Weekly Report, "Ecuador: Naming the Day," 16 December 1977, p. 389.
Mainwaring, Scott and Timothy Scully. 1995. *Building Democratic Institutions. Party Systems in Latin America.* Stanford, CA: Stanford University Press.
Martinez Lara, Javier. 1996. *Building Democracy in Brazil. The Politics of Constitutional Change, 1985–95.* Oxford, Oxfordshire: McMillan Press.
Mejía Acosta, Andrés. 2002. *Gobernabilidad democrática.* Quito: Fundación Konrad Adenauer.
Mills, Nick. 1984. *Crisis, Conflicto y Consenso: Ecuador 1979–84.* Quito: Corporación Editora Nacional.
Negretto, Gabriel. 2004. "Compromising on a Qualified Plurality System," in Josep Colomer, ed., *The Handbook of Electoral System Choice.* Basingstoke, Hampshire: Palgrave, pp. 110–20.
Negretto, Gabriel. 2006. "Choosing How to Choose Presidents: Parties, Military Rulers, and Presidential Elections in Latin America." *Journal of Politics* 68(2): 421–33.
Negretto, Gabriel. 2013. *Making Constitutions. Presidents, Parties, and Institutional Choice in Latin America.* New York: Cambridge University Press.
Nohlen, Dieter (ed.). 2005. *Elections in the Americas* Volumes 1 and 2. New York: Oxford University Press.
Oxford Latin American Economic History Database, http://oxlad.qeh.ox.ac.uk/ (accessed December 2009).
Padilla, Alejandro Jorge. 1986. "Proyectos y Reformas a la Constitución Nacional: Apuntes Sobre el Período 1930–1983." *Criterio* 1975: 586–7.
Perez-Liñan, Anibal and Scott Mainwaring. 2013. "Regime Legacies and Levels of Democracy: Evidence From Latin America." *Comparative Politics* 45(4): 379–397.
Political Database of the Americas, http://pdba.georgetown.edu (accessed November 2010).
Potash, Robert. 1994. *El Ejercito y la Política en la Argentina, 1962–1973: De la Caída de Frondizi a la Restauración Peronista.* Buenos Aires: Emecé.
Przeworski, Adam, Michael E. Alvarez, Jose Antonio Cheibub, and Fernando Limongi. 2000. *Democracy and Development. Political Institutions and Well-Being in the World, 1950–1990.* New York: Cambridge University Press.

Rouquie, Alain. 1986. "Demilitarization and the Institutionalization of Military-Dominated Polities in Latin America," in Guillermo O'Donnell, Philippe Schmitter, and Laurence Whitehead, *Transitions from Authoritarian Rule. Comparative Perspectives*. Baltimore, MD: The John Hopkins University Press, pp. 108–136.

Rouquie, Alain. 1987. *The Military and the State in Latin America*. Berkeley: University of California Press.

Rouquie, Alain and Stephen Suffern. 1998. "The Military in Latin American Politics Since 1930," in Leslie Bethell, *Latin America. Politics and Society since 1930*. New York: Cambridge University Press, pp. 145–216.

Skidmore, Thomas. 1988. *The Politics of Military Rule in Brazil, 1964–1985*. New York: Oxford University Press.

Smith, Peter. 2005. *Democracy in Latin America. Political Change in Comparative Perspective*. New York: Oxford University Press.

Stepan, Alfred (ed.). 1973. *Authoritarian Brazil. Origins, Policies, and Future*. New Haven, CT: Yale University Press.

6

Constitutions in Authoritarian Regimes

The Egyptian Constitution of 1971

*Kristen Stilt**

In the public protests that led to Hosni Mubarak's ouster on February 11, 2011, the abuses that Mubarak had carried out through the Egyptian constitution were part of the litany of complaints. The slogan of "bread, freedom, and social justice," for example, encompassed demands for genuine multicandidate presidential elections, which were impossible under the constitution, and for an end to the constitutionally permissible emergency law. In a final effort to stay in power, on February 10, Mubarak announced that he had appointed a committee to amend the constitutional provisions dealing with the presidential elections and term limits, the election procedures for the People's Assembly, and the use of military courts to try civilians.[1] He also stated that he would not run for re-election in the presidential election that was scheduled for September 2011 (although he did not say that his son Gamal would also refrain from running). For the protestors, this statement of intention to amend the most offensive articles of the constitution was seen as both insincere and insufficient to achieve genuine change in Egypt, and they refused his offer. Sustained public pressure caused senior military officials to assume control of the country.

Mubarak made his mark on the constitution in significant ways such that it was considered his constitution by the protestors, and a fundamental pressing question after his ouster was what place the document would have in the post-Mubarak era. Mubarak did not create the constitution, however; it was written in 1971, at the beginning of Sadat's presidency. As originally promulgated and then amended by Sadat in 1980, it maintained the strong executive that Sadat's predecessor Nasser

* I thank Nathan Brown, Tom Ginsburg, and Tamir Moustafa for helpful comments on this chapter.

[1] Specifically, Mubarak stated that he requested the preparation of amendments to Articles 76 (presidential election procedure), 77 (presidential term limit and renewal), 88 (voting procedure for the People's Assembly), 93 (power to determine validity of the membership of the People's Assembly), and 189 (the constitutional amendment process) in addition to the abolition of Article 179 (use of military courts for civilian prosecutions).

had established, but it was not as authoritarian as the Nasser-era constitutional documents. Amendments adopted in 2005 and 2007 under Mubarak's watch were particularly offensive to Egyptians, especially those changes that entrenched his rule under the guise of promoting multicandidate presidential elections.

As part of Mubarak's ouster, the Supreme Council of the Armed Forces (SCAF) assumed control and immediately announced the suspension of the 1971 constitution. SCAF then began the process of preparing a set of amendments to remove the constitution's most offensive provisions, with the presumption that the constitution would thereafter be returned to force.[2] These amendments were adopted in a national referendum on March 19, 2011, by a wide margin and with a large voter turnout. However, SCAF announced a change in strategy: instead of reinstating the constitution, as amended, SCAF surprisingly issued a constitutional declaration on March 30, 2011, that replaced the 1971 constitution. While technically the constitution was no longer effective as of that date, in practice, the 1971 constitution endures in the sense that many of its provisions were included in the declaration. Further, it served as the basis of the new constitution, which went into effect on December 26, 2012.

This chapter contributes to the larger goals of this volume by asking what purpose the 1971 constitution served, given that both the Sadat and Mubarak regimes were considered authoritarian. The assumption has often been made that constitutions in autocracies are merely meaningless pieces of paper.[3] The introduction of this volume poses a typical question about constitutions in such polities: "how can a sham document generate any legitimacy?" The examples discussed in this chapter will show that the notion of a "sham document" is a misleading one; constitutions in authoritarian regimes serve specific purposes and may fulfill them with great success, but those purposes are often – although not always – different from those of constitutions in democratic societies. Building on the nonexclusive list of possible functions for provisions of authoritarian constitutions, as outlined in the volume's introduction, such as an "operating manual" or a "billboard," this chapter identifies some noteworthy examples from the 1971 Egyptian constitution and discusses why an authoritarian would have included them and with what goals in mind.

The Egyptian case as discussed in this chapter also shows that there are several further nuances that need to be taken into account in the study of authoritarian constitutions. First, the substance of the constitution needs to be treated separately from the process by which the constitution was drafted and adopted. As seen in the

[2] At that early stage, it was not yet known whether a new constitution would be drafted at some future time; the immediate goal was merely to make the most crucial amendments to the 1971 constitution.

[3] Historians of twentieth-century Egypt, for example, rarely discuss constitutions or constitutional documents, and this appears to be the reason. For example, in the *Cambridge History of Egypt: Modern Egypt from 1517 to the End of the Twentieth Century*, M. W. Daly, ed., the term "constitution" appears only once in the index, and it refers to the 1923 constitution.

preparation of the 1971 constitution, the process might serve one purpose while the substance achieves other goals. Second, the constitution should be viewed both as a whole and at the level of each particular article. One provision might describe how different parts of government are to function, with the sincere intention that the rules will be followed because they suit the needs of the ruler. A second provision might be pure fiction, a promise of rights that serves some rhetorical purpose but will not be guaranteed in practice. Even within one article, different parts can serve different purposes, or one article can serve different purposes at different points in time. Third, the constitution needs to be considered in relation to previous constitutions in the country and the same for a particular amendment. If the country is replacing its constitution, then, internally at least, the next constitution will inevitably be viewed in relation to what came before. In the abstract, a constitution might look clearly authoritarian, but as a practical matter to the citizenry of the particular jurisdiction, it might be less authoritarian than its predecessor, perhaps with very tangible consequences on a daily basis.

The 1971 constitution, with its several amendments, is a complicated document. The story of the constitution's formation, amendment, and interpretation by the Supreme Constitutional Court has been likened to an Egyptian soap opera, with all of the dramatic twists and turns befitting the genre.[4] And the cast of characters reaches beyond Egypt: the prompts for the series of amendments came from both internal and external sources. The 1971 constitution is a document of accretion, and its final form at the time of the 2011 revolution can be understood only by taking a careful look at its development over time. Each provision advanced particular goals of the regime, and the interesting questions are what they were and whether they were met. Through a discussion of some key moments in Egypt's constitutional development, this chapter suggests some ways to think about the role of constitutions in an authoritarian regime in general and Egypt in particular. It is not meant to be a comprehensive study of the 1971 constitution, however, although hopefully further work in this area will be prompted by these initial observations.

THE ORIGINS OF THE 1971 CONSTITUTION

The preparation of a new constitution was an obvious task for President Anwar Sadat in the early days of his regime. Nasser's rule saw a series of constitutional documents, beginning with the constitution of 1956, which was adopted four years after the military coup; in the interim, the Revolutionary Command Council had issued constitutional declarations, including one that abolished the 1923 constitution. Nasser based his document on the monarchical constitution of 1923 with some significant changes. He abolished political parties in 1953 but subsequently needed

4 I thank Nathan Brown for this idea.

some kind of political entity to structure and control political life. The 1956 constitution provided for a one-party system in the form of his Arab Socialist Union to serve that purpose (Waterbury 1983: 308). Nasser put the cabinet under the president's control, and the president had the right to issue decrees that functioned as law. While the 1956 constitution included an array of rights and freedoms, they were defined by or subject to law, making them in effect meaningless because of Nasser's control over the legislative branch (Brown 2002: 78–9).[5]

This constitutional philosophy prevailed throughout the subsequent constitutional documents of the Nasser period. The 1958 union between Egypt and Syria resulted in a constitution for the new United Arab Republic that bore much in common with Egypt's 1956 document. When Syria withdrew in 1961, the constitution was also abandoned, and a provisional constitutional declaration concentrated power in the hands of Nasser and his close allies for the interim period. Nasser then turned to preparing a lengthy policy statement, the National Charter (*al-mithaq al-watani*), which identified Arab socialism as official state ideology, and a national congress adopted it in 1962.[6] The National Charter was not meant as a constitution, but rather the next constitution was supposed to give meaning to the principles expressed in it. An elected assembly prepared the 1964 provisional constitution, which was still in force at the time of Nasser's death (Brown 2002: 79–80). While the 1964 constitution provided for a National Assembly, in practice Nasser was the most powerful political actor (Boyle and Sherif 1996: 11). In 1966, a committee began to work on a new permanent constitution but did not make much progress.[7] Nasser's final action in the area of constitutional development was a declaration to the nation (*biyan*) on March 30, 1968 (known as the March 30 Declaration), in which he specified what a permanent constitution should include.[8]

Sadat became president upon Nasser's death on September 28, 1970. At that time, there was growing instability in the political institutions. The ideological basis of the Arab Socialist Union had been weakened as a result of Egypt's losses in the June 1967 war with Israel, and "Egypt's leaders, discredited, dispirited, and stripped of most ideological pretense, could only fall back on their control of institutional power" (Waterbury 1983: 349). Because Sadat "had no institutional base of power and no organized clientele," he was an acceptable president to those who did have

5 As Nathan Brown concluded, with the 1956 constitution, "Egypt had perfected the art of writing anticonstitutionalist constitutions" (Brown 2002: 79).

6 For a discussion of the National Charter, see Roussillon (1988: 346–47).

7 The Minutes of the Preparatory Committee for Drafting the 1971 Constitution refer to records of discussions toward a permanent constitution that were held in 1966.

8 The constitutional history of the Nasser period, with a series of constitutions and constitutional documents promulgated in a short time period, is clearly very different from the Sadat and Mubarak eras, in which the 1971 constitution remained in force until 2011 with only three sets of amendments. To better understand the experiences of constitutions without constitutionalism, the Nasser period is worthy of separate study.

such bases of support because they thought he could be controlled until the time that one of them emerged as a more powerful figure (Waterbury 1983: 349).

Sadat, however, asserted an unexpected degree of independence, moving ahead, for example, with the plan Nasser began to form the Federation of Arab Republics with Libya, Sudan, and Syria and bypassing the authority of the Supreme Executive Committee of the Arab Socialist Union in the process (Waterbury 1983: 350). Sadat faced substantial opposition and potentially even a coup, but he moved first against the "'power centers' that were maneuvering against him," leading to high-ranking dismissals and then collective resignations (Waterbury 1983: 351). May 15, 1971, became known as the beginning of the "corrective revolution" because nearly 100 government and Arab Socialist Union officials were arrested, and most were subsequently convicted (Waterbury 1983: 351).

Sadat then turned to the drafting of a new constitution.[9] In a speech to a special session of the National Assembly on May 20, 1971, Sadat announced his intent to build a new society on the basis of knowledge and belief (*al-'ilm wa-l-iman*); his emphasis on belief was part of a larger strategy to cultivate support among religious segments of society that Nasser had alienated and persecuted (Stilt 2010: 77).[10] Building the country is a service to the battlefield, he said, referring to the conflict with Israel and the losses of 1967 in particular. The new society should be one of freedom and respect in which each individual feels a sense of security today and for the future, and the first step to building this new society is the adoption of a permanent constitution.[11] Sadat charged the National Assembly with carrying out this task and told the members to seek the input and counsel of people at all levels of society throughout the country.[12]

Sadat then gave a short list of specific instructions about what the constitution should include. Some of these comments emphasized continuity with the past. The constitution should affirm Egypt's membership in the Arab community (*umma*) and protect the gains made by socialism in Egypt, including the 50 percent minimum representation for "workers" and "peasants" in all elected popular assemblies,

9 The constitutional preparatory process was documented contemporaneously through extensive notes and minutes, and a set of these documents is held in the Supreme Constitutional Court in Cairo. I thank Adel Omar Sherif for arranging my access.

10 In his opening speech, Sadat also hinted at the state of belief in Nasser's administration when he said that "we have learned that if people want to achieve something that God does not want them to achieve, they will not succeed." Minutes of the Preparatory Committee for Drafting the 1971 Constitution, 3. In August 1965, Nasser believed that the Muslim Brotherhood in Egypt was conspiring with the King of Saudi Arabia to overthrow him, and this led to massive arrests, and there are reports that "27,000 had been swept up in a single twenty-four hour period" (Waterbury 1983: 341). In 1975, Sadat released those still remaining in prison (Waterbury 1983: 341).

11 As Bruce Rutherford explained, Sadat "sought to strengthen the legitimacy of his regime by drafting a new Constitution that would show greater respect for the rule of law and human rights" (Rutherford 2008: 43).

12 Minutes of the Preparatory Committee for Drafting the 1971 Constitution, 3. He praised the morals and values of Egyptian villages in particular, saying that Egyptians in the villages knew when something was simply wrong (*'ayb*). "I want Egypt to be like one big village," Sadat said (Ibid.).

local and national.[13] Further, socialism should be the basis of all state policies and procedures. The constitution should make clear the strong connection between political and social freedom, for if a man is not confident that he will have bread to eat, what is the meaning to him of political freedom, Sadat asked. The principle of one job for one person should be enshrined in the constitution, as should the guarantee of unemployment insurance.[14]

Other aspects of Sadat's instructions to the National Assembly indicated a desire to depart from the practices of Nasser's era.[15] He stated that the nation should be subject to the rule of law, just as individuals should, and that no decision from any authority should be free from judicial review.[16] Related, each individual has the right to seek judicial recourse regarding all state action. While the constitution should affirm the role of the public sector and the cooperative (public-private) sector, it should also give full protection to the private sector. The constitution should provide for press freedoms, Sadat said, while the press itself, as well as other professional societies, should prepare codes of conduct to be agreed on with the relevant national authorities.[17]

The National Assembly's president, Hafiz al-Badawi, served as the chairman of the drafting committee, which was composed of eighty members of the National Assembly. At the first meeting, held on May 29, al-Badawi delivered his own speech, emphasizing aspects of Sadat's instructions and further elaborating on others. He began by enumerating three events crucial to Egypt's success, and he returned to these same themes in every subsequent speech he gave: the Federation of Arab Republics (FAR) among Egypt, Libya, and Syria, because it will forward the cause of unity; the purification of the remaining "power centers" within Egypt; and the treaty of peace and friendship with the Soviet Union. Simultaneous with the Egyptian constitutional drafting process was an effort to prepare a constitution for the FAR, and on several occasions the Egyptian domestic drafters referred to the FAR process

[13] As Sadat mentioned, these affirmative action percentages were established by Nasser in the National Charter. By 1971, they were of questionable value, and some speakers in the town hall meetings said that they should be left out of the new constitution while many others were in support of them; ultimately, they were retained in the 1971 constitution. In 2011, SCAF chose to include these rules in the constitutional declaration.

[14] Minutes of the Preparatory Committee for Drafting the 1971 Constitution, 5–7.

[15] According to Waterbury, "within months of the May 1971 confrontation Sadat moved to release many political prisoners, reinstate civil servants who had been dismissed from their jobs, and to return property that had been sequestered for political reasons. All these measures gained him widespread support among the civilian middle class that had come to chafe under Nasser's police surveillance. Implicitly these moves called into question the quality of Nasser's leadership and planted the seeds for the process of de-Nasserization that Sadat allowed to develop" (Waterbury 1983: 352).

[16] Tamir Moustafa has noted that Sadat constantly used "rule-of-law" rhetoric throughout his presidency (Moustafa 2007: 39).

[17] Minutes of the Preparatory Committee for Drafting the 1971 Constitution, 3. On the idea of professional societies establishing codes of conduct, see the discussion of corporatism in the section on the 1980 amendment, below.

and questioned how it would or should influence what Egypt was expected to include in its own constitution.[18]

Al-Badawi specified some details of the process in his opening speech. They were not starting with a blank slate but rather would begin by consulting the existing basic documents: the National Charter, Nasser's March 30 pronouncement, the 1964 temporary constitution, and the work of the 1966 preparatory committee. President Sadat's speech of May 20 launching the idea of a new constitution would also be a point of reference for the drafters. The country must be involved in the drafting process, al-Badawi said. To achieve that, a committee for receiving suggestions was formed, in addition to committees to work on drafting different parts of the text itself. Further, members of the drafting committee divided into groups and went out into the communities for "town hall" meetings to hear the views of people, including in each governorate of the country and in all of the main universities.

Comments by many of the drafters and their invited guests in the drafting committee meetings along with remarks by Egyptians in the town hall meetings across the country strongly indicated a widespread desire to move away from the political system established under Nasser and to protect personal freedoms in the new constitution.[19] For example, Mustafa Kamil Murad, a member of the drafting committee, criticized Nasser directly and called for a constitution that enshrined the rule of law; guaranteed individual freedoms, including freedom of speech; protected private property; established an independent judiciary and press; and decentralized political powers.[20] Dr. Muhammad al-Qasimi al-Tarshubi, another member of the drafting committee, made an impassioned appeal for a rule of law that is greater than the centers of power and the wishes of individuals. He also called for a legislature that is more powerful than the executive.[21]

Other experts had the opportunity to speak to the drafting committee. When Dr. Mustafa Abu Zayd, chair of the department of constitutional law at Alexandria University and the Socialist Public Prosecutor, suggested to the drafters that a strong executive was necessary, he caused an outcry among the committee members.[22] One said that Abu Zayd's statement forced him to point out to everyone that Egypt already had a pharaoh-like executive and another said that Abu Zayd wanted to

18 Ibid., 30–34. On the FAR, see Bechtold 1971.

19 From the extensive documentation of committee meetings and town hall sessions, I present only a few comments here because of space constraints. A separate article will provide a social history of the drafting of the 1971 constitution based on these detailed records.

20 Minutes of the Preparatory Committee for Drafting the 1971 Constitution, 35.

21 Ibid., 69–70.

22 The position of Socialist Public Prosecutor was also an issue in the drafting process. Public prosecution in Egypt had been entrusted to judicial personnel, acting through a body known as the *niyaba*, but Nasser introduced the idea of public prosecution under the control of the executive branch (Brown 2002: 83). The 1971 constitution both maintained the *niyaba* and provided in Article 179 for the Socialist Public Prosecutor, who was to be supervised by the legislature. Ibid.

bring a dictatorship to Egypt.[23] Dr. Ibrahim Darwish, speaking to the committee, complained that the 1956 and 1964 constitutions concentrated power in the hands of the executive. He called for a strong legislature, an executive limited by law, a balance between executive and legislative power, and an independent judiciary like Egypt used to have, lamenting that the Egyptian judiciary was formerly the model for the whole developing world (at which point the Minster of Justice interjected that Egypt still was such a model).[24]

In town hall meetings across the country, comments by individuals from all walks of life emphasized the need for personal freedoms and for limits on executive power.[25] For example, Mahmud Salah al-Din Jad, a resident of the governorate of Manufiyya, called for the separation of powers, which he thought could be achieved by establishing the rule of law and freedom of expression. (He also called for the death penalty for the crime of embezzling state funds.) In the Giza governorate, Muhammad 'Abd al-Aziz Khalil asked for multicandidate presidential elections for a six-year term with only one possible renewal.[26] A professor in the College of Humanities at Alexandria University warned the committee of the danger of a constitution that is not respected by the people in power.[27] An engineer in the Sharqiyya governorate, Shafi'i 'Abd al-Rahman, asked for the constitution to guarantee personal freedoms and to ensure that arrests would be carried out in accordance with law.[28] And a preacher in Qena asked for freedom of speech, within the bounds of Islam, and for the protection of private property.[29]

These kinds of comments and concerns, however, did not necessarily influence the drafters. While their final draft did take some clear steps away from the constitutional documents of Nasser's era and the 1964 temporary constitution in particular,

[23] Minutes of the Preparatory Committee for Drafting the 1971 Constitution, 60, 68. Abu Zayd defended himself by stating that he merely wanted to prevent conflict among the branches by making sure that one branch was stronger than the others and by noting that the 1956 constitution established an effective balance between the executive and the legislature (Ibid., 49, 62). He was also one of the very few individuals to suggest that the presidency did not need term limits; without limits, the people still retained their power because the president would have to get their approval every six years for renewal, he argued (Ibid., 47).

[24] Ibid., 56–59.

[25] They also displayed great concern about the role of religion in the state, often calling for Islam to be the religion of the state, which had already been included in previous Egyptian constitutions, and sometimes suggesting further language about Islamic law as a source or main source of lawmaking. The way that many individuals presented these two issues together suggests an understanding that Islam requires or perhaps even guarantees justice; a greater allegiance to Islam in the Nasser period might have prevented the intrusions on personal freedoms, many speakers seem to have suggested. Christians who spoke at these meetings almost always expressed concern about Islam as the state religion or other ways of enshrining Islam or Islamic law in the constitution.

[26] Minutes of the Preparatory Committee for Drafting the 1971 Constitution, 247.

[27] Ibid., 289.

[28] Ibid., 336.

[29] Ibid., 392.

it bore many similarities to its predecessors.[30] The Arab Socialist Union was kept as the sole political party, although its reach into other state institutions was curtailed to some extent. Social and economic rights were largely retained, such as the state's guarantees of work (Art. 13), health care and pensions (Art. 17), and education (Arts. 18 and 20). The national economy was subject to a comprehensive development plan (Art. 23) and workers were given a share in the management and profits of projects (Art. 26). The president still held substantial powers, and maintaining the presidential nomination and referendum process (Art. 76) ensured no threat of multicandidate presidential elections. The position's six-year term, with only one renewal (Art. 77), did at least put some limitations on the incumbent.

In some areas, the constitution marked a departure from the past. The security of private property was protected to a much larger extent than before in Articles 34 through 36; although its sanctity was not absolute and could be altered by law, due process was required. Chapter 3, encompassing articles 40 through 72, included protections of freedoms such as belief and the practice of religion (Art. 46), opinion (Art. 47), the press (Art. 48), assembly (Art. 54), and association (Art. 55). However, these protections were easily suspended by a judge or public prosecutor (Kienle 2001: 21). Article 68 prevented the removal of any act or administrative decision from judicial review. Egyptians would have been justified in doubting that these freedoms would be upheld in practice, but Sadat must have hoped that he would be perceived as providing his citizens more guarantees than they had under Nasser. Sadat did not live up to his rule-of-law rhetoric, but he could at least claim to be more of a rule-of-law president than his predecessor.

Articles 174 through 178 provided for a new judicial institution, the Supreme Constitutional Court (SCC), although the implementing legislation was not enacted until 1979. As has been carefully documented by Tamir Moustafa, through the establishment of the SCC, in conjunction with constitutional provisions protecting private property, Sadat was seeking to announce to the foreign community that Egypt had become a safe place for their investments (Moustafa 2007). Finally, the place of Islam in the Egyptian legal system was elevated. In addition to maintaining Islam as the religion of the state, a new source-of-law clause was added in Article 2 to provide that the principles of the Islamic Sharia are a main source of legislation. This addition served the function of a constitutional billboard; it was meant to be as large as the one concerning the protection of private property but was positioned to be seen by a domestic audience. The intensification of constitutional Islam was directed in particular toward the more conservative Islamists whose support Sadat was trying to cultivate (Lombardi 2006: 124–5). It was not until later, however, that the SCC interpreted the clause, giving it a very limited meaning.

30 For a brief description of the constitution's articles, see Kienle (2001: 20–4). Nathan Brown called it "a strange document that gave with the one hand and took away with the other" (Brown 2002: 81).

Separate from the constitution's text, the drafting process throughout the summer of 1971 and the town hall meetings in particular served an important function for Sadat. They allowed for the expression of the flaws and excesses of Nasser's regime, which helped further marginalize Nasser's remaining supporters and diminish the chances that they could seriously threaten Sadat's rule. The demands stated in these sessions for personal freedoms and limitations on executive power were ample and vigorous, but they were only comments on what the constitution in general should include and not on the constitution as actually drafted, which was not presented to the populace until late in the summer just before the referendum. The open process shown to the public was itself somewhat of a "window dressing" for the actual drafting mechanisms and the influence that Sadat and his inner circle exerted over the document's contents.[31] And while freedom of expression seemed fairly unrestricted during these meetings prior to the constitution's drafting, the views of the populace were certainly subject to some manipulation in the constitutional referendum held on September 11, 1971: the constitution was adopted by 99.98 percent of voters, a figure that strongly suggests some official control over the outcome (Moustafa 2007: 70).

AMENDMENTS OF 1980

Throughout the 1970s, Sadat adopted policies that moved away from socialism, while at the same time he allowed for a greater consideration of the place of Islam in state laws and policies. He allowed protoparty "platforms" to form within the Arab Socialist Union, and through them candidates participated in the 1976 parliamentary elections; by 1978, the platforms had become political parties, including the forerunner of the National Democratic Party, and the Arab Socialist Union was essentially dismantled (Waterbury 1983: 355). Sadat was actively cultivating Western support and investment in particular and sought to show investors that Egypt's political and legal systems were in alignment with their expectations (Moustafa 2007). The 1980 constitutional amendments mainly dealt with those parts of the constitution that functioned as an operating manual and updated them in accordance with ideological and political developments. Significantly, in anticipation of a third term, Sadat amended Article 77 to remove the two-term limit on the presidency.

In terms of proclaiming state ideology, one word in Article 2 was changed: "the principles of the Islamic Sharia are *a* main source of legislation" became "the principles of the Islamic Sharia are *the* main source of legislation" (emphasis added). This change reflected, at least in part, an intensification of Sadat's ongoing pragmatic efforts to cultivate Islamist support, which he needed because his domestic

31 According to Kienle, "the constitution of 1971 was not the result of a consensus or compromise among the political actors and forces of the time, but the tool of Sadat and his entourage to defend their interests and consolidate their power" (Kienle 2001: 23).

and foreign policies were increasingly moving away from those of his predecessor and triggering opposition. He substantially limited food subsidies and, significantly, signed a peace treaty with Israel (Lombardi 2006: 130; Moustafa 2007: 107). The seemingly trivial change from the indefinite to the definite article did indeed make for a much larger Islamic billboard. As Moustafa explained, "the simple amendment of one word . . . was interpreted by almost everyone (including SCC justices) as meaning that all laws must be in conformity with Islamic law" (Moustafa 2007: 107).[32]

The amendment of Article 4 is an example of a policy change that angered the remaining Nasserists: the language was modified so that "narrowing the gap between incomes" and "protecting legitimate earnings" became the goals of the state instead of "removing class distinctions." To update the constitution to reflect the changes that had taken place in the political system, mention of the Arab Socialist Union was eliminated from Article 5; instead, "the political regime of the Arab Republic of Egypt is based upon the multi-party system" and "political parties shall be regulated by law." Despite this slight openness in political party formation, the presidential selection system of Article 76 remained the same, such that the People's Assembly nominated the presidential candidate and then submitted that candidate to a national referendum. The candidate only needed approval from a majority of voters in order to become president.

An upper house of Parliament, the Consultative Assembly, was created by adding Articles 194 through 205 to the constitution. Serving for six-year terms and without term limits, two thirds of the members would be elected and one third appointed by the president. The elected members were subject to the same 50 percent worker-peasant quota. The Consultative Assembly's power was largely advisory, although its approval was deemed binding on constitutional amendments, on laws considered complementary to specified constitutional provisions, and on international treaties. Some of the powers of the former Arab Socialist Union were basically transferred to the newly created Consultative Assembly, creating a presidential-dominated check on the lower house (Brown 2002: 84).

Finally, the press received its own set of provisions in new Articles 206 through 211, added to the end of the constitution following the section on the Consultative Assembly. Article 48 had already expressed the principle of freedom of the press, but these articles went much further in specifying the rights and duties of the press in a way that both protected press freedoms and also specified that journalists must behave in a manner consistent with the constitution and law. Article 211 established a Supreme Press Council to deal with all matters concerning the press; some of these functions had previously been carried out by the Arab Socialist Union (Brown 2002: 84). The Press Council and other similar labor and professional unions are indicative of a "corporatist" system of governance, whereby these institutions would add another

[32] On the SCC's Article 2 decisions, see generally Lombardi (2006).

layer of control, including the power to discipline, over the individuals within their purview.[33]

The creation of a multiparty political system raised the hope, domestically and abroad, that Parliament could become a more politically robust institution. However, the addition of a Consultative Assembly, controlled to a substantial degree by the president, was clearly intended to check the lower house's independence. Further, possibilities of multiparty parliamentary elections and a diverse parliament were only real to the extent that parties were able to register and elections were free and fair, and subsequent electoral practices by the regime substantially diminished those hopes.[34] Since the People's Assembly controlled the nomination of the presidential candidate, as long as the president's party dominated the People's Assembly, there was no way for other parties to present their candidates to the public. Further, the removal of presidential term limits meant that the president was secure in office to the degree that he could control his own party.

The package of amendments was mixed, in some cases moving toward a more pluralistic system while in others clearly paving the way for a more authoritarian president. As with the adoption of the constitution itself, there was probably manipulation in the referendum. The amendments were adopted on May 22, 1980, by 98.6 percent of the voters. Sadat, however, did not live to witness their long-term effects on social, political, and economic life. Due in large part to the treaty with Israel, Sadat's relations with the Muslim Brotherhood and offshoot Islamist groups worsened substantially, and he was assassinated by a member of Islamic Jihad on October 6, 1981. Clearly, his efforts with Article 2 did not outweigh his other transgressions in the view of his assassins. His vice president, Hosni Mubarak, the presumptive successor, was elected president in a referendum the next month.

AMENDMENT OF 2005

Mubarak benefitted from the amendments introduced by Sadat and by the removal of term limits on the presidency in particular, and he proceeded with the same constitution for nearly twenty-five years. The absence of amendments during this lengthy period of time is perhaps best explained by the simple assertion that the current constitution suited his needs. The prompts for the 2005 amendment were both internal and external and had much to do with domestic actors agitating, within very narrow limitations, for greater political participation and the U.S. government desperately seeking democratic developments in the region at a time when efforts in Iraq were becoming no less than catastrophic.

The presidential selection system in particular was a growing focal point for prodemocracy advocates, both inside and outside Egypt, and the amendment of

33 On Mubarak's use of corporatism, see generally Bianchi (1989). I thank Tamir Moustafa for pointing this out to me.

34 On the abuses in parliamentary elections, see generally Moustafa (2007: 154–61).

2005 dealt only with this issue. The short Article 76 originally provided that the People's Assembly determines the presidential nominee, who will be submitted to the voters in a referendum. At that time, the People's Assembly was controlled by the National Democratic Party (NDP) because of political party laws and electoral practices that prevented opposition party members or independents from substantial success at the polls. Thus, the outcome of the presidential nomination process was guaranteed, as was, because of the executive's control over the voting process, the result of the referendum itself. Subsequent to taking office in 1981, Mubarak was reelected in this process in 1987, 1993, and 1999, with the official referendum approval votes in the mid to high 90 percent range each time.

In early 2005, Mubarak started the process to amend the presidential election system, intending for the changes to go into effect before the next presidential election, which was scheduled for September 2005. Mubarak did not seek to change the fundamental dynamics of the process, but he was under substantial pressure, domestically and externally, to allow some additional participation by other candidates. American attention to the Middle East was high following the invasion of Iraq, and the U.S. was urging Egypt to present itself as an exemplar of democracy in the region at a time when the democratic project in Iraq was failing. In his 2005 State of the Union address, Bush called on Mubarak directly: "And the great and proud nation of Egypt, which showed the way toward peace in the Middle East, can now show the way toward democracy in the Middle East."[35] Both parliamentary and presidential elections were at issue, but, unlike the parliamentary election system, which was at that time mainly regulated by laws, any real change to the presidential election process required a constitutional amendment to Article 76.[36]

In order to present the amendment as an internal project and not something dictated by the U.S., Mubarak constructed a fictional historical narrative in which Egypt was now ready for this level of democracy. In his communication to the People's Assembly and the Consultative Assembly tasking the bodies with drafting the amendment, Mubarak said that when the 1971 constitution was prepared, the drafters considered two options: direct, popular presidential elections or selection of the president by the parliament. Not wholly satisfied with either, the drafters chose a middle path: the parliament nominates the candidate whom the people then accept or reject. This was a typical presidential selection process for countries undergoing a transition to democracy, Mubarak said, and it had afforded Egypt security and stability until she was able to completely eject the invading enemy from

[35] President George Bush, State of the Union Address, Feb. 2, 2005.

[36] The parliamentary election system was also a major focus of complaint by prodemocracy activists. While some gains had been made in terms of the process of parliamentary elections, largely because of an SCC ruling in 2000 that concluded that Article 88 of the constitution required judges to be present at each polling outlet, there were still significant limitations, both legal and in practice, that prevented parties other than the NDP and independents from substantial success. See the discussion in Moustafa (2007: 154–61).

her soil, referring, of course, to Israel.[37] Having achieved these preparatory steps, the obvious next stage was a system of multicandidate presidential elections, Mubarak concluded.[38]

The amendment to Article 76 did not merely allow for multiple presidential candidates but rather replaced the existing terse language with a long and detailed article that, when read against the prevailing political realities, essentially maintained the status quo under the guise of democratic change. According to the amendment, there are two ways to become a candidate. First, political parties that had been in existence for the preceding five years and had, in the last parliamentary elections, received at least 5 percent of the seats in both the People's Assembly and the Consultative Assembly were able to nominate one of their leaders. However, only the NDP met this threshold of 5 percent.

The second option in the amendment concerned candidates who were either independent or whose party did not have the requisite number of parliamentary seats. Such candidates had to gain the support of at least 250 members from the People's Assembly, Consultative Assembly, and regional parliaments combined, with specific distribution requirements among these bodies. Further, the candidate needed the support of at least ten members from at least fourteen of the twenty-six regional parliaments.

Since the amendment was supposed to look like it was creating multicandidate presidential elections, the true nature would have been obvious if Mubarak were the only candidate eligible for the first election held under the new system. To avoid this, the constitutional amendment contained a waiver of the minimum seat requirement for party-sponsored candidates for the first election held pursuant to it, and each political party was permitted to nominate one member from its leadership body. Mubarak had suggested the need for such a waiver in his initial speech. There was no waiver for independent candidates, many of whom were Muslim Brotherhood affiliates. The candidate who received an absolute majority of votes was the presidential winner under the amendment (Stilt 2006: 349–50).

The amended Article 76 was many times longer than its predecessor and far more detailed, making its style clearly inconsistent with the other constitutional articles. The reasons for this stylistic change relate to the SCC, which had grown to become a powerful force in the 1980s and 1990s that had ruled against the executive and the NDP-dominated legislature on numerous occasions, including in cases regarding the parliamentary election procedure (Moustafa 2007: 154–61). Even though the SCC had come under much tighter executive control by 2005, it was clear that

37 There is no evidence in the drafting records to support this narrative. In 1971, allowing the parliament to select the president would have been a step backward, in terms of popular participation, from the Nasser-era process.

38 Text of the Speech of Mubarak to the Presidents of the People's Assembly and Consultative Assembly, Feb. 26, 2005, published in *al-Ahram*, Feb. 27, 2005.

Mubarak was not going to take a chance with amended Article 76.[39] Putting that level of detail in the constitution shielded it from the SCC; as the speaker of the People's Assembly, Fathi Sorour, commented at the time, part of the constitution cannot be declared unconstitutional.[40] The amended Article 76 also further tied the SCC's hands by requiring that it conduct a prepromulgation review of the new legislation that would implement Article 76, a review process not otherwise in the power of the SCC. It was implied that once the SCC reviewed (and approved) the legislation prepromulgation, it would not – and even could not – subsequently rereview it (Stilt 2006: 371–2).

The amendment to Article 76 also created a Presidential Election Commission. The constitution provided in Article 88 that members of the judiciary should supervise elections to the People's Assembly, but it did not provide for a supervisory body for presidential referenda. The Presidential Election Commission would not consist solely of judges but would be composed of ten members: five judges and five individuals elected by the People's Assembly and Consultative Assembly. Clearly, it would not be a neutral body (Stilt 2006: 350–1).

The amendment was submitted on May 25, 2005, to a national referendum, which was boycotted by the three main opposition parties, the coalition called the Egyptian Movement for Change (known as *kifaya*, meaning "enough"), and many others because it did not create genuine presidential elections.[41] Perhaps the only positive aspect of the 2005 amendment is that some of the Kifaya-led demonstrations at the time of the referendum and later during the presidential campaign were tolerated by the regime, which helped the political opposition develop and gain momentum. According to the Ministry of the Interior, 54 percent of the nation's voters participated in the referendum and 83 percent of voters accepted the amendment.[42] The first (and, because of the events of 2011, only) presidential election held pursuant to this amendment on September 7, 2005, resulted in a sweeping victory for Mubarak over his opponents. According to official reports, the second-place candidate, Ayman Nur, received only 7.3 percent of the votes (Stilt 2006: 335).

Article 76 as amended provided a detailed instruction manual for exactly how presidential elections would take place, elections that would look different but, as every Egyptian knew, would achieve the same result as under the old system. And yet the amendment was presented to a foreign audience as a democratic billboard. The complicated language was intended to give Mubarak the ability to claim in front of the international community that he was establishing a democratic process, because in the abstract, without knowing the political realities in Egypt, the change appeared

[39] For the process by which the executive exerted control over the SCC, see Moustafa (2007: 178–218).

[40] Noha El-Hennawy, "The Race Is On," *Egypt Today*, June 2005.

[41] The three parties issued a joint statement that the amendment "sanctifies the permanent monopoly of the ruling party over the post of the republic's president" (Noha El-Hennawy, "The Race Is On," *Egypt Today*, June 2005).

[42] "Approval of the Amendment to the Constitution by a Sweeping Majority," *al-Ahram*, May 27, 2005.

to actually offer a viable path to a non-NDP candidate.[43] The U.S. did not publicly recognize this double-talk, however, and instead Secretary of State Condoleezza Rice praised the new system as "one step in the march towards the full democracy that the Egyptian people desire and deserve."[44]

AMENDMENTS OF 2007

In late 2006, Mubarak launched a lengthy set of thirty-four constitutional amendments that dealt again with the presidential election process and also reached into the areas of state ideology, political party formation, parliamentary elections, military courts, the distribution of power within the executive branch, and the power of the People's Assembly vis-à-vis the executive.[45] As in 2005, Mubarak framed these amendments as important steps in Egypt's path toward democracy, asserting that the purpose was to "strengthen our constitutional framework, deepen our process of democratic development and support our democratic process" (Bernard-Maugiron 2008: 398). But a careful look at the text of the amendments in the Egyptian social and political context reveals far more complex intentions. One goal was simply to align the constitution with prevailing state ideology, which had firmly departed from socialism, and another was to provide new rules regarding parties and elections that were intended to be followed because they benefitted Mubarak and the NDP generally. The few provisions that looked like a liberal development created minimal real change, allowing Mubarak to call them a further step toward democracy while actually giving up very little on the ground.

On the level of state ideology, eleven amendments were made to remove references to socialism, either literally or implicitly. Article 1 was amended to replace "the Arab Republic of Egypt is a Socialist Democratic State based on the alliance of the working forces of the people" with "the Arab Republic of Egypt is a state with a democratic system that is based on citizenship," and Article 4, on the economic foundations of the state, was further revised to remove "socialist" as a descriptor and other language such as the intent to narrow the gap between income levels. Reference to the people "controlling all means of production" was removed from Article 24, and the concept of "public ownership" was deleted from several articles.

43 In a March 15, 2005, editorial, the *Washington Post* called the amendments "an act of minimalism intended to deflect domestic and international pressure." Acknowledging that the amendments were a minimal improvement fails to recognize that, when taken as a package and in the context of the political realities in Egypt, they were not an improvement at all; they were a step backward.

44 Press Release, Condoleezza Rice, Secretary of State of the United States, Sept. 10, 2005.

45 A short publication by the Carnegie Endowment for International Peace contains Nathan Brown, Michele Dunne, and Amr Hamzawy (2007), "Egypt's Controversial Constitutional Amendments," which is a succinct guide to the most significant of these amendments; Amr Hamzawy, "Political Motivations," which is a helpful brief analysis of the political context of the amendments; and a translation of some of the amendments.

Two amendments targeted, without naming, the Muslim Brotherhood, a large and powerful group without political party status but whose members had performed very well as independent candidates in the 2005 People's Assembly elections.[46] Article 5 on political parties, which was amended in 1980 to adopt a multiparty system, was supplemented by a new clause: "Citizens have the right to form political parties in accordance with law. It is not permitted to pursue any political activity or establish political parties with a religious frame of reference, on a religious basis, or on the basis of gender or origin." Laws regulating political parties had prevented the Muslim Brotherhood from recognition and had blocked the formation of parties on the basis of religion; the amendment significantly expanded these prohibitions. The Brotherhood had long stated that it did not operate on the basis of religion but rather under the broader notion of a religious frame of reference; the amendment carefully tracked the group's self-description.

An amendment to Article 62 created the possibility for a change in the way that parliamentary elections would take place, also to the detriment of the Muslim Brotherhood but to the benefit of formal opposition parties.[47] Since an SCC decision in 1990 striking down a party list system as unconstitutional, parliamentary elections were held using a system of individual districts; voters in each district were presented with two lists, one containing individuals who qualified as "workers" or "peasants" and one list that contained all other candidates (Moustafa 2007: 99–100). The amendment added the statement that a system may be adopted that combines an individual district and a party list system in any ratio specified by law. As a result, the number of districts that use individual lists could be minimized dramatically.

Although worded neutrally, this amendment was clearly aimed at the Muslim Brotherhood. Brotherhood-affiliated candidates running as independents had been able to achieve some electoral success despite the electoral fraud carried out by the state. Even with considerable state interference, independent candidates affiliated with the Brotherhood won 88 out of 444 seats in the 2005 elections for the People's Assembly (Stilt 2010: 74). This victory clearly alarmed the regime. By reducing or even eliminating the independent candidate option, the only way for Brotherhood members to run for office would be to join legal opposition parties, as they had sometimes done in the past. However, other parties would be concerned that allowing a Brotherhood member to run on its ticket would invite additional state interference. On the surface, then, the amendment appeared neutral, but given the obstacles to party formation, it served to continue to keep out candidates and parties unless the regime deemed them acceptable.

46 For a discussion of their performance in 2005, see Stilt (2010: 79).

47 As Amr Hamzawy noted, this amendment "serves the regime's purpose of widening the gap between the Brotherhood and legal opposition parties" with the intention of "trying to thwart the opposition's efforts to form a united front that includes Islamists and liberals." In order to try to meet the parliamentary membership threshold for nominating a presidential candidate, these parties "have a vested interest in allying themselves with the regime to marginalize the Brotherhood and expand their own legal space as opposition parties" (Hamzawy 2007).

Article 76, the sole provision at issue in the 2005 amendment, was further amended to make it slightly easier for a party other than the NDP to nominate a presidential candidate. As amended in 2005, Article 76 required an existing party to have 5 percent of the seats in the People's Assembly and Consultative Assembly in order to have the right to nominate, although an exception was made for the 2005 presidential election to allow each preexisting party to nominate one candidate. After 2005, however, the general rule would apply, and no party other than the NDP would be able to meet it. The 2007 amendment to Article 76 reduced the seat requirement to 3 percent and also extended for ten years the exception used in 2005 allowing any registered party with one seat in either house to nominate a party leader as a candidate.[48] The strict rules for independent candidates remained in place unmodified, essentially precluding an independent (and in particular a Muslim Brotherhood member) from running for president.

The powers of the cabinet of ministers and the prime minister in particular were expanded vis-à-vis the president in the 2007 amendments. Article 138 as amended required the president to consult with the cabinet on certain constitutional powers and get the cabinet's approval on others. The process for assumption of executive power in the event of the president's temporary inability was clarified by an amendment to Article 82. Formerly, the president could only delegate his powers to a vice president, but Mubarak had failed to appoint any vice presidents. As amended, the president may delegate his powers to a vice president or the prime minister. The president still appointed and dismissed the prime minister at will, and so these changes were far more about adjusting the details of the constitution in its function as an operational manual rather than shifting power away from the president.

Article 88 was amended to remove judicial supervision from parliamentary elections. This supervision had been a major irritant to Mubarak, because the SCC had determined that Article 88 required full judicial supervision over the entire voting process, including having a judge present at each polling station. Since there were not enough judges to accomplish this in one day, in 2000 the government adopted a new election law that required parliamentary elections be held over a series of days, so that only about one third of the polls were open on each day. But there was still a shortage of judges, so the government recruited prosecutors and other quasi-judges to assist in the process, which drew questions about their independence. Judges still complained that their presence in the polling stations could not prevent or even detect the fraud that took place elsewhere, such as intimidation of candidates or voters before or during the election (Moustafa 2007: 192–8). Amended Article 88 simply eliminated judicial supervision over parliamentary elections and created an election commission, similar to the one created in 2005 for presidential elections. Opposition parties and the Muslim Brotherhood alike were highly critical of this

48 The requirement that the nominee be a party leader was largely meant to preclude one party from choosing as its candidate a member of the Muslim Brotherhood who had not, prior to that time, been involved in the party.

change in particular. While it is, generally speaking, unusual for judges to oversee elections at this level of depth, and election commissions are common in most countries, in Egypt "the public has grown increasingly convinced that the regime is intent on rigging the elections and that only judges can uncover such practices and prevent their spread" (Hamzawy 2007).

Amendments to Article 179 were considered the "big disaster" by Egyptians (Hamzawy 2007). As explained by Mubarak, Article 179, which provided for a Socialist Public Prosecutor, needed amendment to establish a system that would allow for the prosecution of terrorists and other threats to national security; such a system and its related implementing legislation would ultimately replace the state of emergency that had been in place since 1981, he claimed. The amendment stated that procedures for the investigation and identification of suspects of terrorist activities will be provided for by law and then specified that such procedures do not need to comply with Article 41 (protection from arbitrary detention and arrest), Article 44 (sanctity of the home from intrusion without judicial warrant), or Article 45 (privacy rights that may not be violated without judicial warrant). Amended Article 179 also added a stunning clause at the end: the president has the right to refer any crime of terrorism to any judicial authority created by the constitution or by law, meaning that civilians could, consistent with the constitution, be tried in military courts.

The final set of amendments concerned the People's Assembly. The body received some additional powers: it must receive the annual budget for review in advance and then vote on it one article at time rather than on the whole package (Article 115). It may also dismiss the prime minister by a vote of the majority of its members (Article 127). However, Article 136 was amended to allow the president to dissolve the People's Assembly, in a case of necessity, on his own initiative. Previously, dissolution could only take place with the approval of the electorate expressed through a national referendum. The amendments giving the People's Assembly more power were largely meaningless without the structural changes that would allow for a more politically diverse People's Assembly.

This lengthy list of amendments was finalized and presented to the voters in a quick process, and voters had to approve or reject the whole slate. A draft of the amendments was available in late January 2007, and then Parliament approved all of them on March 19 after a few weeks of consideration. Opposition members said that their concerns about the contents were summarily rejected, and they refused to vote on them as a result (Brown, Dunne, and Hamzawy 2007).[49] After parliamentary approval, the amendments were quickly presented to the country and the referendum was held on March 26. According to official reports, 27.1 percent of the registered voters turned out and the amendments were approved by 75.9 percent

[49] Muslim Brothers in the People's Assembly walked out of the discussion in protest and returned wearing black banners with the statement "no to the constitutional coup d'etat." NDP members responded with their own green equivalents that stated that "modernizing the constitution is modernizing Egypt" (Bernard-Maugiron 2008: 399).

of those voting, but opposition groups estimated that less than 10 percent of Egyptians actually participated (Bernard-Maugiron 2008: 399).[50]

Because of the length and complexity of the amendments, the extent to which Egyptians understood their actual details is not clear, but it does seem that their overall nature was widely understood based on the level of street protests that took place at the time. Sizable protests were held or were attempted in cities across the country, but unlike in 2005 when some demonstrations were tolerated, in 2007 the governmental response was far more severe. While the protesters had no chance of stopping the adoption of the amendments, the protests did serve the important function of raising public consciousness about the way that authoritarian policies were carried out through the constitution. This consciousness continued to grow, culminating in the 2011 revolution.

For the regime at the time of the amendments, each individual change provided some benefit; in addition, the vastness and complexity of the amendments as a whole served certain other goals. Some appeared, in the abstract, to be democratic developments, however slight, and these were the ones that were highlighted for the international community. They served as "window dressing" in the sense that they helped distract from the authoritarian entrenchment accomplished by the amendments overall. Egyptians knew that they were not improvements given the larger political power structures, but viewed from a distance the most egregious ones could seem diluted among the changes to eliminate socialist references, for example. The U.S. response to the 2007 amendments was not as sanguine as in 2005, but criticism was muted. Secretary of State Condoleezza Rice expressed "disappointment" but recognized that "the process of reform" will "have its ups and downs."[51]

POSTREVOLUTION CONSTITUTIONAL DEVELOPMENTS

Soon after assuming control of the country, the Supreme Council of the Armed Forces (SCAF) suspended the constitution and formed a committee of eight men to prepare amendments to modify or remove the most offensive provisions.[52] Even though the constitution was viewed by some of the revolutionaries as irredeemably

[50] Since voters had only two choices and could not vote separately on each amendment, it is possible that the package was appealing to those Egyptians who wanted to stem the growing political strength of the Muslim Brotherhood and were willing to trade off other restrictions for the provisions that harmed the Brotherhood in particular.

[51] "Egypt Dials Back Political Reform," *The Christian Science Monitor*, March 26, 2007. There also has been ample speculation that the U.S. government became less interested in pushing for democratic reform in Egypt after the Muslim Brotherhood's success in the 2005 parliamentary elections gave some indication of what democracy in Egypt might look like. Thus, President Mubarak became confident that the pressure from the U.S. that he was under in 2005 had lifted, and he proceeded with the 2007 amendments.

[52] The Arabic text of the referendum as presented to Egyptian voters can be found on the website of the Egyptian Supreme Judicial Council at http://referendum.eg/constitutional-amendments/2011-03-11-22-19-08.html. An English-language analysis of the referendum along with a summary of

tainted by Mubarak, the prospect of drafting a new document as the first step in the transition apparently seemed to SCAF to be too time consuming and unwieldy and perhaps completely unnecessary. The committee quickly completed its task, and the amendments were released to the public just before the scheduled referendum on March 19, 2011. Supporters and opponents tended to disagree over the practical implications of adopting or rejecting the amendments rather than over the actual substance of the changes.[53]

Just days before the referendum, SCAF announced that it would also issue a "constitutional declaration."[54] Egyptians had assumed that if the referendum passed, and thus the constitution was amended and returned to force, the declaration would merely be a straightforward statement of the timetable for parliamentary and presidential elections. If the referendum failed, such a declaration would announce a new plan. Although SCAF obviously supported the amendments and the referendum it arranged, at some point late in the referendum process it seemed to develop second thoughts about the viability of salvaging the 1971 constitution. This realization came a little too late, since SCAF had just held a nationwide referendum – that Egyptians approved in large numbers – to amend and reinstate that very document.

On March 30, 2011, SCAF utilized a favored communication method of the Tahrir revolutionaries and posted on its Facebook page a surprising constitutional declaration. At a length of sixty-three articles, it effectively superseded the 1971 constitution while at the same time recycling many of its provisions. But it was also much shorter than the 1971 constitution and left many topics simply unaddressed. The declaration consisted of:

> articles from the 1971 constitution as amended in the referendum; articles from the 1971 constitution as amended in the referendum with additional changes made by SCAF; articles from the 1971 constitution that were not part of the referendum, some of which were included verbatim and some of which were amended by SCAF; and several new articles that specifically recognize and give powers to SCAF. (Stilt 2012: 48)

The constitutional declaration was subsequently modified several times. On June 17, 2012, SCAF issued a short supplement to the declaration to give itself additional powers, including the legislative power that was normally exercised by the People's Assembly.[55] The timing of that announcement was significant: on June 14, the SCC had announced its ruling that resulted in the dissolution of the elected People's Assembly, but the winner of the presidential elections, the final rounds of which

the amendments as adopted can be found in Brown and Dunn (2011; see also Moustafa 2011; Stilt 2012).

[53] For a discussion of the debates around the referendum, see Stilt (2011).

[54] For a discussion of the declaration, see Brown and Stilt (2011).

[55] For a discussion of the supplement to the declaration, see Brown (2012).

had been held June 16 through 17, had not yet been announced. In a further complication, newly elected President Morsi issued his own constitutional supplement on August 12, 2012, in which he abrogated SCAF's June supplement and assigned legislative powers to the president along with control over the constitutional drafting process, which had previously been appropriated by SCAF.[56] President Morsi issued an additional and highly controversial supplementary declaration on November 22, 2012, in which he claimed for himself extensive powers, including immunity from judicial review for his decisions. Violent protests ensued, causing Morsi to withdraw the most provocative aspects of his statement.[57]

It is difficult to determine where to place the constitutional declaration: should it be considered the final phase of the 1971 constitutional period, departing from it in some ways while also sharing with it key authoritarian attributes? In terms of procedure, the constitutional declaration was adopted in a nondemocratic process, and it is not even clear who drafted it; it was merely released by SCAF. Further, the declaration was an explicit affront to the democratic process that resulted in the amendment of the 1971 constitution in the March 2011 referendum. The results of the referendum approving those amendments were implicitly rejected in SCAF's decision to issue the declaration. And yet at the same time, the declaration contains many of the guarantees of rights and freedoms that would be expected in any democratic constitution and does not include the egregious provisions seen in the 1971 constitution.

In terms of content, SCAF repurposed extensive portions of the 1971 constitution for the constitutional declaration. It may seem counterintuitive that a revolutionary movement would eject a dictator under whose watch, and that of his predecessor, a constitution was drafted and amended in ways that allowed for and indeed supported authoritarian policies, and then accept, at least in part, the provisions of that constitution. Does this signal that the revolution failed? Or, does it indicate that provisions that seem desirable on their face were not irrevocably destroyed by the way they were implemented or not implemented in the previous regime?

Some of the provisions retained in the declaration deal with the structure of government, such as identifying the two houses of parliament, and serve a simple coordinating function. The section on fundamental rights and freedoms is similar to the 1971 constitution, providing, for example, for freedom of expression. While the situation is complicated by the fact that SCAF, the author of the declaration, has certainly placed limits on expression, presumably no one accepts the idea that the freedom of expression as provided for in the declaration is the same, in text and in practice, as that which existed under Mubarak. Provisions that were "window dressing" in one context can, in another, prove potentially meaningful.

[56] The short text of President Morsi's August supplement can be found at http://english.ahram.org.eg/News/50248.aspx.

[57] The November supplement is discussed in David Kirkpatrick, "Backing Off Added Powers, Egypt's Leader Presses Vote," *The New York Times*, Dec. 8, 2012.

The constitutional declaration was replaced by a new constitution that went into force on December 26, 2012, after a lukewarm electoral turnout of about 33 percent approved the document by a margin of 64 percent.[58] While an analysis of the 2012 constitution is beyond the scope of this chapter, it is clear that the process and substance of the document have proven controversial and divisive in Egypt. The time pressures imposed on the drafting process meant that the 1971 constitution was relied on heavily as a model for the new constitution, and the result is a document "that human rights groups and international experts said was full of holes and ambiguities."[59] Before the final vote within the drafting commission, many of the liberal and Christian delegates left in protest.[60] President Morsi then rushed the national referendum on the document, leaving little time for Egyptians to evaluate and discuss it, and the voting process was criticized for irregularities that suggest that the electoral manipulations of the Mubarak era have not been relegated to the past.[61] The extent to which the 2012 constitution marks a new constitutional phase in Egypt remains a significant question for future analysis.

CONCLUSIONS

The example of the Egyptian constitution of 1971 shows that a constitution in an authoritarian regime can serve many diverse purposes and is not merely a "sham document," unworthy of attention or study. Egypt's two presidents throughout the course of the life of the 1971 constitution, Sadat and then Mubarak, were directly responsible for the text and its amendments, and so a study of constitutional change is one of how these two authoritarian leaders used the constitution for their own purposes. While ultimately those purposes connected to larger self-serving political ambitions, constitutional provisions did not always merely reflect blatant assertions of raw power. A careful look at the constitutional text and the processes by which the text and amendments were adopted reveal a more complex account of constitutional events in Egypt, in which provisions served, for example, billboard, operating manual, and coordinating functions and were aimed at both internal and foreign audiences.

The 1971 constitution was born in the immediate post-Nasser period, when Sadat was just beginning to distance himself from his predecessor and his policies. The absence of a permanent constitution at the time of Nasser's death gave Sadat the natural opportunity to make the adoption of a new one a matter of national priority, asking the parliament to draft it and calling on Egyptians to voice their opinions about what it should include at town hall meetings. The public aspects of the drafting

58 "Egyptian Voters Back New Constitution in Referendum," BBC News, Dec. 25, 2012.

59 David Kirkpatrick, "Egyptian Islamists Approve Draft Constitution Despite Objections," *The New York Times*, Nov. 29, 2012.

60 Ibid.

61 See "Egypt's Constitutional Referendum, A Dubious Yes," *The Economist*, Dec. 22, 1012.

process served the important function for Sadat of allowing the nation to express, in a controlled and managed manner, disapproval and anger over the authoritarian excesses of Nasser. At the same time, Sadat cultivated his image as the "rule of law" and "believing" president in an effort to show Egyptians that his regime would be just and pious – or at least more so – than that of his predecessor. And he sought to make the constitution reflect those attributes in articles that protected private property; created a new judicial institution, the SCC; promised more individual freedoms and liberties; instituted presidential term limits; and intensified the place of Islam in the constitution. These kinds of provisions were to some extent instructions for how the country would actually operate, but they were also meant to attract support, at home and abroad, for his presidency, even if subsequent full implementation was not actually intended.

By 1980, Sadat's own style of leadership and vision for the country were becoming more pronounced, and he initiated a slate of amendments to update the constitution accordingly. These changes went in many directions. He was actively cultivating Islamist support, and so he began to phase out the remaining Nasserite language while also making a small but significant change to the source-of-law clause of Article 2 to intensify the place of Islam in the legal system. A slight political opening came with the institution of a pluralistic political party system (although the formation of parties was heavily regulated by law), but Sadat also lifted the term limits on the presidency in anticipation of his third term. Moving ideologically toward the West and away from the Soviet Union, Sadat used the constitution to signal this shift, and Western governments and investors did respond favorably. But Sadat's internal Islamic billboard with the amendment to Article 2 was just not enough to overcome the criticisms that extremists lodged against him due, in large part, to the peace treaty with Israel that he signed.

After Sadat's assassination, Mubarak inherited a constitution that largely suited his purposes; there was no reason to write a new one or even rush to amend the existing one. The constitution provided that many issues were to be "regulated by law," and so Mubarak and his National Democratic Party could achieve most of their goals through legislation. The formation of political parties was tightly regulated, elections for both houses of Parliament were under Mubarak's control, and the presidential selection system guaranteed that Mubarak would be nominated and then approved in a national referendum. The SCC did become a powerful institution and struck down some legislation that Mubarak supported, but Mubarak worked to decrease the SCC's independence rather than, at least until 2007, to amend the constitution to counter unfavorable SCC rulings.

In 2005, after serving as president for twenty-four years, Mubarak suddenly sought to amend the constitution to change the presidential selection system from a one-candidate referendum to a multicandidate election. Mubarak did not become a democrat overnight, nor did he actually want to lose his position to another candidate in a free and fair election. Instead, he was trying to preempt the growing internal opposition to his authoritarian rule as well as respond to increasing pressure from the U.S. At that time, democratization in the Middle East was an American priority, but the process in Iraq was proceeding very badly. President Bush was seeking a success story, and he turned to Egypt in the hopes of creating one positive example of the new Middle Eastern order. Presumably using the substantial aid relationship as leverage, Mubarak was encouraged to loosen his grip on the presidential selection process. The 2005 amendment to Article 76 was a masterful creation of authoritarianism in democratic clothing – and a perfect example of a constitutional provision serving as a detailed operating manual – and earned him the praise of the U.S. government.

Subsequent to the 2005 amendment of the presidential election system, elections for the People's Assembly saw a substantial victory for independent candidates affiliated with the Muslim Brotherhood, even with a fair amount of state-perpetrated electoral fraud. Concerned about this showing, and no longer under as much American scrutiny, Mubarak turned to a sweeping set of thirty-four constitutional amendments. The 2007 amendments served a wide range of goals, including the removal of the last remaining references to socialism in the constitution. Several amendments sought to push the Muslim Brotherhood further out of the political process. Overall, these amendments were designed to further entrench Mubarak's reign and that of his successor, who was expected to be his son Gamal. To gain further powers over domestic opposition, one amendment explicitly allowed the president to refer anyone suspected of threatening national security to a military or any other court.

By this time, Mubarak saw a benefit in actively using the constitution for his own purposes, but this use also increasingly angered Egyptians. Forcing the 2007 amendments as a package on Egyptians was clearly an authoritarian move, prompting opposition that was responded to harshly by the government. The more extensive range of amendments in 2007 only further provoked the opposition that had been generated in 2005 and helped galvanize public opposition to Mubarak. The 2007 amendments also certainly drew increasing attention to ways in which the constitution was an instrument of his authoritarianism. And thus, at the beginning of the 2011 revolution, in a last-minute effort to appease the protesters, Mubarak offered to amend the worst of the provisions from 2005 and 2007, along with some of the provisions, such as the lack of presidential term limits, inherited from Sadat.

The 1971 constitution was replaced in March 2011 by SCAF's constitutional declaration, but its content was not rejected wholesale. Many of the provisions of the 1971 constitution are, on their face, acceptable and even desirable in a democratic society. They simply were not enforced under Sadat's and Mubarak's regimes and were seen by Egyptians as hollow promises. The newly adopted December 2012 constitution – discussion of which is beyond the scope of this chapter – has also repurposed many provisions from the 1971 constitution. As with the 1971 constitution, the process by which the 2012 constitution was drafted and adopted demands careful study as part of understanding the extent to which the 2012 document marks a significant departure from that of 1971. Whether the 2012 constitution will adequately serve Egypt remains, at the time of the writing of this chapter, an open question.

REFERENCES

Bechtold, Peter. 1971. "New Attempts at Arab Cooperation: The Federation of Arab Republics, 1971–?." *Middle East Journal* 27(2): 152–72.

Bernard-Maugiron, Nathalie. 2008. "The 2007 Constitutional Amendments in Egypt and Their Implications on the Balance of Power." *Arab Law Quarterly* 22: 397–417.

Bianchi, Robert. 1989. *Unruly Corporatism*. New York: Oxford University Press.

Boyle, Kevin and Adel Omar Sherif. 1996. "The Road to the 1971 Constitution – A Brief Constitutional History of Modern Egypt," in idem, eds., *Human Rights and Democracy: The Role of the Supreme Constitutional Court of Egypt*. London; Boston: Kluwer Law International, pp. 3–12.

Brown, Nathan. 2002. *Constitutions in a Nonconstitutional World*. Albany: State University of New York.

Brown, Nathan. 2012. "The Egyptian Political System in Disarray," Carnegie Endowment for International Peace, available at http://carnegieendowment.org/2012/06/19/egyptian-political-system-in-disarray/c073.

Brown, Nathan and Dunn, Michele. 2011. "Egypt's Draft Constitutional Amendments Answer Some Questions and Raise Others," Carnegie Endowment for International Peace, available at http://www.carnegieendowment.org/2011/03/01/egypt-s-draft-constitutional-amendments-answer-some-questions-and-raise-others/fr.

Brown, Nathan, Dunne, Michele, and Hamzawy, Amr. 2007. "Egypt's Controversial Constitutional Amendments," Carnegie Endowment for International Peace, available at http://www.carnegieendowment.org/files/egypt_constitution_webcommentary01.pdf.

Brown, Nathan and Stilt, Kristen. 2011. "A Haphazard Constitutional Compromise," Carnegie Endowment for International Peace, available at http://www.carnegieendowment.org/2011/04/11/haphazard-constitutional-compromise/2q1.

Daly, M. W. (ed.). 1998. *The Cambridge History of Egypt: Volume Two: Modern Egypt from 1517 to the End of the Twentieth Century*. Cambridge: Cambridge University Press.

Hamzawy, Amr. 2007. "Political Motivations," Carnegie Endowment for International Peace, available at http://www.carnegieendowment.org/files/egypt_constitution_webcommen tary01.pdf.

Kienle, Eberhard. 2001. *A Grand Delusion: Democracy and Economic Reform in Egypt*. New York: I. B. Tauris.

Lombardi, Clark. 2006. *State Law as Islamic Law in Modern Egypt*. Leiden; Boston: Brill.

Moustafa, Tamir. 2007. *The Struggle for Constitutional Power*. New York: Cambridge University Press.

Moustafa, Tamir. 2011. "It's Not a Revolution Yet," The Middle East Channel, available at http://mideast.foreignpolicy.com/posts/2011/02/28/it_s_not_a_revolution_yet.

Roussillon, Alain. 1988. "Republican Egypt: Revolution and Beyond," in M. W. Daly, ed., *The Cambridge History of Egypt: Volume Two: Modern Egypt from 1517 to the End of the Twentieth Century*. Cambridge: Cambridge University Press, pp. 334–93.

Rutherford, Bruce. 2008. *Egypt after Mubarak*. Princeton, NJ: Princeton University Press.

Stilt, Kristen. 2006. "Constitutional Authority and Subversion: Egypt's New Presidential Election System." *Indiana International and Comparative Law Review* 16: 335–73.

Stilt, Kristen. 2010. "'Islam Is the Solution': Constitutional Visions of the Egyptian Muslim Brotherhood." *Texas International Law Journal* 46: 73–108.

Stilt, Kristen. 2011. "What the Egyptian Constitutional Amendment Referendum Is Really About," available at http://www.comparativeconstitutions.org/2011/03/dispatch-from-cairo-what-egyptian.html.

Stilt, Kristen. 2012. "The End of 'One Hand': The Egyptian Constitutional Declaration and the Rift between the 'People' and the Supreme Council of the Armed Forces." *Yearbook of Islamic and Middle Eastern Law* 16: 43–52.

Waterbury, John. 1983. *The Egypt of Nasser and Sadat: Law, Politics, and Economic Development in Egypt*. Princeton, NJ: Princeton University Press.

PART III

Contents of Authoritarian Constitutions

7

The Content of Authoritarian Constitutions

Zachary Elkins, Tom Ginsburg, and James Melton

"What is the difference," went an old joke in the Soviet Union, "between the Soviet and U.S. constitutions? The Soviet constitution guarantees freedom of speech; the U.S. constitution guarantees freedom *after* speech." The joke captures the common intuition about the function (or *dysfunction*, rather) of constitutions in authoritarian regimes. Many other examples abound: citizens of North Korea might be surprised to learn that they are guaranteed rights to free speech, assembly, and association,[1] while the constitution of Niger guarantees each citizen the right to health and education, notwithstanding the fact that the country ranks 182nd out of 182 countries rated by the Human Development Index.[2]

If we are to generalize from these phenomena, we might expect that there is little difference between constitutions written by dictators and those written by democrats. There is certainly anecdotal evidence to support this expectation. The entrenchment of human rights in constitutions has been nearly universal, with both authoritarian and democratic constitutions incorporating an increasing number of rights. Similarly, the vast majority of constitutions at least mention the word "democracy" (approximately 90 percent of those in force in 2006). We are not the first to note the commonality between institutions in authoritarian and democratic regimes. An entire literature in comparative politics has evolved to understand why dictators adopt multiparty legislatures (Gandhi and Przeworski 2007), elections (Schedler 2006), and relatively autonomous judiciaries (Ginsburg and Moustafa 2008). In general, it is thought that such institutions provide information that is used by dictators to prolong their tenure.

It seems that, on paper, dictatorship looks remarkably similar to democracy, at least that is the presumption in much of the scholarly literature (for an exception, see Brown 2002). Still, a casual inspection of authoritarian constitutions reveals some

[1] Art. 67, "Citizens shall have freedom of speech, press, assembly, demonstration, and association."
[2] Art. 11. Human Development Index 2009.

very apparent and very important differences. For instance, the Soviet constitutions left little doubt that the communist party was the "leading and guiding force of Soviet society" (1977 constitution; Brown 2002: 6). The preamble of North Korea's constitution declares Kim Il-Sung's genius, a reflection of the personality cult of politics in that country. Coup makers routinely adopt interim constitutions that explicitly suspend the regular operations of government institutions and instead agglomerate power to a junta or revolutionary council. Each of these examples suggests a concentration of (executive) power, a key indicator of authoritarian rule. Is this a general feature of constitutions written by dictators or a stereotype based on a few well-known examples (e.g., the Soviet Union and North Korea)? One cannot answer this question without a systematic, cross-national investigation of the content of authoritarian constitutions.

This inquiry is relevant not only to our understanding of the regime practices of authoritarianism and of institutional convergence but also to our understanding of the conditions under which formal constitutions correspond with reality. The Soviet joke highlights the common assumption that law only "matters" if it matches reality. However, this assumption is too simplistic. Most would probably describe the constitutions of North Korea or the USSR as façades or "window dressing" because each guaranteed the protection of human rights that were later repressed by public officials. However, as those examples illustrate, even facade constitutions can give some clues as to actual political practice. Take the 1936 constitution of the Soviet Union, for instance. The rights guaranteed in that constitution were oppressed, often brutally, but the institutional provisions – the "operating manual" – were taken seriously in some moments (Getty 1991). In short, it is readily apparent that some parts of authoritarian constitutions match reality while others are meaningless. Understanding where differences between authoritarian and democratic constitutions exist can give some indication about which sections are likely to match practice and which do not.

In this chapter, we examine the formal characteristics of constitutions and use the Comparative Constitutions Project (CCP) database to engage some basic comparisons of authoritarian and democratic constitutions. The CCP records data on more than 600 different features of constitutions, including government structure, rights, and form. If the Soviet joke is correct, we should see no systematic differences between constitutions in authoritarian and democratic regimes. Alternatively, we might find that there are systematic differences across regime type, controlling for other factors that are determinative of the contents of constitutional text, such as region, era, and colonial heritage (Elkins, Ginsburg, and Melton 2009). One way to summarize these intuitions is as follows: if all provisions in constitutions were operating manuals, we would expect that democratic and authoritarian constitutions would diverge. If all provisions were window dressing, we might expect convergence. Oddly, if we find that constitutional *texts* are similar across regime type, it implies that the *practices* of constitution making may be playing very different functions.

The same terms may be genuine promises in democracies and mere obfuscation or window dressing in the authoritarian context.

This chapter is organized as follows. We first develop the concept of the authoritarian constitution. We then provide our theory, which is that authoritarian constitutions will differ from democratic ones with regard to institutional structures but not necessarily with regard to rights provisions. Our expectation is of selective or partial convergence. We next examine the empirical evidence, finding that there are very few statistically significant differences between authoritarian and democratic constitutions when controlling for other factors. In addition, the magnitude of the observed differences is small: an authoritarian constitution will have only marginally fewer rights, specificity, or judicial independence than will a democratic constitution. We find, somewhat surprisingly, that there is less formal executive power in authoritarian constitutions. Moreover, we find evidence that authoritarian constitutions tend to converge toward democratic constitutions over time. We speculate that this indicates a continual process of lagged adaptation by authoritarians, who seek to model their texts on those of their democratic counterparts. Democrats innovate in the formal constitution, while dictators tend to imitate formal democratic institutions, saving their innovations for the informal realm. Our findings provide evidence that regime type is a relatively minor determinant of the form of constitutions relative to region, era, and the constitutional legacy of the country.

WHAT IS AN "AUTHORITARIAN" CONSTITUTION?

The concept of an authoritarian constitution is not self-defining. To begin, it should be obvious by now – though it is worth emphasizing – that we do not classify authoritarian constitutions as such based on what they say; on the contrary, understanding what they say is our very goal. Rather, we mean the term to refer to constitutions drafted by dictators, but even then, a number of conceptual challenges lurk beyond that seemingly straightforward idea. One important challenge is that of timing, inasmuch as the characterization of drafters during a constitutional moment may not be representative of their true colors. Rather than a snapshot, we might look for a *pattern* of behavior over time in order to distinguish a consolidated dictatorship from episodes of authoritarian behavior (i.e., an authoritarian "situation" [O'Donnell et al. 1986]). In that sense, a look further back in a ruler's track record might provide a better sense of regime type, but so too would looking forward at his future behavior, which at least in a retrospective study we have the luxury to do. But if a constitution lasts long enough such that its stewards display both authoritarian and democratic traits, interesting classification problems arise. If a "dictatorship" eventually transforms itself into a "democracy" (e.g., as in Mexico's 1917 constitution), was it truly a dictatorship (say, such as Libya's Gadhaffi), or would it make more sense to recognize the regime's dynamic character? Thus, one might identify the initial stewards of Mexico's 1917 document as dictators with democratic ambitions – a distinction that might have dramatic differences for what the leaders might have written into their formal constitution. Conversely, if seemingly democratic actors draft a constitution and then reveal themselves to be decidedly more authoritarian, how should we label their product? The Venezuelan constitution of 1999, written by Chavez during a comparably more democratic time, might be such an example.

Another way to think about the challenges of timing with respect to regimes and constitutions is to recognize that democrats and authoritarians, even after an abrupt regime change, sometimes share the same constitution. That democrats and authoritarians work under the same institutional framework may simply be an interesting phenomenon, but it may also alter the way we characterize the constitution and its authors. Consider the 1980 constitution of Chile, drafted by the Pinochet government. Few would suggest that the Pinochet regime was anything less than authoritarian across most dimensions. Still, compelling accounts of the Pinochet-authored constitution and its implementation suggest that the document was designed *not* to perpetuate that rule but to provide for an orderly transition to democracy by entrenching a downstream veto point for the military (e.g., Barros 2002). In fact, the constitution oversaw the return to democracy and continues to govern Chile, albeit with significant amendments. Is a constitution "authoritarian" if it began its life under an authoritarian situation but evolved to reflect, ultimately, many of the document's democratic promises?

Of course, related to the difficulty in fixing the character of an evolving regime are the well-known challenges that come with the conceptualization and measurement of the root concepts themselves. It is very likely that each of the two categories includes cases with considerable variation across important dimensions. The literature on the conceptualization and measurement of democracy and authoritarianism makes this variation abundantly clear (e.g., Collier and Adcock 1999; Collier and Levitsky 1997; Linz 1978; Munck and Verkuilen 2002). The within-class variation is manifest, among other dimensions, in the level of competitiveness or inclusion, as well as in the architecture of formal structures, such as whether the central power takes the form of a political party, a monarch, or a junta.

To fix ideas, we treat regime type as a binary concept and measure it, using the Unified Democracy Scores (UDS) (Pemstein et al. 2010).[3] Conceptualizing

[3] We use the UDS because constitutions are often promulgated during periods of political transition, when individual measures of democracy are most likely to give divergent estimates about the level of democracy. The UDS gives a more reliable estimate of the level of democracy during these periods because it utilizes information from multiple measures, weighting those measures based on their reliability. In choosing to use the UDS, we had two important measurement decisions to make: (1) the cut-point to use for transforming the continuous UDS into a binary measure and (2) whether and (if so) how to impute the UDS for the time period from 1789 to 1946.

For the former decision, we use a cut-point of 0.16 because this is the point where Przeworski et al.'s (2000) measure of democracy falls on the UDS. Thus, country-years with a UDS score greater than or equal to 0.16 are coded as democratic, and country-years with a UDS score less than 0.16 are coded as authoritarian.

democracy as binary allows us to demarcate clearly the periods of authoritarian rule and regime transition and facilitates a simple operational definition of an authoritarian constitution: *an authoritarian [democratic] constitution is one that was promulgated in a year in which its country was coded as authoritarian [democratic].*

Each constitutional system is examined in the year it was adopted, ignoring subsequent amendments to and shifting interpretations of the system.[4] Focusing on the inaugural draft, of course, ignores the fluid nature of constitutional systems, which often grow by accretion and could be argued to be written and rewritten constantly. Still, a focus on the constitutional system's inaugural draft ensures that we match the writing with its authors. Admittedly, even inaugural drafts will contain many ideas not conceived by the authors (constitutions are heavily borrowed instruments, after all). Still, an inaugural draft is arguably the document most associated with the actors in power, who, at a minimum, have the ability to pick and choose what they borrow from other constitutions.

An alternative conceptualization of "the constitution" might entail some sort of country-year analysis, in which one would connect the constitution in force with the regime type in any given year. In that sense, the Mexican constitution would have been an authoritarian one in 1993 but a democratic one in 1995. This sort of approach is too fluid; it assumes that leaders reevaluate their constitution regularly and ignores the costs associated with constitutional change (see Elkins et al. 2009). Constitutions are quite sticky (i.e., they exhibit a high degree of serial correlation), so evaluating the initial version makes sense with respect to the analytical issues associated with time dependence. Otherwise, long-lived constitutional systems would flood the analysis with observations dependent on one another.

Defining a constitution as we do, we find that a vast majority of them since 1789 could be considered authoritarian: a whopping 695 of the 846 constitutional systems for which we have data on regime type.[5] Not surprisingly, the share of constitutions "born democratic" at any given time has increased with the rise of democracy itself over this period (see Figure 7.1). As of 2008, 44 percent (79) of the world's constitutions in force are categorized as democratic and the remaining

For the imputation decision, we decided to impute the UDS. To do so, we used Amelia II (King et al. 2001) to impute ten data sets using the three measures of democracy that span back to 1800 (i.e., Boix and Rosato [2012], Polity [Marshall et al. 2011], and VanHanen [2002]), year, and all possible interactions between these variables as covariates in the imputation. We assessed the reliability of the imputed data by comparing the imputed data to Boix and Rosato's (2012) measure of regime type and a binary version of Polity (Marshall et al. 2011) – using a cut-point of 6. Of the 310 constitutions promulgated from 1800 to 1946, the three measures only categorize the regime type of fourteen constitutions differently (~5%). The decision to use the UDS over other measures of democracy matters much more in the 1946 through 2008 time period. During the later time period, 57 out of 434 (~13%) constitutions are not classified the same by all three measures.

4 We follow Elkins et al. (2009) in our definition of a constitutional system. Thus, a new "system" incorporates an original draft as well as any amendments and nontextual modifications.

5 The universe of constitutional systems from 1789 to 2008 numbers 911; we have regime-type data for 846 of these.

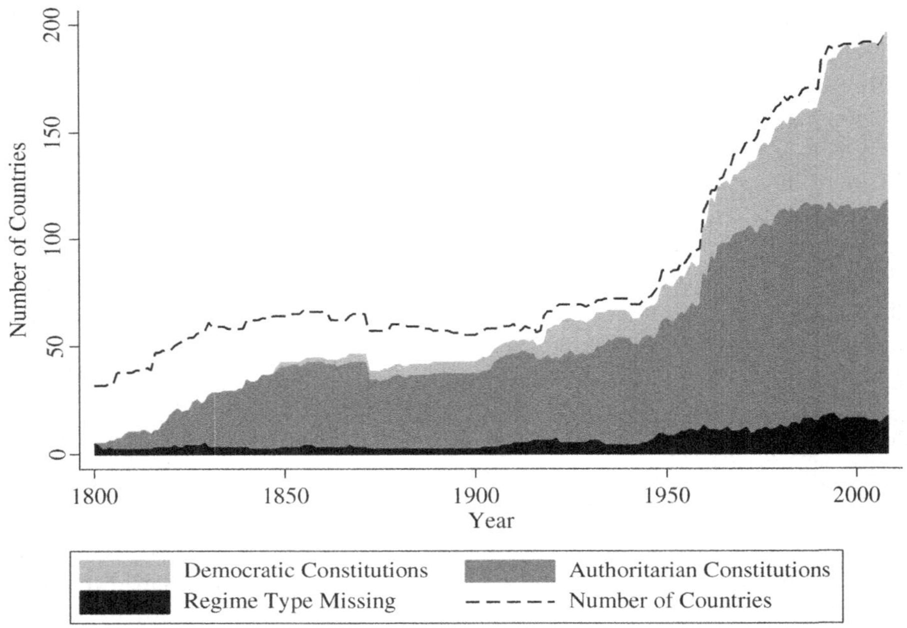

FIGURE 7.1. Number of Constitutions Born Authoritarian or Democratic. *Universe: 907 constitutions promulgated in independent states from 1800 to 2008.*

56 percent (99) categorized as authoritarian.[6] Even in an indisputably democratic moment, almost three fifths of constitutions in force are "authoritarian." Hardly an exotic species, "authoritarians" are apparently the garden-variety constitution.

On its face, there is something profoundly alarming about this balance. In part, the skewed distribution may stem from a preponderance of authoritarian regime-years in the sample (i.e., in statistical terms, an issue of increased exposure). Today, fewer than half of the world's countries are considered authoritarian, but for most of the modern constitutional era, authoritarian regimes were the norm. Before the third wave of democracy, roughly 80 percent of countries were considered authoritarian, and throughout much of the nineteenth century, when the first modern constitutions were written, more than 90 percent of independent countries were considered authoritarian.

However, the prevalence of authoritarian regimes over the last 225 years is only part of the story. The large number of authoritarian constitutions also reflects differences in fertility across regime types. Authoritarians tend to exhibit a stronger appetite for constitutional replacement than do democrats. Indeed, authoritarians are not only more likely to rewrite a *democratic* constitution but they are also more likely

[6] Fifteen constitutions are uncategorized because of missing data on regime type.

to rewrite their own – that is, one drafted by themselves or another authoritarian leader. A democratic constitution has a 0.14 probability of being replaced by an authoritarian leader in any given country-year, compared with a 0.05 probability that a democratic leader will replace an authoritarian constitution. Looking within regimes, authoritarian leaders replace authoritarian constitutions with a probability of 0.05, while the probability that a democratic leader will replace a democratically written constitution is only 0.01.

The probabilities in the previous paragraph corroborate our earlier work on the repudiation or retention of constitutions drafted by the *other* regime (Elkins et al. 2009). In a highly specified model that assesses the effect of regime change on replacement within two years of the change, we estimate a replacement rate of about 0.03 for constitutions following a regime change in either direction, but they find that democratic transitions trigger replacement slightly more frequently than do authoritarian ones. It is important to revisit this subtopic here, if only because it serves as another criterion by which to narrow the broad field of authoritarians to hardline – or at least nontransplantable – authoritarians. One would expect, perhaps, that a truly authoritarian product is one that would *not* be retained and reused by a subsequent democratic group, though of course there are reasons other than content that might lead democrats – through negotiation or duress – to retain authoritarian products (again, the Pinochet constitution provides an example). Figure 7.2 provides some sense of the distribution of constitutions based on these criteria over time. The large dark-gray area in the middle represents what we might think of as the "intolerable" authoritarian documents – that is, those that were born authoritarian and did not survive the transition to democracy (i.e., they were repudiated by the new democrats). The smaller light-gray area below "intolerable" authoritarian constitutions represents those constitutions that were written by authoritarian leaders but survived a transition to democracy at some point in their life span. Although this smaller group makes up only 10 percent of historical constitutions, nearly 20 percent of constitutions in force today are of this variety.

These data contain many potentially interesting digressions, but let us recap and refocus. We discover that a large percentage of historical constitutions is, by the measure discussed, authoritarian. One analytic implication of this large population is that it may be worth analyzing and describing subtypes. In particular, in an effort to maximize differences between democratic and authoritarian constitutions, it may be useful to isolate (and study) "hardline" authoritarian constitutions. We can define this category as containing constitutions that were born authoritarian and either subsequently replaced by democrats who assume control after a regime transition or are still in force today. Such constitutions are, arguably, more obviously the work of authoritarians if the behavior of democrats is any guide.[7]

[7] We combine democratic constitutions that experience a regime transition and those that do not into one category because there are so few that survive a regime transition (only two in force in 2008).

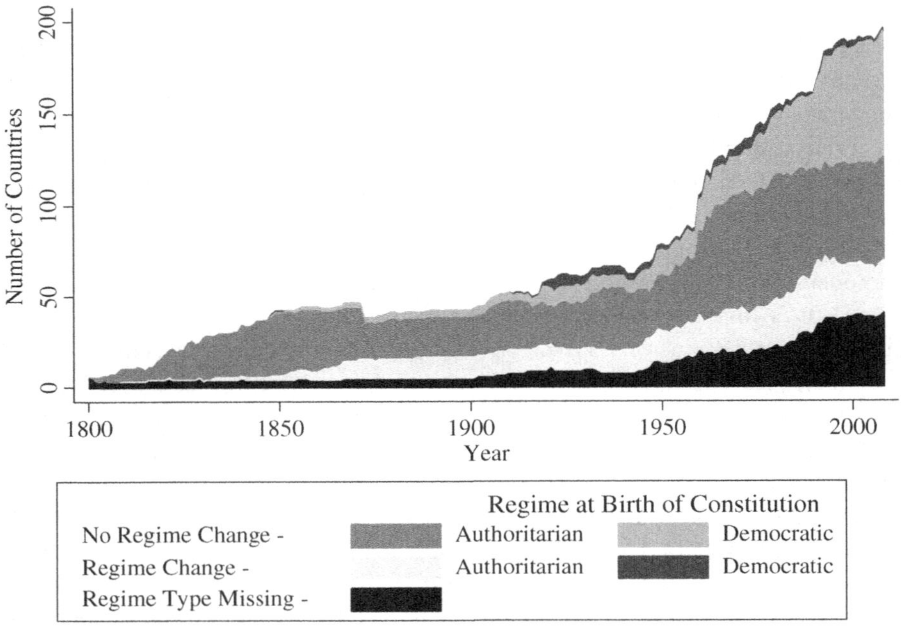

FIGURE 7.2. Number of Constitutions Born Authoritarian or Democratic by Subsequent Regime Change. *Universe: 907 constitutions promulgated in independent states from 1800–2008. Illustration*: Constitutions that are "born democratic with no regime change" are those that were promulgated in a democratic setting and spent their entire history in a democratic setting. Those "born democratic with regime change" were promulgated in a democracy but lived under authoritarianism as well. And so on.

THEORY: WHY (AND HOW) MIGHT AUTHORITARIAN CONSTITUTIONS BE DIFFERENT?

Scholars and practitioners alike have come to associate constitutions with democracy. For these individuals, the idea of an authoritarian constitution may sound farcical. However, as we describe shortly, *some* of the basic objectives of constitution making do not vary appreciably across regime type. Most writing on constitutions ascribes a relatively small number of functions to them. A central one is precommitment: "becoming committed, bound or obligated to some course of action or inaction or to some constraint on future action . . . to influence someone else's choices" (Schelling 2006: 1). While authoritarians, at least those with long time horizons, may have less need for formal precommitment devices than would democrats who are certain to be replaced (at least by other democrats) at some point, they still need to make credible promises to their supporters, and constitutions might be one mechanism for doing so.

Written constitutions are also symbolically costly and, as a result, can serve as signals of the actual intentions of the rulers. Beyond their role in establishing institutions, constitutions are "billboards" that can emit communicative signals of government policy (Yu 2010). They play this function because they are politically encumbering. Constitutions are typically, though not always, more entrenched than ordinary law, which means they are also more costly to change. Even if not manifestly entrenched (because of capricious decision making by authoritarians), constitutions are "hallowed vessels" and adorned with political and ceremonial weight. Drafting a constitution consumes significant political energy on the part of the governing elite and provides a repository of regime rhetoric. The costly nature of constitution making supports the idea that a constitution can be a credible signal of political intentions, even for autocrats.

Another purpose of constitutions in authoritarian regimes is to serve as a simple coordination device among the elites within the regime (Barros 2002). In any political system, the relevant subjects of the constitution need to coordinate among themselves about the prerogatives and limits of power. The subjects may have strong shared intuitions about these matters, but they may not have intersubjective agreement on the precise definitions of what counts as an abuse or on procedures for identifying and punishing violations. A written constitution can provide a focal point to generate this intersubjective understanding (Carey 2000; Hardin 1989; Ordeshook 1992; Przeworski 1991; Weingast 1997). Intersubjective understanding is a necessary, though not sufficient, condition for the enforcement of constitutional terms.

These functions of precommitment, signaling, and coordination suggest where we might observe differences in formal constitutions across regime type. Consider first the distinction between, on the one hand, constitutional rules that describe and empower institutions and on the other, rights provisions and limitations on government. Some autocracies might adopt rights as "cheap talk," but on balance, we should expect that autocracies would be less willing to adopt formal limitations on government power, such as judicial checks. However, even autocracies need established rules to coordinate the ruling elite. We thus might expect that there will be a greater congruence between text and practice in the authoritarian setting with regard to governmental institutions. This might lead us to expect that authoritarian regimes would have more executive power and less judicial power than democracies. We also might expect less formal power of the legislature, which is generally associated with democratic rule.

The intuition is consistent with the idea that constitutions matter in terms of setting up institutions that will then be able to act in their own defense, but constitutions cannot serve to protect rights any more than the "people themselves" demand. A related argument is that the text matters by initiating basic institutions and reducing decision costs for choices that do not matter very much (Strauss 2003). One might call this the *institutional priority* thesis. Every regime needs to have institutions, and even the worst dictator may want to establish formal bodies that match conventional categories: an executive, a legislature, courts. Rights provisions, on the other hand, may be more a matter of fashion and whim, in which cheap talk might be a dominant motivation for dictators.

The expectation that constitutions matter more for institutional design than rights accords with the Madisonian point that institutional structures are themselves important instruments for the protection of liberty. All regimes, whether democratic or autocratic, must rely on a coalition of supporters, but the size of this group varies from country to country (Bueno de Mesquita et al. 2003). Winning coalitions need to coordinate their own expectations internally about the mechanisms of rule, and constitutions can play an important role in aligning such expectations. But the importance of different constitutional mechanisms may vary across regime type. Rights limitations may only be important when the winning coalition is large (i.e., in democracies), because small winning coalitions have less trouble solving the collective action problem and punishing executives that violate the bargain. Institutional limits, on the other hand, may be important everywhere, since every winning coalition needs some rules to restrain the leader.

For many, civil and political rights constitute a central dimension of the concept of democracy. Certainly, some scholars adopt a narrower, procedural definition that excludes rights, but even these scholars will likely admit to a strong elective affinity between rights and democracy, if not a definitional one. We therefore expect authoritarian constitutions – almost by definition – to include fewer rights. Although we are mindful of the conditional hypothesis that it is precisely this area of the constitution (rights) in which authoritarians are likely to misrepresent themselves, we believe the expected probability that constitutional rights will be enforced at some future point in is greater than zero, regardless of regime type. As a result, even authoritarian regimes face an expected cost from the entrenching rights in their constitutions and will do so only sparingly and when there is an expected benefit (e.g., signaling a commitment to human rights to international audiences).

Consider another variable: constitutional specificity (Elkins et al. 2009). We use this concept to capture the breadth and depth of constitutional language; we refer to these as scope and detail, respectively. We assume that specifying details in the constitution is costly and so is only undertaken in response to real needs of some kind. One of the major determinants of constitutional specificity is audience heterogeneity (Ginsburg 2010). If all subjects of the constitution share a set of baseline and unwritten understandings about politics, there is less need to articulate details in the formal text. On the other hand, when audiences are heterogeneous, we should expect that there will be a greater need for formal mechanisms of coordination. *Ceteris paribus*, democratic constitutions have more heterogeneous audiences than do autocratic constitutions: the winning coalition is larger and less bound by shared ideological or normative commitments. One would thus expect that there would be higher levels of constitutional specificity in democratic constitutions.

To summarize, we expect authoritarian constitutions to be less specific, protect fewer rights, give the executive more power and the legislature less power, and provide for less judicial independence. Since we expect that the fit between text and practice will be tighter in the institutional arena as opposed to the rights arena, we expect that any differences between regimes in the latter category will be more muted.

OPERATIONALIZING CONSTITUTIONAL ATTRIBUTES

We operationalize many of the concepts discussed previously, using indices developed by the principal investigators of the Comparative Constitutions Project (CCP). For instance, to measure executive power, we use a measure developed in an earlier paper (2011), in which we create an additive index that captures how many of the following powers are granted to the executive: initiate legislation, issue decrees, declare states of emergency, propose amendments to the constitution, veto legislation, challenge the constitutionality of legislation, and dissolve the legislature.[8] In addition, we use a measure of judicial independence created by Ginsburg and Melton (2013). The measure is additive and captures the number of aspects of the constitution that are generally thought to enhance the autonomy of the judiciary: an explicit declaration of independence, selection, and removal procedures that involve multiple bodies, whether the conditions on which judges can be removed from office are explicitly mentioned, life tenure for judges, and protection of judges' salaries. Lastly, we use two measures of specificity developed in our earlier book. The first measure is scope, which is the percentage of topics addressed in the constitution out of a set of fifty-eight key topics from the CCP's survey instrument; the second measure is detail, which is the number of scope topics addressed in the constitution divided by the length (in words) of the constitution.

In addition to the measures created by Elkins, Ginsburg, and Melton, we create two new measures of constitutional rights. The CCP's survey instrument asks about the presence of 116 constitutional rights. Recall that we expect dictators to only adopt rights when there is some benefit from doing so. One such benefit is to signal their commitment to international human rights norms. Thus, we suspect that authoritarian leaders can signal this commitment by adopting rights that are commonly agreed on by the international community. As a result, they are more likely to incorporate rights commonly found in other countries' constitutions and are less likely to incorporate rights found only rarely in other countries' constitutions. To test this hypothesis, we need measures of "common" rights and "rare" rights. We consider a right "common" if it is incorporated into half or more of the constitutions in force at the time a constitution is drafted. We consider a right "rare" if it is incorporated into fewer than half of the constitutions in force at the time a constitution is drafted.

[8] The measure of executive power described in Elkins et al.'s (2011) aggregates the subcomponents of the measure using weights derived inductively from a regression model. Here, we adopt an unweighted version of that measure, because the sample in this paper is drastically different from that elaborated in Elkins et al.'s (2011).

We then measure the percentage of common and rare rights incorporated each constitution. Notably, the number of common and rare rights (the denominator when calculating this percentage) depends on when the constitution is promulgated. For instance, in 1850, only 10 of the 116 rights recorded by the CCP are counted as common, but by 2008, the number of common rights had increased to 40, a fourfold increase.

These indices, six in total, constitute the set of dependent variables for the analyses conducted below. Each is rescaled to range from 0 to 1, with higher values indicating more of the titular dimension. The summary statistics for each are provided in Table 7.1. The middle columns in the table provide the summary statistics for authoritarian constitutions, and the columns on the right provide the summary statistics for democratic constitutions. Looking at the means in Table 7.1, there are already a few notable differences between authoritarian and democratic constitutions. The largest differences are related to judicial independence and rare rights, where the means differ by about 0.11. The smallest difference between the means is for executive power, where the means differ by only 0.03. This initial look at the data suggests that executives are granted about the same amount of power regardless of regime type but that there are fewer explicit limits on their power in authoritarian constitutions. This is preliminary evidence to support the hypotheses presented above. In the next section, we use regression analysis to assess if the differences in means reported in Table 7.1 are robust to conditioning on the effect of several factors typically associated with the contents of constitutions (e.g., region, period, and constitutional history).

REGRESSION MODELS

We assess the validity of the hypotheses by regressing the six *de jure* indices listed in Table 7.1 on the regime type of the constitution. The unit of analysis in the models below is the constitution. Each model includes an indicator of the constitution's regime type and some control variables to account for other factors we associate with the contents of constitutions.

We use two measures of regime type, both of which were discussed previously. Our primary measure is binary and coded 1 if the country is coded as authoritarian in the year the constitution was promulgated. The secondary measure captures differences between authoritarian constitutions that experience a transition to democracy and those that do not. We include two binary variables to capture the difference between these two types of authoritarian constitutions. For all of the models estimated in the following discussion, the reference category for the authoritarian constitution variable(s) is constitutions promulgated in democratic country-years.

We include several variables to control for factors that we generally associated with the contents of constitutions. Region is associated with a number of variables that one might suspect affect the contents of constitutions (e.g., colonial heritage, legal

TABLE 7.1. *Summary statistics for constitutional attributes*

	Authoritarian constitutions				Democratic constitutions			
Constitutional attribute	Mean	S.D.	Range	Obs.	Mean	S.D.	Range	Obs.
Executive Power	0.53	0.24	0.00–1.00	546	0.56	0.24	0.00–1.00	136
Judicial Independence	0.26	0.21	0.00–1.00	546	0.37	0.25	0.00–1.00	136
Common Rights	0.72	0.22	0.00–1.00	546	0.77	0.22	0.03–1.00	136
Rare Rights	0.16	0.11	0.00–0.59	546	0.27	0.14	0.00–0.62	136
Scope	0.49	0.11	0.09–0.74	546	0.55	0.10	0.23–0.80	136
Detail	0.09	0.07	0.01–0.65	537	0.16	0.11	0.03–0.51	135

origin, religion, etc.). We include a series of binary variables for different regions (Latin America is the reference category) to help control for all of these factors while saving as many degrees of freedom as possible. Countries' constitutional histories also have a strong influence on the content of their present constitutions. Constitutional provisions tend to favor some individuals' interests over others, so once an attribute is entrenched, it often exhibits a high degree of path dependence, as those who are benefited by a provision fight for its continued inclusion. To control for this path dependence, we include the value of the dependent variable from the countries' previous constitutions as an independent variable.[9] Yet another factor associated with a constitution's contents is the time period in which it is written. Certain constitutional provisions are fashionable in some time periods and not others. Take constitutional rights, for instance. We already noted that many more rights are included in constitutions today than were included in constitutions 200 years ago. To control for period effects, we include year fixed effects in many of the estimates reported below. Lastly, we include country random effects and robust standard errors clustered on country to account for unobserved heterogeneity between countries in the constitutional attributes.[10]

Tables 7.2 through 7.5 report the results of the regression models. In general, we estimate three models for each constitutional attribute. The first reports the results when only a binary variable for authoritarian constitutions is included in the model, the second adds covariates to the model, and the third breaks authoritarian constitutions into those that experience a transition and those that do not. The next four sections describe the results of these models for the different constitutional attributes.

Executive Power

Table 7.2 assesses if executive power is affected by a constitution's regime type. Only in model 1 are authoritarian constitutions significantly different from democratic

9 The lagged dependent variable is missing for each country's first constitution. Rather than omitting all of these observations because of listwise deletion, we substitute our best estimate of the expected level of the dependent variable for countries' first constitutions: the mean level of the dependent variable from all other constitutions in force the year prior to promulgation of the first constitution. To illustrate, Brazil's first constitution was written in 1824, so the lagged value of executive power is missing for Brazil's constitution of 1824. To ensure this constitution is included in the analysis, we replace the missing value for executive power with 0.29, which is the mean level of executive power in all constitutions in force in 1823.

10 Typically, one does not include country random effects and a lagged dependent variable in the same model because the lagged dependent variable is presumed to be correlated with the random effect in the error term, which can introduce bias into the coefficient estimates. Recent research finds that, although such estimators are not unbiased, they are consistent (Ashley 2010). Thus, we include a random-effects term in our main model because we have a relatively large sample and want to control for unobserved heterogeneity between countries without the inefficiency associated with fixed effects.

TABLE 7.2. *Effect of regime-type at drafting on executive power (1800–2008)*

Variables	(1)	(2)	(3)
Authoritarian constitution	−0.05*	0.01	
	(0.03)	(0.03)	
Auth. Const. (w/ Transition)			0.05
			(0.05)
Auth. Const. (No Transition)			0.01
			(0.03)
Executive Power$_{(t-1)}$		0.19***	0.21***
		(0.06)	(0.06)
Western Europe		0.10**	0.10*
		(0.05)	(0.05)
Eastern Europe		0.06	0.07*
		(0.04)	(0.04)
Sub-Saharan Africa		0.04	0.05
		(0.05)	(0.05)
Middle East/N. Africa		0.16*	0.17**
		(0.08)	(0.08)
South Asia		−0.07	−0.07
		(0.07)	(0.07)
East Asia		−0.12*	−0.12*
		(0.06)	(0.06)
Oceania		−0.18***	−0.17**
		(0.07)	(0.07)
ρ	0.19	0.30	0.26
R^2	0.01	0.43	0.45
Year FE		Y	Y
Countries	189	173	169
Observations	682	526	515

Notes: Coefficient estimates are from ordinary least squares models with country random-effects. Clustered, robust standard errors are in parentheses. Statistical significance is denoted as follows: $p < 0.1$ = *; $p < 0.05$ = **; $p < 0.01$ = ***.

constitutions. Perhaps surprisingly, the coefficient estimate in model 1 is negative, which suggests that dictators might provide themselves slightly less constitutional power (on average) than democratic leaders. However, this effect is small and not robust. When covariates are included in models 2 and 3, authoritarian constitutions are expected to include more executive power than democratic constitutions, but this effect is not statistically significant. Thus, there is little evidence that executive power varies much between constitutions written by dictators and those written by democrats. Factors like the level of executive power in a country's past constitutions, region, and period are far better predictors of executive power than regime type.

TABLE 7.3. *Effect of regime-type at drafting on judicial independence (1800–2008)*

Variables	(4)	(5)	(6)
Authoritarian Constitution	−0.13***	−0.10***	
	(0.02)	(0.04)	
Auth. Const. (w/ Transition)			0.00
			(0.05)
Auth. Const. (No Transition)			−0.17***
			(0.04)
Judicial Independence$_{(t-1)}$		0.23***	0.23***
		(0.06)	(0.07)
Western Europe		−0.03	0.03
		(0.05)	(0.07)
Eastern Europe		0.03	0.09
		(0.05)	(0.06)
Sub-Saharan Africa		0.06	0.11**
		(0.05)	(0.05)
Middle East/N. Africa		0.04	0.15**
		(0.06)	(0.07)
South Asia		0.23***	0.27***
		(0.09)	(0.08)
East Asia		−0.04	0.03
		(0.05)	(0.05)
Oceania		0.13	0.13
		(0.10)	(0.09)
ρ	0.19	0.25	0.31
R^2	0.03	0.43	0.39
Year FE		Y	Y
Countries	189	173	151
Observations	682	526	318

Notes: Coefficient estimates are from ordinary least squares models with country random-effects. Clustered, robust standard errors are in parentheses. Statistical significance is denoted as follows: $p < 0.1 = {}^{*}$; $p < 0.05 = {}^{**}$; $p < 0.01 = {}^{***}$.

Judicial Independence

Table 7.3 assesses how the autonomy of the judiciary is affected by a constitution's regime type. Judiciaries are granted far less autonomy in authoritarian constitutions than in democratic constitutions. This effect is consistent across models 4 and 5. Model 6 suggests that this effect is present only in constitutions that never experience a transition to democracy. Authoritarian constitutions that never experience a transition to democracy score −0.17 less than democratic constitutions on the measure of judicial independence used here. In other words, hardline dictators include (on average) one fewer protection of judicial autonomy than democrats in their constitutions. This leaves hardline dictators a gap in the judiciary's protection that,

TABLE 7.4. *Effect of regime-type at drafting on rights (1800–2008)*

	Common rights (≥50% of consts.)			Rare rights (<50% of consts.)		
Variables	(7)	(8)	(9)	(10)	(11)	(12)
Authoritarian Constitution	−0.05**	−0.02		−0.12***	−0.04***	
	(0.02)	(0.03)		(0.02)	(0.02)	
Auth. Const. (w/ Transition)			0.04			0.03
			(0.03)			(0.02)
Auth. Const. (No Transition)			−0.05			−0.07***
			(0.04)			(0.02)
Common Rights$_{(t-1)}$		−0.01	−0.01		0.20***	0.20***
		(0.06)	(0.06)		(0.07)	(0.07)
Western Europe		−0.07	−0.08		−0.03	−0.02
		(0.06)	(0.06)		(0.03)	(0.03)
Eastern Europe		−0.09**	−0.08**		−0.03	−0.02
		(0.04)	(0.04)		(0.03)	(0.03)
Sub-Saharan Africa		−0.13***	−0.13***		−0.10***	−0.09***
		(0.03)	(0.03)		(0.02)	(0.02)
Middle East/N. Africa		−0.01	0.00		−0.09**	−0.07**
		(0.05)	(0.05)		(0.03)	(0.03)
South Asia		−0.17***	−0.17***		−0.10***	−0.10***
		(0.06)	(0.06)		(0.03)	(0.03)
East Asia		−0.19***	−0.19***		−0.09***	−0.08***
		(0.05)	(0.05)		(0.03)	(0.03)
Oceania		−0.03	−0.04		−0.07**	−0.09***
		(0.05)	(0.05)		(0.04)	(0.03)
ρ	0.13	0.00	0.00	0.18	0.08	0.06
R^2	0.01	0.36	0.38	0.11	0.61	0.64
Year FE		Y	Y		Y	Y
Countries	189	173	169	189	173	169
Observations	682	526	515	682	526	515

Notes: Coefficient estimates are from ordinary least squares models with country random-effects. Clustered, robust standard errors are in parentheses. Statistical significance is denoted as follows: $p < 0.1$ = *; $p < 0.05$ = **; $p < 0.01$ = ***.

if necessary, they can exploit to curtail its independence (Melton and Ginsburg 2013).

Constitutional Rights

Table 7.4 assesses the effect of authoritarian constitutions on constitutional rights. The dependent variable in models 7, 8, and 9 is the proportion of common rights in the constitution, and the dependent variable in models 10, 11, and 12 is the proportion of rare rights in the constitution. There is an interesting asymmetry between common rights and rare rights. The regime type of the constitution seems to have no effect

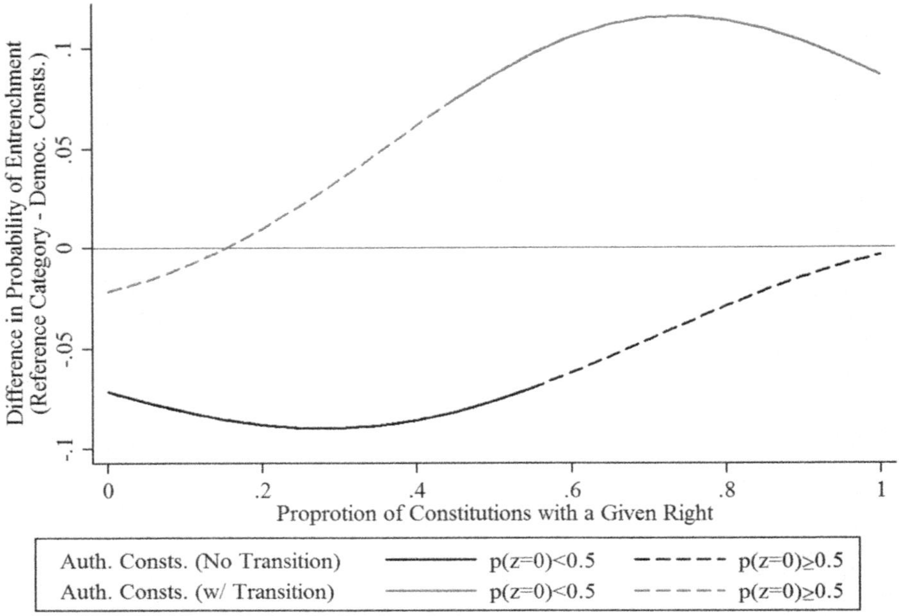

FIGURE 7.3. Effect by Rights and Subsequent Regime Change

on the proportion of common rights included in the constitution. The authoritarian constitution variable only has a statistically significant effect on the proportion of common rights in model 7, when no covariates are included in the model, and even in that model, the effect is small. The regime type of the drafter matters far more for rare rights. Dictators include far fewer rare rights in their constitutions than democrats. This effect is consistent across models 10, 11, and 12. The estimates in model 12 suggest that the proportion of rare rights is the fewest in authoritarian constitutions that do not experience a regime transition. Such constitutions have (on average) between five and seven fewer rare rights than do democratic constitutions.

Figure 7.3 captures the effect graphically. The figure shows the difference in the probability of adopting any given right between democracies and authoritarians that experience transition (in the upper line) and those that do not (the lower line). The *x*-axis is the general popularity of the right. As one can see, for some very popular rights, authoritarians that experience transition are actually *more* likely to adopt a right than are democracies on average. But stable authoritarians are never more likely to do so.

Specificity

Table 7.5 presents the last set of results. The table contains the estimates of the effect that authoritarian-drafted constitutions have on constitutional specificity. Scope is

TABLE 7.5. *Effect of regime-type at drafting on specificity (1800–2008)*

	Scope			Detail		
Variables	(13)	(14)	(15)	(16)	(17)	(18)
Authoritarian Constitution	−0.06***	−0.03**		−0.05***	−0.03***	
	(0.01)	(0.01)		(0.01)	(0.01)	
Auth. Const. (w/ Transition)			0.02			−0.01
			(0.02)			(0.02)
Auth. Const. (No Transition)			−0.04***			−0.05***
			(0.01)			(0.01)
$Scope_{(t-1)}$		0.15**	0.14**		0.16**	0.19***
		(0.07)	(0.07)		(0.07)	(0.07)
Western Europe		−0.02	−0.02		−0.07**	−0.07***
		(0.02)	(0.03)		(0.03)	(0.03)
Eastern Europe		−0.05**	−0.04**		−0.11***	−0.10***
		(0.02)	(0.02)		(0.02)	(0.02)
Sub-Saharan Africa		−0.06***	−0.06***		−0.04	−0.04
		(0.02)	(0.02)		(0.03)	(0.03)
Middle East/N. Africa		−0.01	−0.00		−0.10***	−0.09***
		(0.03)	(0.02)		(0.02)	(0.02)
South Asia		−0.04	−0.05		0.01	0.01
		(0.04)	(0.04)		(0.06)	(0.06)
East Asia		−0.08***	−0.08***		−0.07*	−0.06
		(0.02)	(0.02)		(0.03)	(0.03)
Oceania		−0.13***	−0.14***		0.07	0.06
		(0.03)	(0.03)		(0.05)	(0.05)
ρ	0.05	0.00	0.00	0.84	0.82	0.79
R^2	0.04	0.50	0.52	0.13	0.37	0.42
Year FE		Y	Y		Y	Y
Countries	189	173	169	188	169	165
Observations	682	526	515	672	511	500

Notes: Coefficient estimates are from ordinary least squares models with country random-effects. Clustered, robust standard errors are in parentheses. Statistical significance is denoted as follows: $p < 0.1 = *$; $p < 0.05 = **$; $p < 0.01 = ***$.

the dependent variable in models 13, 14, and 15, and detail is the dependent variable in models 16, 17, and 18. The results in Table 7.5 are very similar to those presented in Table 7.3, in which judicial independence is the dependent variable, and in Table 7.5 pertaining to rare rights. Authoritarian constitutions are significantly less specific than democratic constitutions. They cover fewer topics, and the topics they cover are addressed in less detail. Once again, the effect of authoritarian constitutions is limited to authoritarian constitutions that do not experience a transition to democracy. Notably, the findings related to specificity correspond to our general impression of constitutions written in authoritarian regimes: they tend to be relatively short.

Robustness Checks

To summarize our findings thus far, authoritarian constitutions are the same as democratic constitutions in terms of the amount of power allocated to the executive and the number of common rights guaranteed. Authoritarian constitutions diverge from democratic constitutions, though, when analyzing the independence of the judiciary, rare rights, and specificity. Importantly, the results suggest that these differences are limited to authoritarian constitutions that never experience a transition to democracy. The results indicate that authoritarian constitutions that do experience a transition to democracy at some point during their life span are no different in substance than constitutions written by democrats, at least in terms of the six constitutional attributes we analyze. Even authoritarian constitutions that do not experience a regime transition, though, do not differ too much from democratic constitutions. Our estimates suggest that such constitutions, on average, contain one less feature that protects the autonomy of the judiciary (out of six), guarantee 5 to 7 fewer rare rights (out of between 80 and 110), addresses two fewer scope items (out of fifty-eight) and contain 5 percent fewer words on each topic than democratic constitutions.

In addition to the estimates reported in Tables 7.2 through 7.5, we have estimated a number of additional models to assess the robustness of our results.[11] We have estimated models with fixed effects instead of random effects and with neither fixed nor random effects. We have used the continuous version of the UDS to operationalize the regime type of the constitution, broken up authoritarian constitutions by the type of authoritarian regime (i.e., civilian or military), and used two alternative measures of democracy. We have also restricted the time period under analysis to the post–World War II era, when there is both better data on the level of democracy and more variance in whether constitutions were written by democrats or dictators. With two exceptions, these permutations of the models reported have no substantive effect on the results.

The first exception is when fixed effects are used in the models instead of random effects. When fixed effects are included, the effect of authoritarian constitutions on scope and detail shrinks dramatically and loses statistical significance. The other change relates to executive power. The coefficient for authoritarian constitutions becomes more negative and statistically significant when fixed effects are included in the model, suggesting that authoritarian constitutions provide less power to the executive than democratic constitutions.

The finding that executive power decreases when constitutions are written by dictators seems counterintuitive. If anything, we would expect the opposite: that executives in authoritarian constitutions are given more power. In unreported

[11] The full estimates from these models are available from the authors on request.

regressions, we find basically the same pattern with indices of legislative power developed in our earlier work (Elkins, Ginsburg, and Melton 2009). While reduced legislative power accords with intuitions about authoritarian incentives, it might also help explain reduced executive power. Authoritarian constitutions simply seem to specify less power overall: judiciaries are less independent and legislatures less powerful. If residual power in the system is within the control of the executive, there would be less need to specify the explicit powers of the executive, and we would observe lower levels of power relative to democracies. This is consistent with the idea that the source of authoritarian power is, in many cases, informal and extra-constitutional.

The other differences in the results pertain to the analyses focused on constitutions drafted since World War II. Authoritarian constitutions that did not experience a regime transition and that were drafted in the post–World War II period contain two or three fewer common rights than democratic constitutions drafted during this time period. Authoritarian constitutions that experienced a regime transition during this time period had significantly more rare rights (about four or five) and addressed significantly more topics (two or three) than democratic constitutions. In other words, the substantive differences between authoritarian constitutions that experienced a regime transition and those that did not are larger in the post–World War II era than they were prior to World War II. Of course, this could be attributable to the small number of authoritarian constitutions that experienced a regime change from 1800 to 1946.

These period differences are not totally unexpected. It is well known that the contents of constitutions have changed over time. Since the United States's constitution was written in 1787, constitutions have become significantly longer and more detailed (Elkins et al. 2009). In addition, more recent constitutions have a variety of new provisions: for example, many more rights are part of the drafters' menu in 2010 than were contemplated in 1910 or even 1810. Given this variation over time, it is unsurprising that we find authoritarian and democratic constitutions have adapted to modern norms differently.

In summary, we consistently observe important differences between authoritarian constitutions that never experience a transition to democracy and both authoritarian constitutions that do experience a democracy transition and democratic constitutions. The former have less autonomous judiciaries, guarantee fewer rights (especially rare rights), and are less specific. Authoritarian constitutions that survive a regime change, in other words, are closer to democratic constitutions in content than are those authoritarian documents that are not retained. It is unclear whether this is a result of a selection effect, in that authoritarians a la Pinochet are writing more "democratic" documents in preparation for regime transition. Regardless, it does appear that the content of the authoritarian document is related to the new democrats' decision to keep or scrap it.

CONCLUSION

We have demonstrated that there are few systematic differences across the formal constitutions of democracies and dictatorships, but there are some. At the margin, authoritarian constitutions tend to be less specific, protect fewer rights (especially those rights that are less common), and provide for less judicial independence. We do not, however, see higher levels of executive power in authoritarian texts, probably because executive power is residual in authoritarian systems. But none of these differences is very large across the entire set of cases.

Instead, the most important determinants of constitutional form are the era and the region in which the constitution was written and the set of institutions chosen for the first constitution in the country's history. There is a good deal of serial dependence in constitutional texts.

If we assume that authoritarian institutions and rights protections differ systematically from democratic ones, our aggregate result of overall similarity in formal texts calls into question the simple version of what we labeled the institutional priority thesis: that authoritarian constitutions would be more congruent with authoritarian practice as to executive and legislative power and less congruent with regard to rights provisions. Even when we disaggregated the authoritarian constitution into subtypes, there are few observable differences between authoritarian and democratic constitutions. We do find some evidence that staunchly authoritarian constitutions (i.e., those that do not survive a regime change) are different from both democratic constitutions and authoritarian constitutions that survive regime changes. This suggests that one might be able to predict the possibilities of a transition, simply from the constitutional text. Similarly, we observe some differences in authoritarian and democratic constitutions written between 1974 and 1991. However, the end of the Cold War and the ensuing wave of constitution making appear to have eradicated even these minor differences. Constitutions have converged in form, if not in function.

REFERENCES

Ashley, Richard A. 2010. "A Reconsideration of Consistent Estimation of a Dynamic Panel Data Model in the Random-effects (Error Components) Framework." Working Paper, Virgina Polytechnic Institute. Available at http://ashleymac.econ.vt.edu/working_papers/random_effects_note.pdf.

Barros, Robert. 2002. *Constitutionalism and Dictatorship*. New York: Cambridge University Press.

Boix, Carles and Sebastian Rosato. 2012. "A Complete Dataset of Political Regimes 1800–1999." *Comparative Political Studies*.

Brown, Nathan. 2002. *Constitutions in a Nonconstitutional World: Arab Basic Laws and the Prospects for Accountable Governmen*t. New York: SUNY University Press.

Bueno de Mesquita, Bruce, Alastair Smith, Randolph M. Siverson, and James D. Morrow. 2003. *The Logic of Political Survival*. Cambridge: MIT Press.

Carey, John. 2000. "Parchment, Equilibria and Institutions." *Comparative Political Studies* 33(6/7): 735–61.

Collier, David, and Robert Adcock. 1999. "Democracy and Dichotomies: A Pragmatic Approach to Choices about Concepts." *Annual Review of Political Science* 2: 537–65.

Collier, David, and Steven Levitsky. 1997. "Democracy with Adjectives: Conceptual Innovation in Comparative Research." *World Politics* 49(3): 430–51.

Elkins, Zachary, Tom Ginsburg, and James Melton. 2009. *The Endurance of National Constitutions*. New York: Oxford University Press.

Elkins, Zachary, Tom Ginsburg, and James Melton. 2011. "Constitutional Constraints on Executive Lawmaking." Working Paper.

Gandhi, Jennifer and Adam Przeworski. 2007. "Authoritarian Institutions and the Survival of Autocrats." *Comparative Political Studies* 1279–301.

Getty, J. Arch. 1991. "State and Society under Stalin: Constitutions and Elections in the 1930s." *Slavic Review* 50: 18–35.

Ginsburg, Tom. 2010. "Constitutional Specificity, Unwritten Understandings and Constitutional Agreement." pp. 66–93 in Andras Sajo and Renata Utz, eds., *Constitutional Topography: Values and Constitutions*. The Hague: Eleven Publishing.

Ginsburg, Tom and Tamir Moustafa. 2008. *Rule by Law: The Politics of Courts in Authoritarian Regimes*. Cambridge: Cambridge University Press.

Hardin, Russell. 1989. "Why a Constitution?" in Bernard Grofman and Donald Wittman, eds., *The Federalist Papers and the New Institutionalism*. New York: Agathon Press, pp. 100–20.

King, Gary, James Honaker, Anne Joseph, and Kenneth Scheve. 2001. "Analyzing Incomplete Political Science Data: An Alternative Algorithm for Multiple Imputation." *American Political Science Review* 95(1): 49–69.

Linz, Juan. 1978. *The Breakdown of Democratic Regimes: Crisis, Breakdown and Reequilibration*. Baltimore, MD: The Johns Hopkins University Press.

Marshall, Monty G., Keith Jaggers, and Ted Robert Gurr. 2011. *Polity IV Project: Political Regime Characteristics and Transitions, 1800–2010*. Available at http://www.systemicpeace.org/inscr/inscr.htm.

Melton, James, and Tom Ginsburg. 2013. "Does De Jure Judicial Independence Really Matter?: A Reevaluation of Explanations for Judicial Independence." Working Paper.

Munck, Gerardo and Jay Verkuilen. 2002. "Conceptualizing and Measuring Democracy: Evaluating Alternative Indices." *Comparative Political Studies* 35(1): 5–34.

O'Donnell, Guillermo, Philippe Schmitter, and Laurence Whitehead. 1986. *Transitions from Authoritarian Rule*. Baltimore, MD: The Johns Hopkins University Press.

Ordeshook, Peter. 1992. "Constitutional Stability." *Constitutional Political Economy* 3(2): 137–75.

Pemstein, Daniel, Stephen Meserve, and James Melton. 2010. "Democratic Compromise: A Latent Variable Analysis of Ten Measures of Regime Type." *Political Analysis* 18(4): 426–49.

Przeworski, Adam. 1991. *Democracy and the Market*. Cambridge: Cambridge University Press.

Schedler, Andreas. 2006. *Electoral Authoritarianism: The Dynamics of Unfree Competition*. Boulder, CO: Lynne Rienner.

Strauss, David. 2003. "Common Law, Common Ground, and Jefferson's Principle." *Yale Law Journal* 112: 717–55.

VanHanen, Tatu. 2002. *Polyarchy Dataset: Measures of Democratization 1800–2000*. Available at http://www.prio.no/Data/Governance/Vanhanens-index-of-democracy/.

Weingast, Barry. 1997. "The Political Foundations of Democracy and the Rule of Law." *American Political Science Review* 91: 245–63.

Yu, Guanghua. 2010. "The Other Roles of Law: Signaling, Self-Commitment and Coordination." *Australian Journal of Asian Law*.

8

Constitutional Variation among Strains of Authoritarianism

David S. Law and Mila Versteeg[*]

INTRODUCTION

Legend has it that Russian Field Marshall Potemkin built the façades of nonexistent villages along the banks of the river Dnieper to impress visiting dignitaries, such as the Empress, with the illusion of prosperity. Some constitutions are the equivalent of Potemkin villages: they neither constrain nor accurately describe the powers of the state but instead exist primarily to present an attractive face to the world (see, e.g., Law and Versteeg 2013; see also Brown 2002: 4, 91–2; Howard 2009: 13; Lane 1996: 122; Law 2010: 382–3; Marcos 2003: 259; Murphy 1993: 8–9, 2007: 14; Nolutshungu 1993: 366; Sakwa 1996: 118; Sartori 1962: 861; Zhang 2010: 952). It is not difficult to see why authoritarian states might choose to adopt sham constitutions. On the one hand, countries that openly defy the values of "world society" (Meyer et al. 1997) by refusing to pay lip service to human rights and democracy invite ostracism from the international community. On the other hand, there are no constitutional enforcement mechanisms at either the domestic or international level to prevent authoritarian states from making empty promises.

Not all authoritarian constitutions, however, can be dismissed as window-dressing. Some are relatively accurate reflections of a country's legal and political institutions, to the point of brutal candor. The Saudi constitution, for example, expressly obligates the media to "employ courteous language" and conform to state regulation,[1] while the first Soviet constitution explicitly committed the state to "deprive individuals and sections of the community of any rights used by them to the detriment of the interests of the Socialist Revolution."[2] Even an authoritarian regime may have rational reasons

* We are grateful to Tom Ginsburg, Alberto Simpser, and all of the participants at the University of Chicago conference on authoritarian constitutionalism; to Jud Mathews, Kenneth McElwain, and Wayne Sandholtz for very helpful suggestions given at the 2013 annual meeting of the Midwest Political Science Association in Chicago; and to our anonymous reviewer. We thank Elizabeth Mohan Drake and Trevor Moore for excellent research assistance. Collaboration between the authors and extension of the data set on formal constitutions to encompass the years 2007 and 2008 was made possible by grants from the Center for Empirical Research in the Law at Washington University in St. Louis.

1 Saudi Arabia Const. art. 39 (1993); see Brown 2002: 7.

2 Konstitutsiia RSFSR [RSFSR Const.] arts. 9, 23 (1918).

for practicing a form of constitutional modesty. Making empty promises can be costly, and an accurate constitution may perform useful functions for the regime. It has been argued, for example, that a constitution can solve coordination problems among members of the regime itself.[3]

In this chapter, we address a combination of theoretical and empirical questions concerning the constitutional choices that authoritarian regimes make. First, to what extent do authoritarian regimes adopt relatively candid constitutions as opposed to sham constitutions, and for what reasons? Second, are certain types of authoritarian regimes more likely to practice constitutional candor, and if so, why?

The descriptive framework for our discussion is a typology of constitutions and authoritarian regimes that distinguishes among four types of constitutions (strong, sham, modest, and weak) and three strains of authoritarianism (monarchical, military, and civilian).[4] We conceptualize authoritarian regimes as rational actors that choose which type of constitution to adopt by balancing the costs and benefits of each option. A descriptively accurate constitution may help an authoritarian regime overcome internal coordination problems but can also expose the regime to delegitimating criticism from domestic and international audiences. We hypothesize that the three varieties of authoritarianism possess distinctive characteristics that lead them to balance the competing demands of legitimacy and coordination in different ways, and to pursue divergent constitution-writing strategies as a result.

Our empirical findings confirm the existence of meaningful constitutional differences not only between authoritarian and democratic regimes, but also among the three strains of authoritarianism. On the whole, authoritarian states are more likely than democratic states to adopt sham constitutions containing a panoply of constitutional rights that are not respected in practice. However, a sizeable minority of authoritarian regimes pursue a different strategy of adopting weak constitutions that promise relatively few rights in the first place. Consistent with our overarching hypothesis, monarchical and military regimes are more likely than civilian regimes to follow this strategy.

A TYPOLOGY OF CONSTITUTIONS AND AUTHORITARIAN REGIMES

In democratic as well as authoritarian states, there is bound to be a degree of divergence between the content of the formal or "large-C" constitution, on the one

3 See, for example, Elkins et al. 2014: 149; Moustafa and Ginsburg 2008: 8 (citing Pinochet's Chile as "the most lucid example of how constitutions have been used to formalize pacts among competing factions within authoritarian regimes").

4 We use the term "authoritarian regime" in the widely understood sense of an unelected regime that exercises pervasive control over society. However, the empirical measure that we use to identify authoritarian regimes is a binary indicator of dictatorship drawn from Cheibub et al. (2010) that captures only whether a state lacks fair and competitive elections. This indicator does not attempt to account for the repressiveness of the regime.

TABLE 8.1. *A typology of constitutions*

A country . . .	*. . . delivers little in practice (low* de facto *rights protection)*	*. . . delivers much in practice (high* de facto *rights protection)*
. . . promises much in its constitution (high de jure *rights protection)*	**"sham constitution"** (e.g., Sudan)	**"strong constitution"** (e.g., Finland)
. . . promises little in its constitution (low de jure *rights protection)*	**"weak constitution"** (e.g., Saudi Arabia)	**"modest constitution"** (e.g., Australia)

hand, and the informal or "small-c" constitution that captures the actual organization and behavior of the government, on the other (Law 2010). In the case of a sham constitution, the formal commitments found in a country's formal constitution overstate the country's actual commitments. For example, a country may promise free and fair elections and universal secondary education while in practice holding rigged elections and failing to promote basic literacy. But the opposite scenario is also possible: A country's formal constitution may understate its actual constitutional commitments. A genuinely democratic country that respects a full range of rights in practice might possess a relatively modest constitution that lacks any formal constitutional promise of regular elections, as in the United Kingdom, or a bill of rights, as in the case of Australia (Mayer and Schweber 2008: 229–30; Williams 2004: 306).

This divergence between parchment and practice can be modeled as the product of strategic choice. In conceptual terms, a state can be understood as making two types of constitutional choices, *de jure* and *de facto*. On paper, a regime can promise a wide range of rights and democratic institutions, or it can refrain from making such promises. Likewise, it can in practice uphold a wide range of rights and democratic institutions or none at all. As a result, a regime's *de facto* commitments can equal, exceed, or fall short of its *de jure* commitments.

Variation along these two dimensions of constitutional commitment yields the two-by-two typology of constitutions set forth in Table 8.1 (Law and Versteeg 2013). Along the horizontal axis, countries in the left-hand column respect a wide range of rights in practice, while those in the right-hand column do not. Along the vertical axis, countries in the top row set a high standard for themselves by adopting fairly ambitious constitutions, whereas those in the bottom row include relatively few commitments in their constitutions. In the upper-right quadrant are *sham constitutions*. This category includes countries such as Sudan that promise a wide variety of rights in their constitutions but uphold few of those rights in reality (Law and Versteeg 2013). In the lower-left quadrant, by contrast, are countries such as Australia with constitutions that understate the government's actual commitments. These are labeled *modest constitutions*.

In the two remaining quadrants are those countries that deliver roughly what their constitutions promise. Even among such countries, however, there remains a meaningful distinction to be drawn. In the upper-left quadrant are countries that deliver what their constitutions promise, in spite of the fact that their constitutions promise a good deal. Countries in this category, such as Finland, possess what might be called *strong constitutions* in the sense that they respect a broad range of constitutional commitments both on paper and in practice. In the lower-right quadrant, by contrast, are countries such as Saudi Arabia that also succeed at respecting their formal constitutions but do so for the reason that their constitutions impose little constraint on the government and contain few commitments that the government might be reluctant or unable to uphold. Countries in this category possess what we call *weak constitutions*. In such cases, the formal constitution is not a sham because its content aligns reasonably well with actual practice, but that alignment is attributable to the fact that the constitution sets low standards that are easily satisfied.

Authoritarian states are not known for upholding a wide range of personal and political freedoms and are therefore less likely to possess constitutions that could be classified as either strong or modest. They do, however, face a choice between the two types of constitutions in the right-hand column. Will they adopt constitutions that are weak but candid about the power and organization of the state? Or, will they instead adopt sham constitutions?

The answer may depend in part on the type of authoritarian regime at issue. The relevant political science literature distinguishes among three types of authoritarian regimes – monarchical, military, and civilian. Historically, those of a civilian variety have been most common, while monarchical regimes have been least common. All three types of authoritarian regimes, in turn, are increasingly outnumbered by democratic regimes. Figure 8.1 depicts the relative proportion of each type of authoritarian regime over time, as well as the extent to which authoritarian states are increasingly outnumbered by democratic states.[5]

Each type of authoritarian regime is characterized by a distinctive power base and structure for resolving internal conflict, controlling regime outsiders, and coordinating action (see, e.g., Geddes 1999; Hadenius and Teorell 2007; Levitsky and Way 2002). Monarchical regimes rely on family and kinship networks to resolve succession issues and to govern. Military dictatorships seize power with the help of the military and, once in power, harness the organizational apparatus of the armed forces to consolidate their rule. Civilian dictatorships typically rely on a political party structure to mobilize popular support and keep regime opponents in check. In exchange, the party offers regime collaborators a vehicle for personal advancement within a stable system of patronage (Cheibub et al. 2010).

[5] The data underlying Figure 8.2, including the binary indicator that we use to distinguish between democratic and authoritarian regimes, are drawn from Cheibub et al. (2010).

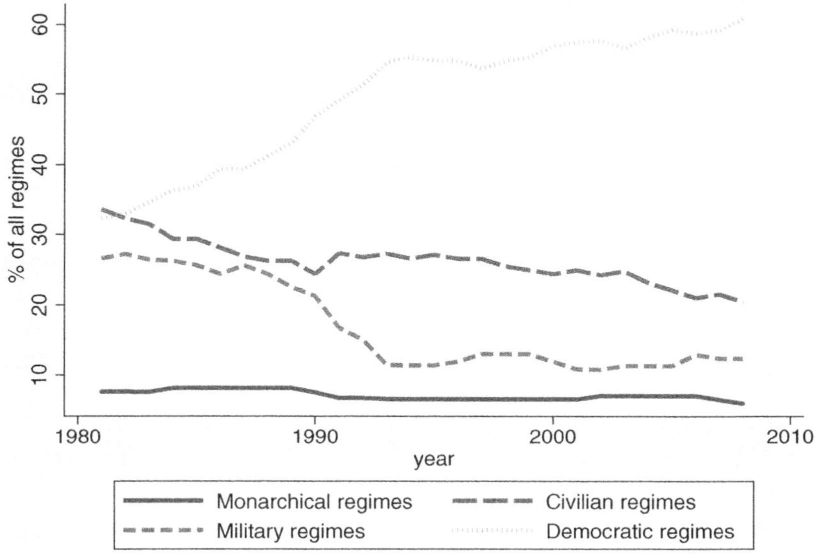

FIGURE 8.1. Prevalence of Different Regime Types

These differences among authoritarian regimes have been found to account for variance over a wide range of outcomes, including economic growth and investment, conflict behavior, political survival, and prospects for democratization (*ibid.*: 90). In the next section of this chapter, we identify several reasons why these differences might also make certain types of authoritarian regimes more prone to sham constitution-writing than others.

THREE HYPOTHESES ABOUT THE CONSTITUTIONAL CHOICES OF AUTHORITARIAN REGIMES

Our theoretical premise is that authoritarian regimes can be understood as self-interested, rational actors whose constitution-writing choices are shaped by the respective costs and benefits of each option. Furthermore, the outcome of this cost-benefit calculus will depend in part on characteristics unique to each type of authoritarian regime. In this section, we identify several factors that might influence the relative attractiveness of sham constitutionalism as opposed to constitutional honesty, and we propose three competing hypotheses as to why certain types of authoritarian regimes might be more likely to practice constitutional candor than others. These are the world society hypothesis, the domestic political economy hypothesis, and the coordination hypothesis.

The World Society Hypothesis

One possibility is that authoritarian regimes approach constitution-making as a rhetorical exercise in which certain principles and promises must be recited in order to appease the demands and satisfy the expectations of the international community. The international community is increasingly characterized by standardized models of statehood: as Meyer et al. (1997) put it, "many features of the contemporary nation-state derive from worldwide models constructed and propagated through global cultural and associational models" (144–5; see also Frank et al. 2000). More specifically, the growing global popularity of both "rule of law" discourse and an internationally defined human rights paradigm have equipped the international community with explicit and formal constitutional standards against which states can be evaluated (Klug 2000: 58).

States conform to such standardized models to secure recognition from the international community. The notion that states adopt laws with an eye toward securing acceptance from other states is hardly new. As Hegel observed nearly two centuries ago, if a civilized nation lacks "in its own eyes and the eyes of others a universal and universally valid embodiment in laws . . . it fails to secure recognition from others" (Hegel 1820: 218). At the dawn of the twenty-first century, a formal constitution that embodies certain values and principles has become both a sign of modernity and a statement of conformity to the values of "world society" (Meyer et al. 1997). In order to secure membership in international institutions and win the acceptance and recognition of the international community, states must at least purport to accept the values of world society by reciting a standard constitutional script that pays allegiance to such notions as democracy, human rights, and the rule of law (Chimni 2004: 15; Law and Versteeg 2011: 1228–30; Meyer et al. 1997: 153).

It is clear, however, that constitution-writing in authoritarian regimes is not driven solely by the goal of appeasing the international community with appropriate rhetoric. Were that the sole consideration, all authoritarian regimes would choose to adopt sham constitutions. In reality, many authoritarian constitutions are relatively candid, as demonstrated by parts of the Arab world (Brown 2002). Constitutional candor can be an entirely rational strategy for an authoritarian regime to pursue because of the costs and risks associated with sham constitutionalism. There is always the possibility that a sham constitution can be turned against the regime: the commitments made in a constitution can become a rallying point for domestic opposition and provide the basis for national and international nongovernmental organizations (NGOs) to engage in naming and shaming (Epp 1998; Simmons 2009). The 1971 Egyptian constitution, for example, has been described as "the joke that turned serious" for the Mubarak regime (El-Ghobashy 2008: 1598). Likewise, the adoption of judicially enforceable bills of rights in Georgia, Ukraine, and Kyrgyzstan backfired on authoritarian leaders by paving the way for judicial invalidation of rigged election results that ultimately brought down the leaders themselves (Trochev 2013).[6]

Any regime contemplating adoption of a sham constitution thus faces a trade-off between the benefits of international legitimacy and the political risks that come with a sham constitution. Certain types of authoritarian regimes, in turn, may be more willing to forego international approval than others. Monarchical regimes may find it relatively unnecessary to justify their rule by adopting the legalistic trappings of the modern nation-state. Monarchies typically enjoy some combination of deeply rooted historical and religious claims to authority. Both religion and tradition provide normative foundations for the state that are alternatives to, and compete with, legal modernity (Arjomand 1992; de Maistre 1810; Hassall and Saunders 2002: 120). To the extent that religious and historical claims to authority satisfy domestic audiences, monarchical regimes may experience less need to pursue international acceptance by adhering to the latest fashions in constitutional drafting.

Military regimes typically do not possess the historical or religious legitimacy of monarchical regimes. However, their control of the state can instead rest on their capacity to employ brute force. Insofar as this capacity for force is an adequate substitute for traditionalist claims to legitimacy, military dictators may also feel relatively little need to curry the favor of world society by paying tribute to the constitutional norms and standards of world society.

By contrast, civilian or party-based dictatorships may be unable either to take the backing of the military for granted or to assert their legitimacy on traditionalist grounds. They must instead find some other basis on which to command allegiance, such as ideology or charismatic leadership, that may be neither as tangible nor as well established. Although monarchs and military rulers are also capable of possessing ideological or charismatic appeal, their ability to do so merely reinforces the hold on political power that they already enjoy for other reasons. Civilian dictators do not have the same range of options for securing acceptance of their rule. In theory, this vulnerability may give them a greater incentive to seek international legitimacy. One way in which they may do so is by adopting constitutions that signal conformity to the values and expectations of world society. The world society hypothesis thus yields the prediction that, of the three types of authoritarian regimes, civilian dictatorships have the greatest incentive to adopt constitutions that espouse broadly popular norms, even if they have little intention of honoring those norms in practice.

THE DOMESTIC POLITICAL ECONOMY HYPOTHESIS

A related but analytically distinct hypothesis is that authoritarian constitutions are written primarily to appease *domestic* audiences. Faced with challenges to

[6] See also, for example, Reale 1939: 153–54 (discussing Mussolini's suspension of the Italian constitution).

their authority, autocrats choose between strategies of repression and appeasement (Acemoglu and Robinson 2006: 681; Cook 2006: 68; Howard and Roessler 2006: 365). A regime that chooses repression may find it advantageous to adopt a brutally honest constitution. A constitution that forthrightly describes the allocation and extent of state power generates clear expectations that may not only help the regime overcome internal coordination problems, but also deprive the regime's opponents of the ability to rally potential opposition around the constitution or criticize the regime for behaving unconstitutionally. A regime that promises too many constitutional rights, by contrast, must beware the possibility that it may one day face pressure to live up to those commitments (Simmons 2009).

Alternatively, authoritarian regimes may pursue an appeasement strategy that includes a constitutional component. This tactic was prominently on display in the context of the recent Arab Spring, in which various dictators sought to appease popular uprisings and remain in power by offering concessions in the form of constitutional reforms (Brown 2012; see, e.g., BBC 2011; Hirschl 2013). A regime may, of course, renege on these concessions once challenges to its rule have subsided. If political pressure persists, however, even an authoritarian regime may find itself forced to respect rights in practice as well as on paper.

The choice between repression and appeasement – and thus between promising few or many rights – will reflect a regime's need to secure popular support and bolster its domestic legitimacy. The more that a regime needs popular support in order to remain in power, the less plausible that a strategy of repression becomes, and the more concessions that the regime must make to the people (Bueno de Mesquita et al. 2003). Civilian regimes, in turn, are likely to be in greater need of popular support than either monarchical or military regimes because they cannot rest to the same degree on tradition or brute force. One way in which a civilian dictatorship can cultivate popular support is by making ideologically or normatively appealing commitments in constitutional form. If those commitments are not upheld in practice, however, the result will be a tendency toward sham constitutionalism.

The Coordination Hypothesis

It has long been recognized that constitutions play an important role in coordinating social and political behavior (Hardin 1989; Ordeshook 1992; Przeworski 1991; Weingast 1997). Scholars writing in this vein emphasize that the very act of writing a constitution can create conventions that are hard to change in the future. Indeed, the efficacy of a constitution rests on its ability to generate such conventions. Because constitutions lack third-party enforcement, they must be self-enforcing, and they accomplish this feat by coordinating behavior in ways that "raise the costs of doing things some other way" and form "an obstacle to re-coordination" (Hardin 2013). If this account is correct, a constitution will be effective if it actually coordinates behavior, regardless of whether its content is normatively appealing (Ginsburg 2012; Hardin 2013).

Authoritarian regimes are not immune to internal division and coordination problems. A descriptively accurate constitution that clarifies the allocation of power and the roles that different actors or factions within the regime are supposed to play may be useful to the regime as a means of signaling the expectations and desires of the leadership to subordinate officials, and of resolving conflict within the regime. A constitution that successfully coordinates government action and defines popular expectations can also help consolidate the regime's grip on power by inhibiting recoordination on a different set of arrangements (Hardin 2013).

Such coordinating functions are most obviously performed by structural constitutional provisions that define the institutions of government and allocate power among them. However, the rights-related constitutional content of a constitution can also shape beliefs and coordinate behavior in ways that enhance regime stability. The constitutional omission or repudiation of basic rights can foster and reinforce popular beliefs about the ubiquity of government control and the futility of opposition or dissent. Such beliefs can, in turn, become self-fulfilling: A belief that challenges to the regime will not be tolerated, for example, discourages challenges to the regime. Conversely, a constitution that contains a host of unfulfilled rights can backfire by coordinating regime opponents, who may employ the constitution as both a source of formal legitimacy for their actions and a common set of goals.

Thus, even the most ruthless of authoritarian regimes interested only in its own survival may find that sham constitution-writing has its disadvantages. A constitution that consists merely of pretty lies will not be an effective device for coordinating social and political behavior in ways that consolidate the regime. This disadvantage may be outweighed, however, by other considerations. From the perspective of a rational authoritarian regime, the potential coordination benefits of a relatively candid approach to constitution-writing must be weighed against the loss of legitimacy resulting from adoption of a constitution that fails to meet the normative expectations of domestic and international audiences.

Different types of authoritarian regimes, in turn, have reason to strike this balance differently. Monarchical and military regimes inherently possess effective internal coordination mechanisms (family relations and military command structure, respectively) that may obviate coordination devices of a constitutional variety (Cheibub et al. 2010). Party-based civilian regimes, by contrast, lack the benefit of such mechanisms yet face formidable coordination problems. The maintenance of a party apparatus is a coordination-intensive activity involving popular mobilization, recruitment, and large-scale organization. In the face of such challenges, constitution-writing may prove an appealing coordination strategy.

The coordination and world society hypotheses thus yield conflicting predictions. To the extent that authoritarian regimes rely on constitutions to solve coordination problems, their constitutions should accurately reflect reality, and this tendency toward candid constitution-writing should be stronger for civilian regimes than for monarchical or military regimes. Conversely, to the extent that authoritarian regimes employ constitutions as a means of paying lip service to globally imposed values and principles that they have little or no interest in honoring, their constitutions should bear little resemblance to reality. This should be especially true of civilian regimes, insofar as their inherently weaker grip on power leaves them especially in need of international approval.

The preceding hypotheses and the competing predictions that they yield for different types of authoritarian regimes can be summarized as follows:

> *H1: The world society hypothesis.* – Authoritarian regimes adopt sham constitutions to signal conformity to the norms of world society. Among the three types of authoritarian regimes – monarchical, military, and civilian or party-based dictatorships – civilian regimes will be most inclined to pursue such a strategy because they can neither take the backing of the military for granted nor invoke the tradition-based claims to authority and legitimacy that are available to monarchical regimes. The unavailability of these other forms of support may increase the relative attractiveness of other approaches to securing acceptance, such as constitution-writing that appeals ideologically to international audiences.

> *H2: The domestic political economy hypothesis.* – Authoritarian regimes make constitutional promises to enhance their appeal and consolidate support. Civilian or party-based regimes in particular cannot make the same religious or historical claims to authority as monarchical regimes and cannot rely on sheer force to the same extent as military regimes. Instead, they must construct governing party structures by mobilizing and organizing supporters. To do so, they will adopt constitutional provisions that are normatively or ideologically appealing to potential supporters.

> *H3: The coordination hypothesis.* – Authoritarian regimes face internal coordination problems, which they address by adopting constitutions that are sufficiently genuine to function as coordinating devices. All other things being equal, coordination problems of this kind are likely to be more acute among civilian dictatorships than either monarchical regimes (which can coordinate via familial ties) or military regimes (which already enjoy a highly disciplined and hierarchical organizational infrastructure with clearly defined lines of authority, in the form of the military itself). Civilian regimes should therefore be more likely than monarchical or military regimes to adopt relatively candid constitutions.

Measuring Constitutional (Dis)Honesty

To explain the gap between what authoritarian regimes promise in their constitutions and how they behave in practice, we must first devise a way of measuring the gap itself. We do so by matching data on the content of the world's constitutions against empirical indicators of actual human rights practice. Our data span the written constitutions of 188 countries from 1946 onward. The full data set contains 237 variables that cover the rights-related content of each constitution.[7]

The next step was to collect indicators of the extent to which rights are upheld in practice. We rely primarily on the widely used measures of human rights performance compiled by Cingranelli and Richards (2011) from the annual human rights country reports issued by Amnesty International (2011) and the U.S. State Department (Law and Versteeg 2013).[8] Because these indicators are not available on a consistent basis prior to 1981 or subsequent to 2008, we confine our analysis to the twenty-eight-year period from 1981 through 2008.

In total, we identified fifteen empirical indicators of *de facto* human rights performance that correspond to fifteen of the *de jure* rights covered by our data on formal constitutions. The fifteen rights for which we were able to compile both *de jure* and *de facto* data are as follows: prohibition of arbitrary arrest and/or detention, prohibition of torture, right to habeas corpus, fair trial rights, prohibition of the death penalty, freedom of assembly and/or association, freedom of movement, freedom of religion, right to vote, freedom of press or expression, right to health, right to education, gender equality in marriage, gender equality in labor relations, and protection of minority rights.[9] The manner in which a country's level of *de facto* and *de jure* respect for each of these fifteen rights was coded is explained in Appendix 1.

Combining the de facto and de jure data enables us to calculate, for any given country in any given year, (1) how many of the fifteen rights were promised on paper, (2) how many of the same fifteen rights were upheld in practice, and (3) the degree of overlap between what was promised and what was upheld (Law and Versteeg 2013). Figures 8.2 through 8.4 are graphs that simultaneously depict the de facto and de jure performance of all countries for the years 1986, 1996, and 2006, respectively.[10] Each country occupies a position in two-dimensional space: its position on the horizontal dimension equals the number of rights that it promises on paper, while its position on the vertical dimension equals the number of rights that it upholds in practice.

Constitutional Variation between Democratic and Authoritarian Regimes

As expected, the data show that authoritarian regimes are, on the whole, more prone to sham constitutionalism than democratic regimes. However, authoritarian

[7] For an introduction to the data on formal constitutions, see Goderis and Versteeg 2011; Law and Versteeg 2011.

[8] The other sources of data on human rights performance on which we relied were Amnesty International (2013) for our death penalty data; the Minorities at Risk dataset (2011) to capture minority rights; Hathaway (2002) for the fair trial data; the World Bank Development Indicators (2013) for data on life expectancy rates; and Vanhanen (2003) for illiteracy rates.

[9] For an explanation of how these fifteen rights were selected, see Law and Versteeg (2013).

[10] These graphs depict the total number of rights upheld in practice by each country, rather than the number of rights contained in the constitution that were also upheld in practice.

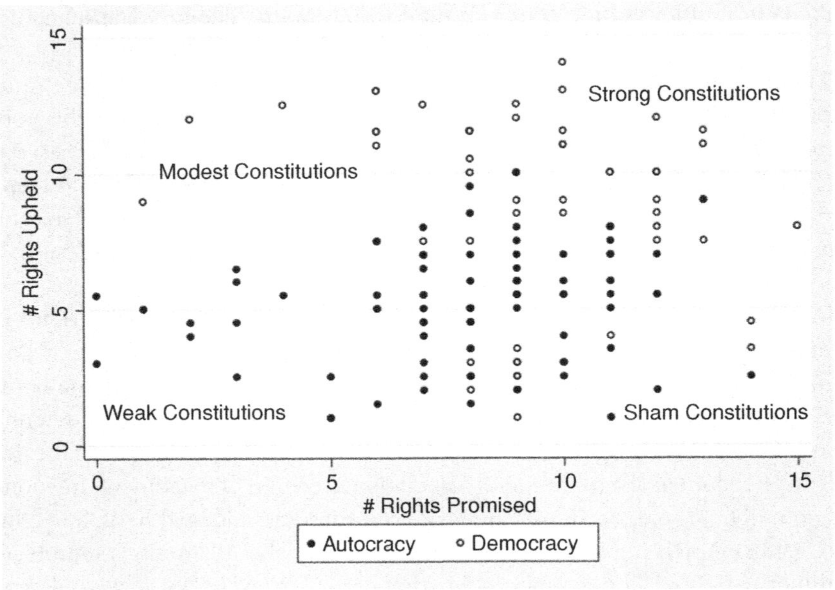

FIGURE 8.2. Types of Constitutions Among Authoritarian and Democratic Regimes, 1986

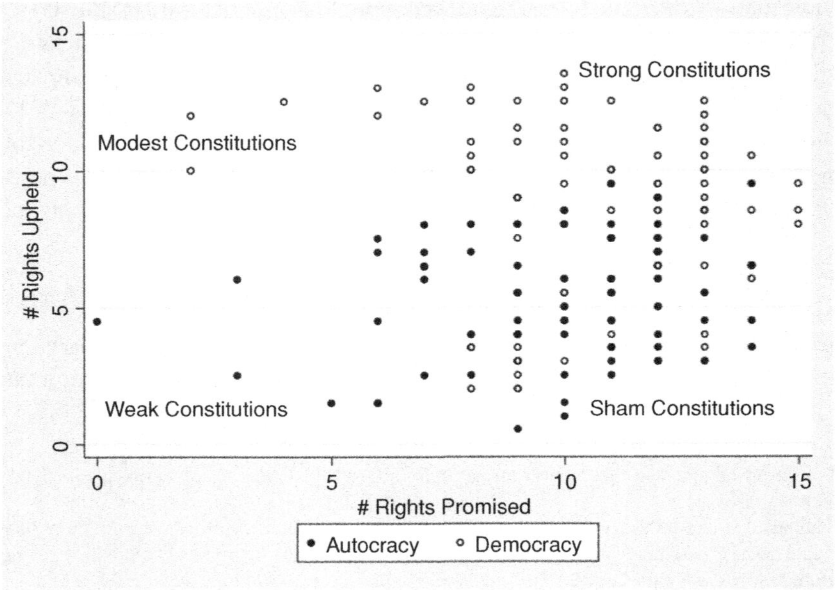

FIGURE 8.3. Types of Constitutions Among Authoritarian and Democratic Regimes, 1996

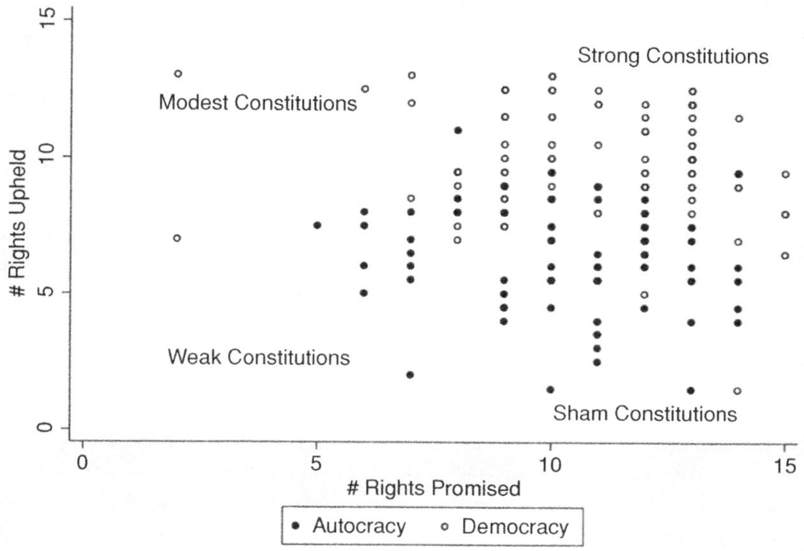

FIGURE 8.4. Types of Constitutions Among Authoritarian and Democratic Regimes, 2006

regimes also vary considerably from one another. In Figures 8.2 through 8.4, authoritarian regimes are represented by solid black dots, while democratic regimes are represented by hollow circles.

Democratic regimes are largely clustered in the top half of each graph, which corresponds to respect for a greater number of rights in practice. By contrast, authoritarian regimes are overwhelmingly clustered in the bottom half of each graph. The finding that autocratic regimes are characterized by less respect for rights should not come as a surprise: as an empirical matter, if not also by definition, democratic countries are more likely to respect rights than authoritarian countries (Poe et al. 1999). Authoritarian constitutions can be further divided into two camps: those in the bottom right of each graph promise a relatively large number of rights and can thus be classified as sham constitutions, while those in the bottom left refrain from promising too many rights and can thus be classified as weak constitutions. In each graph, the quadrants that correspond to sham and weak constitution-writing are overwhelmingly populated by authoritarian as opposed to democratic regimes.

The graphs also suggest a degree of migration by authoritarian regimes from the weak category to the sham category. This migration is a result of the fact that countries tend to add rights to their constitutions over time (Law and Versteeg 2011: 1195). This phenomenon of "rights creep" is not unique to authoritarian regimes but also characterizes democratic countries (*ibid.*). Among authoritarian regimes in particular, however, actual respect for rights has not kept pace with growth in the number of rights promised, and the result has been a tendency toward increasingly sham constitutions.

Regression analysis confirms that authoritarian regimes are more likely than democratic regimes to adopt sham or weak constitutions, even if one controls for potentially relevant variables such as economic development and population size. To control for these variables, we estimate a multinomial logit model in which the predictor variable captures whether a nation is authoritarian and the dependent variable is the type of constitution that a country possesses. Our measure of authoritarianism is a dichotomous variable devised by Cheibub and colleagues (2010) that distinguishes between democracies and dictatorships.[11]

The coding of the dependent variable follows the typology of constitutions introduced in Table 8.1. Each constitution was classified as sham, strong, modest, weak, or average. Constitutions that contained more than nine of the fifteen rights were classified as either strong (if a majority of the promised rights were actually upheld) or sham, while those containing fewer than nine rights were classified as either modest or weak (depending again on the number of rights actually upheld). Constitutions containing nine rights – the global average from 1981 through 2008 – were classified as average.[12]

To isolate the effect of authoritarianism on a country's choice of constitutional type, we include a number of control variables that we have previously found to be correlated with sham constitution-writing (Law and Versteeg 2013). These control variables are as follows:

(1) Whether a country is experiencing *civil war* (Gleditsch 2007).[13] Civil war is often associated with suspension of the constitutional order and rights infringement and is therefore expected to dampen constitutional compliance

[11] Cheibub et al. (2010), in turn, rely on earlier work by Przeworski et al. (2000). Experimentation with two alternative measures of authoritarianism did not affect our results. The first alternative was a more granular measure of authoritarianism derived from the Polity IV data set that ranges from +10 (strongly democratic) to −10 (strongly autocratic) (Marshall and Jaggers 2007). The second alternative was a binary version of the same variable that we constructed by selecting the values of 4 and 6 as cutoffs to separate democracies from autocracies. (For a similar approach to constructing a binary indicator of democracy, see Simmons (2009).)

[12] To be precise, our numerical criteria for assigning a constitution to one of the five categories were as follows. A country was classified as possessing a *strong* constitution if it promises at least ten of the fifteen *de jure* rights in its constitution *and* it upholds more than half of the included rights in practice. Conversely, a country was instead classified as possessing a *sham* constitution if it promises at least ten of the fifteen rights but actually upholds less than half of the promised rights. Countries that promise fewer than nine rights and uphold less than half of the unpromised rights were classified as possessing *weak* constitutions, while countries that promise fewer than nine rights but uphold at least half of the unpromised rights were categorized as possessing *modest* constitutions. Finally, constitutions that promised exactly nine rights were classified as average.

[13] The presence of civil war is captured by a dummy variable that takes a value of 1 if civil war affects a country in a given year and 0 otherwise.

(Hafner-Burton and Tsutsui 2005, 1388; Poe et al. 1999, 305; Poe and Tate 1994, 865).

(2) The country's level of *economic wealth*, as measured by the natural log of its gross domestic product (GDP) per capita (World Bank 2013). Scholars have identified several reasons why a country's level of economic wealth may influence the degree to which it meets its constitutional obligations. Conflict over scarce resources can generate instability that in turn triggers government repression (Blasi and Cingranelli 1996: 225). In addition, wealthier countries are inherently more capable of honoring constitutional obligations of a socioeconomic variety that entail government expenditures, such as a right to education or health (Cingranelli and Richards 2011: 215). Consistent with such theories, studies have repeatedly found that wealthy countries tend to possess superior human rights practices (Blasi and Cingranelli 1996: 225–6).

(3) Whether a country is located in a particular *geographic region*. Our expectation that regional patterns affect constitutional performance is in line with existing scholarship on policy diffusion, which emphasizes the tendency of neighboring jurisdictions to adopt similar policies for reasons related to sheer proximity (Elkins and Simmons 2005: 34; Rogers 2003: 276–77). To the extent that governments within a particular region serve as benchmarks and sources of inspiration for one another (Elkins and Simmons 2005: 45), it is unsurprising that they adopt similar approaches to the drafting and implementation of constitutions. In previous work, we found that North Africa and the Middle East, Sub-Saharan Africa, and South Asia are characterized by relatively high levels of constitutional noncompliance, even after controlling for a variety of political and economic variables (Law and Versteeg 2012, Tbl. 13; see also Brown 2002).

(4) The natural log of the country's *population size* (World Bank 2013). The existing empirical literature suggests that more populous countries are more prone to human rights violations. Rapid population growth can place stress on a country's limited resources, and governments may resort to repression to manage the resulting friction (Hafner-Burton and Tsutsui 2005: 1388; Henderson 1993: 330; Poe and Tate 1994: 861; Poe et al. 1999: 305). Methodological considerations also lead us to control for population size. The Cingranelli and Richards indicators on which we rely purport to measure the absolute number of rights violations in a country rather than the per capita incidence of rights violations, which can have the effect of penalizing more populous countries.

(5) A variable that captures the *passage of time*. Inclusion of a linear time trend enables us to evaluate the possibility that there exists a gradual trend toward constitutional dishonesty among authoritarian regimes, as suggested by Figures 8.1 through 8.3.

The resulting model takes the following form[14]:

$$Y^*_{itj} = \beta_{1j} Autocracy_{it} + \beta_{2j} Civilwar_{it} + \beta_{3j} GDP_{it} + \beta_{4j} Region_i + \beta_{5j} Population_{it} + \beta_{6j} Time_t + \varepsilon_{itj} \quad (1)$$

where y^*_{itj} is a latent variable for y_{itj},

$$j = \{Strong,\ Sham,\ Modest,\ Weak,\ \text{or}\ Average\} \quad (2)$$

Because the dependent variable consists of discrete categories (strong, sham, modest, weak, or average), we employ multinomial logit regression. However, the coefficients from a multinomial logit regression do not lend themselves to substantive interpretation. Accordingly, we report relative-risk ratios in lieu of regression coefficients. These relative-risk ratios capture the change in the probability that a particular type of country will adopt a particular type of constitution relative to some baseline probability (Greene 2011: 720–23). The baseline for comparison in the present case is the probability that a democratic country adopts an average constitution. If a variable carries a relative-risk ratio of less than 1, this means that the variable's effect on the probability that a country adopts a specific type of constitution (compared to the probability of an average constitution) is negative, while a relative-risk ratio greater than 1 means that the effect is positive.[15] Suppose, for example, that the relative-risk ratio associated with dictatorship is 0.8 for a modest constitution and 12 for a weak constitution. In this example, the relative-risk ratios indicate that a country that switches from democracy to dictatorship becomes 20 percent less likely than before to possess a modest constitution (given the corresponding relative-risk ratio of less than 1) but twelve times more likely than before to possess a weak constitution (given the corresponding relative-risk ratio that is much greater than 1).

The relative-risk ratios confirm that authoritarian countries are more likely than democracies to choose a sham or weak constitution over an average constitution, even if one controls for all of the other variables in the model. As indicated in Table 8.2, the relative-risk ratio for an authoritarian regime to choose a *sham* constitution over an average constitution is 4.22 (meaning that a country that switches from democracy to authoritarianism becomes 4.22 times more likely than before to choose a sham constitution over an average constitution, holding all other variables constant). However, that same country becomes 12.53 times more likely than before to choose a weak constitution over an average constitution. In other words, the probability that a newly authoritarian regime will adopt a weak constitution is about three times larger than the probability that it will adopt a sham constitution. Even though a growing number of authoritarian regimes have migrated to the sham category in

14 In this model, we calculate robust standard errors clustered at the country level to correct for heteroskedasticity and serial correlation over time.

15 The multinomial logit model is estimated in Stata using the "mlogit" command, and the relative-risk ratios are obtained by including the "rrr" option.

TABLE 8.2. *Authoritarian versus democratic regimes: relative-risk ratios (computed from multinomial logit regression)*

	1 Sham constitution	2 Strong constitution	3 Modest constitution	4 Weak constitution
Dictatorship	4.224***	0.563	0.852	12.527***
GDP per capita (ln)	0.563***	0.762*	1.684**	1.005
Population (ln)	1.843***	1.378**	1.590***	1.414*
Sub-Saharan Africa region	0.238**	0.194***	2.489	1.448
South Asia region	0.656	0.126***	0.727	0.196
North Africa/Middle East region	0.684	0.196**	1.294	1.296
Civil war	4.604***	0.579	0.064**	1.333
Time trend	1.114***	1.086***	0.995	0.983

$n = 3{,}385$
*** $p < 0.01$, ** $p < 0.05$, * $p < 0.10$

recent decades, the phenomenon of the weak constitution – wherein few rights exist either on paper or in practice – remains largely unique to authoritarian regimes.[16]

The effects of the control variables also comport with our expectations. A higher GDP per capita simultaneously decreases the likelihood of a sham constitution that overstates the country's actual commitment to rights, and increases the likelihood of a modest constitution that does precisely the opposite. Conversely, civil war is strongly associated with sham constitutionalism. The regression model also confirms the existence of regional differences: countries in Sub-Saharan Africa, South Asia, and North Africa and the Middle East are all less likely than those in other regions to possess strong constitutions.[17] Finally, all other things being equal, countries have become more likely over time to fall in the strong or sham category, which is to say that countries are promising a growing number of constitutional rights but not always upholding them as well.

Constitutional Variation among Different Types of Authoritarian Regimes

More noteworthy than the differences between authoritarian and democratic regimes, however, are the differences among various types of authoritarian regimes. Tables 8.3 and 8.4 offer a numerical breakdown of the constitutional choices made by each type of authoritarian regime – monarchical, military, and civilian – for the first and last year of our sample period (1981 and 2008, respectively),[18] while Figures 8.5 through 8.7 depict the overall trend for each type of regime over the entire period.

16 As of 2008, 83% of all weak constitutions belonged to authoritarian regimes.

17 We do not include all possible geographic regions in the model because inclusion of all regions creates a sparse indicator problem and renders the logit model unable to reach convergence.

18 For a detailed explanation of how constitutions were assigned to the five categories, see note 12 above.

TABLE 8.3. *The constitutional choices of each regime type as of 1981*

	Strong constitution	Sham constitution	Modest constitution	Weak constitution	Average constitution
Authoritarian regimes (n=81):	7 (8.6%)	13 (16.0%)	6 (7.5%)	19 (23.5%)	36 (44.4%)
Monarchical (n=8):	0 (0%)	0 (0%)	0 (0%)	4 (50%)	4 (50%)
Military (n=36):	7 (19.4%)	6 (16.7%)	3 (8.3%)	9 (25%)	11 (31%)
Civilian (n=37):	0 (0%)	7 (18.9%)	3 (8.1%)	6 (16.2%)	21 (26.8%)
Democratic regimes (n=39):	12 (30.7%)	1 (2.6%)	10 (25.6%)	2 (5.1%)	14 (35.8%)
TOTAL (n=120):	19 (7.5%)	14 (11.7%)	16 (13.3%)	21 (17.5%)	50 (41.7%)

TABLE 8.4. *The constitutional choices of each regime type as of 2008*

	Strong constitution	Sham constitution	Modest constitution	Weak constitution	Average constitution
Authoritarian regimes (n=70):	15 (21.4%)	28 (40.0%)	5 (7.1%)	10 (14.3%)	12 (17.1%)
Monarchical (n=11):	3 (27.3%)	1 (9.1%)	2 (18.2%)	2 (18.2%)	3 (27.3%)
Military (n=23):	2 (8.7%)	8 (34.8%)	2 (8.7%)	6 (26.1%)	5 (21.7%)
Civilian (n=36):	10 (27.8%)	19 (52.8%)	1 (2.8%)	2 (5.6%)	4 (11.1%)
Democratic regimes (n=108):	62 (57.4%)	14 (13.0%)	7 (6.5%)	2 (1.9%)	23 (21.3%)
TOTAL (n=178):	77 (43.3%)	42 (23.6%)	12 (6.7%)	12 (6.7%)	35 (19.6%)

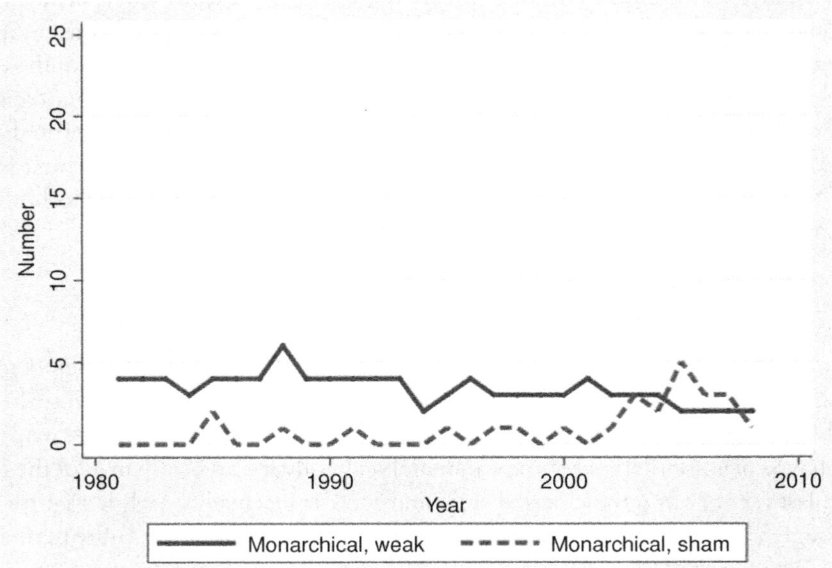

FIGURE 8.5. Raw Number of Sham and Weak Constitutions among Monarchical Regimes

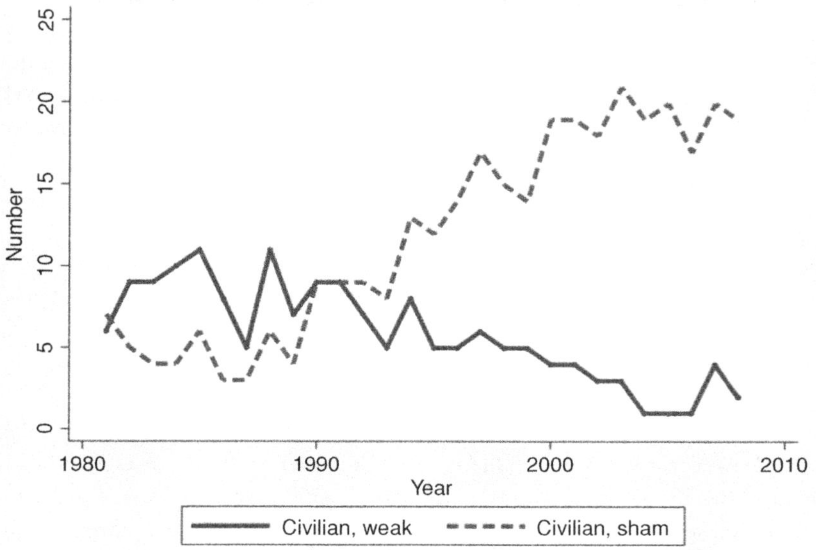

FIGURE 8.6. Raw Number of Sham and Weak Constitutions Among Civilian Regimes

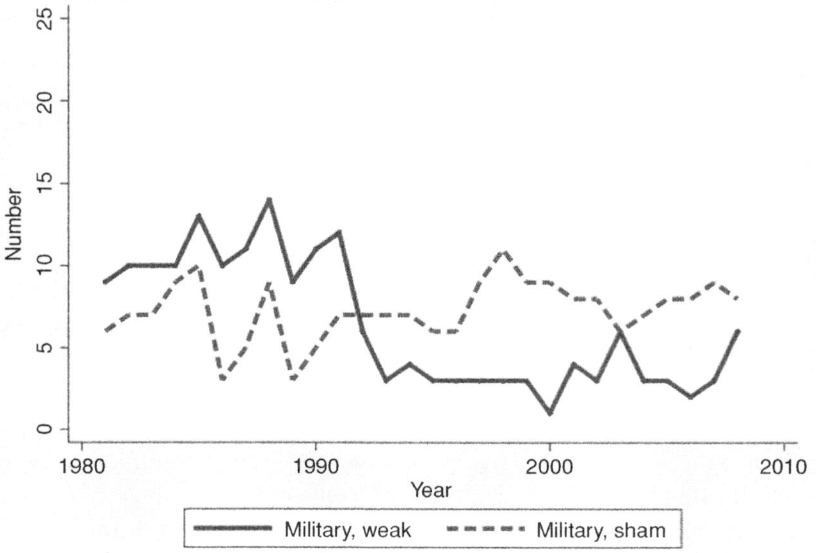

FIGURE 8.7. Raw Number of Sham and Weak Constitutions Among Military Regimes

On the whole, civilian dictatorships tend to favor sham constitutions over weak constitutions, whereas monarchical and military regimes have been more evenly divided between the two categories. As of 2008, 52.8 percent of civilian regimes fell in the sham category, as compared to 34.8 percent of military regimes and only 9.1 percent of monarchical regimes. Moreover, this tendency toward sham constitution-writing has been building over time. In 1981, out of thirty-seven civilian dictatorships, nine fell in the weak category and only six in the sham category. By 2008, however, out of a total of thirty-six civilian regimes, only two remained in the weak category, as compared to nineteen in the sham category.

This shift toward sham constitutions reflects the phenomenon of rights creep. In 1981, the constitutions of civilian dictatorships contained an average of 7.5 rights; by 2008, the average had grown to 11.2, an increase of nearly 50%. Unsurprisingly, many civilian regimes failed in practice to uphold this increasingly expansive set of rights and consequently shifted from the weak category to the sham category. Others, however, rose to the challenge that they had set for themselves and shifted instead in the direction of strong constitutionalism: as of 2008, ten of the thirty-six civilian regimes covered by our data were classified as possessing strong constitutions.

Historically, monarchical regimes have refrained from promising an abundance of constitutional rights, with the result that they have been characterized by a higher degree of constitutional candor than civilian regimes. As of 1981, the eight monarchical regimes in our data were evenly divided between the weak and average categories. However, this pattern has shown signs of reversal in recent years. By 2008, only two out of eleven monarchical regimes still belonged in the weak category; of the remainder, three fell in the strong category and one fell in the sham category. As in the case of civilian regimes, this shift away from weak constitutions reflects growth in the number of rights promised. Between 1981 and 2008, the average number of rights in monarchical constitutions increased by 37%, from 6.8 to 9.3.[19] This increase pushed a number of regimes from the weak category into either the strong category or the sham category, depending upon whether their real-world performance kept pace with their constitutional promises.

Like monarchical regimes, military regimes were historically characterized by weak constitutions, but like civilian regimes, they have shifted noticeably toward sham constitutions. Out of the thirty-six military regimes for which we have data as of 1981, nine (25 percent) had weak constitutions and six (17 percent) had sham constitutions, while another 11 (31 percent) possessed average constitutions. By 2008, however, the number of military regimes had declined to twenty-three, of which eight (35 percent) had sham constitutions and six (26 percent) had weak constitutions. This shift toward sham constitutionalism appears to reflect not only rights creep, but also a

[19] Because our analysis covers 15 rights, both figures are out of a maximum of 15.

decline in the population of military regimes. From 1981 to 2008, the average number of rights in the constitutions of military regimes rose only modestly, from 8.8 to 9.3 (a 6% increase). Since the 1990s, however, there has also been a steep drop in the number of military regimes, and those that have survived have disproportionately been in the sham category. The decline in the population of military regimes can be seen in Figure 8.1.

Regression analysis confirms the existence of statistically significant differences among the three types of authoritarian regimes that cannot be explained by variables such as economic development or civil war. To explore the differences among authoritarian regime types, we estimate a modified version of the regression model set forth in Table 8.2. As in the earlier version of the model, the dependent variable is the type of constitution that a country adopts (strong, sham, modest, weak, or average), and the control variables included remain the same.[20] However, instead of a binary predictor variable that distinguishes only between democracies and dictatorships, we include a set of predictor variables that distinguish among the three strains of authoritarianism – monarchical, military, and civilian — as well as between democratic and authoritarian regimes. In lieu of regression coefficients, we again report relative-risk ratios that capture the change in the probability of a country adopting a particular type of constitution relative to some baseline probability. The baseline for purposes of comparison in this case is the probability that a civilian dictatorship adopts an average constitution.

The regression results reported in Table 8.5 confirm that both monarchical and military regimes are more likely than civilian regimes to adopt weak constitutions. Holding all other variables constant, a state that switches from civilian dictatorship to monarchical rule becomes 15.4 times more likely than before to choose a weak constitution over an average constitution. The difference between military and civilian regimes is not as pronounced but still statistically significant: a state that changes from civilian dictatorship to military rule becomes 1.7 times more likely than before to choose a weak constitution over an average constitution. By a statistically significant margin, military regimes are also more likely than civilian regimes to choose modest constitutions. An authoritarian state that switches from civilian to military rule becomes 3.5 times more likely than before to choose a modest constitution over an average constitution. In absolute terms, however, modest constitutions are a rarity, and neither military regimes nor other states are very likely as a practical matter to adopt constitutions that understate their actual commitment to rights.

[20] With one minor exception, these modifications of the model did not change any findings with respect to the control variables. In the modified model, the regional variable for South Asia reaches a conventional level of statistical significance ($p = 0.10$), whereas in the original model, it falls slightly short ($p = 0.12$). In both models, however, the variable has the same predicted effect: a country located in South Asia is more likely than those in other regions to choose an average constitution over a weak constitution.

TABLE 8.5. *Differences among strains of authoritarianism: relative-risk ratios (computed from multinomial logit regression)*

	1 Sham constitution	2 Strong constitution	3 Modest constitution	4 Weak constitution
Monarchical regime	0.612	1.922	1.093	15.401***
Military regime	0.967	0.778	3.250**	1.695***
Democratic regime	0.227***	1.723	1.773	0.116***
GDP per capita (ln)	0.563***	0.759*	1.839**	0.918
Population (ln)	1.846***	1.392**	1.588***	1.622**
Sub-Saharan Africa region	0.237**	0.199***	2.810	1.211
South Asia region	0.692	0.119***	0.880	0.043**
North Africa/Middle East region	0.691	0.152**	1.266	0.280
Civil war	4.556***	0.575	0.072**	1.370
Time trend	1.113***	1.084***	0.996	0.98

$n = 3{,}385$
*** $p < 0.01$, ** $p < 0.05$, * $p < 0.10$

These findings support our overarching hypothesis that authoritarian regimes face competing incentives when deciding what constitution-writing strategy to pursue, and that different types of authoritarian regimes possess distinctive characteristics that lead them to weigh these incentives differently. On the one hand, adoption of a constitution that contains a plethora of rights can bolster a regime's legitimacy by appealing to the ideological sensibilities of domestic and international constituencies. On the other hand, such a strategy is not without its costs. Adoption of a sham constitution can backfire by depriving regime members of a device for overcoming internal coordination problems while simultaneously providing regime opponents with a coordination device of their own.

For military and monarchical regimes, the costs of sham constitutionalism may outweigh the benefits, which would explain their propensity for adopting candidly weak constitutions. For civilian or party-based regimes, however, the strategic calculus appears to be different. Civilian rulers possess neither the traditional claims to authority enjoyed by monarchs nor the convenient recourse to force enjoyed by military rulers and must therefore find other ways of consolidating their rule. Adoption of a constitution that incorporates a wide range of popular human rights is one strategy by which a civilian regime can muster domestic and international approval. Consistent with what we have termed the world society and domestic political economy hypotheses, our findings support the view that civilian regimes face greater pressure than either monarchical or military regimes to adopt formal constitutions that satisfy the expectations of domestic and international audiences.

CONCLUSION

There can be a considerable gap between what a country promises in its constitution and how it actually behaves (Law and Versteeg 2013). Not surprisingly, our analysis reveals this gap to be larger in authoritarian states than in democratic states: authoritarian regimes are less likely to uphold the rights found in their constitutions. An obvious explanation for this finding is that authoritarian regimes have a tendency to promise rights for the sake of appearances rather than out of genuine commitment.

It is also clear, however, that not all authoritarian regimes adopt sham constitutions. Many choose to write constitutions that are relatively candid about their lack of respect for a variety of basic rights. The notion that authoritarian regimes approach constitution-writing as merely an exercise in cheap talk or window dressing cannot account for the existence of weak or modest constitutions that explicitly provide low levels of rights protection.

We find, moreover, that this form of constitutional candor is associated with specific varieties of authoritarianism. By a statistically significant margin, monarchical and military regimes are more likely than civilian regimes to adopt weak constitutions that promise relatively few rights. We attribute this pattern to strategic constitution-writing behavior rooted in the distinctive features of each type of regime. Even for the most ruthless of authoritarian regimes, there are benefits to constitutional candor. Adoption of a weak but descriptively accurate constitution can help a regime to solve internal coordination problems, whereas adoption of a sham constitution filled with empty promises can backfire by coordinating opponents of the regime instead. In the case of civilian regimes, however, these considerations may be outweighed by a heightened need for ideological legitimacy that is served by promising a variety of rights on paper.

Our findings highlight several questions for further research. One such question is whether authoritarian regimes are more likely to comply with the structural provisions of their constitutions, such as those pertaining to the allocation of power between legislative and executive institutions or between national and subnational governments, than with the rights-related provisions considered in this study. Given that authoritarian regimes are defined in large part by their control over society, it is plausible to think that they are more likely to violate provisions limiting their power over individuals than provisions concerning their internal structure (Elkins et al. 2009: 55; Law 2011: 282).[21] Although some studies suggest that constitutional provisions relating to legislative power and federalism tend to reflect actual practice, it is questionable whether the same could be said of other structural provisions, such as those concerning judicial independence (Feld and Voigt 2003: 267; Law 2010).

[21] Indeed, a number of studies have found a negative relationship between formal rights protection and actual rights observance (Boli-Bennett 1976; Keith 2002; Law and Versteeg 2011; Pritchard 1986).

Another question concerns the impact of political competition on authoritarian constitutionalism. As various scholars have observed, not all authoritarian states are devoid of political competition (Ginsburg and Moustafa 2008; Levitsky and Way 2010; Schedler 2009). Consistent with the logic of the domestic political economy hypothesis, authoritarians exposed to electoral pressures may make constitutional concessions in the form of more rights. Although a full exploration of this hypothesis is beyond the scope of this chapter, our tentative analysis of the data suggests that authoritarian states with multiple political parties are no more likely to adopt sham or weak constitutions than authoritarian states with only a single party.[22] The extent to which authoritarian regimes make empty constitutional promises may ultimately depend more on the type of authoritarian regime at issue than on the existence of a modicum of political competition.

APPENDIX 1

DE JURE RIGHT	*DE FACTO* RIGHT
I. Personal Integrity	
1. *Prohibition of Arbitrary Arrest and/or Detention* 0 = not mentioned in constitution 1 = mentioned in constitution	1. *Disappearances* 0 = disappearances occur frequently 0.5 = disappearances occur occasionally 1 = no disappearances are reported
2. *Prohibition of Torture* 0 = not mentioned in the constitution 1 = mentioned in the constitution	2. *Torture* 0 = torture occurs frequently 0.5 = torture occurs occasionally 1 = no torture is reported
3. *Right to Habeas Corpus* 0 = not mentioned in the constitution 1 = mentioned in the constitution	3. *Extrajudicial Killings* 0 = extrajudicial killings occur frequently 0.5 = extrajudicial killings occur occasionally 1 = no extrajudicial killings are reported

[22] We performed a test of the difference between one-party and multi-party authoritarian regimes by estimating a modified version of the multinomial logit model reported in Table 8.1. Once again, the dependent variable is the type of constitution that a country adopts, and the control variables remain the same. However, we replaced the binary autocracy predictor variable with a set of predictor variables that distinguish among one-party authoritarian states, multi-party authoritarian states, and democratic states. The data that we use to distinguish between one-party and multi-party authoritarian states is drawn from Henisz (2002). According to this data, 36% of the authoritarian states in our data are multi-party states. Estimation of this model revealed no statistically significant difference between the two types of authoritarian states in terms of their propensity to adopt sham or weak constitutions.

4. Fair Trial Rights 0 = constitution contains fewer than three of the following eight trial-related rights: the right to counsel, the right to present a defense, a presumption of innocence, the right to an appeal, the right to an interpreter, protection from ex post facto laws, a public trial; and the right to a timely trial[23] 1 = constitution contains at least three of the preceding eight trial-related rights	*4. Fair Trial Rights* 0 = a score of 4 out of 4 on Hathaway (2002)'s aggregated fair trial index (the worst possible score) 0.5 = a score of 2 or 3 out of 4 on the aggregated fair trial index 1 = a score of 1 out of 4 on the fair trial index (the best possible score)
5. Prohibition of Death Penalty 0 = not mentioned in the constitution 1 = constitution explicitly prohibits the death penalty	*5. Death Penalty Abolition* 0 = death penalty is allowed 0.5 = death penalty is abolished for ordinary crimes 1 = death penalty is abolished for all crimes
II. Civil and Political Freedoms	
6. Freedom of Assembly and/or Association 0 = neither right is mentioned in the constitution 1 = either or both rights are mentioned in the constitution	*6. Freedom of Assembly and/or Association* 0 = freedom of assembly and/or association is severely restricted or denied completely to all citizens 0.5 = freedom of assembly and/or association is limited for all citizens or severely restricted or denied for select groups 1 = freedom of assembly and/or association is virtually unrestricted and freely enjoyed by practically all citizens
7. Freedom of Movement 0 = not mentioned in the constitution 1 = mentioned in the constitution	*7. Freedom of Movement* 0 = domestic travel is severely restricted 0.5 = domestic travel is somewhat restricted 1 = domestic travel is unrestricted
8. Freedom of Religion 0 = not mentioned in the constitution 1 = mentioned in the constitution	*8. Freedom of Religion* 0 = government restrictions on religious practices are severe and widespread 0.5 = government restrictions on religious practices are moderate 1 = government restrictions on religious practices are practically absent

(*continued*)

[23] The mean number of fair trial rights found in all constitutions from 1946 to 2010 is 3.47.

9. Right to Vote 0 = not mentioned in the constitution 1 = mentioned in the constitution	*9. Free and Fair Elections* 0 = right to self-determination through free and fair elections does not exist under law or in practice 0.5 = although citizens have the legal right to self-determination, there are some limitations on the exercise of this right in practice, and political participation is only moderately free and open 1 = political participation is very free and open, and citizens have the right to self-determination through free and fair elections in both law and practice
10. Freedom of the Press and/or Expression 0 = neither freedom is mentioned in the constitution 1 = constitution protects either or both freedoms	*10. Freedom of Speech* 0 = complete government censorship of the media 0.5 = some government censorship of the media 1 = no government censorship of the media
III. Socioeconomic and Group Rights	
11. Right to Health 0 = not mentioned in the constitution 1 = mentioned in the constitution	*11. Life Expectancy at Birth* 0 = life expectancy is less than 52 years[24] 0.5 = life expectancy is between 52 and 72 years[25] 1 = life expectancy is more than 72 years
12. Right to Education 0 = not mentioned in the constitution 1 = mentioned in the constitution	*12. Literacy Rates* 0 = less than 36%[26] of the population is literate 0.5 = literacy rate is between 36% and 93%[27] 1 = more than 93% of the population is literate

[24] Fifty-two years is the twenty-fifth percentile on the life expectancy measure.
[25] Seventy-two years is the seventy-fifth percentile on the life expectancy measure.
[26] Thirty-six percent is the twenty-fifth percentile on the literacy rates measure: in other words, only 25% of countries had a literacy rate lower than 36%.
[27] Ninety-three percent is the seventy-fifth percentile on the literacy rates measure.

13. Gender Equality in Marriage 0 = not mentioned in the constitution 1 = mentioned in the constitution	*13. Women's Social Rights* 0 = the law contains no social rights for women, and systematic discrimination based on sex may be embedded in the legal system; or, women enjoy some social rights by law, but they are not effectively enforced 0.5 = the government effectively upholds some social rights of women in practice but still allows a low level of discrimination against women in social matters 1 = nearly all women's social rights are guaranteed by law, and the government fully and vigorously enforces these laws in practice
14. Gender Equality in Labor Relations (e.g., Equal Wages for Equal Work) 0 = not mentioned in the constitution 1 = mentioned in the constitution	*14. Women's Economic Rights* 0 = the law contains no economic rights for women, and systematic discrimination based on sex may be embedded in the legal system; or, women enjoy some economic rights by law, but they are not effectively enforced 0.5 = the government effectively upholds some economic rights of women in practice but still allows a low level of discrimination against women in economic matters 1 = nearly all women's economic rights are guaranteed by law, and the government fully and vigorously enforces these laws in practice
15. General Protection of Minority Rights, or Right of Minorities to Be Represented in Government 0 = not mentioned in the constitution 1 = constitution either contains a general protection of minority rights or explicit provision for minorities to be represented in government	*15. Minority Rights* 0 = government policy substantially restricts the largest minority group's political participation relative to other groups; or, the largest minority group is substantially underrepresented because of prevailing social practice by dominant groups and a lack of adequate remedial policies 0.5 = the largest minority group experiences substantial underrepresentation in political office and/or low levels of political participation, but policies are in place to improve the group's political status; or, the largest minority group experiences substantial underrepresentation even though government policy is neutral 1 = no discrimination in the political system against minorities

REFERENCES

Acemoglu, Daron and James Robinson. 2006. "Paths of Economic Development," in Barry Weingast and Donald Wittman, eds., *Oxford Handbook of Political Economy*. Oxford, UK: Oxford University Press, pp. 673–92.

Amnesty International. 2011. *Amnesty International Report 2011: The State of the World's Human Rights*. Available at http://files.amnesty.org/air11/air_2011_full_en.pdf.

Amnesty International. 2013. *Abolish the Death Penalty*, AMNESTY INT'L, http://www.amnesty.org/en/death-penalty (last visited May 5, 2013).

Arjomand, Saïd. 1992. "Constitutions and the Struggle for Political Order: A Study in the Modernization of Political Traditions." *European Journal of Sociology* 33: 39–82.

BBC. 2011, June 18. *Morocco's King Mohammed Unveils Constitutional Reforms*. http://www.bbc.co.uk/news/world-africa-13816974.

Blasi, Gerald and David Cingranelli. 1996. "Do Constitutions and Institutions Help Protect Human Rights?" in David Cingranelli, ed., *Human Rights and Developing Countries*. Greenwich, CT: JAI, pp. 223–37.

Boli-Bennet, John. 1976. "The Expansion of Nation State. 1870–1970." Ph.D. Dissertation, Stanford University.

Brown, Nathan. 2002. *Constitutions in a Nonconstitutional World: Arab Basic Laws and the Prospects for Accountable Government*. New York: State University of New York Press.

Brown, Nathan. 2012. Constitutionalizing Authoritarianism and Democracy in Egypt and Tunisia. Unpublished manuscript, on file with author.

Bueno de Mesquita, Bruce, Alastair Smith, Randolph M. Siverson, and James D. Morrow. 2003. *The Logic of Political Survival*. Cambridge: MIT Press.

Cheibub, José, Jennifer Gandhi, and James Vreeland. 2010. "Democracy and Dictatorship Revisited." *Public Choice* 143: 67–101.

Chimni, B. S. 2004. "International Institutions Today: An Imperial Global State in the Making." *European Journal of International Law* 15: 1–37.

Cingranelli, David and David Richards. 2011. *The Cingranelli-Richards (CIRI) Human Rights Dataset*, version 2011.12.09, http://www.humanrightsdata.org.

Cook, Steven. 2006. "Getting to Arab Democracy: The Promise of Pacts." *Journal of Democracy* 17: 63–74.

de Maistre, Joseph. 1810. "Essay on Generative Principles of Constitutions," in Jack Lively, ed., *The Works of Joseph de Maistre*. New York: Schocken Books, pp. 147–83.

Epp, Charles. 1998. *The Rights Revolution: Lawyers, Activists, and Supreme Courts in Comparative Perspective*. Chicago: University of Chicago Press.

El-Ghobashy, Mona. 2008. "Constitutional Contention in Contemporary Egypt." *American Behavioral Scientist* 51: 1590–1610.

Elkins, Zachary and Simmons, Beth. 2005. "On Waves, Clusters, and Diffusion: A Conceptual Framework." *Annals of the American Academy of Political and Social Science* 598: 33–51.

Elkins, Zachary et al. 2009. *The Endurance of National Constitutions* (Cambridge: Cambridge University Press).

Elkins, Zachary, Tom Ginsburg, and James Melton. 2014. "The Content of Authoritarian Constitutions," in Tom Ginsburg and Alberto Simpser, eds., *Constitutions in Authoritarian Regimes* 141–64.

Frank, David, Ann Hironaka, and Evan Schofer. 2000. "The Nation-State and the Natural Environment Over the Twentieth Century." *American Sociology Review* 65: 96–116.

Feld, Lars P. and Voigt, Stefan. 2003. "Economic growth and judicial independence: cross-country evidence using a new set of indicators." *European Journal of Political Economy*, Elsevier, 19: 497–527.

Geddes, Barbara. 1999. "What Do We Know About Democratization After Twenty Years?" *Annual Review of Political Science* 2: 115–44.

Ginsburg, Tom. 2013. "Constitutions as Charters, Constitutions as Covenants," in Denis Galligan and Mila Versteeg, eds., *The Social and Political Foundations of Constitutions*, 182–204.

Gleditsch, Kristian. 2007. *Expanded War Data*, version 1.52 (May 23, 2007). Available at http://privatewww.essex.ac.uk/~ksg/expwar.html.

Goderis, Benedikt and Mila Versteeg. 2011. *Transnational Constitutions*. 6th Annual Conference on Empirical Legal Studies. Available at http://ssrn.com/abstract=1865724.

Greene, William. 2011. *Econometric Analysis*. Boston, MA: Prentice Hall.

Hadenius, A. and J. Teorell. 2007. "Pathways from Authoritarianism." *Journal of Democracy* 18(1): 143–56.

Hafner-Burton, Emilie and Kiyoteru Tsutsui. 2005. "Human Rights in a Globalizing World: The Paradox of Empty Promises." *American Journal of Sociology* 110: 1373–1411.

Hardin, Russell. 1989. "Why a Constitution?" in Bernard Grofman and Donald Wittman, eds., *The Federalist Papers and the New Institutionalism*. New York: Agathon Press, pp. 100–20.

Hardin, Russell. 2013. "Why a Constitution?" in Denis Galligan and Mila Versteeg, eds., *The Social and Political Foundations of Constitutions*, 51–72.

Hassall, Graham and Cheryl Saunders. 2002. *Asia-Pacific Constitutional Systems*. Cambridge, UK: Cambridge University Press.

Hathaway, Oona. 2002. "Do Human Rights Treaties Make a Difference?" *Yale Law Journal* 111: 1935–74.

Hegel, G.W.F. The Philosophy of Right (T.M. Knox trans., Oxford University Press 1st ed. 1952) (1820).

Henderson, Conway. 1993. "Population Pressures and Political Repression." *Social Science Quarterly* 74: 322–33.

Henisz, Witold J. 2002. The Institutional Environment for Infrastructure Investment." *Industrial and Corporate Change* 11: 355–89.

Hirschl, Ran. 2013. "The Strategic Foundations of Constitutions," in Denis Galligan and Mila Versteeg, eds., *The Social and Political Foundations of Constitutions*, pp. 157–181.

Howard, Marc and Philip Roessler. 2006. "Liberalizing Electoral Outcomes in Competitive Authoritarian Regimes." *American Journal of Political Science* 50: 365–81.

Howard, Dick A. E. 2009. "A Traveller from an Antique Land: The Modern Renaissance of Comparative Constitutionalism." *Virginia Journal of International Law* 50: 3–29.

Keith, Linda C. 2002. "Constitutional Provisions for Individual Human Rights (1977–1996): Are They More Than Mere 'Window Dressing'?" *Political Research Quarterly* 55: 111–43.

Klug, Heinz. 2000. *Constituting Democracy: Law, Globalism and South Africa's Political Reconstruction*, Cambridge, UK: Cambridge University Press.

Lane, Jan-Erik. 1996. *Constitutions and Political Theory*. Manchester, UK: Manchester University Press.

Law, David. 2010. "Constitutions," in Peter Cane and Herbert Kritzer, eds., *The Oxford Handbook of Empirical Legal Research*. Oxford, UK: Oxford University Press, pp. 379–98.

Law, David and Mila Versteeg. 2011. "The Evolution and Ideology of Global Constitutionalism." *California Law Review* 99: 1163–1257.

Law, David and Mila Versteeg. 2012. "The Declining Influence of the United States Constitution." *New York University Law Review* 87: 762–858.

Law, David and Mila Versteeg. 2013. "Sham Constitutions." *California Law Review* 101: 863–952.

Levitsky, S. and L. A. Way. 2002. "The Rise of Competitive Authoritarianism." *Journal of Democracy* 13: 51.

Marcos, Miguel. 2003. "Comparative Law at the Service of Democracy: A Reading of Arosemena's Constitutional Studies of the Latin American Governments." *Boston University International Law Journal* 21: 259–323.

Marshall, Monty and Keith Jaggers. 2007. *Polity IV Project: Dataset User's Manual*. Available at http://home.bi.no/a0110709/PolityIV_manual.pdf.

Mayer, Kenneth and Howard Schweber. 2008. "Does Australia Have a Constitution? Part I: Powers – A Constitution Without Constitutionalism." *UCLA Pacific Basin Law Journal* 25: 228–64.

Melton, James, Zachary Elkins, Tom Ginsburg and Kalev Leetaru. 2013. "On the Interpretability of Law: Lessons from the Decoding of National Constitutions." *British Journal of Political Science* 43: 399–423.

Meyer, John, John Boli, George Thomas, and Francisco Ramirez. 1997. "World Society and the Nation-State." *American Journal of Sociology* 103: 144–81.

Minorities at Risk. 2011. Minorities at Risk Project (last updated Mar. 10, 2011), http://www.cidcm.umd.edu/mar).

Moustafa, Tamir and Tom Ginsburg. 2008. "Introduction: The Function of Courts in Authoritarian Politics," in Tom Ginsburg and Tamir Moustafa, eds., *Rule by Law: The Politics of Courts in Authoritarian Regimes*. Cambridge, UK: Cambridge University Press, pp. 1–22.

Murphy, Walter. 1993. "Constitutions, Constitutionalism, and Democracy," in Douglas Greenberg et al., eds., *Constitutionalism and Democracy: Transitions in the Contemporary World*. New York: Oxford University Press, pp. 3–25.

Murphy, Walter. 2007. *Constitutional Democracy: Creating and Maintaining a Just Political Order*. Baltimore, MD: Johns Hopkins University Press.

Nolutshungu, Samuel. 1993. "Constitutionalism in Africa: Some Conclusions," in Douglas Greenberg et al., eds., *Constitutionalism and Democracy: Transitions in the Contemporary World*. New York: Oxford University Press, pp. 366–78.

Ordeshook, Peter. 1992. *A Political Theory Primer*. New York: Routledge Press.

Poe, Steven and C. Neal Tate. 1994. "Repression of Human Rights to Personal Integrity in the 1980s: A Global Analysis." *American Political Science Review* 88: 853–72.

Poe, Steven, Neal Tate, and Linda Keith. 1999. "Repression of the Human Right to Integrity Revisited: A Global Cross-National Study Covering the Years 1976–1993." *International Studies Quarterly* 43: 291–313.

Pritchard, K. 1986. "Comparative Human Rights: An Integrative Explanation." *Policy Studies Journal* 15: 110–22.

Przeworski, Adam. 1991. *Democracy and the Market: Political and Economic Reforms in Eastern Europe and Latin America*. Cambridge, MA: Cambridge University Press.

Reale, Egidio. 1939. "The Italian Constitution Under Fascism." *Foreign Affairs* 18: 1953–57.

Rogers, Everett. 2003. *Diffusion of Innovations*. New York: Free Press.

Sakwa, Richard. 1996. "The Struggle for the Constitution in Russia and the Triumph of Ethical Individualism." *Studies in East European Thought* 48: 115–57.

Sartori, Giovanni. 1962. "Constitutionalism: A Preliminary Discussion." *American Political Science Review* 56: 853–64.

Schedler, Andreas. 2009. The New Institutionalism in the Study of Authoritarian Regimes. Centro de Investigación y Docencia Económicas, División de Estudios Políticos, 2009. Working Paper # 215.

Simmons, Beth. 2009. *Mobilizing for Human Rights: International Law in Domestic Politics*. Cambridge, MA: Cambridge University Press.

Trochev, Alexei. 2013. "Fragmentation? Defection? Legitimacy? Explaining judicial roles in post-communist 'colored revolutions," in Diana Kapiszewski et al., eds., *Consequential Courts: New Judicial Roles in Global Perspective*. Cambridge: Cambridge University Press, pp. 67–92.

Vanhanen, Tatu. 2003. Democratization and Power Resources 1850–2000 (dataset ver. 1.0).

Weingast, Barry. 1997. "The Political Foundations of Democracy and the Rule of Law." *American Political Science Review* 91: 245–63.

Williams, George. 2004. "Human Rights and Judicial Review in a Nation Without a Bill of Rights: The Australian Experience," in Grant Huscroft and Ian Brodie, eds., *Constitutionalism in the Charter Era*. Markham, ON: LexisNexis, pp. 305–34.

World Bank. 2013. *World Development Indicators*. Available at http://data.worldbank.org/indicator.

Zhang, Qianfan. 2010. "A Constitution Without Constitutionalism? The Paths of Constitutional Development in China." *International Journal of Constitutional Law* 8: 950–76.

PART IV

Consequences of Authoritarian Constitutions

9

The Role of Presidential Power in Authoritarian Elections

*Jennifer Gandhi**

INTRODUCTION

Authoritarian regimes usually operate under an official legal order, either maintaining a past democratic constitution (e.g., the 1935 constitution during Marcos's early years in the Philippines) or creating a new constitution (e.g., Yushin constitution under Park in South Korea). While constitutions in these contexts often are viewed as "shams" or a form of "window dressing," this may, in fact, not always be the case. Barros (2002) details how the 1980 constitution in Chile – the military's own creation – constrained the junta and ultimately paved the way for the transition to democracy. Albertus and Menaldo (2011), more generally in Latin America, find that some dictators construct greater institutional constraints to their authority through constitutions and, as a result, survive in power longer. In this way, constitutions are another power-sharing device that enables authoritarian leaders and elites to prolong their rule (Myerson 2008; Svolik 2009).

Incumbents, however, are not the only ones influenced by constitutional rules under authoritarianism. Constitutions also shape the strategies of opposition parties when they compete in authoritarian elections. While authoritarian incumbents attempt to use their "menu of manipulation" to ensure electoral victory, opposition parties must decide how best to challenge these regimes (Schedler 2006). One decision parties must make is whether to form preelectoral pacts in an effort to defeat the incumbent (Howard and Roessler 2006; Van de Walle 2006). In the case of presidential elections, coalitions form when several parties agree to support

* Thanks to the participants of the Conference on Constitutions under Authoritarianism, University of Chicago School of Law (October 21–22, 2011), for their comments and suggestions; to Zach Elkins, Tom Ginsburg, and James Melton for sharing data from the *Comparative Constitutions Project*; and to Pascael Barclay, Jana Marie Hutchinson, and Andrew Kirkpatrick for their excellent research assistance.

one candidate for the election in exchange for cabinet positions and other political appointments.[1]

Opposition parties in authoritarian regimes sometimes manage to maintain a cohesive front in challenging incumbents. In the Philippines, for example, Salvador Laurel, head of the largest opposition party, agreed to support Corazon Aquino's candidacy in snap presidential elections called by Ferdinand Marcos in 1985. In Kenya, opposition leaders formed the National Rainbow Coalition (NARC) in support of Mwai Kibaki, leading to his victory in 2002 over the regime-sponsored candidate, Uhuru Kenyatta. Yet for every instance of successful coalitions, there are spectacular cases of noncoordination among opposition parties, and these failures enable authoritarian incumbents to use elections to perpetuate their rule. In South Korea, for example, neither Kim Dae Jung nor Kim Young Sam was willing to yield in his quest to become president, clearing the way for the regime candidate, Roh Tae Woo, to win the 1988 election with only 36 percent of the vote. In the 1992 presidential elections in Kenya, seven opposition candidates ran against the fourteen-year incumbent, Daniel Arap Moi, allowing him to squeak by with 37 percent of the vote.

The variation in opposition unity points to an underlying tension facing these parties. As Przeworski (1991: 67) observes, the struggle for democracy "creates a dilemma: to bring about democracy, anti-authoritarian forces must unite against authoritarianism, but to be victorious under democracy, they must compete with each other. Hence, the struggle for democracy always takes place on two fronts: against the authoritarian regime for democracy and against one's allies for the best place under democracy." Constitutions under authoritarianism influence how parties decide to resolve this tension.

The chapter proceeds as follows. In the next section I introduce the empirical puzzle of preelectoral coalitions among opposition parties. In the third section I discuss how constitutions can influence the problem of coordination confronting opposition parties. In the fourth section I provide an empirical test of the argument followed by a discussion of the results. The chapter closes with a brief conclusion.

ELECTIONS UNDER AUTHORITARIANISM

Multiparty elections in nondemocracies are increasingly common. Yet these are elections that "violate the liberal-democratic principles of freedom and fairness so profoundly and systematically as to render elections instruments of authoritarian rule" (Schedler 2006). Some of the ways in which nondemocratic incumbents violate the spirit of "free and fair" elections include manipulation of electoral rules,

[1] In legislative coalitions, preelectoral coalitions form when parties agree to joint lists of candidates or not to run against each other in electoral districts.

state control of the media and other campaign resources, intimidation of candidates and their supporters, and electoral fraud (Levitsky and Way 2010).

Against this backdrop, opposition parties must consider how to effectively compete against an authoritarian incumbent. One way is to form preelectoral coalitions. A preelectoral coalition is an agreement among political parties to coordinate their efforts to maximize their seats and/or votes in elections. Coordination in elections among opposition parties can take a variety of forms, including the issuing of joint statements or the creation of joint electoral lists for legislative elections. In the context of presidential elections, it requires opposition parties to unite behind a single candidate. To pursue such actions, opposition parties contract with each other, and in deciding whether to "sign" a contract with others, each party must weigh the costs and benefits of doing so.

The decision to form a preelectoral coalition is an important one because it directly influences election results, which, in turn, may affect the stability of the authoritarian regime. Even though autocratic incumbents use manipulation, fraud, and violence to control electoral processes, opposition parties sometimes manage to maintain a cohesive front and go on to win. Coalitions resulted in Aquino's victory in the Philippines and Kibaki's in Kenya. Howard and Roessler (2006) argue that more generally, preelectoral coalitions lead to liberalizing outcomes, including those that fall short of a full democratic transition. Before understanding the effects of coalitions, however, it is useful to understand why preelectoral coalitions would form in the first place (Van de Walle 2006). While this has been studied in the context of democracies (Carroll and Cox 2007; Golder 2006), it has been rarely examined in the context of nondemocracies.

Table 9.1 provides cases in which the regime candidate, facing more than one opposition candidate, received less than 50 percent of the total votes in a presidential election. Assuming that voters who cast their ballots for separate opposition candidates would have supported a single representative of the opposition, coordination among opposition parties would have resulted in an opposition victory.

Probably some voters made strategic decisions in supporting the incumbent, preferring not to bear the costs of opposing the regime when the opposition was so divided and unlikely to win. These voters might have switched their vote to an opposition candidate who headed a unified coalition. Their actions could have made the difference in a number of other elections in which the regime candidate obtained just more than a majority. All together, the regime candidate polled less than 60 percent of the vote in 43 percent of the elections. That the regime allowed for opposition candidates to come so close to achieving victory indicates that in these cases, incumbents may have been willing to step down. These cases beg the question: Why did opposition parties fail in forming a united electoral front? Or more generally, under what conditions do opposition parties form coalitions to present a unity candidate in presidential elections?

TABLE 9.1. *"Failures" to form opposition coalitions in authoritarian presidential elections, 1946–2008*

Country-year	Regime candidate*	Regime votes, percentage of total**	Opposition candidates, number	Runoff
Angola 1992	Jose Eduardo dos Santos	49.6	10	No
Belarus 1994	Alyaksandr Lukashenko	44.8	4	Yes
Bolivia 1979	Hernan Siles Zuazo	36	7	No
Bolivia 1980	Hernan Siles Zuazo	38.7	12	No
Bosnia-Herzegovina 1996	Alija Izetbegovic	42.3	3	No
Burkina Faso 1978	Sangoule Lamizana	42.2	3	Yes
Cameroon 1992	Paul Biya	40.0	5	No
Chad 1996	Idriss Deby	43.8	14	Yes
Comoros 2002	Azali Assoumani	39.8	8	Yes
Dem. Rep. of Congo 2006	Joseph Kabila	44.8	32	Yes
El Salvador 1972	Arturo Armando Molina	43.4	3	No
Guatemala 1958	Miguel Ydigoras Fuentes	40.8	3	No
Guinea-Bissau 1994	Joao Bernardo Vieira	46.2	7	Yes
Honduras 1954	Tiburcio Carias Andino	30.8	2	No
Iran 2005	Mahmoud Ahmadinejad	20.3	6	Yes
Kenya 1992	Daniel Arap Moi	36.6	7	No
Kenya 1997	Daniel Arap Moi	40.4	14	No
Korea, South 1963	Park Chun Hee	46.6	4	No
Korea, South 1987	Roh Tae Woo	35.9	4	No
Korea, South 1992	Kim Young Sam	42	6	No
Moldova 1996	Mircea Snegur	38.7	4	Yes
Niger 1993	Mamadou Tandja	34.3	7	Yes
Niger 1999	Mamadou Tandja	32.3	6	Yes
Nigeria 1983	Shehi Shegari	47.5	5	No
Panama 1948	Domingo Diaz Arosemena	38.5	4	No
Panama 1984	Nicolas Ardito Barletto	46.9	6	No
Peru 2000	Alberto Fujimori	49.9	8	Yes
Zambia 2001	Levy Patrick Mwanawasa	29.1	10	No
Zambia 2006	Levy Patrick Mwanawasa	43.0	4	No
Zambia 2008	Rupiah Banda	40.1	3	No
Zimbabwe 2008	Robert Mugabe	43.2	3	Yes

* Refers to either the incumbent or the candidate supported by the incumbent who ultimately wins the election.

** For cases in which a runoff occurs, refers to the regime candidate's vote share in the first round.

THE PROBLEM OF COOPERATION

Consider a simplified version of the world in which there are two opposition candidates (or parties), *A* and *B*, who are deciding whether to form a coalition in an authoritarian election. Because they are contesting a presidential election, formation of a coalition will require one of the parties (say, *B*) to agree not to contest the election and support the other party's candidate (A) as the opposition standard bearer. In exchange, *B* will receive an important ministry in A's cabinet should A win the election. This is the nature of the power-sharing agreement that underlies the electoral coalition.

Assume that the candidates are located close enough to each other in the policy space so that ideology does not present an obstacle to coordination and that the regime's actions are constant so that any type of action by the opposition parties will result in a cost that is borne equally by both parties. In other words, the expected value of pursuing cooperative action for either party is determined primarily by what the other party does (rather than what the authoritarian regime might do).

If opposition candidate A wins the election, he becomes president. Under the preelectoral agreement, *B* becomes a cabinet member. Whether A and *B* actually achieve office depends on the voters. If voters do not support A in the election, he does not become president, which, in turn, means that *B* cannot become a minister. But while A's capture of political office depends only on the voters, in order for *B* to obtain political power, he relies also on A to appoint and keep him as a minister. As a result, *B* should enter into a preelectoral agreement with A only if he believes that A can and will honor their original bargain once A wins the presidency.

Why is abiding by the terms of the original agreement so important? Presumably, the preelectoral agreement over the division of political offices reflects the parties' respective bargaining powers: A became the presidential candidate and *B* was only promised a ministry because A is a more powerful candidate/party than *B*. Power, however, may also be a function of political office. In presidential systems, the holding of formal office may enable a political leader to maintain a following through access to informal networks and the distribution of patronage (Hale 2011). Upon A's victory, then, *B*'s concern is whether he will obtain the position he was promised in order to maintain the balance of power between the two parties. If A does not appoint *B* to office, *B*'s power will diminish from *before* to *after* the election. What is problematic for the candidates/parties, then, is the postelectoral enforcement of their preelectoral agreement over the distribution of political offices. The degree to which enforcement is problematic affects how hard parties will bargain in the first place (Fearon 1998). The enforcement problem may sow enough seeds of distrust among opposition parties that coalitions do not form.

Indeed, the inability to trust their bargaining partners is endemic in negotiations among opposition parties in authoritarian regimes. In 2005, the chief opposition party in Zimbabwe, the Movement for Democratic Change (MDC), split into two factions because of a disagreement over the party's decision to contest Senate elections that year. After a close internal party vote resulted in the decision to participate (rather than boycott), party leader Morgan Tsvangirai demanded the vote be ignored, precipitating the departure of Arthur Mutambara (and his followers) amid accusations that Tsvangirai was behaving undemocratically. Mutambara's fears appeared to be confirmed when Trudy Stevenson, a parliamentarian and member of his faction, accused Tsvangirai's supporters of a machete attack in 2006. As one political commentator observed: "If you are prepared to beat people up when you are still in opposition, what would happen if you have the state machinery at your disposal – you have the CIO, the army, police – would anybody be able to stand up against you?" (Nyaira 2006). When presidential elections in 2008 presented the opposition with the opportunity to take down a weakened Robert Mugabe, the two sides could not find a way to address their mutual mistrust. Talks to create a coalition broke down, and both Tsvangirai and Mutambara offered themselves as presidential candidates. "Had the MDC entered the presidential round in lockstep with Mutambara, Tsvangirai might have got the crucial extra votes to win the presidency outright" in the first round (Chan 2008).

The fears and failures of opposition forces in Zimbabwe are experienced by opposition challengers in many authoritarian states. In Kyrgyzstan, for example, a comprehensive survey of opposition leaders from several parties found that "a lack of trust of other members of the opposition (an inability to take others at their word)" complicates efforts to cooperate (Huskey and Iskakova 2010). Similarly, in Egypt, when a member of an opposition party was asked why his party did not cooperate with others in protesting the 1995 election results, he answered: " . . . but how can we work with other groups when we don't know about their intentions?" (Sahgal 2008: 130–1). Finally, the Democratic Party (DP) in Uganda declined to join an opposition formation, the Inter-Party Coalition (IPC), in its attempt to defeat the incumbent, Yoweri Museveni, in a 2011 presidential contest. The DP's candidate, Norbert Mao, explained the controversial decision, claiming that while his party and those in the IPC shared similar preferences on many issues, he was forced to ask himself: "Is the solution only to change the presidential portrait that hangs on a wall?"[2] Opposition leaders from Zimbabwe to Kyrgyzstan to Egypt to Uganda voice the same concern: the uncertainty about the future intentions and behavior of potential partners can create an impediment to cooperating when challenging authoritarian incumbents in elections.

THE ROLE OF CONSTITUTIONS

How do authoritarian constitutions enter this picture? Whether the future occupant of the presidency can and will abide by the power-sharing agreement depends on the type and strength of the powers attached to the office of chief executive. Because pre-electoral coalitions rest on promises of political offices, the nature of the president's power to select his cabinet or make other political appointments is important. Some presidents have the power to unilaterally appoint cabinet members, while others face

[2] "History Will Absolve Us on IPC Question" (http://www.democraticparty.ug/; downloaded November 28, 2010).

institutional constraints on their powers to choose (usually in the form of legislative participation). What presidents endowed with strong appointment powers may do is unclear. On the one hand, the ability to unilaterally make political appointments may enable the new president to better fulfill the preelectoral agreement. Without having to negotiate with the assembly, *A* easily can appoint *B* to the cabinet. Knowing this, *B* should enter into a preelectoral coalition when he expects *A* to inherit a presidency with strong appointment powers. On the other hand, unilateral appointment power implies unchecked power for the president, which possibly makes it easier for him to renege on a preelectoral deal. Anticipating that this may happen, *B* should not enter into agreement with *A* under strong presidential powers of appointment. Indeed, the quote from Mutambara's supporter – "If you are prepared to beat people up when you are still in opposition, what would happen if you have the state machinery at your disposal . . . " – suggests that parties worry about the president's power to renege – and in even more sinister forms. If the constitution provides the president with unilateral control over the coercive apparatus of the state, parties may worry that a victory of one of their peers may just lead to another dictatorship.

In order for current constitutional rules to serve as a cue to opposition parties about the type of presidency they stand to inherit, parties must anticipate that these are the rules with which they might govern. While major constitutional change commonly accompanies democratic transitions, it usually seems to occur before elections. For the 1989 to 2006 period, for example, of the forty-nine transitions to democracy, there were twenty-one cases in which a new constitution was adopted. Yet in seventeen of these cases, the new constitution was adopted before the presidential election, thereby allowing parties to condition their expectations on the new document. In the remaining cases, the new government governs with the old authoritarian constitution, but amendments often occur before the election. The timing of these legal changes enables parties to use constitutional provisions at the time of the election to form their expectations about the strength of the presidency they stand to inherit after the election.

If parties are intent on betraying their coalition partners and establishing a new dictatorship, why would they allow the constitution to constrain their behavior in doing so? In other words, why would parties expect that these provisions would be anything more than "parchment boundaries" for a new president? A new president comes to office under the burden of having to construct a new regime and gain legitimacy for it. As a result, while he may want to pass on advantages to his political forces, he may feel constrained by constitutional rules that may serve as a coordinating device for potential opposition within his regime (Weingast 1997). If the president exceeds constitutional limits on his power in trying to gain political advantages, his transgressions may serve to mobilize opposition to his rule.[3]

[3] Of course, if some candidates or parties already have the intention of dismantling their opponents once they come to power, the constitutional powers – weak or strong – will do little to constrain them. If this is the case, we should observe no relationship between legal rules and preelectoral coalitions.

The notion that strong presidential powers impede coordination among the opposition is consistent with another theory of coalition formation. It may be the case that opposition parties run separately because each views the office of the presidency as a prize too large to give up. Because formation of a preelectoral coalition for a presidential election requires some parties to give up their presidential aspirations, when the office comes endowed with strong powers, parties may be unwilling to make the sacrifice, especially if they each believe they have a good chance of winning. While this theory produces a similar prediction – that strong presidential powers should be correlated with nonformation of electoral coalitions – it fails to capture the mistrust that appears to characterize the attitudes of opposition parties toward their peers.

EMPIRICAL ANALYSIS

To examine the relationship between presidential powers and coalition formation, I examine all direct multicandidate presidential elections from 1946 to 2008 held under the auspices of an incumbent who came to power through nondemocratic means (i.e., coup, revolution, *autogolpe*). The sample includes 264 elections from eighty-five countries.[4] In each presidential election, there must be at least one challenger, and both political parties and electoral coalitions must be legal.[5] To identify authoritarian elections, I follow Przeworski et al.'s (2000) minimalist definition.[6] Because regime type of a country is coded as of December 31 of the year, the sample includes all presidential elections in dictatorial years and in the first year of a democratic spell if the election occurred prior to the regime change. This procedure ensures that all elections in the sample were held under the auspices of authoritarian incumbents.

The dependent variable is a proxy to measure the degree of cooperation among opposition parties: the vote share of the largest opposition party in the first round of the election (if there are two rounds).[7] If parties do not enter or withdraw from the race in order to support a unity candidate, the vote share obtained by this candidate should be larger (Van de Walle 2006).[8] Voting results come from Nohlen et al. (1999, 2002, 2005), the African Elections Database, and the IFES Election Guide.

4 For a list of the countries and election years, see Appendix I.

5 Therefore, plebiscites and referenda on the incumbent are not included. The condition that parties and coalitions must be legal excludes thirty-eight elections from the list in Appendix I.

6 Nondemocracies include all regimes that (1) do not have competitive legislative elections, (2) do not have competitive executive elections, (3) do not allow for more than one political party, and/or (4) do not allow for alternation in office. For an updated version of the data, see Cheibub and colleagues (2010).

7 In presidential elections, it is not obvious what should be the universe of all possible coalition partners because any single individual can declare himself/herself as a candidate. Therefore, creating dichotomous measures of cooperation between party dyads as Golder (2006) does in examining democratic legislative elections is not feasible.

8 Descriptive statistics of all variables in the analysis are in Appendix II.

The power of the presidency that opposition parties expect to inherit is found in the constitution under which the election occurs. Given that negotiations over the formation of preelectoral coalitions usually focus on the distribution of political office, I include the power of the president to appoint and dismiss cabinet ministers. *Cabinet appointment* is a dichotomous measure, taking the value of 1 when the president has unilateral power to approve his ministers, 0 when he must share this power with other institutions (e.g., legislative chambers, the majority party) or must act on the basis of electoral results. *Cabinet dismissal* is a dichotomous indicator with the value of 1 when the president has unilateral power to dismiss members of his cabinet, 0 otherwise. These measures of presidential power are constructed from data from the *Comparative Constitutions Project*. If strong presidential powers are necessary to enable opposition winners to fulfill their preelectoral commitments, then the sign of these variables should be positive. If, however, opposition parties expect that unilateral control over political offices will allow the winner to renege, they may be less likely to enter into an agreement under strong presidential powers. Negative signs on these indicators would constitute evidence of a commitment problem among opposition parties.

One indicator of the president's coercive powers is his institutional capacity to declare states of emergency. *Emergency power* is dichotomous, coded 1 when the president has sole power to declare a state of emergency, 0 when he must share this power with another institution (usually a legislature and sometimes an unelected body, such as a national security council). This variable also is constructed from information from the *Comparative Constitutions Project*. Since the coercive powers of the state would be used only to renege on any preelectoral agreement, the variable is expected to take a negative sign.

Table 9.2 provides a first look at the relationship between presidential powers and opposition coordination. The table shows the mean vote share of the largest opposition candidate under weak and strong powers of appointment, dismissal, and state of emergency. Consistent with the theory, the average vote share of the largest opposition candidate is significantly larger when the president's powers to dismiss cabinet members and to call a state of emergency are weak. When the president's powers to appoint are weak, the average vote share is higher, although the difference-in-means is not significantly different from zero.

I use regression analysis to determine whether *de jure* presidential powers still have an effect after controlling for electoral institutions, social cleavages, past interactions among the parties, and actions by the regime.

Parties trying to form a coalition for the presidential election may be helped or hindered by negotiations over concurrent legislative elections. On the one hand, forming a legislative preelectoral coalition should be easier than a presidential one because of the divisibility of gains in the former. So the momentum gained from forming a legislative coalition may spill over into concurrent presidential elections.

TABLE 9.2. *Difference-in-means of opposition vote share under weak and strong presidential powers*

	Vote share of largest opposition candidate		
	Mean	Std error	N
Weak appointment power	24.738	1.930	76
Strong appointment power	27.433	1.406	124
Combined samples	26.409	1.140	200
Difference between samples	–2.695	2.388	
Weak dismissal power	28.705	2.038	70
Strong dismissal power	25.173	1.361	130
Combined samples	26.409	1.140	200
Difference between samples	3.531*	2.451	
Weak emergency power	30.613	2.276	60
Strong emergency power	25.704	1.230	163
Combined samples	27.025	1.095	223
Difference between samples	4.909**	2.587	

For independent samples with unequal variances
* One-tailed test ($t = 1.4406$; $p = 0.0760$); ** One-tailed test ($t = 1.8973$; $p = 0.0304$)

On the other hand, concurrent elections mean that parties may feel compelled to form a coalition encompassing both elections. An increasing number of issues on the table may present more potential stumbling blocks for parties attempting to reach agreement. *Concurrent election,* a dichotomous variable coded 1 if there are presidential and legislative elections within twelve months of each other, 0 otherwise, is included.

Provisions regarding runoffs if no candidate succeeds in securing a majority in the first round should affect the decision of candidates to enter in the first place. Runoff elections should result in more presidential challengers, or less opposition coordination, for two reasons. First, under plurality, only one candidate can win, while under two-round runoff, two can move past the first stage. As a result, a challenger who might anticipate winning enough votes for second place might not enter an election with plurality rule but will if he knows that a second round is possible (Cox 1997). Second, candidates might enter the race with the goal of obtaining enough votes so that they can bargain for benefits in exchange for their endorsement (Jones 1999). With the possibility of reaching a second round, these candidates might be in a better position to bargain for benefits. *Runoff,* a dichotomous variable coded 1 if electoral rules allow for a second-round runoff among top candidates from the first round, 0 for plurality formula, is expected to have a negative impact on the vote share of the largest opposition candidate.[9]

9 Second-round polling usually consists of just the top two vote getters from the first round but in rare cases may include more than just these two (e.g., Tanzania). These unusual cases are included on

Electoral rules work in tandem with social cleavages to determine the number of competitors in elections (Cox 1997; Mozaffar et al. 2003; Ordeshook and Shvetsova 1994). A greater number of social cleavages, all else being equal, should encourage the entrance of more opposition candidates. To capture the effect of social cleavages on opposition strategies, *Ethnic fractionalization* is included. It is constructed as $1 - \Sigma(p_i^2)$, where p_i is the share of the population that belongs to ethnic group *i* and is from Alesina and Ferrara (2005). It is expected to have a negative effect on the largest party's vote share.

The interaction among opposition parties probably differs in countries in which elections take place infrequently from those in which contests for the presidency are regular events. In countries such as Burundi, Cambodia, Egypt, and Uruguay, presidential elections under the auspices of an authoritarian incumbent occurred only once during the postwar period. In contrast, in states such as Azerbaijan, Gambia, Mexico, and Senegal, presidential elections occurred at regular intervals, allowing opposition parties to interact repeatedly. While repeated interaction may help parties "learn" how to cooperate, it also may teach them to mistrust their peers – depending on the nature of their interactions. To capture the effects of past interactions and the frequency of those situations, I include *Previous elections*, the number of presidential elections that occurred prior to the election at hand.[10] In addition, I include the *Previous opposition share*, the vote share of the largest opposition candidate in the previous presidential election.

The actions of authoritarian regimes may deter or facilitate coordination by opposition parties. Much of the literature on electoral authoritarianism focuses on how dictators use techniques such as the intimidation of candidates and votes to discourage opposition efforts. To capture some of these coercive tactics, I include *Harassment*, a dichotomous variable based on whether there is evidence that the government harassed the opposition in the lead-up to the elections (Hyde and Marinov 2011). Its effect is expected to be negative. In addition, I control for the type of authoritarian regime under which elections are being held because military dictatorships are more likely to give way to democratic transitions. *Military dictatorship* is coded 1 if the effective head of government is from the armed forces, 0 otherwise (Cheibub et al. 2010). If military regimes are more likely to preside over transitional elections, they are likely to experience less opposition cooperation as each party jockeys to protect its position for the future.

Ordinary least squares is used to estimate the models with standard errors clustered by country. Table 9.3 provides results from models with different specifications. Model 1 includes only the relevant presidential powers, providing a baseline with

the grounds that as long as the second round admits fewer candidates than the first, the strategic winnowing out of candidates should still occur, if only in lesser degrees.

10 It also may be the case that in nondemocracies with regular elections, ideological cleavages are more salient, impeding cooperation. In this case, the expected effect of *Previous elections* is negative.

TABLE 9.3. *Effect of presidential powers on opposition coordination*

	Dependent variable: vote share of largest opposition candidate		
	(1)	(2)	(3)
Cabinet approval	5.564**	4.100	2.285
	(2.464)	(2.484)	(3.684)
Cabinet dismissal	−6.045**	−6.718***	−6.087*
	(2.357)	(2.417)	(3.344)
Emergency power	−5.578**	−7.269**	−7.201*
	(2.282)	(2.734)	(3.749)
Concurrent election		7.574***	7.065*
		(2.542)	(3.804)
Runoff		0.046	−0.564
		(2.541)	(3.560)
Ethnic fractionalization		6.075	9.050
		(4.358)	(5.404)
Previous elections		0.659	1.284
		(0.598)	(0.919)
Previous opposition share			0.106
			(0.137)
Military dictatorship			0.479
			(3.019)
Harassment			−4.507
			(3.862)
Constant	31.101***	23.930***	19.659**
	(2.726)	(3.308)	(7.551)
Prob > F	0.0060	0.0012	0.0006
R-sq	0.0494	0.1116	0.1683
No. observations	200	196	116
No. countries	78	75	55

*** $p \leq 0.01$; ** $p \leq 0.05$; * $p \leq 0.10$

which to compare other specifications that include controls. Model 2 also incorporates control variables whose inclusion does not result in much listwise deletion of observations. Finally, model 3 includes all the variables discussed here.

In Table 9.3, the effect of presidential powers in all three models is broadly consistent with the difference-in-means results of Table 9.2: strong presidential powers to dismiss cabinet members and declare states of emergency are correlated with a decrease in opposition coordination (i.e., a decrease in the vote share of the largest candidate). These effects retain their significance at conventional levels even after the inclusion of several control variables. In addition, their effects are of substantial magnitude in comparison to the effects of other variables. Unilateral power to appoint cabinet members is correlated with an increase in the vote share of the largest opposition candidate, but this effect is not always significantly different from zero.

Of the control variables, very few of them consistently affect the degree of cooperation among opposition candidates in presidential elections. The type of regime does not have a significant impact on the vote share of the largest candidate. Also noteworthy is that while the magnitude of the coefficient on ethnic fractionalization is large, its effect is not significantly different from zero. Interaction among the parties in previous elections does not affect the likelihood that they will cooperate. This may be because previous interactions teach both good and bad lessons about the ability to trust other parties. Alternatively, it may be that there is sufficient volatility within party systems that the same parties are not interacting with each other over time. Because the frequency of past interactions does not have an impact on current strategies, it seems unlikely that ideological considerations play a major role in determining coalition behavior. Even in regimes in which multiple elections may have given parties the chance to emphasize distinct ideologies, the antiregime dimension overwhelms any standard ideological or policy cleavages (Tucker 2006). Only the concurrency of elections has a significant impact: simultaneous legislative elections make coordination more likely in presidential races.

Why might concurrent elections facilitate opposition cooperation? One possibility is that concurrent elections may provide parties with the opportunity to create enforcement mechanisms to guard against reneging by the future president. If parties that give up their presidential aspirations know that they can secure a large enough proportion of seats in the legislature through concurrent elections, they may believe that their power within the legislature would enable them to check the power of the president. Presidents with strong powers may dissuade parties from cooperating, but concurrent elections may mitigate this effect. In these situations, the president may have powers to unilaterally control political appointments and emergency powers, but he will think twice about using them when faced with an assembly dominated by his coalition partners. Even though he has the capacity to renege on the power-sharing agreement, he may resist doing so out of fear of turning his allies into powerful foes on other issues.

The connection between presidential and legislative elections may explain what happened in the case of Kenya in 2002, for example. After two elections in which Daniel Arap Moi, the long-standing incumbent, had won with a plurality of votes, all eyes were on the opposition to see whether it could overcome its traditional divisions and present a unity candidate. Three opposition parties agreed to throw their support behind Mwai Kibaki, leader of the Democratic Party (Howard and Roessler 2006). Their promises of power sharing were made concrete in a secret memorandum of understanding (Kasara 2005). In exchange for the presidency, Kibaki promised to be president for only one term and to advocate constitutional changes that would reduce the powers of the presidency and create the post of prime minister, which would be given to Raila Odinga, the head of another major opposition party. Odinga and other opposition leaders, in turn, agreed to give up their presidential aspirations in order to support Kibaki as head of the coalition, NARC. Kibaki then proceeded to win the election with 62.2 percent of the vote.

What followed in Kenya directly points to the enforcement problem that parties face. After having promised constitutional reform and not to run for reelection in order to persuade Odinga and others to support him, Kibaki, after ascending to the presidency, proceeded to renege on his preelectoral promises. He stayed largely silent on the issue of constitutional reform, condemning it to failure in a referendum. When his term ended in 2007, Kibaki sought reelection, using his powers of incumbency, amid accusations of electoral fraud and intimidation, to win another term. The resulting postelectoral violence between supporters of Kibaki and Odinga directly stemmed from the sitting president's attempts to renege on the terms of the original preelectoral coalition in 2002.

Kibaki's maneuvers to stay in power prompt an obvious question: if everyone knew that Kibaki were to inherit a strong presidency, why did they sign an agreement with him solely on the basis of promises to reform the constitution? Odinga and others should have perceived these promises as not credible and, as a result, not entered into a coalition with Kibaki in the first place. Perhaps Kibaki's coalition partners anticipated their victory over his Democratic Party in concurrent assembly elections: of the 125 seats won by NARC (a majority within the assembly), 86 were won by parties other than Kibaki's. It could be that parties believe they can "solve" problems of postelectoral enforcement when concurrent elections allow for a relative balance of power among opposition parties as reflected in interbranch relations. In the case of Odinga and his partners, this appears to have been a mistake. The result may point to a general phenomenon: if coalitions form despite inappropriate constitutional conditions, they may break up in spectacular fashion, as NARC did in Kenya.

CONCLUSION

Elections under dictatorship typically are viewed as mere instruments by which incumbents perpetuate themselves in power. Yet the empirical record is more mixed: multiparty elections sometimes lead to democratic transitions (Lindberg 2008; Teorell 2010). The challenge is in determining how.

The electoral process does present moments when the opposition can organize itself in order to better challenge authoritarian rulers. One such moment that opposition parties can seize is the period before elections when they must decide whether to form a coalition. In deciding on the best strategies to pursue, however, opposition parties face competing pressures. Forming a preelectoral coalition may hold the promise of securing the "best place" for opposition parties: if cooperation results in electoral victory, then a coalition should be Pareto optimal for all parties to the agreement (even if some parties gain more than others). Yet this scenario depends crucially on the ability of parties to enforce their agreements – something that becomes problematic because parties are bargaining over the political positions endowed with powers that will enable them to affect the distribution of power in the future.

Parties in established democracies form coalitions, but they appear not to suffer from these problems of trust. This may be attributable to the importance of repeated interaction. Party systems in established democracies are relatively stable and, as a result, parties interact with each other frequently. If parties expect that they will be interacting in the future, they have interests in safeguarding their reputations for cooperation. In addition, the publicity of preelectoral agreements in democracies might also make them costly to break; voters might punish parties for reneging (Laver and Schofield 1998: 28). As a result, reneging on preelectoral agreements almost never happens in established democracies, leading most scholars of coalitions in democracies to disregard the enforcement problem (Carroll and Cox 2007; Golder 2006).

Because of the structure of the problem facing opposition parties in authoritarian elections, in contrast, the *de jure* powers of the president are important. Presidencies endowed with strong powers to affect parties' future political positions pose the greatest problem for opposition forces trying to form a preelectoral coalition. In the extreme, parties may fear that upon victory, one side will use the coercive institutions of the state to consolidate its rule. Or parties, absent the fear of violence, may simply worry that one side may be able to monopolize political offices.

In this context, authoritarian constitutions are more than just parchment. Like other types of formal political institutions, such as legislatures and parties, constitutions influence the behavior of political actors and the types of outcomes generated – even in authoritarian regimes. While recent work has examined how formal institutions affect the behavior of authoritarian incumbents (Barros 2002; Gandhi 2008; Lust-Okar 2005; Wright 2008), this analysis suggests that they have effects on the opposition as well. Written rules do matter: even if they do not perfectly constrain authoritarian incumbents, they influence the behavior of opposition parties that are striving to become future incumbents.

APPENDIX I. PRESIDENTIAL ELECTIONS IN AUTHORITARIAN REGIMES, 1946–2008

Afghanistan 2004	Korea (South) 1952, 1956, 1963, 1967, 1971, 1987, 1992
Algeria 1995, 1999, 2004	Kyrgyzstan 1995, 2000, 2005
Angola 1992	Liberia 1955, 1959, 1985, 1997, 2005
Argentina 1958, 1963, 1983	Madagascar 1982, 1989, 1992
Azerbaijan 1992, 1993, 1998, 2003, 2008	Malawi 1994

(*continued*)

APPENDIX I (*continued*)

Bangladesh 1978, 1981, 1986
Belarus 1994, 2001, 2006
Benin 1968, 1970, 1991
Bolivia 1951, 1956, 1960, 1964, 1966, 1978, 1979, 1980
Bosnia-Herzegovina 1996
Burkina Faso 1978, 1998, 2005
Burundi 1993
Cambodia 1972
Cameroon 1992, 1997, 2004
Cape Verde 1991
Central African Republic 1981, 1993
Chad 1996, 2001, 2006
Colombia 1949, 1958
Comoros 1996, 2002, 2006
Congo (Rep. of) 1992, 2002
Costa Rica 1948
Cote d'Ivoire 1990, 1995, 2000
Cuba 1958
Cyprus 1968
Dem. Rep. of Congo 2006
Djibouti 1993, 1999
Dominican Republic 1947, 1962, 1966
Ecuador 1948, 1968, 1978, 2002
Egypt 2005
El Salvador 1950, 1956, 1967, 1972, 1977, 1984
Equatorial Guinea 1968, 1996, 2002
Gabon 1993, 1998, 2005
Gambia 1982, 1987, 1992, 1996, 2001, 2006
Georgia 1991, 1995, 2000
Ghana 1960, 1979, 1992
Guatemala 1957, 1958, 1966, 1985
Guinea 1993, 1998, 2003
Guinea-Bissau 1994, 1999
Haiti 1957, 1988, 1990, 1995, 2000, 2006
Honduras 1948, 1954, 1971, 1981
Iran 1980, 1981 (2), 1985, 1989, 1993, 1997, 2001, 2005
Kazakhstan 1999, 2005
Kenya 1992, 1997, 2002
Maldives 2008
Mali 1992
Mauritania 1992, 1997, 2003, 2007
Mexico 1946, 1952, 1958, 1964, 1970, 1982, 1988, 1994, 2000
Moldova 1996
Montenegro 2008
Mozambique 1994, 1999, 2004
Namibia 1994, 1999, 2004
Nicaragua 1947, 1950, 1957, 1963, 1967, 1974, 1984
Niger 1993, 1996, 1999
Nigeria 1979, 1983, 1993, 1999, 2003, 2007
Panama 1948, 1952, 1968, 1984, 1989
Paraguay 1963, 1968, 1973, 1978, 1983, 1988
Peru 1956, 1963, 1980, 1995, 2000, 2001
Philippines 1969, 1981, 1986
Portugal 1949, 1958, 1976
Russian Federation 1991, 1996, 2000, 2004, 2008
Rwanda 2003
Senegal 1978, 1983, 1988, 1993, 2000
Serbia-Montenegro 2000
Seychelles 1993, 1998, 2001, 2006
Sierra Leone 1996
Sri Lanka 1982, 1988
Sudan 1996, 2000
Taiwan 1996, 2000
Tajikistan 1991, 1994, 1999, 2006
Tanzania 1995, 2000, 2005
Togo 1993, 1998, 2003, 2005
Tunisia 1999, 2004
Turkmenistan 2007
Uganda 1996, 2001, 2006
Uruguay 1984
Uzbekistan 1991, 2000, 2007
Venezuela 1958
Yemen 1999, 2006
Zambia 1968, 1991, 1996, 2001, 2006, 2008
Zimbabwe 1990, 1996, 2002, 2008

APPENDIX II. DESCRIPTIVE STATISTICS OF VARIABLES

Variable	Mean	Standard deviation	Minimum	Maximum	N
Dependent variable					
Vote share of largest opposition candidate	25.571	16.966	0	84	260
Independent variables (presidential powers)					
Cabinet appointment	0.631	0.483	0	1	236
Cabinet dismissal	0.644	0.480	0	1	236
Emergency power	0.693	0.462	0	1	264
Control variables					
Concurrent election	0.716	0.452	0	1	261
Ethnic fractionalization	0.529	0.265	0	0.930	259
Harassment	0.310	0.464	0	1	197
Military dictatorship	0.429	0.496	0	1	261
Previous election	1.655	1.744	0	8	264
Previous opposition share	24.650	16.560	0	84	176
Runoff	0.598	0.491	0	1	261

REFERENCES

African Elections Database. Available at http://africanelections.tripod.com.

Albertus, Michael and Victor Menaldo. 2011. *Dictators as Founding Fathers? The Role of Constitutions under Autocracy*. Manuscript.

Alesina, Alberto and Eliana La Ferrara. 2005. "Ethnic Diversity and Economic Performance." *Journal of Economic Literature* 43(3): 762–800.

Barros, Robert. 2002. *Constitutionalism and Dictatorship*. New York: Cambridge University Press.

Carroll, Royce and Gary Cox. 2007. "The Logic of Gamson's Law: Pre-election Coalitions and Portfolio Allocations." *American Journal of Political Science* 51(2): 300–13.

Chan, Stephen. 2008. "The Tragedy of Tsvangirai." *Prospect* 149(August). Available at http://www.prospect-magazine.co.uk/pdfarticle.php?id=10310. Downloaded November 11, 2008.

Cheibub, José Antonio, Jennifer Gandhi, and James Vreeland. 2010. "Democracy and Dictatorship Revisited." *Public Choice* 143(1–2): 67–101.

Cox, Gary. 1997. *Making Votes Count: Strategic Coordination in the World's Electoral Systems*. New York: Cambridge University Press.

Elkins, Zachary, Tom Ginsburg, and James Melton (national directors). *Comparative Constitutions Project*. Available at http://www.comparativeconstitutionsproject.org/index.htm.

Fearon, John. 1998. "Bargaining, Enforcement, and International Cooperation." *International Organization* 52(2): 269–305.

Gandhi, Jennifer. 2008. *Political Institutions under Dictatorship*. New York: Cambridge University Press.

Golder, Sona Nadenichek. 2006. *The Logic of Pre-Electoral Coalition Formation*. Columbus: Ohio State University Press.
Hale, Henry. 2011. "Formal Constitutions in Informal Politics: Institutions and Democratization in Eurasia." *World Politics* 63(4): 581–617.
Howard, Marc Morje and Philip G. Roessler. 2006. "Liberalizing Electoral Outcomes in Competitive Authoritarian Regimes." *American Journal of Political Science* 50(2): 365–81.
Huskey, Eugene and Gulnara Iskakova. 2010. "The Barriers to Intra-Opposition Cooperation in the Post-Communist World: Evidence from Kyrgyzstan." *Post-Soviet Affairs* 26(3): 228–62.
Hyde, Susan and Nikolay Marinov. 2011. "Which Elections Can Be Lost?" *Political Analysis*. First published online November 18, 2011. doi:10.1093/pan/mpr040.
International Foundation for Electoral Systems (IFES) Election Guide. Available at http://www.electionguide.org/.
Jones, Mark. 1999. "Electoral Laws and the Effective Number of Candidates in Presidential Elections." *Journal of Politics* 61(1): 171–84.
Kasara, Kimuli. 2005. *A Prize Too Large to Share: Opposition Coalitions and the Kenyan Presidency, 1991–2002*. Manuscript. Department of Political Science, Stanford University.
Laver, Michael and Norman Schofield. 1998. *Multiparty Government: The Politics of Coalition in Europe*. Ann Arbor: University of Michigan Press.
Levitsky, Steven and Lucan A. Way. 2010. *Competitive Authoritarianism: Hybrid Regime after the Cold War*. New York: Cambridge University Press.
Lindberg, Staffan. 2008. *Democracy and Elections in Africa*. Baltimore, MD: The Johns Hopkins University Press.
Lust-Okar, Ellen. 2005. *Structuring Conflict in the Arab World: Incumbents, Opponents, and Institutions*. New York: Cambridge University Press.
Mozaffar, Shaheen, James Scarritt, and Glen Galaich. 2003. "Electoral Institutions, Ethnopolitical Cleavages, and Party Systems in Africa's Emerging Democracies." *American Political Science Review* 97: 379–90.
Myerson, Roger. 2008. "The Autocrat's Credibility Problem and Foundations of the Constitutional State." *American Political Science Review* 102(1): 125–39.
Nohlen, Dieter (ed.). 2005. *Elections in the Americas: A Data Handbook, Volumes 1 and 2*. Oxford: Oxford University Press.
Nohlen, Dieter, Florian Grotz, and Christof Hartmann (eds.). 2002. *Elections in Asia and the Pacific: A Data Handbook, Volumes 1 and 2*. Oxford: Oxford University Press.
Nohlen, Dieter, Michael Krennerich, and Berhard Thibaut (eds.). 1999. *Elections in Africa*. Oxford: Oxford University Press.
Nyaira, Sandra. 2006. *Of Mutambara Rally and the MDC Split*. Association of Zimbabwe Journalists in the UK (May 16). Available at http://www.zimbabwejournalists.com/story.php?art_id=398&cat=3. Downloaded March 20, 2008.
Ordeshook, Peter and Olga Shvetsova. 1994. "Ethnic Heterogeneity, District Magnitude, and the Number of Parties." *American Journal of Political Science* 38: 100–23.
Przeworski, Adam. 1991. *Democracy and the Market*. New York: Cambridge University Press.
Przeworski, Adam, Michael Alvarez, José Antonio Cheibub, and Fernando Limongi. 2000. *Democracy and Development: Material Well-Being in the World, 1950–1990*. New York: Cambridge University Press.
Sahgal, Neha. 2008. *Divided We Stand, but United We Oppose? Opposition Alliances in Egypt and Pakistan*. Dissertation. Department of Political Science, University of Maryland–College Park.

Schedler, Andreas (ed.). 2006. *Electoral Authoritarianism: The Dynamics of Unfree Competition*. Boulder, CO: Lynne Rienner.

Svolik, Milan. 2009. "Power-Sharing and Leadership Dynamics in Authoritarian Regimes." *American Journal of Political Science* 53(2): 477–94.

Teorell, Jan. 2010. *Determinants of Democratization: Explaining Regime Change in the World, 1972–2006*. New York: Cambridge University Press.

Tucker, Joshua. 2006. *Regional Economic Voting: Russia, Poland, Hungary, Slovakia, and the Czech Republic, 1990–1999*. New York: Cambridge University Press.

Van de Walle, Nicolas. 2006. "Tipping Games? When Do Opposition Parties Coalesce?" In Andreas Schedler, ed., *Electoral Authoritarianism: The Dynamics of Unfree Competition*. Boulder, CO: Lynne Rienner, pp. 77–92.

Weingast, Barry. 1997. "The Political Foundations of Democracy and the Rule of Law." *American Political Science Review* 91(June): 245–63.

Wright, Joseph. 2008. "Do Authoritarian Institutions Constrain? How Legislatures Affect Economic Growth and Investment." *American Journal of Political Science* 52(2): 322–43.

10

The Informal Politics of Formal Constitutions

*Rethinking the Effects of "Presidentialism" and "Parliamentarism" in the Cases of Kyrgyzstan, Moldova, and Ukraine**

Henry E. Hale[1]
George Washington University

How do formal constitutions impact prospects for democratization? Most answers focus on how rules of the game in place during a transition process guide behavior in ways facilitating democratic stability, progress, or breakdown.[2] At the same time, a growing body of work calls this entire enterprise into question by arguing that formal institutions rarely operate as assumed.[3] The literature on hybrid regimes – political systems combining authoritarian and democratic elements – is particularly eager to stress the ways in which actual behavior deviates from the democratic formal content of a country's constitution and body of law.[4] What matters instead is said to be *informal* politics, the "real" workings of politics, those unwritten and officially uncodified norms, habits, and practices that actually guide political behavior.[5] While it is tempting to place these literatures in opposition, "formal institutions versus informal politics," this obscures the possibility that formal institutions may impact

* This chapter draws heavily (though does not reproduce everything) from but adds important new theoretical and empirical material to Hale (2011).

1 For helpful feedback on earlier drafts, the author thanks, along with others, Li Bennich-Bjorkman, Christofer Berglund, Charlotta Friedner-Parrat, Jordan Gans-Morse, Vsevolod Gunitskiy, Danielle Lussier, Israel Marques, Kelly McMann, Oxana Shevel, Oleksandr Fisun, and participants in: the Conference on Constitutions in Authoritarian Regimes co-sponsored by the University of Chicago Law School, the Chicago Initiative on Regime Practices, and the Center for Latin American Studies; Columbia University's Comparative Politics Seminar; the Uppsala Forum at Uppsala University's Department of Government; and a workshop of the Program on New Approaches to Research and Security in Eurasia.

2 Some classics in this voluminous literature include the exchange on constitutional design in the *Journal of Democracy*, republished in Diamond and Plattner (1996); Fish (2006); Linz and Stepan (1996); Shugart and Carey (1992); Skach (2005).

3 E.g., Bratton and van de Walle (1994); O'Donnell (1994); Wilson (2005b).

4 E.g., Carothers (2002); Magaloni (2006); Schedler (2002); Way (2005).

5 Informal institutions are "socially shared rules, usually unwritten, that are created, communicated, and enforced outside of officially sanctioned channels" and formal institutions are "rules and procedures that are created, communicated, and enforced through channels widely accepted as official"; Helmke and Levitsky (2004: 727).

regime change in part by altering patterns of informal politics. Indeed, an emerging body of research is now focusing on how formal rules and informal institutions interact,[6] and recent theoretical work suggests that one of the ways that formal institutions can have political effects is by inducing change in informal rules.[7] That is, formal institutions may still matter, but not in the way theories and practitioners often assume.

This chapter advances the latter research agenda with respect to basic formal constitutional design and the prospects for nondemocratic regimes to develop more democratic features. It proceeds from the familiar insight that constitutions influence an individual's behavior primarily by shaping that individual's expectations as to the behavior of others.[8] But the way such expectations are shaped differs fundamentally depending on whether the underlying social context is characterized by high degrees of *patronalism*, a syndrome typically manifesting itself in weak rule of law, high levels of corruption, strong patronage politics, and low levels of social capital. More specifically, all other things being equal, constitutions that stipulate a directly elected president as the single most powerful office (presidentialist constitutions) tend to generate expectations of future political power that encourage patronalistic networks to coordinate their activities around a single dominant political machine led by the directly elected president. Constitutions formalizing two independent holders of roughly equal executive power (divided-executive constitutions), however, will complicate coordination around a single patron, thereby working against the amassing of formal and informal power around the president. Divided-executive constitutions must not be confused with parliamentarist constitutions, which are found capable of producing "single-pyramid systems" in much the way that presidentialist ones can, though in a "softer" way.

To isolate the impact of formal constitutions from that of the many other factors that can influence both democratization and the arrangement of patronalistic networks, this study adopts a focused process-tracing comparison of three cases. The first two, Ukraine and Kyrgyzstan in 2005 through 2010, constitute a carefully controlled paired comparison: Ukraine, because of an essentially exogenous set of events, wound up with a divided-executive constitution following an electoral revolution, whereas Kyrgyzstan retained a presidentialist constitution after experiencing its own electoral revolution just a few months later. The comparison indicates that the presence of this formal constitutional change in Ukraine and its absence in Kyrgyzstan explains the more democratic configuration *of informal institutions* in Ukraine during 2005 through 2010, while Kyrgyzstan's revolution was soon followed by a new concentration of informal power around the president. The case of Moldova, however, shows that we cannot simply boil this story down to the formal powers of

6 Lauth (2000); Levitsky and Helmke (2006); Sakwa (2011).

7 Helmke and Levitsky (2004: 732–33). A complementary approach explores how informal institutions impact formal rules: Grzymala-Busse (2010).

8 North and Weingast (1989); Veitch (1986); Weingast (1997).

parliament. Moldova's constitution has been parliamentarist since 2000, and it is demonstrated that it had many of the same "autocratizing" effects in Moldova as did the presidentialist constitution in Kyrgyzstan. This is because, as with presidentialist constitutions, Moldova's parliamentarist one stipulated a single source of executive power that promoted the coordination of elite networks in a closed arrangement, though some moderating nuances of parliamentarist constitutions are also discussed.

CONSTITUTIONS IN PATRONALISTIC SOCIETIES

Patronalism is a social equilibrium in which political exchange tends to be characterized far more by concrete punishments and rewards meted out to specific individuals than by broad policies that are not targeted at individuals and that instead impact different parts of society according to relatively explicit, generalized rules.[9] It can be conceived of as a kind of collective action problem, a vicious cycle whereby individuals understand politics as an arena of personal wealth redistribution and targeted coercion and therefore reproduce these very practices themselves for fear of being "suckers," those feckless souls who act on principle but only succeed in impoverishing their own families, marginalizing themselves, and accomplishing nothing. For individuals in highly patronalistic societies, what matters most for achieving material welfare is belonging to a coalition that has access to – and hence can pay out – resources. There is thus a very important process of *coordination* at the core of political competition in patronalistic societies: which side individuals of all levels choose to support depends very much on which side these individuals expect other individuals to support – or, more precisely, which side they expect not to wind up losing access to resources for patronage and coercion because of a lack of support.

In highly patronalistic hybrid regimes, constitutions influence people's expectations as to whether any one single network is likely to be dominant in the foreseeable future, thereby helping resolve or instead complicate the problem of coordination that actors in the polity face.[10] Of particular interest is whether the constitution signals a concentration or a relatively equal division of executive authority. A presidentialist constitution, one that has a directly elected presidency with substantial executive powers capable of nominating and/or removing the other most significant formal holders of executive power, is the most obvious example of a constitution signaling a concentration of executive authority. But very importantly, parliamentarist constitutions can also fall into this category to the extent that they provide for a top executive post that is not formally constrained or selected/removed by another

9 A full elaboration of this concept and how it differs from related concepts like clientelism (e.g., Grzymala-Busse 2008; Kitschelt 2000) can be found in Hale 2013. [Note: Hale 2013 refers to: Henry E. Hale, *Great Expectations: Patronal Politics and Regime Dynamics in Eurasia*, draft book manuscript, 2013.]

10 "Highly patronalistic" communicates the idea that the higher are levels of patronalism, the more pronounced and observable the dynamics discussed in this article should be.

executive office with a basis outside parliament, as in the classic Westminster system in which the winning party obtains the prime ministership and there is no counterbalancing presidency. In systems that have both a president and a prime minister with substantial formal powers, whether one post is seen as the bigger prize is likely to be determined by whether one of the offices is formally dependent on the other, as when a president with substantial other formal executive powers has the right to nominate or remove the prime minister while the prime minister has no such right with respect to who occupies the presidency.

To understand how such formal constitutional provisions can meaningfully shape informal political configurations, let us consider a hypothetical country that has two large, rival patron–client networks perceived by all to wield equal informal power. Let us further assume that there is no history of a national government and no previous constitution and then introduce to this mix a constitution that formally stipulates a directly elected presidency to be the most powerful executive office in the land. At the moment the constitution is introduced, it is purely formal: there is nothing more behind the presidency than the piece of parchment on which it is described because the rival patrons' power is based solely on informal authority.

We can identify both an *information effect* and a *focal effect* by which such a constitution will encourage elites in such a context to gravitate more to the occupant of the office of president than to the nonoccupant. The information effect arises from the nature of the presidency as an *indivisible good*: only one patron can occupy it.[11] Somehow, a decision must be made as to who will occupy the post. Because power depends on convincing individuals that one's network is currently powerful enough to deliver resources and will continue to be able to do so in the future, both of our hypothetically equal rival networks can be assumed to have an interest in occupying a post that a visible, widely accessible document deems to be superior to one deemed to be subordinate. The fact that one network occupies the presidency and another does not, then, signals a marginal superiority of the former. The focal effect proceeds from the presidentialist constitution's conferral of the symbolism of supreme power upon its occupant and has its strongest effect at moments when people otherwise have no idea who is actually more powerful. To wit, a formal presidentialist constitution can turn the presidency's occupant into a focal point for elites who do not otherwise have grounds for deciding whose network other elites will be most likely to support.

By generating expectations that the presidential network is likely to be marginally more powerful now (information effect) and in the future (focal and information effects), the presidentialist constitution affords the patron who occupies the presidency an opportunity to accumulate ever greater *informal* power. Eventually, as coordination dynamics play themselves out, the president can construct a system in which s/he dominates the political system by virtue of *both* formal and informal authority (usually in tight combination). Alternative "pyramids" of power under rival

[11] Stepan, Linz, and Yadav (2011: 20, 199).

patrons generally face one of the following fates: liquidation as their most marginal members progressively defect to the dominant network, co-optation into the larger pyramid, or operation at the margins of the system. Presidentialist constitutions, then, foster something like a self-fulfilling prophecy in patronalistic societies, encouraging expectations as to current and future balances of power that then make themselves true. When all this happens, the informal power structure in the polity might be characterized as a kind of *single pyramid* in which the president administers society through an ever-broadening conglomeration of vertical networks of subpatrons and clients. To casual observers, such a polity simply looks authoritarian.

Many constitutions, however, do not concentrate the preponderance of formal executive authority in a single state office and instead divide it in some way, usually between a president and a prime minister. Of specific interest here is the situation when formally the prime minister is neither nominated/appointed nor removed by the president, meaning that the prime minister is selected by a parliament independently (formally) of the president and is assigned a package of executive powers roughly equal to those of the president.[12] Returning to the hypothetical country just discussed, introducing a divided-executive constitution instead of a presidentialist one (and assuming that each major network occupies one of the posts) would weaken the tendency to single-pyramid systems by encouraging expectations that there will be at least two patrons in the polity with roughly equal power. In terms of the information effect, the fact that one network occupies the presidency no longer signals that network's relative strength over all other networks, and in terms of the focal effect, it supplies no obvious way for elites to determine what other elites are likely to do and thereby coordinate their actions. In particular, the divided-power constitution provides a specific *alternative* focal point (the prime minister) around which patronalistic actors can coordinate should they not be satisfied with the "deal" offered to them by the presidential network. And this, in turn, can have a multiplier effect by creating maneuvering room for "third" networks to become powerful by playing one network off against the other. Such a configuration of informal politics can be usefully called a *competing-pyramid system*. It resembles a more democratic outcome by virtue of vigorous competition and political openness, although the competition is typically fought by patronalistic means and is thus highly corrupt and far from the liberal ideal.

Of course, in the real world, all other things are not equal as they are in the hypothetical country discussed so far. Preexisting power configurations influence the design and adoption of constitutions,[13] and context shapes how signals are interpreted.[14] Thus, a formally presidentialist constitution suddenly superimposed

12 The first requirement means that a divided-executive constitution does not equate with a semipresidentialist constitution, which may or may not empower the president to nominate, appoint, or remove the head of government. On semipresidentialism, see Duverger (1980); Shugart and Carey (1992).

13 Knight (1992); Przeworski (1991: 79–88).

14 Geertz (1973).

on two obviously unequal informal networks might initially be seen as providing no useful signals as to which network will be the more powerful. Moreover, the wide variety of specific provisions on the distribution of numerous itemized formal powers between a chief executive and other officeholders that real-world constitutions typically stipulate can also cloud or clarify the signals sent to elites, as can court rulings on these provisions. Rival networks have incentives to take advantage of any ambiguities by overestimating the status and power of any offices they hold and asserting limits on any posts held by their rivals. And to make things even more complicated, elite expectations as to which networks will be dominant can clearly be influenced by factors other than the constitution. For example, when a long-dominant patron becomes incapacitated by illness with no clear successor in place, an ensuing succession crisis may call into question earlier expectations as to his network's ability to maintain its dominance.[15]

These considerations do not supply grounds for neglecting the study of the effects of formal constitutions, but they do pose quite a challenge for isolating these effects in empirical studies. For example, let us take the finding that dominant actors tend to create presidentialist instead of divided-executive constitutions and to augment rather than diminish executive power to suit their own needs.[16] On the one hand, this observation reinforces the argument here: surely dominant actors do this because they sense that formal constitutions are able over time to reinforce or alter power configurations, and the information effect is likely to be substantial because the occupant of a very powerful presidency is empirically likely to be someone with great informal as well as formal power. But on the other hand, all this makes it very hard to determine what the effect of formal constitutional design itself is because prior distributions of power (and potentially many other contextual factors)[17] may be (a) determining whether a system is a competing-pyramid or a single-pyramid one and (b) at the same time causing the adoption of constitutions to reflect more than produce these systems. These difficulties are exacerbated to the extent that other factors might overpower, obscure, or even alter (through interaction) the effects of formal constitutions.

A strong test of the impact of formal constitutions on informal political arrangements relevant to democratization, therefore, would require holding maximally constant the aforementioned contextual variables as well as other factors reasonably believed to influence regime type, while at the same time introducing a clear difference in formal constitutions that cannot itself be attributed to the factors influencing regime type. Such a strong test would also require demonstrating in detail that precisely the processes described here, rather than actual obedience to formal constitutional rules, was what generated the observed difference.

15 Hale (2005).
16 Easter (1997).
17 See Cheibub, Elkins, and Ginsburg (2011).

EMPIRICAL STRATEGY

This chapter adopts a focused three-case study that begins with a comparison between Ukraine and Kyrgyzstan during 2005 through 2010, which helps us isolate the effect of divided-executive constitutions relative to presidentialist ones, and concludes with a study of Moldova to illustrate that these effects do not simply boil down to "parliamentarism" but are a result precisely of the constitutionally divided executive rather than formal parliamentary powers per se. Kyrgyzstan and Ukraine provide a strikingly fortuitous opportunity (arguably as good as can be expected in the real world) to deal with the empirical difficulties and isolate the effects of formal constitutional design through a process-tracing paired comparison.[18] In keeping with the logic already outlined, both Kyrgyzstan and Ukraine

- have been enduringly highly patronalistic societies, as defined previously.[19]
- had presidentialist constitutions from at least the mid-1990s up until their revolutions.
- had single-pyramid systems dominated by a president relying on both formal and informal powers.[20]

Because these countries were so similar in regime type and constitution prior to 2005, we cannot explain any dramatic post-2005 differences by citing factors that did not change dramatically in either country in 2005, including religious heritage, historical legacy, extent of kinship-based politics, or political culture. Moreover, the specific events in these two countries during and immediately following 2005 are strikingly similar in important details that help isolate the effects of formal constitutions. In both cases:

- The old strongman presidents were toppled by "electoral revolutions" during the same span of a few months, with both new presidents assuming a five-year term of office in 2005 – these terms define the period of this study (2005–2010).[21]
- Emerging victorious was not a single leader but a "tandem" of leaders who each represented separate but allied patronalistic networks (Viktor Yushchenko and Yulia Tymoshenko in Ukraine and Kurmanbek Bakiev and Feliks Kulov in Kyrgyzstan).

18 George and Bennett (2005); Tarrow (2010).

19 As indicated by Kitschelt's coding of these countries as featuring the most "patrimonial" kind of communist legacy, a concept close to patronalism as discussed in Hale (2013). Kyrgyzstan and Ukraine fall into the same, most patronalistic category in the postcommunist world. See Kitschelt and colleagues (1999). Corroborating this are Ukraine's and Kyrgyzstan's persistently high ratings on levels of corruption perception and problems with rule of law in global indices: Kaufmann, Kraay, and Mastruzze (2008); Transparency International (2008).

20 McFaul (2005).

21 The vast literature on the revolutions includes Bunce and Wolchik (2010); and Kuzio (2008).

- A deal was struck in which one member of each tandem became president (Yushchenko and Bakiev) and the other became prime minister (Tymoshenko and Kulov).
- The future president, unable to win the presidency outright, was forced to accept a power-sharing arrangement that involved transferring significant powers to a prime minister.

The crucial "treatment" that differentiates the two cases is as follows. *In Ukraine, the power-sharing arrangement became anchored in the adoption of a formal divided-executive constitution. In Kyrgyzstan, by contrast, the power-sharing deal was based only on the rough balance of informal power* that each tandem mate wielded at the time of the revolution without changing the presidentialist nature of the formal constitution to make the prime minister independent of the president.[22] At the time, Bakiev described his deal with Kulov thus: "This is not a legal document, but a political document. Of course, the word of a politician is worth nothing, but I gave my word as a man."[23]

Importantly, this difference in "treatment" (whether or not constitutional reform occurred) was for our purposes exogenous, not the product of other forces that might have also produced the observed difference in democratization prospects. Ukraine reformed because, in the heat of the moment, it already had immediately available a draft constitutional reform that could be pulled off the shelf to resolve the crisis. After consistently working to strengthen presidential powers during the 1990s and early 2000s, incumbent president Leonid Kuchma grew worried that he might become vulnerable to his successor after he personally left the presidency in 2004. Thus in August 2002, he reversed himself and proposed a constitutional reform that would greatly weaken the presidency, minimizing his own vulnerability to the next president. Importantly, his concerns were not only that an opposition figure like Yushchenko could become president but also that he did not fully trust his own choice for successor, Prime Minister Yanukovych, who represented the ambitious eastern-based Donetsk network (not Kuchma's own) and had business and political interests in tension with those of some key Kuchma allies (including chief of staff Viktor Medvedchuk, the constitutional reform's chief advocate within the administration).[24] The reform was never adopted, however, but it remained predrafted, ready to be pulled off the shelf in the heat of the moment to resolve the Orange Revolution stalemate. This is exactly what happened, as it was this "very same draft" that was brought in to become the basis for the presidential power-sharing arrangement that ended Ukraine's standoff.[25]

22 Christensen, Rakhimkulov, and Wise (2005).
23 *RFE/RL Newsline*, May 18, 2005.
24 D'Anieri (2007: 88–98); Kudelia (2010: 172–3); Wilson (2005a: 80).
25 Kudelia (2010: 172–3, 182).

This prior availability of a constitutional reform bill in Ukraine cannot by itself explain why Ukraine would be more open politically than Kyrgyzstan during 2005 through 2010. If anything, it owed its existence to the old regime's self-perceived *weakness* in 2002 through 2004, and weak old-regime authorities should if anything have made it *easier* for Yushchenko than for Bakiev to establish his own revolutionary power because he would face weaker resistance from the outgoing authorities. One might posit that Kuchma's weakness reflected a more general pluralism in Ukrainian society, making it harder for any Ukrainian president to consolidate power than it would be for any Kyrgyz president. But here we must recall that the old regime was still strong enough *during the late 2004 standoff* to force the deal on Yushchenko, who did not want it. Moreover, the notion that Ukrainian political society is somehow *generally* more fractious than Kyrgyzstan's rings rather hollow to Kyrgyzstan experts, who frequently question whether any political consolidation is possible there at all and characterize it as a classic weak or outright failed state.[26] Indeed, a detailed tracing of the actual events that produced and sustained competing-pyramid politics in Ukraine and that led to the reconsolidation of single-pyramid politics in Kyrgyzstan during 2005 through 2010 confirms that it was the fact of the constitutional reform itself, not any general sociopolitical fractiousness or any factors initiating the original constitutional reform bill back in 2002 (or any other difference between Ukraine and Kyrgyzstan, for that matter), that was the direct and decisive cause of Kyrgyzstan's and Ukraine's divergent political paths in the period under consideration.

The third case study of Moldova reinforces the argument by demonstrating that we cannot attribute Ukraine's post-2005 political opening to greater formal parliamentary powers per se and that Kyrgyzstan's post-2005 political closure is not unique to presidentialism but can arise from any constitutional form that establishes a single chief source of executive authority, including parliamentarism. Indeed, Moldova was the only post-Soviet country in which the parliament eventually won the transitional power struggle between president and parliament, adopting a parliamentary constitution in 2000. This reform did stipulate a formal presidency, but this post was to be filled by a three-fifths vote among parliamentary deputies rather than by direct election. Whoever controlled the parliament, then, could control the most important executive posts in the country, most prominently the presidency. Standard theories emphasizing the importance of formal parliamentary power for democracy[27] would consider Moldova to be a most likely case for a democratic outcome, both because it had a parliamentary system and because it had not yet experienced the development of a single-pyramid system prior to the 2000 reform. Yet a perspective focused on the informal effects of formal constitutions would lead us to expect that if a single network won a majority in the parliament, we would be likely to see the development of a single-pyramid system here much like we did in Kyrgyzstan after its revolution.

[26] E.g., McGlinchey (2010).
[27] E.g., Fish (2006).

KYRGYZSTAN: PRESIDENTIALIST CONSTITUTION AND SINGLE-PYRAMID POLITICS

That Kyrgyzstan would return to its earlier levels of authoritarianism was not immediately or universally evident.[28] But the fact that Kyrgyzstan retained its presidentialist constitution would have major consequences for the Kyrgyz political system. The constitution conferred on Bakiev the symbolic attributes of power and communicated that because he occupied this post, he was in fact the more powerful of the two partners. As a result, he proved better able than his tandem-mate Kulov (who occupied the premiership) at attracting clients, punishing the disloyal, and gradually stripping his rival of authority and clients by using both informal and formal powers. By early 2007, Kulov had been maneuvered out of office and had ceased to be considered a serious rival, capping the postrevolutionary reemergence of a single-pyramid system.

Bakiev accomplished this in a number of ways, sending signals through his use of formal and informal powers to induce elite coordination around his personal and formal authority and to marginalize those who resisted. One of the first things he did was to use his formal powers of appointment to replace senior figures in the Interior Ministry, the secret police, and territorial governments in both North and South.[29] The president also took a number of steps designed to establish his control over financial operations and much economic activity in Kyrgyzstan, including issuing decrees to create both a Financial Intelligence Service (September 2005) and a new Financial Police Service (November 2005).[30] These formal personnel arrangements then structured the informal process whereby these agents acted contrary to law – providing legal pretexts or cover – to secure the transfer of key economic assets to Bakiev's own family members and close allies. These assets included but were not limited to many of those formerly controlled by the Akaev family, as has been documented in a number of studies.[31] Understanding the importance of good relations with the president, many business and other elites who had previously been loyal to Akaev worked to seek accommodation with the new president. Regine Spector's detailed case studies of some of Kyrgyzstan's biggest businesses describe a pattern by which, for example, the co-owner of Kyrgyzstan's massive and rich Dordoi Bazaar, Askar Salymbekov, had carefully developed positive relations with Akaev's family during the prerevolutionary period but switched to cultivating ties with Bakiev's family almost immediately after the revolution. Through a conscious business-preservation strategy of maintaining good relations with whichever president's family happened to be in place, Salymbekov thus managed to keep his business holdings despite not

[28] Compare McFaul (2005); Radnitz (2006); Silitski (2005).
[29] *Gazeta.Kg*, June 30, 2005, 19:59; RFE/RL *Newsline*, February 7, 2006; RFE/RL *Newsline*, January 30, 2006.
[30] RFE/RL *Newsline*, September 12, 2005; RFE/RL *Newsline*, November 29, 2005.
[31] Marat (2008); Ozcan (2010).

being related to the Bakievs. By contrast, his co-owner, Kubatbek Baibolov, went into political opposition and was consequently forced out.[32]

Both during and after the revolution, Bakiev had publicly supported constitutional amendments to formalize a weaker presidency,[33] but he did not act to implement such reforms immediately, and by early 2006 he was sounding a different note. After several clashes with parliament over the president's growing authority, Bakiev's administration reportedly began drawing up its own draft constitution independently of the parliament or civil society organizations that were originally promised a role. Bakiev's constitution would retain "all the powers that Akaev had," and a referendum was planned for November 2006.[34] Opposition forces rallied over the course of that year. Two large protests in April and May 2006 prompted Bakiev to reshuffle his cabinet and remove officials whose resignations were demanded by the opposition.[35] Of course, such reshuffling also served the key presidential purpose of dividing and conquering his own supporters, preventing any from becoming too entrenched in their posts (e.g., by shaping the arrangement of informal institutions – in this case ministry-based networks – such that they could not easily organize against him). Bakiev was also on the offensive. The prominent opposition leader Omurbek Tekebaev was arrested in Warsaw for allegedly carrying drugs, an incident widely regarded as a setup arranged by the National Security Service (SNB), which just happened to be headed by the president's brother.[36] Once again, we see formal institutional arrangements linked to the formal presidency (in this case the presidentially appointed SNB leadership) shaping arrangements of informal politics by disrupting rival networks (such as Tekebaev's) and arranging others in an increasingly tight hierarchical configuration dominated by the person at the top.

Revelatory of how the formal constitution had rendered Kulov unable to act independently of Bakiev were events surrounding the opposition's last major attempt to force Bakiev to live up to his promise not to govern as Akaev had. In November 2006, a group of opposition figures under the banner of the For Reforms movement mobilized several straight days of protests in Bishkek to demand a constitution that reduced presidential power.[37] One of the chief rally organizers, Temir Sariev, reports in a memoir that Kulov had contacted him and other key opposition figures and communicated that he was "in complete solidarity" with the opposition in making these demands and planning the rally but puzzled organizers by acting secretly and refusing to come out in public.[38] Surely, this was not the mark of a man who expected he could mobilize the government he formally headed against a president

32 Spector (2008).
33 E.g., RFE/RL *Newsline*, April 28, 2005.
34 Pritchin (2006).
35 RFE/RL *Newsline*, May 11, 2006; *Polit.Ru*, May 10, 2006, 11:08, 10:01, 17:02.
36 RFE/RL *Newsline*, September 11, 14, and 25, 2006.
37 RFE/RL *Newsline*, October 3, 2006.
38 Sariev (2008: 71–2).

he opposed, and the behavior stood in marked contrast to that of Ukrainian prime ministers who were similarly dissatisfied with presidential attempts to usurp some of their authority. Indeed, organizers report that no significant support was forthcoming from Kulov.[39] That is, Kulov as prime minister appears to have been unable (or unwilling because of his own dependence on Bakiev's powers of appointment and removal) to provide actual political cover for opposition politics and instead could only covertly hint at support while toeing the presidential line in public. Sariev's account also indicates that Kulov was not expected to be a significant counterweight to Bakiev's presidential authority because of his position. Bakiev initially agreed to the November 2006 protesters' demands, but once they had gone home thinking they had won, he turned around (by at least one account, cutting a variety of deals to pay off or co-opt former opposition members[40]) and passed an even more presidentialist constitution, then removing Kulov from the prime ministership and soon installing a former opposition leader (evidently co-opted) in this post.[41]

Kulov, now without his prime ministerial post, tried in a much-heralded April 2007 rally to mobilize popular resistance through what was left of his own network, but he enticed virtually no other high figures from within the Bakiev administration or even from the government that Kulov had formally headed for well over a year to cast their lots with him instead of with Bakiev. Bakiev's forces thus put the protest down with a decisive show of coercion. As a final humiliation, Bakiev in May 2008 offered Kulov a minor state post with lucrative patronage potential: head of the directorate of the Project on Development of Small and Medium Energy. Bowing to his own utter defeat, Kulov accepted.[42] Kulov himself, then, becomes one of the starkest examples of a major elite being co-opted to Bakiev's side in recognition of the latter's dominance. Kulov had in essence been co-opted from himself.

Huskey's and Iskakova's survey of opposition politicians in Kyrgyzstan in 2008 helps us get into the minds of at least some Kyrgyz elites, demonstrating that Kulov's calculus in joining Bakiev even after having been blatantly betrayed by him in fact reflects a calculus common to at least opposition elite politicians. These elites at that time indeed regarded Bakiev's ability to dole out rewards and mete out punishments to be a critical reason opposition figures were unable to join forces to mount any sort of effective opposition to the president. Very interestingly, the survey finds that this perception of the centrality of state authority in dividing the opposition is decidedly highest among opposition figures who had previously served within the government as executive branch officials, strongly suggesting that this perception is not held primarily by the opposition but rather is held by elites more generally.[43]

39 For example, along with Sariev's account, that given by another opposition leader, Edil Baisalov, in an interview with the author on June 14, 2011, in Bishkek.

40 Sariev (2008).

41 Details on these complex events can be found in Kulov (2008); *Polit.Ru*, December 30, 2007, 10:43, 12:38; RFE/RL *Newsline*, January 16, 2007; Sariev (2008); *Utro.ru*, December 19, 2006, 13:40.

42 *AKIpress*, May 6, 2008, 13:15.

43 Huskey and Iskakova (2010: 237).

Indeed, Huskey and Iskakova refer to a "long list of opposition politicians who have succumbed to the temptations of *vlast'* [power] and abandoned their colleagues in the opposition for high-ranking positions in government."[44]

Kulov's 2007 defeat consolidated the expectation that the power of the Bakiev network would not be effectively balanced by anyone in state executive power, and accordingly that point in time marked an acceleration in the consolidation of a single-pyramid system around Bakiev's presidency. The elite expectations involved are explicitly articulated by a "veteran leader of the opposition" in Huskey's and Iskakova's 2008 elite interview project: after Kulov left the political scene and Atambaev was co-opted, there was a general perception that the "last chance to unite the opposition" was lost, and "people simply turned away in disgust, saying the opposition is no different from the government."[45] With little coordinated elite resistance from inside or outside his regime, the consolidation of Bakiev's power pyramid was rapid. His loyalists passed an even more strongly presidentialist constitution by referendum, then forced early parliamentary elections in December 2007 and filled seventy-one of its ninety seats with a newly created propresidential party, the Ak Zhol (True Path) Party.[46] Minority fractions went only to parties considered to be pliable, the Party of Communists and Atambaev's Social Democratic Party, and the territorial breakdowns of the vote were never released.[47] The Central Election Commission chief who certified these results later admitted to having been subjected to unrelenting pressure from the president and his family to influence election results.[48] Trying to catch the opposition off guard and to win reelection before the effects of the 2008 financial crisis could hit hard, Bakiev secured a Constitutional Court ruling moving the election date up to summer 2009 instead of 2010. The opposition tried to unite, but Atambaev and Sariev both wound up running, the latter accusing the former of collaborationism. Neither managed to mobilize much elite or mass support, and Bakiev won the official count with 76 percent of the official vote count, far ahead of Atambaev's 8 and Sariev's 6 percent, respectively.[49] Postelection protests were easily put down, though they were mostly just ignored because they found few supporters among either the elite or the masses. Kulov supported Bakiev's campaign.[50] This regression to single-pyramid politics is generally reflected in the wide variety of scholarly efforts to systematically measure the degree to which countries display the attributes of democracy from year to year.[51]

44 Ibid., 238.
45 Ibid., 247–8.
46 RFE/RL *Newsline*, October 24, 2007.
47 AKI*press*, December 18, 2007, 17:14; RFE/RL *Newsline*, December 27, 2007.
48 AKI*press*, September 26, 2008, 10:19, 15:22, 17:17, 17:41, 18:50.
49 AKI*press*, July 21, 2009, 19:15.
50 AKI*press*, June 19, 2009, 14:23.
51 Economist Intelligence Unit (2008); Freedom House (2010); Goehring (2008: 44); Kekic (2007); Marat (2009); Marshall (2008).

UKRAINE: DIVIDED-EXECUTIVE CONSTITUTION AND COMPETING-PYRAMID POLITICS

A detailed look at post–color revolution Ukraine presents a dramatic contrast, a clear postrevolutionary move toward open, competing-pyramid politics. Regardless of their measures or definitions of democracy, all of the indices just discussed for Kyrgyzstan point in the same direction: Ukraine was much more democratic during the five years after its revolution than it had been before it, with no trend toward authoritarianization straight through the 2010 presidential election.[52] Equally importantly, these measures *also* record no significant improvement in levels of corruption and governance.[53] Taken all together, this pattern strongly confirms theoretical expectations: the important "outcome" that changed was not the *level* of patronalistic politics but the *arrangement* of patronalistic networks into more competitive rather than more closed configurations. While evidence indicates that Ukraine started a slide back toward single-pyramid politics after its 2010 presidential election and with a subsequent reversion to the old presidentialist constitution, the stark difference between Ukraine and Kyrgyzstan during their first postrevolutionary presidential terms deserves explanation.[54] The argument presented here is that Ukraine's new divided-executive constitution complicated and ultimately undermined the elite coordination necessary for any one power pyramid to emerge dominant for half a decade.

As noted above, the Orange Revolution's standoff in the streets resulted in a constitutional change that the team of outgoing President Leonid Kuchma forced Yushchenko to accept in return for a peaceful transition to the presidency in early 2005: the presidency Yushchenko inherited would be weakened as of January 2006, with the prime minister gaining direct control over key ministries (including the police) and, most importantly, becoming exclusively beholden to Parliament rather than being nominated or removed at the whim of the president.[55] The fact that the new division of power formally went into effect only in January 2006 helps us separate the "informal" effects of the constitutional reform from the formal effects. Despite the formality of Yushchenko's wielding the powers of Kuchma during 2005, the adoption of the constitutional reform to resolve the Orange Revolution standoff had already created the expectation that the president would not be the single dominant authority as of 2006. Thus Yushchenko did use his formal power to try to subordinate the prime minister after they clashed publicly, replacing Tymoshenko in September 2005 with the more pliable Yury Yekhanurov. But the constitutional reform meant that observers already regarded Yekhanurov as a "caretaker" prime minister from the outset, expecting that the March 2006 parliamentary election would determine an

52 Economist Intelligence Unit (2008); Kekic (2007); Marshall (2008); Sushko and Prystayko (2009).

53 See Economist Intelligence Unit (2008); Sushko and Prystayko (2009).

54 Walker and Orttung (2011).

55 Christensen, Rakhimkulov, and Wise (2005).

independent prime minister and that the president might thus not be in a position after that point to follow through on promises or threats made before.[56] Tymoshenko voiced (and sought to reinforce) these expectations rather dramatically just before the 2006 elections, saying the prime ministership was worth fighting for in the election because "under the new constitution, the president has practically lost all of his powers."[57] Despite the falling out with the president that had led to her dismissal, she ran for parliament in 2006 again as part of a "democratic" coalition with Yushchenko. This election returned the man Yushchenko had defeated in the 2004 presidential battle, Viktor Yanukovych, to the premiership.

Close analysis of political events after this reveals a history of all major political networks flouting formal rules and employing patronalistic practices to gain power at the expense of their rivals, using and claiming state executive authority wherever possible. Prime Minister Yanukovych wasted little time. One of his first and most creative moves was to unilaterally claim the right to invalidate presidential decrees by refusing to countersign them as required by procedural regulations.[58] Even more momentous was his 2006 to 2007 push for a new Law on the Council of Ministers that would have significantly augmented prime ministerial power at the president's expense. These determined moves, along with widely rumored material blandishments, induced a growing stream of elites (especially parliamentary deputies) to defect from Yushchenko and join Yanukovych's coalition. The prime minister's allies bragged that they would soon get the three hundred parliamentary votes needed to amend the constitution unilaterally, potentially emasculating or even eliminating the presidency. This led many to forecast a new single-pyramid "vertikal" of power, now operating out of the premier's office instead of the president's.[59]

What stopped Yanukovych in 2007? Here we see a pattern that occurs repeatedly in the Ukraine of 2005 through 2010: efforts by one arm of the divided executive to flout formal rules and usurp power from the other were defeated by similarly patronalistic political practices undertaken in response by the occupant of the rival executive post. In this case, President Yushchenko became the focal point for opposition to Yanukovych, renewing his alliance with Tymoshenko and rallying other elites, as he issued and enforced a decree of extremely dubious constitutionality in April 2007 to dissolve the parliament.[60] This decree was not simply "followed" according to

56 RFE/RL *Newsline*, September 12, 2005.

57 RFE/RL *Newsline*, February 28, 2006.

58 *Ukraiins'ka Pravda*, September 21, 2006, 13:31, 15:42.

59 *Ukraiins'ka Pravda*, April 6, 2007, 17:10; *Korrespondent*, January 20, 2007, 20.

60 The president's status as a "guarantor of the Constitution," he asserted, implied the duty to dissolve parliament if it acted in a way that the president unilaterally deemed unconstitutional. This justification, to say the least, did not appear among the three circumstances that the constitution explicitly stipulated as the only grounds for the president to dissolve parliament. See Ukaz prezydenta Ukraiiny, "Pro dostrokove prypynennia povnovazhen' Verkhovnoi Rady Ukraiiny." In *Ofitsiinyi Visnyk Prezydenta Ukraiina*, April 2, 2007, no. 1, 3–5. At http://www2.pravda.com.ua/news/2007/4/5/56948.htm, accessed April 26, 2011; Maksymiuk (2007).

formal legal procedures but enforced through the extensive coordination of informal networks around the president. The defense minister, who by Ukraine's divided-executive constitution was appointed by the president, quickly made it clear that should Yanukovych attempt to resist by using force, "the army will only carry out orders from the commander in chief" (Yushchenko).[61] The parliamentary coalition behind Yanukovych nevertheless sought to block any new elections by passing a resolution to disband the Central Election Commission.[62] In early May, while the case was still being decided by the eighteen-member Constitutional Court, Yushchenko issued decrees unilaterally removing three of the justices that had been appointed by his predecessor, Kuchma.[63] As the month went by, Yushchenko took direct control of antiriot police troops and then ordered more of them into the capital city. At that point, Yanukovych conceded, with new elections bringing Tymoshenko back as premier in fall 2007 as part of an alliance with Yushchenko.[64]

Power grabs were not limited to Yanukovych but were undertaken by Yushchenko as well. The most dramatic occurred in 2008. Shortly after she became prime minister, Tymoshenko experienced another falling out with Yushchenko as he sought to augment the power of the presidency at the prime minister's expense, especially over control of the economy. Yushchenko's team systematically issued bogus constitutional challenges so as to stall or undermine government decisions[65]; sought to revoke the citizenship of a prominent critic on the grounds that he had falsified his application back in 1999[66]; pressured certain television outlets to influence political content (driving the famous former Radio Liberty journalist Savik Shuster to leave one such channel)[67]; and even ordered the Ukrainian Security Service (SBU) to open a case against Tymoshenko in 2008 for treason over an alleged secret deal with Russian President Vladimir Putin.[68] The culmination was his attempt to force a new dissolution of the parliament and new elections in 2008 so as to get a new, more pliable government. Trying to enforce this move, Yushchenko's administration was found to have removed judges who had decided against him or were expected to do so,[69] dissolved an entire court that ruled against him so as to get the desired decision from one of the two courts he created to replace it,[70] and sent state guard troops under his authority to "protect" a court making a decision important to Yushchenko.[71] Interior Minister Yury Lutsenko, elected atop the party list that Yushchenko himself had

61 Maksymiuk (2007).
62 RFE/RL *Newsline*, April 3, 2007.
63 See Trochev (2010: 134).
64 RFE/RL *Newsline*, May 29, 2007.
65 Yatsenko (2008: 1, 3).
66 Korduban (2008); *Ukraiins'ka Pravda*, July 21, 2008, 19:31.
67 Savik Shuster, interview, *Segodnia*, August 7, 2008, 7; *Segodnia*, July 30, 2008, 4; Naiiem and Leshchenko (2008).
68 *Ukraiins'ka Pravda*, August 21, 2008, 11:50; *Ukraiins'ka Pravda*, February 11, 2009, 20:02.
69 *Segodnia*, October 17, 2008, 3; *Kommersant Ukraiina*, November 24, 2008.
70 *Ukraiins'ka Pravda*, October 17, 2008, 15:55.
71 *Kommersant Ukraina*, October 15, 2008.

supported, reported that the Presidential Secretariat had put through several phone calls to judges during the precise times of key court deliberations.[72]

President Yushchenko's power grab was rebuffed in much the same way Prime Minister Yanukovych's had been: the occupant of the opposite branch of executive power became a rallying point for those elites who wished to restrain the overstepping branch and accordingly was able to employ "political machine" tactics effectively enough to defeat the effort. This focal effect helped Prime Minister Tymoshenko coordinate efforts with some unlikely tactical allies, including Yanukovych's Party of Regions, which joined with her bloc to deny funding for the early elections Yushchenko had decreed. Tymoshenko's supporters also physically blocked the work of courts thought likely to rule in favor of Yushchenko.[73] She also went on the counterattack by entering into negotiations with Yanukovych's party on a plan to pool their parliamentary votes to amend the constitution and eliminate the directly elected presidency, subordinating the office instead to the parliament. Yushchenko, in turn, countered by warning that he would call a referendum on the issue or even force early direct presidential elections before the change could be effected, and the plan was shelved during 2009 as the regularly scheduled presidential elections took their course in early 2010.[74] This division of executive authority, importantly, went on to ensure that Ukraine's 2010 presidential elections were widely determined to be free and fair, the best evidence of which may be that Yanukovych managed to win them while the unpopular sitting president, Viktor Yushchenko, came in a distant fifth place.[75]

The constitutionally underpinned expectations that there were two independent centers of executive power rather than just one, along with the constitutionally provided alternative focal point for elites dissatisfied with either center, gave elite networks of various kinds a great deal of latitude to pursue their own games by switching sides at opportune moments or playing one side against the other. This is quite evident in the behavior of major business groupings. Ihor Kolomoisky and his Pryvat group, for example, went from being key Tymoshenko supporters to Yushchenko supporters over the course of 2005 to 2010, while Petro Poroshenko switched in the reverse direction. Vitaly Haiduk had been Yanukovych's deputy prime minister in 2002 to 2003 and backed him for president in the 2004 election but switched to become Yushchenko's national security and defense council secretary afterward, only to leave Yushchenko after a policy dispute and ultimately wind up supporting Tymoshenko's 2010 presidential campaign.[76] Yanukovych's Party of Regions, when occupying neither the presidency nor the prime ministership, also

72 *Ukraiins'ka Pravda*, October 16, 2008, 14:49.

73 *Ukraiins'ka Pravda*, October 11, 2008, 16:08; *Segodnia*, October 17, 2008, 3; *Kommersant-Ukraiina*, November 24, 2008.

74 *Ukraiins'ka Pravda*, May 27, 2009, 15:26; *Segodnia*, June 7, 2009, 12:30.

75 Herron (2011).

76 *KyivPost*, January 22, 2010, 6–7; RFE/RL *Newsline*, May 14, 2007; *Ukraiins'ka Pravda*, October 10, 2006, 11:55; Wagstyl and Oleachyk (2010).

played both sides against each other. Thus while it joined Tymoshenko to block Yushchenko's 2008 early election decree, it initiated a no-confidence vote against Tymoshenko earlier that same year. This opportunity for business and political elites to switch sides and find new political cover when one side ceased to be useful to them was precisely what was missing in Kyrgyzstan, forcing "oligarchs" either to toe the official line or to surrender key assets to the president's circle – just recall the contrast between the fates of Kyrgyz big businessmen Salymbekov and Baibolov discussed previously.[77]

The course of events since Yanukovych's 2010 election calls attention to the importance of formal constitutions at the same time that it establishes some of the limits of their effects. The fact that Yanukovych felt it desirable to change the constitution indicates he himself saw the divided-executive constitution as potentially complicating his future consolidation of power. At the same time, these events show that emerging victorious in a head-to-head contest against the rival network can at least temporarily resolve the coordination problems generated by divided-executive constitution, generating a wave of defections to the ascending network and thereby creating a window of opportunity to fundamentally change the constitution.[78] Even recognizing that constitutions are not all-powerful and impervious to change, however, the analysis presented here shows that the effects of the divided-executive constitution remain significant: the very same Yanukovych tried twice to create his own power pyramid rooted in state executive power, once in 2006 to 2007 and once starting in 2010, but was only successful once. And these pages show how the divided-executive constitution also hindered similar attempts by both Yushchenko and Tymoshenko. This stands in stark contrast to the record of post–Soviet presidentialist constitutions, which underpin single-pyramid systems not only in the Kyrgyzstan of 2005 to 2010 but also in every other post–Soviet country that has one.[79]

MOLDOVA: PARLIAMENTARIST CONSTITUTION AND SINGLE-PYRAMID POLITICS

It is important that the preceding analysis not be boiled down to a restatement of the old argument that presidentialism is bad for democracy while parliamentarism is good.[80] The case of Ukraine has already provided some indication that the effects of formal constitutions in highly patronalistic societies are not so simple. Indeed, when Yanukovych controlled the parliamentary majority and consequently the government in 2006 to 2007, it was him and his parliamentary base that were considered the primary threat to democracy, as documented previously. Accordingly, in that case it was the *president* who successfully blocked this autocratizing

77 As documented in Ozcan (2010); Spector (2008).
78 Trochev (2011); *Ukraiins'ka Pravda*, September 21, 2011, 11:01.
79 Fish (2005); Hale (2005).
80 A powerful new version of this argument is Fish (2006).

gambit by forcing early elections and a new government; a weaker presidency would not have been able to do so and an even stronger parliament would not have succumbed to this obstacle. It was thus precisely the *balance* of informal authority that the divided-executive constitution induced that protected political contestation in Ukraine from a parliament-based threat. The case of Moldova makes the argument even more strongly, since here we find a parliamentarist constitution adopted in a situation in which there was no single-pyramid system already in place, and we can trace the emergence of one to focal and information effects created by this basic formal law.

After defeating President Petru Lucinschi in a long power struggle, the parliament that adopted the new parliamentarist constitution was not dominated by any single party, and those who designed the reform did not anticipate that it would be dominated by the party that wound up controlling it, the Communist Party of the Republic of Moldova. The Communists – who were in opposition to the incumbent leadership – at that time had just 40 of the 101 seats in parliament and so were unable to get the 61 votes necessary to elect their candidate president. Instead, the expectation was that the parliament would choose a compromise president agreed among the major forces.[81] But the parliament deadlocked, which led to early elections in 2001. Surprisingly to most observers, the Communists won these overwhelmingly, claiming – thanks to the electoral system – 71 of the 101 seats with only about 50 percent of the vote. The Communists thus assumed control under the newly parliamentarist constitution without any previous control over the central executive branch in Moldova, and so in essence faced a task of building a single-pyramid system from scratch.

Communist Party leader Vladimir Voronin then had his pick of three leadership posts that the changed constitution had endowed with some formal executive power and that were each to be filled by parliamentary vote: the presidency, the prime ministership, and the parliamentary speakership. He opted for the presidency, which became understood to be the chief seat of both formal and informal power in Moldova. From this position, we find him using some of the same levers that Bakiev used to build a single-pyramid system in Moldova despite the parliamentary source of his formal mandate. One method was to gain influence over the business community that could at least potentially become involved in politics. For example, the big businessman Boris Birshtein, a major figure under the previous president, found his contract with the Information Ministry expired.[82] At the same time, the president's own son's business holdings were reputed to have grown rapidly, ranging from banking to pharmaceuticals to metallurgy to wine to media.[83] Other major businessmen with roots in Moldova, such as Anatol Stati and his ASCOM group,

[81] Dumitru D'iakov (chair of the parliament that adopted the reform), "Novaia konstitutsionnaia real'nost': neskol'ko soobrazhenii," *Nezavisimaia Moldova*, July 13, 2000, p. 1.

[82] Dumitru (2011: 63).

[83] *Kommersant – Vlast'*, no. 36, September 15, 2009, online at www.kommersant.ru.

were said to quickly reach accommodation with Voronin's emerging machine.[84] Still other business groups emerged as major players through what were widely believed to be close ties to Voronin's inner circle, such as Vladimir Plahotniuc, who came to control a large holding of gas stations and mass media, including Moldova's biggest television outlet, Prime-TV.[85]

Formal powers of the presidency also proved potent in reinforcing or augmenting Voronin's informal powers as patron-in-chief in ways that tightened the coordination of the country's major networks around his own patronage. State-owned media increasingly came to reflect the official administration line, and in an event unprecedented in recent Moldovan history at that time, an opposition newspaper was shuttered.[86] Voronin used his appointment powers to replace nearly three quarters of lower-level court heads and increased his power over who became a judge of the Constitutional Court.[87] The presidency also proved to be a potent position from which to manipulate policy positions so as to co-opt or marginalize the pro-Romanian nationalist forces that had remained its primary source of idea-based opposition, in particular shifting from relatively pro–Russian foreign policy orientation to a rejection of Russian influence and a concomitant push to move closer to the European Union.[88] These growing machine assets were deployed in the 2005 parliamentary elections, which produced a new majority for Voronin's Communists.[89] Voronin's adoption of a more nationalistic stance helped facilitate his co-optation of the country's main nationalist opposition party at the time, the Christian Democratic Party, right after the election. This trend toward political closure is evident in Freedom House's measure of political rights, which are found to have declined between 2000 and the end of Voronin's tenure in office.[90]

At the same time, the case of Moldova also illustrates that there nevertheless remain some important differences between parliamentarist and presidentialist constitutions in their effects on the coordinated arrangement of patronalistic networks in a country. Of particular importance are differences in the information effect of the constitution. This is because the chief patron in a parliamentarist system, to obtain the formal leadership post, must obtain not only a formal victory in a popular vote (as in a presidentialist system) but also a formal victory in a vote among newly

[84] Kseniia Il'ina, "La Famiglia," *Kishinevskii Obozrevatel'*, October 21, 2010, http://www.ko.md/main/view_article.php?issue_date=2010-10-21&issue_id=2021&PHPSESSID=dedbd418020bb49ec72a4f3dba69f1f5, accessed May 27, 2012.

[85] Stack (2012).

[86] Way (2002: 131).

[87] Ibid.

[88] Cashu (2005).

[89] *RFE/RL* Newsline, March 8, 2005.

[90] Freedom House, *Freedom in the World*, Excel file for "Country ratings and status, FIW 1973–2011," posted at http://www.freedomhouse.org/template.cfm?page=439 (accessed October 19, 2011); the most recent version can be found at http://www.freedomhouse.org/report-types/freedom-world, accessed August 13, 2013. Polity IV, however, records no change during Voronin's tenure.

elected members of parliament. This effectively provides different networks in the patron's power pyramid a new chance to bargain with the patron for resources and position. This in effect loosens the pyramid, both because networks within it have greater incentive to hold out in order to gain bargaining position and because the occupation of posts other than the presidency is more likely to be interpreted as involving significant potential influence. In short, there is more cause for various networks in the system to consider it potentially profitable not to toe the presidential line as demonstratively as in presidentialist systems.

Thus we see that while Voronin in 2005 was able to secure a new majority for the Communists in parliament, to get himself elected president (which required a three-fifths rather than a simple majority), he needed to strike deals with other political forces that had won seats in Parliament, in this case, key members of the moderate Democratic and Social Liberal Parties as well as the nationalist Christian Democrats. That Voronin was able to do this illustrates that the constitution still tended to promote network coordination around his leadership, but in the process he had to make greater concessions than he would have had just winning a direct presidential election been sufficient. In particular, he agreed to commit even more strongly to a pro–Europe foreign policy and to a series of formal institutional reforms that the Christian Democrats required as the price for a deal. Whether these reforms had any effect is a topic hotly debated in Moldova, and while it is beyond the scope of this chapter to delve into this dispute, suffice it to say that Christian Democratic leaders to this day insist that the Communists did in fact follow through on these reforms and that some of them, including granting parties other than the dominant one representation in key oversight institutions like election commissions and media monitoring, did in fact prevent the Communists from tightening their political machine to the degree seen in presidentialist countries.[91]

Thus the case of Moldova, when related to the paired comparison of Ukraine and Kyrgyzstan, indicates that parliamentarist constitutions in highly patronalistic societies are perfectly capable of underpinning the emergence of single-pyramid politics and that their democratizing effects are likely to be weaker than those of divided-executive constitutions. At the same time, however, they are likely to facilitate a somewhat weaker form of coordination of patronalistic networks around the chief patron in comparison with presidentialist constitutions.

[91] Mihai Adauge, Secretary of the Christian Democratic Party, author's interview, December 20, 2008; Vlad Cubreacov, head of Christian Democratic Party parliamentary fraction and party VP, author's interview, Chisinau, Moldova, March 28, 2009; Iurie Rosca, Christian Democratic Party leader, author's interview, Chisinau, Moldova, July 7, 2010. Some independent experts regard these claims of Christian Democratic influence through bargaining to be credible: Igor Botan, executive director of the analytical center ADEPT, author's interview, Chisinau, Moldova, June 30, 2009; Viorel Cibotaru, director of the European Institute for Political Studies of Moldova, author's interview, Chisinau, Moldova, March 23, 2009.

CONCLUSION

The preceding discussion has shown, through a process-tracing comparison of Kyrgyzstan, Moldova, and Ukraine, that formal constitutions can have an important impact even in societies in which rules are not reliably followed and in which institutions are routinely corrupted – as in highly patronalistic societies. They matter in different ways than they do in other countries, however. Presidentialist constitutions have their effect not so much because they are "followed" as because (all other things being equal) they signal that whichever patronalistic network captures presidential office is likely to be the most powerful one in the country and make the occupant of the presidency a singular focal point for elite coordination. Such signals better enable the president to set informal rules and practices and to selectively give life to formal rules that other networks must acknowledge or risk political or economic isolation, creating a strong tendency to single-pyramid politics. Conversely, divided-executive constitutions complicate this process, creating uncertainty as to which network will be dominant and incentivizing rivalry among networks based in top state executive offices, primarily the premiership and the presidency, a process that tends to promote political opening. This does not boil down to an argument that increasing parliamentary power tends to produce democracy while presidential power tends toward autocracy; parliamentarist systems are also found under at least some conditions to promote the coordination of elite networks around chief patrons in a closed arrangement that resembles authoritarianism. While the degree of coordination induced by formal parliamentarist constitutions is likely to be somewhat weaker than that encouraged by presidentialist ones because the former add a second vote that a chief patron must win to assume the top formal office,[92] divided-executive constitutions are likely to be far more effective in disrupting the coordination processes central to the development of a strong political machine.

These findings have significant implications for debates about the role of constitutions in regime change. For one thing, the careful paired comparison between Kyrgyzstan and Ukraine successfully isolates an important effect of presidentialist constitutions on the degree of democracy. In two countries emerging from an electoral revolution with a standoff between two regionally based networks with roughly equal informal power, the one that retained a presidentialist constitution experienced a reconsolidation of single-pyramid politics while the other – for essentially exogenous reasons – wound up adopting a new divided-executive constitution that significantly complicated attempts by all major players to reestablish single-pyramid politics through the processes described here. This should caution us not to take too far arguments that constitutions are often epiphenomenal, having no

92 While not explored here, parliamentarist constitutions can also underpin more open political outcomes when the majority constitutes a coalition of separate networks (parties) that are roughly even in strength, with no single one playing the leading role. See Hale 2013.

independent impact on democratization.[93] Further comparative process-tracing research and large-*N* research designs carefully tailored to test for specific causal mechanisms will be required to know for sure how far such arguments travel.

The findings also reveal a democracy-promoting side to divided-executive constitutions even under the condition of "cohabitation" (control over different executive posts by rival factions), usually cited for negative effects like political infighting, policy paralysis, and regime instability.[94] We do in fact find these negative effects in Ukraine during 2005 through 2010, and it may be that observers ultimately judge them to outweigh the positive effects. While such judgment is beyond the scope of this analysis, we can conclude that the democratizing effects of divided-executive constitutions in highly patronalistic societies should be taken into consideration. Indeed, a divided-executive constitution sustained a period of political openness in Ukraine that lasted half a decade – the post–Soviet region's only such sustained opening, apart from the Baltic countries, during over twenty years of postcommunism. Moreover, this success stands out positively against the yardstick of democracy relative to Moldova's experience of a parliamentarist constitution during much of the 2000s, which underpinned democratic erosion. And it may be that future research will help us identify conditions under which divided executive power can function effectively even in highly patronalistic societies, making the democracy it promotes more stable and attractive. With Georgia and Kyrgyzstan as of 2013 now having adopted reforms creating divided-executive constitutions, we are likely to gain new analytical leverage on this question in the future. This study is thus intended as a step toward better understanding how constitutions actually and potentially matter in highly patronalistic societies based on post–Soviet history as it has developed so far.

REFERENCES

Bratton, Michael and Nicolas Van de Walle. 1994. "Neopatrimonial Regimes and Political Transitions in Africa." *World Politics* 46(4): 453–89.

Bunce, Valerie J. and Sharon L. Wolchik. 2010. "Defeating Dictators: Electoral Change and Stability in Competitive Authoritarian Regimes." *World Politics* 62(2): 43–86.

Carothers, Thomas. 2002. "The End of the Transition Paradigm." *Journal of Democracy* 13(1): 5–21.

Cashu, Ilian. 2005. "What Makes an Orange Revolution Unlikely in Moldova?" End Note, *RFE/RL Newsline*, March 4.

Cheibub, Jose Antonio. 2007. *Presidentialism, Parliamentarism, and Democracy*. New York: Cambridge University Press.

Cheibub, Jose Antonio, Zachary Elkins, and Tom Ginsburg. 2011. "Latin American Presidentialism in Comparative and Historical Perspective." *Texas Law Review* 89(7): 1707–39.

93 E.g., Cheibub (2007).

94 E.g., Shugart and Carey (1992: chap. 4). For an argument that certain forms of semipresidentialism (such as what Stepan calls "parliamentarized semi-presidentialism") can have more promising effects, see Stepan (2009); and Colton and Skach (2009).

Christensen, Robert K., Edward R. Rakhimkulov, and Charles R. Wise. 2005. "The Ukrainian Orange Revolution Brought More Than a New President: What Kind of Democracy Will the Institutional Changes Bring?" *Communist and Post-Communist Studies* 38(2): 207–30.

Colton, Timothy and Cindy Skach. 2009. "The Predicament of Semi-Presidentialism," in Alfred Stepan, ed., *Democracies in Danger*. Baltimore, MD: The Johns Hopkins University Press, pp. 121–36.

D'Anieri, Paul. 2007. *Understanding Ukrainian Politics: Power, Politics, and Institutional Design*. Armonk, NY: M. E. Sharpe.

Diamond, Larry and Marc Plattner, eds. 1996. *The Global Resurgence of Democracy*. Baltimore, MD: The Johns Hopkins University Press.

Dumitru, Razvan. 2011. "Politics and Practices in Post-Soviet 'Business': Between Shame and Success." *Revista Martor* 16: 52–66.

Duverger, Maurice. 1980. "A New Political System Model: Semi-presidential Government." *European Journal of Political Research* 8: 165–87.

Easter, Gerald M. 1997. "Preference for Presidentialism: Postcommunist Regime Change in Russia and the NIS." *World Politics* 49(2): 184–211.

Economist Intelligence Unit. 2008. *Index of Democracy 2008*. Available at http://a330.g.akamai.net/7/330/25828/20081021185552/graphics.eiu.com/PDF/Democracy%20Index%202008.pdf. Accessed March 1, 2009.

Fish, M. Steven. 2005. *Democracy Derailed in Russia: The Failure of Open Politics*. New York: Cambridge University Press.

Fish, M. Steven. 2006. "Stronger Legislatures, Stronger Democracy." *Journal of Democracy* 17(1): 5–20.

Freedom House. 2010. *Freedom in the World*. At http://www.freedomhouse.org/template.cfm?page=22&year=2010&country=7856. Accessed June 24, 2010.

Geertz, Clifford. 1973. *The Interpretation of Culture*. New York: Basic Books.

George, Alexander L. and A. Bennett. 2005. *Case Studies and Theory Development in the Social Sciences*. Cambridge, MA: MIT Press.

Goehring, Jennifer, ed. 2008. *Nations in Transit 2008: Democratization from Central Europe to Eurasia*. New York: Freedom House.

Grzymala-Busse, Anna. 2008. "Beyond Clientelism: Incumbent State Capture and State Formation." *Comparative Political Studies* 41(4–5): 638–73.

Grzymala-Busse, Anna. 2010. "The Best Laid Plans: The Impact of Informal Rules on Formal Institutions in Transitional Regimes." *Studies in Comparative International Development* 45(3): 311–33.

Hale, Henry E. 2005. "Regime Cycles: Democracy, Autocracy, and Revolution in Post-Soviet Eurasia." *World Politics* 58(1): 133–65.

Hale, Henry E. 2011. "Formal Constitutions in Informal Politics: Institutions and Democratization in Eurasia." *World Politics* 63(4): 581–617.

Hale, Henry E. 2013. *Great Expectations: Patronal Politics and Regime Dynamics in Eurasia*, draft book manuscript.

Helmke, Gretchen and Steven Levitsky. 2004. "Informal Institutions and Comparative Politics: A Research Agenda." *Perspectives on Politics* 2(4): 725–40.

Herron, Erik S. 2011. "How Viktor Yanukovych Won: Reassessing the Dominant Narratives of Ukraine's 2010 Presidential Election." *East European Politics and Societies* 25(1): 47–67.

Huskey, Eugene and Gulnara Iskakova. 2010. "The Barriers to Intra-Opposition Cooperation in the Post-Communist World: Evidence from Kyrgyzstan." *Post-Soviet Affairs* 26(3): 228–62.

Kaufmann, Daniel, Aart Kraay, and Massimo Mastruzze. 2008. *Governance Matters VII: Aggregate and Individual Governance Indicators 1996–2007*. Available at http://www-wds.worldbank.org/external/default/WDSContentServer/IW3P/IB/2008/06/24/000158349_20080624113458/Rendered/PDF/wps4654.pdf. Accessed August 21, 2009.

Kekic, L. 2007. *The Economist Intelligence Unit's Index of Democracy*. Available at http://www.economist.com/media/pdf/democracy_index_2007_v3.pdf. Accessed December 1, 2010.

Kitschelt, Herbert. 2000. "Linkages between Citizens and Politicians in Democratic Polities." *Comparative Political Studies* 33(6–7): 845–79.

Kitschelt, Herbert, Zdenka Mansfeldova, Radoslaw Markowski, and Gabor Toka. 1999. *Post-Communist Party Systems*. New York: Cambridge University Press.

Knight, Jack. 1992. *Institutions and Social Conflict*. New York: Cambridge University Press.

Korduban, Pavel. 2008. "Ukrainian Prosecutors Target Self-Defense Leaders." *Eurasia Daily Monitor*. May 30.

Kudelia, Serhiy. 2010. "Betting on Society: Power Perceptions and Elite Games in Ukraine," in *Orange Revolution and Aftermath: Mobilization, Apathy, and the State in Ukraine*, edited by Paul D'Anieri. Washington, DC: Woodrow Wilson Center Press.

Kulov, Feliks. 2008. *Na perevale*. Moscow: Vremia.

Kuzio, Taras. 2008. "Democratic Breakthroughs and Revolutions in Five Postcommunist Countries: Comparative Perspectives on the Fourth Wave." *Demokratizatsiya* 16(1): 97–112.

Lauth, Hans-Joachim. 2000. "Informal Institutions and Democracy." *Democratization* 7(4): 21–50.

Levitsky, Steven and Gretchen Helmke. 2006. *Informal Institutions and Democracy: Lessons from Latin America*. Baltimore, MD: The Johns Hopkins University Press.

Linz, Juan J., and Alfred Stepan. 1996. *Problems of Democratic Transition and Consolidation: Southern Europe, South America and Post-Communist Europe*. Baltimore, MD: The Johns Hopkins University Press.

Magaloni, Beatriz. 2006. *Voting for Autocracy: Hegemonic Party Survival and Its Demise in Mexico*. New York: Cambridge University Press.

Maksymiuk, Jan. 2007. "Ukraine Faces Crisis as President Dissolves Parliament." End Note in RFE/RL *Newsline*. April 3.

Marat, Erica. 2008. "Need for More Transparency in Kyrgyz and Tajik Energy Sectors to Avoid Future Crises." *Eurasia Daily Monitor* 5 (December 19).

Marat, Erica. 2009. "Kyrgyzstan." *Nations in Transit 2009*. Available at http://www.freedomhouse.org/report/nations-transit/2009/kyrgyzstan (accessed August 13, 2013).

Marshall, Monty G. 2008. *Polity IV Project: Political Regime Characteristics and Transitions 1800–2007*. Available at http://www.systemicpeace.org/polity/polity4.htm. Accessed February 25, 2009.

McFaul, Michael. 2005. "Transitions from Communism." *Journal of Democracy* 16(3): 5–19.

McGlinchey, Eric. 2010. "Running in Circles in Kyrgyzstan." *New York Times*. April 10: A23.

Naiiem, Mustafa and Serhy Leshchenko. 2008. "Oliharkhichni viiny: Khoroshkovskyi iak maska Firtasha?" *Ukraiins'ka Pravda*. July 30, 22:05.

North, Douglass C., and Barry R. Weingast. 1989. "Constitutions and Commitment." *Journal of Economic History* 49(4): 803–32.

O'Donnell, Guillermo. 1994. "Delegative Democracy." *Journal of Democracy* 5(1): 55–69.

Ozcan, Gul Berna. 2010. *Building States and Markets: Enterprise Development in Central Asia*. Houndmills: Palgrave-Macmillan.

Pritchin, Stanislav. 2006. "Vtoroi Akaev?" *Oazis*, no.3 (February). Available at http://www.ca-oasis.info/oasis/?jrn=24&id=171. Accessed February 9, 2006.

Przeworski, Adam. 1991. *Democracy and the Market*. Cambridge: Cambridge University Press.
Radnitz, Scott. 2006. "What Really Happened in Kyrgyzstan?" *Journal of Democracy* 17(2): 132–46.
Sakwa, Richard. 2011. *The Crisis of Russian Democracy: The Dual State, Factionalism and the Medvedev Succession*. Cambridge: Cambridge University Press.
Sariev, Temir. 2008. *Shakh Kyrgyzskoi demokratii [The Shah of Kyrgyz Democracy]*. Bishkek, Kyrgyzstan: Salam.
Schedler, Andreas. 2002. "The Menu of Manipulation." *Journal of Democracy* 13(2): 36–50.
Shugart, Matthew Soberg and John M. Carey. 1992. *Presidents and Assemblies: Constitutional Design and Electoral Dynamics*. New York: Cambridge University Press.
Silitski, Vitali. 2005. "Preempting Democracy: The Case of Belarus." *Journal of Democracy* 16(4): 83–97.
Skach, Cindy. 2005. *Borrowing Constitutional Designs: Constitutional Law in Weimar Germany and the French Fifth Republic*. Princeton, NJ: Princeton University Press.
Spector, Regine A. 2008. "Securing Property in Contemporary Kyrgyzstan." *Post-Soviet Affairs* 24(2): 149–76.
Stack, Graham. 2011. "The Talented Mr Plahotniuc." *BNE Business New Europe* (April 11). At http://www.bne.eu/story2610. Accessed June 17, 2012.
Stepan, Alfred. 2009. "Introduction: Undertheorized Political Problems in the Founding Democratization Literature," in Alfred Stepan, ed., *Democracies in Danger*. Baltimore, MD: The Johns Hopkins University Press, pp. 1–14.
Stepan, Alfred, Juan J. Linz, and Yogendra Yadav. 2011. *Democracy in Multinational Societies: India and Other Polities*. Baltimore, MD: The Johns Hopkins University Press.
Sushko, Oleksandr and Olena Prystayko. 2009. "Ukraine." *Nations in Transit 2009*. Available at http://www.freedomhouse.org/report/nations-transit/2009/ukraine. Accessed August 13, 2013.
Tarrow, Sidney. 2010. "The Strategy of Paired Comparison." *Comparative Political Studies* 43(2): 230–59.
Transparency International. 2008. *2008 Corruption Perceptions Index*. Available at http://www.transparency.org/news_room/in_focus/2008/cpi2008/cpi_2008_table. Accessed April 11, 2009.
Trochev, Alexei. 2010. "Meddling with Justice: Competitive Politics, Impunity, and Distrusted Courts in Post-Orange Ukraine." *Demokratizatsiya: The Journal of Post-Soviet Democratization* 18(2): 122–47.
Trochev, Alexei. 2011. "A Constitution of Convenience in Ukraine." *Jurist-Forum*, January 18. Available at http://jurist.org/forum/2011/01/jurist-guest-columnist-alexei-trochev.php. Accessed April 24, 2011.
Veitch, John M. 1986. "Repudiations and Confiscations by the Medieval State." *Journal of Economic History* 46(1): 31–6.
Wagstyl, Stefan and Roman Oleachyk. 2010. "Ukraine Election Divides Oligarchs." *Financial Times*. January 15. In Dominique Arel, ed., *The Ukraine List (UKL)*, 438, January 16, 2010.
Walker, Christopher, and Robert Orttung. 2011. "From Revolution to Democracy." *Wall Street Journal Europe*. March 7. Available at http://online.wsj.com/article/SB10001424052748703529004576159802566388940.html?mod=WSJ_Opinion_LEFTTopBucket, accessed April 9, 2011.
Way, Lucan A. 2002. "Pluralism by Default in Moldova." *Journal of Democracy* 13(4): 127–41.
Way, Lucan A. 2005. "Authoritarian State Building and the Sources of Regime Competitiveness in the Fourth Wave: The Cases of Belarus, Moldova, Russia, and Ukraine." *World Politics* 57(2): 231–61.

Weingast, Barry R. 1997. "The Political Foundations of Democracy and the Rule of Law." *American Political Science Review* 91(2): 245–63.
Wilson, Andrew. 2005a. *Ukraine's Orange Revolution*. New Haven, CT: Yale University Press.
Wilson, Andrew. 2005b. *Virtual Politics: Faking Democracy in the Post-Soviet World*. New Haven, CT: Yale University Press.
Yatsenko, N. 2008. "Konstitutsiina 'balalaika.'" *Dzerkalo Tyzhnia*. July 19–August 1: 1, 3.

11

The Party's Leadership as a Living Constitution in China

Xin He

Like most countries, China has a well-written constitution. China's constitution, however, does not tell how the state actually operates (Cohen 1978: 839; Jones 1985: 710). We all know that the state apparatus, the military, and the congresses are subordinate to China's Communist Party (the CCP).[1] Unfortunately, the literature on Chinese constitutional studies has paid only scant attention to this fundamental principle. This has been true even for scholars who demand greater study of China's unwritten constitutions. For instance, in "Written and Unwritten Constitutions: A New Approach to the Study of Constitutional Government in China," Jiang did not even mention the Party's leadership at all (2010: 12–46). Moreover, according to Clarke (2010: 87–99), Jiang's discussion remains primarily formalistic and thus is limited in capturing the essence of China's living constitution.

If the most important issue in constitutionalism is the division of power, the penetrating nature of the CCP's leadership poses several thorny questions: What is the relationship among the party and the congress, the state administration, and the judiciaries? Is there any meaningful division of power among the state apparatuses in China? What is the relationship between the central and the local? To what extent are the basic rights of citizens provided in the Constitution meaningful? It is the pattern of exercise of the party's power to which the rest of the chapter will turn.

One might answer these questions with one sentence: the CCP has unconstrained power and can penetrate any aspect of the state operation and citizens' activities. After all, every important position in the state is staffed by a party member; there is thus no meaningful division of power, and any discussion of it is doomed to be futile. Such a response, however, is problematic. First, although the CCP's power

[1] Traditionally there are four cardinal principles enshrined in the 1982 Constitution: the Socialist Road, the Party's Leadership, the Dictatorship of Proletarians, and the Marx-Leninism and Mao's Thoughts. For a discussion of these principles, see Lin Feng, *Constitutional Law of the PRC* (2000: 23–34). But all of these principles, with the exception of the party's leadership, have been challenged, abandoned, or severely eroded.

is theoretically unconstrained, it might not be capable of exercising it fully, or for its own interests, it may not *want* to do so (Ginsburg and Moustafa 2008). For example, there is a great deal of privacy in reform-era China (Wang 1995: 149–72, 2008: 56–87). If the view of total Party hegemony over all of society had some merit in the Maoist period, it has lost much of it in the reform era. Second, as Dowdle argues, such a response conflates party affiliation with party control (1997). When the interests of the two conflict, there is no reason to give priority to those of the Party. Finally, as shown in the history of the CCP's or any other one-party state, intraparty conflicts and compromises are common. Different state apparatuses will almost certainly become arenas for power struggles and competition over agenda setting. Assuming unlimited state capacity and seamless united leadership is thus reminiscent of a totalitarian approach long abandoned by political scientists.[2] An important task for Chinese constitutional studies, indeed, is to identify the patterns of struggles and compromises. Accepting the party's godlike position as a formal matter, the real questions become: How does the CCP actually exercise its leadership? How does it deal with other state apparatuses? How does it establish and negotiate the central-local relationship? What room for basic rights does it leave for citizens?

To answer these questions, it would be naive to rely on the text of the Constitution or the law. The answers, instead, are to be found in CCP documents, party practices, speeches of party leaders, and empirical evidence. This chapter will first examine how the party leads. It will then explore the role of the party's leadership in four constitutional areas: the relationship between the party and the legislatures, party-court relations, central-local relations, and citizens' basic rights.

HOW THE PARTY LEADS

How does the CCP actually lead? In particular, how is the party's leadership structured inside the party and how does it deal with other state apparatuses? Despite constant fluidity and much evolution, some rough sketches can be drawn.

The primary mechanism of party leadership is the Party Central Committee, which instructs the National People's Congress (NPC) as to whom to elect to the most important posts of the state, such as the chair of the NPC standing committee, head of state, chair of the military, ministers, and presidents of the Supreme People's Court and Supreme People's Procuratorate. This arrangement is largely replicated at all levels (Nathan 1997: 43–57).

Moreover, the Party Central Committee, through the Politburo and its Standing Committee, make and enforce the major policy decisions through a strong coordination system. Furthermore, central groups, such as the Political-legal Affairs Commission and the Finance and Economics Leading Group, usually chaired by a Politburo Standing Committee member, are responsible for policy planning, command,

[2] Cf. Zheng Shiping, *Party vs. State in Post 1949 China* (1997).

coordination, and supervision of personnel and implementation (Hamrin 1992: 97–101). As Hamrin stated:

> [N]ormally, internal security, along with the legislative and judicial functions, is channeled through a Political and Legal Affairs Commission or LG (leading group), which oversees the NPC, the procuratorate and the court systems, as well as the police and intelligence forces. Currently, the ministries of state security, justice, public security, and probably civil affairs and supervision are in this arena, judging from official cabinet lists. (1992: 112–3)[3]

In each nonparty organization, party core groups are set up and entrusted with supervising administrative work (Lin 2000: 198–204). At the same time, party core groups in each organization are directly responsible to the next higher level for policy implementation. Thus, the way in which the party's leadership is structured inside the party is more crucial for understanding outcomes. After all, the party subcommittees in all of these nonparty organizations regularly execute the orders of the party.

The party committee apparently leads collectively. The Party Charter (Art. 10.5) states that "party committees at all levels lead with a collective leadership combined with individual division of labor. For significant problems, the decisions are made through a principle of collective leadership, democratic centralism, individually conceived ideas, and meetings discussed by the members." At the heart of this collective leadership is "democratic centralism." Its official interpretations, according to the Party Charter, require that the minority obey the majority. With "democratic" in its name, this institution implies that decisions shall be made by the majority rule. But in reality, in the words of Deng Xiaoping:

> Patriarchy is a social phenomenon with long history and it had caused huge damage in the party's History. Chen Duxiu, Wang Min, Zhang Guotao were all practitioners of patriarchy. From the Zunyi Meeting[4] to the Socialist Reform Period, the Central party Committee and comrade Mao have been leading collectively, implementing democratic centralism, and the democratic life within the party was fairly normal. Unfortunately, these good traditions did not survive, nor was a rigid and perfect institution formed. For example, when discussing significant questions of the party, often democracy and preparation were not fully developed, and decisions were made by a few persons, rarely by voting in accordance with the majority rule. (Deng 1994: 330)

While Deng's reforms may have decreased the concentration of power, the power structure has remained largely unchanged. The decisions are still made behind closed doors and there are no detailed procedures for the proceedings. Nor are the "significant problems" defined. It is no secret that cliques exist and the members'

3 For a more detailed description, see Hamrin (1992: 121–2).

4 A party plenary meeting held in Zunyi, Guizhou province, 1935, en route to the Long March, in which Mao assumed the supreme power of the party.

power in the party committee remains unequally distributed. When one member, usually the first secretary, becomes powerful, he has little difficulty in setting the agenda and pushing it through in the meetings. A telling example may be the succession of power from Jiang Zemin to Hu Jintao. While Jiang could not prevent Hu from being his successor, who had been appointed by Deng and thus countenanced by many senior leaders, Jiang not only placed five of his protégés on the next Politburo Standing Committee but also expanded its membership from seven to nine (Cheng and White: 2006: 81–118). It is hard to imagine that individual members cast their votes independently of others' influence. In making the 1989 crackdown decision, for example, the members were under significant pressure from others, including the nonmember senior leaders (Vogel 2011: 617; Zhang 2001).

Democratic centralism, as the party Charter stipulates (Art. 10.5), has another leg: the division of labor among committee members. Deng said, "[O]nce a decision is made collectively, each member shall do his part to carry it out and bear his own responsibility; kicking balls around is not allowed. . . . Among other members of the party committees, individual division of labor and responsibility shall be emphasized" (Deng 1994: 341).

The use of the term "division of labor" instead of "division of power" or "power sharing" reveals a key aspect of the principle of the party's leadership. It means that there is no real division of power between the party and other state apparatuses. If anything, there only exists division of labor. Of course, division of labor implies a division of power. But when division of power is not a constitutional principle, any division of power that may exist in division of labor is secondary. There is no meaningful separation of power and independence among the state apparatuses and the party. Whenever a dispute arises from a power struggle, the final arbiter, according to the principle of democratic centralism, will simply be the higher-level party committee.

With all these institutional arrangements and long-established norms, it is clear that the party can have iron control over all the major policies. Once the division of labor becomes a principle in dealing with the relationships among political and state organizations, the situations have become subtle and dynamic in light of China's evolving political and socioeconomic conditions.

THE PARTY AND THE CONGRESSES

The relationship between the party and the NPC has never been static. According to the Constitution, the NPC is sovereign and all state organs report to the NPC. But in its first twenty-five years, the NPC did little more than reify the party's will. The heads of the NPC were important figures (Liu Shaoqi, Zhu De, Ye Jianying), but only because they held other influential positions in the state, the party, or the military. Their positions as the NPC head were just honorary. The political irrelevance of the NPC was also evinced by its organizational structure and staff. Its standing committee and even the congresses did not meet regularly, and there were no established procedures for doing so. Prior to 1978, the permanent support staff of the NPC never numbered more than a dozen (Dowdle 1997: 4).

The reform period, however, has brought the steady institutional development of the NPC and local people's congresses (the LPC). The NPC, over the past thirty years, has "grown from insignificance to a potent constitutional force in China's political system" (Dowdle 2002: 2). Many scholars have argued that the LPCs have been transformed from a rubber stamp to an iron one (Cho 2008; O'Brien 1990; Xia 2008). Low approval rates for government reports and the CCP's nominees for public office are taken seriously by national political actors; it has assumed primary authority over China's legislative development, so much so that it once forced the CCP to change a constitutional amendment draft; it also is able to discipline other political actors through the use of its parliamentary investigations (Dowdle 1997: 3–11, 2002: 2–4).

All these developments, however, do not suggest that the NPC and LPCs have in any way challenged the party's leadership. Indeed, it is still not realistic for the NPC to veto a bill or a nominee proposed by the party (although this has occasionally happened at some LPCs). Similar to its dwarf-like political position before the reform, its current development is also orchestrated by the party. Even Dowdle, who insists that the NPC has become an important constitutional player, admits: "The NPC's institutional emergence owes much to a corresponding decrease in the CCP's own willingness to intervene in or otherwise oversee a wide range of constitutional activities" (Dowdle 1997: 13). He continues: "This is not to imply that the CCP is unable to reach into the NPC to pick at political irritations. . . . However, at the very least, the party appears significantly less willing to or interested in censuring political opposition in the NPC than in other political bodies" (Dowdle 1997: 13).

Although Deng Xiaoping rarely explicitly discussed the political function and position of the NPC and the NPC seemed to him a very marginal institution, he did say, at the very beginning of the reforms, in 1978:

> We shall devote concerted effort to legislating criminal laws, civil laws, procedural laws, and other necessary laws, such as factory laws, people's commune laws, forest laws, grassland laws, environmental laws, labor laws, foreign investment laws, etc. passing them through certain democratic discussion; we shall strengthen the procuratorate and judicial institutions, making the laws available and strictly enforcing the laws. The relationships between the state and the enterprises, between the different enterprises, and between the enterprises and individuals shall also be determined by the laws; their disputes shall be resolved by the laws. (Deng 1994: 146–7)

His enthusiasm for law was clearly evinced by his words on legislative work, which have been regarded as the Bible for generations of legislators:

> Nowadays the legislative work is onerous, lacking adequate personnel. So the legal statutes can be broad initially and be perfected later. Some local statutes can be

> legislated first, and then with experience and improvement would a national law be passed. When modifying and complementing laws, complement one article at a time once ready; do not wait for the readiness of "the whole machine." In a word, a law available is better than none; sooner is better than later. (Deng 1994: 147)

This change was formally confirmed in a 1991 internal party document titled "Several Opinions of the Central Committee on Strengthening Leadership over Lawmaking Work." The CCP for the first time set out explicit normative limits on its own authority to oversee legislative drafting. This move limited the CCP's legislative input to one of broad policy direction and increased the NPC's legislative role.

This was done because, to achieve the goals of the economic reforms, the party had to retreat from the society, abandoning the traditional governance via political campaigns and ideological indoctrination. Instead, it needed to rely on laws and legal institutions to govern the society (Shue 1988). As observed by Zheng,

> [A]s China has moved away from revolution and class struggle to economic reform and construction, the Party's ideological work and organizational control can no longer effectively meet the challenge of a new and dynamic economy and an increasingly diverse society. State-building, such as revitalizing the institution of the people's congress and enhancing the legal system, becomes necessary, if not inevitable. (1997: 188)

This changed mode of governance determined the increased political status of the NPC. This trend only became more salient after Jiang Zemin assumed power. In 1999's constitutional amendment, the rule of law has been written into the constitution (Art. 5).

If this amendment does not provide much detail about law and the NPC's position in party governance, the political status of the NPC chairs speaks volumes on its increasing importance in China's political structure in the reform era. When Peng Zhen and Wan Li were the chairmen, in 1983 and 1988, respectively, they were members of the Politburo but of the Politburo's Standing Committee. But when Qiao Shi assumed the position in 1993, he was not just a member of the Politburo's Standing Committee but also the No. 3 politically most powerful person in the country. Five years later, it was Li Peng, the No. 2 person of the party, who assumed the position. And this practice has been routinized when Wu Bangguo took the position in 2003 and 2008. If the NPC chair was only a nominal position for important political figures, the post of the NPC chair has now become a major post held by Qiao Shi (1993–1998), Li Peng (1998–2003), and Wu Bangguo (2003–2013). It is clear that the party has taken the NPC seriously and has thus appointed a most important figure to it. The development of the NPC and LPCs is thus no more the bootstrap development of the institution as the result of the party's changed mode of governance. The low approval rates and some disapproval, similar to some objections and conflicts inside the party, only serve as another layer in the candidate selection process. Rather than harm or challenge the party's leadership, it is intended to perfect and thus strengthen the party's leadership.

All this suggests that although the NPC might have been used by some politicians to advance their agendas, the development of the NPC and LPCs occurs mainly under the auspices of the party's leadership. Peng Zhen, the conservative party leader and the chair of the NPC from 1983 to 1988, was the most influential figure in the NPC's development and was also believed to have used the NPC as an institutional base to temper Deng Xiaoping's liberal policies (Tanner 1994: 74–5). He tacitly placed his agenda under the leadership of the party. He said:

> The party's leadership and following the laws are consistent. The party leads the people in legislating the Constitution and the Laws, and the party also leads the people to comply with, and enforce the Constitutions and the Laws. The party Charter clearly stipulates that the party organizations and party members shall conduct activities inside the Constitution and the Laws. (Peng 1982)

Peng also claimed that the NPC is the principal repository for the government's constitutional legitimacy; therefore, a stronger, more independent, and more assertive NPC is a precedent for China's political development (Peng 1982, 1983; Tanner 1994: 75). Whatever Peng's agenda, his arguments for the development of the NPC are not at all inconsistent with the party's leadership or interests; if anything, the developments have consolidated and perfected the party's leadership in the reform period.

The fact that the development of the NPC is the desired outcome of the party can be corroborated by the way in which the Urban Custody and Repatriation Rules were abolished. After the Sun Zhigang incident, in which a college graduate was beaten to death in Guangzhou, there was an outcry among netizens to abolish the Rules, which, allegedly, had been unconstitutionally promulgated by the State Council (Hand 2009: 221–42). While the power to review constitutionality is clearly vested in the NPC, it did not take the initiative to do so. Indeed, it has never actually exercised the power to declare laws unconstitutional (Peerenboom and He 2009: 1–61). The State Council itself, the promulgator of the Rules, abolished the statute. This was regarded as a tactic to avoid setting a precedent for the NPC, in exercising its reviewing power, to abolish an unconstitutional administrative statute (Hand 2009: 221–42). This was obviously a step coordinated by the party. In so doing, it avoided the appearance of a rift between the NPC and the State Council. In other words, the party controlled the pace of the NPC's development and even provided scripts for its detailed steps. As the preamble of the party Charter states, "The party must make sure that the legislative, judicial, administrative apparatuses, economic and cultural and people's entities actively, independently and responsibility, and consistently work together."

THE PARTY AND THE COURTS

To what extent are the courts able to really exercise adjudicative power independently of administrative organizations, social entities, and individuals, as provided by the Constitution in Article 126? To what extent does the party tolerate the development of the judiciary? Is there any room for judicial innovation? These are familiar questions for China's legal scholars. This section will examine these issues in relation to the party's leadership.

Compared to the people's congresses, the courts are in a much lower position in China's political hierarchy. The president of the Supreme People's Court (SPC) is only a member of the Party Central Committee, not of the Politburo. Although its administrative ranking is higher than the ministries, its political status inside the party is not, and it is in fact lower than the ministries of Public Security, Finance, and the Planning Commission. The lower status of the SPC and other courts can also be seen from the composition of the party's Leading Group of Political-legal Affairs. The group is chaired by a member of the Politburo's Standing Committee, while a Politburo member and the minister of the Public Security serve as the vice chairs. The president of the SPC, similar to the president of the Supreme Procuratorate, is just a regular member. The lower rank accorded to the head of the SPC shows that the judiciary is not so important in the party.

How have the party and its political-legal affairs committees affected the judicial decision-making process? The Notice that the Party must Firmly Support the Socialist Rule by Law, issued by the Party Central Committee in 1986, which is intended to strengthen the authority of the judiciaries, states, "[I]n the significant and difficult cases that the party committee in the judiciaries seek the opinions of the party committee, the party committee shall thoroughly express its opinions according to laws and policies. *The judiciaries shall take the opinions of the party committee seriously*" (Central Committee of the CPC 1986; emphasis added). While it does not define significant and difficult cases, nor does it say whether the party committee of the judiciaries must always seek opinions in such cases, it is a matter of course that the courts would seek opinions for all the cases that they regard as appropriate in a way to avoid potential responsibilities. After all, the presidents and major leaders of the judiciary are actually appointed by the party committee, even though these appointments require nominal approval by the people's congresses. Recent empirical studies on the functioning of the adjudication committee, the highest decision-making body of Chinese courts, show that the adjudication committee has no way of resisting the external interference of upper-level courts, the party, and the government. Indeed, the courts have taken the initiative to seek opinions on whatever cases they feel are difficult and significant to avoid potential responsibility (He 2012). This arrangement makes it clear that Article 126 of the constitution, requiring independent adjudication, does not cover the party, nor is the party included in the "social entities" referenced in the Article.

It is, then, not surprising that there is a clear pattern of dualism in the cases heard by the Chinese courts.[5] For routine and minor cases, the courts seem competent, consistent, and efficient (He 2009: 419–56, 2011: 253–75). But for complicated and important cases, such as those involving collective labor disputes, the courts are led by the party, together with other relevant party and government agencies, to handle the cases, often at the expense of procedural and substantial justice (Su and He 2010: 157–84). While these cases are hard to define *ex ante*, all sorts of politically sensitive cases are listed as vulnerable to external interference in the framework suggested by Fu and Peerenboom (2010: 95–133) to understand judicial independence in China.

This is not to suggest that there is no judicial independence or judicial innovation at all. Indeed, judicial innovation does occur.[6] Viewing the development from a political perspective, Peerenboom suggests that the Chinese judiciary, similar to any other political actors, has pursued its institutional interests strategically and increased its status and authority (Peerenboom 2010: 15). In this sense, there is always a certain degree of judicial independence and the line between mundane cases and politically sensitive cases is evolving. But the point is that judicial independence or judicial innovation, if any, must occur under the umbrella of the party's leadership. As suggested by Peerenboom,

> PRC courts cannot continue to enhance their authorities and independence without party support for legal reforms in general, and for the courts in particular, as they struggle to professionalize and carve out space in the still evolving political order. (2009: 197)

There is empirical support for this statement. In a study of judicialization of administrative governance in East China, I find that the local courts have been successful in regulating administrative behavior (He 2013). The foremost strategy of the courts, however, is to marshal the support of the party, pointing out the potential damage of unruly behavior to social stability, which is the party's number-one concern. In particular,

> [t]he court struck a cautious note, making it clear that in seeking support for administrative litigation, it was not claiming independence. Indeed, it insisted that it remains an integral and loyal branch of the municipal party and government, and

5 Cf. Robert Sharlet (1977: 155–79).

6 In education litigation, for example, Kellogg demonstrates that Chinese courts have been innovative in expanding their own jurisdiction, striking down regulations that are inconsistent with national law, and creating legal requirements that have little legislative basis (Kellogg 2007); cf. Shen Kui (2003). Others observe that some Chinese courts, despite severe limitations on their power, have displayed creative activism and innovative initiative employing the due process principle. He Xin (2012). Examining how courts handled land compensation and welfare disputes in which rural women married outside their village sued their home village collectives, He (2007) argues that "there is room for courts to maneuver in the current political structure" and "under the seemingly peaceful surface of iron control exists dynamic turbulences of conflict, repression, resistance, competition, compromise, and cooperation." One political scientist even declares there is a "rise of local courts in China" (Yu Xiaohong 2009).

> by so doing, it was taking the initiative in sharing the worries of the party (为党分忧). The strengthening process should be initiated by the court, facilitated by the party, and directed by the municipal government (法院推动, 党委促成, 政府主导) . . . If it wanted any form of independence, it is independence from other administrative agencies at the same level, free from illegal interference in the litigation process. (He 2013)

Most importantly, judicial innovation, just like the balance between judicial independence and party interference, has also conformed to the interests of the party. If allowing the courts to handle mundane cases independently and efficiently improves certainty in investment and boosts the legitimacy of the regime, some judicial innovation in regulating administrative behavior helps the upper-level government and ultimately the Central Party Committee oversee the administrative agencies. As the socioeconomic and political environments evolve, the party needs to adjust the division of labor between the party and the courts (the scope of difficult and significant cases, for instance) and between the courts and administrative agencies (the scope and depth of judicialization of administrative behavior). In other words, the form and level of judicial innovation are under party control.

This pattern is clearly demonstrated by looking at the opposite side of the coin: once the judiciary oversteps the line tolerated by the party, it will be rectified, although the influence may or may not be directly conveyed through the party's institutional channels. One example is the 2001 Qi Yuling case, which involved identity theft. The SPC issued a legally thorny document that seemed to indicate that the Constitution could be directly applied to civil cases, which was clearly against traditional practice. The case soon led to an explosion of academic and popular commentary, with many legal scholars calling for the creation of some sort of constitutional review mechanism. This certainly went too far. Subsequently, there was strong political pressure from the central government on the SPC to abandon its attempts to push forward on constitutional development. On December 18, 2008, the SPC quietly withdrew its 2001 interpretation: the Qi Yuling interpretation was "no longer applied," according to the Court's terse explanation, and was therefore withdrawn. This occurred not long after the former vice president Huang Shongyou, the orchestrator of the 2001 interpretation, was convicted of corruption and removed from office. No constitutional litigation can lead to legal or policy change unless a higher-up has consented: even if it is unclear exactly which level or institution the higher-up is, it is definitely directly or indirectly related to the party (Kellogg 2009: 215–46). This is true even if the issue involves some obviously unconstitutional local regulations.

CENTRAL-LOCAL RELATIONS

A large body of literature suggests that the localities have enjoyed significant power in the reform period, in areas such as legislation, tax, finance, project approval, social administration, and personnel appointment (Xie et al. 1998; Zhou 2008). Some contend that although China is formally a unitary country, it is practicing de facto fiscal federalism (Qian and Weingast 1997: 83–92; Shirk 1992: 59–94; Zheng 2007: 213–41). In a similar vein, that the central government has difficulties getting its policy implemented is well documented (Zhou 2010: 47–78). "Heaven is high and the emperor far away" and "the above have policies but the below have countermeasures" are just two popular sayings in describing the difficulty of implementing central policy. Some commentators even claim that the orders of the center may not go beyond Zhongnanhai, the Kremlin of China. Indeed, while the central government retains all the reserved power and the final say on policy making, the local governments enjoy the vast power of enforcing the policies in all the areas except national defense, diplomatic relationship, and currency and bond issuance (Zhou 2008: 202).

This has led some scholars to believe that "initiatives from two sources," a statement written into the Constitution (Art. 3.4), is the constitutional principle governing China's central-local relations (Jiang 2010: 12–46; Zhu 2004). In China's highly centralized political system, emphasizing initiatives from two sources simply suggests that localities enjoy significant power.

But does this really suggest a *division* of power, as a constitutional principle, between the central and the local? As Zhou (2008: 202) aptly points out, there is a distinction between, on the one hand, administrative decentralization and de facto discretion enjoyed by the localities as a result of supervision difficulty inherent in a principal-agent relationship and, on the other, a political division of power in the constitutional sense. It is true that the localities enjoy power in the areas of taxation and fiscal arrangements. But viewed from the perspective of the political power structure, the fact that the localities enjoy some power is just reification of the party's leadership and especially the principle of the democratic centralism.

Whatever is written in the Constitution, the power structure of the party is clearly provided in the party Charter (Art. 10. 1):

> Individual party members are subordinate to the party organization, the minority is subordinate to the majority, the lower party organizations are subordinate to the higher party organization, and all the constituent organizations and members of the party are subordinate to the National Congress and the Central Committee of the party.

This power structure is characterized by hierarchy and democratic centralism. With an absolute party leadership, even if a political system has strong local governments, it still retains a highly centralized character. That is why in the PRC's prereform history, many efforts to expand the initiative of the localities failed, despite "consulting to settle the matter" and democratic processes repeatedly claimed by Mao (1977).

The situation has been somewhat changed after Deng's relentless emphasis that the localities shall be given more room for decision making in the reform period.

For example, the Economic Special Zones, Coastal Port Cities, and Specially Listed Cities were created, which enjoy tremendous autonomy from both the central and provincial governments. Furthermore, before the reform, the personnel appointment system had been "to control the two levels below (下管两级)," meaning that the party at the central level makes personnel appointments for both the provincial and the prefectural levels. The system has now changed to "controlling one level below (下管一级)," which means the party at the central level will only make appointment decisions for the provincial-level cadres, and the provincial party shall have the power to appoint cadres at the prefectural level (Xie et al. 1998). This certainly has been a huge delegation of power from the center to the localities, but the principal-agent nature of the personnel control system remains largely intact. At the heart of the party's power structure sit party primacy and discipline. Given the power structure and the primacy of the party's leadership, "the localities have limited autonomy by design, and initiative from below occurs mainly during implementation" (O'Brien 2010: 84).

Similar to the development of the people's congresses and courts, the center's initiative to release power to the localities is necessitated by the need of economic reforms and social modernization (Deng 1994: 330). This is what Shirk called "the political logic of economic reforms" (1993) and thus also conforms to the party's interests. The process and degree of power release are also well under the control of the party. Zhou uses "the political tournament," which means the lower-level officials have to compete for promotion according to the criteria set by the upper-level party, to characterize how the center has motivated and controlled the lower-level officials (Zhou 2008). In this process, the center has always retained the final say on personnel appointments and promotions for the provinces. The de facto fiscal federalism is guaranteed by the political centralization (Oliver and Shleifer 2001: 171–9). Or, only with the iron control over local officials' political careers can the center be comfortable releasing the fiscal and administrative power to the localities. The release of power and encouragement of various initiatives, political and economic,[7] is possible only in a highly centralized political system (Cai and Treisman 2006: 505–35). In other words, the local initiative is subject to the central initiative; no division of power, only a division of labor, exists between the center and the localities. As Shirk observed: "as the ultimate principles, the top Party leader retained the power to take policy initiatives, set the ideological line, and replace government cadres" (Shirk 1992: 86–7). And the de facto power enjoyed by the localities only indicates the inherent problems in a principle/agent framework in

7 One of the most interesting phenomena in China's political arena is the different governance tactics between Wang Yang and Bo Xilai. Wang Yang, the party chief of Guangdong, stresses economic upgrade and transformation, while Bo Xilai, the party chief of Chongqing municipality, promotes revolutionary ideologies. It is widely believed that the two are competing for a seat in the next Politburo Standing Committee. Obviously both tactics are, at least, not forestalled by the center. Bo even claimed that of the nine incumbent members of the Politburo Standing Committee, six supported his new way of governance (Mingpao News 2011).

which the center lacks effective means to eliminate lower-level discretion (He 2009: 143–62).

CITIZENS' BASIC RIGHTS

While there is a debate among scholars whether citizens' basic rights shall be regarded as a constitutional principle (Chen 2008: 485–511), the 2004 constitutional amendment did stipulate that "The State respects and protects human rights" be written into the Constitution (Art. 33.3). The Constitution also contains a chapter on "Citizens' Basic Rights and Obligations," enshrining rights that can be found in most constitutions of the developed world. This chapter is even placed before the chapters on state apparatuses to show the importance of citizens under the Constitution. Once again, however, the laws on the books are at best the starting point of exploration: What are the basic rights actually enjoyed by the Chinese citizens?

Chinese citizens have generally enjoyed a significant level of basic rights in the reform era and significantly more than they did under Mao. Let us take the right of association as an example. According to the laws, most civic associations are required to register with the Ministry of Civil Affairs and its local bureaus. To do so, an association has to find a party/state agency that is willing to serve as its official sponsor. Otherwise, it must dissolve itself. Regardless of such a control mechanism, according to Wang:

> The past two decades have witnessed an unprecedented associational revolution in China. By March 2007 there were over 190,000 associations of various types registered with government civil affairs departments at the county level and above. However, those registered associations account for only a small fraction of China's associational landscape, as a large number of associations choose either to register as business organizations or not to register at all. . . . If the unregistered are included, it is estimated there are at least 500,000 associations operating in China. (Wang 2008: 74–5)

Moreover, some of these associations, such as the nongovernmental organizations (NGOs) aimed at environmental protection, have played roles in setting the agenda and thus making decisions on relevant policies (Wang 2008: 56–87).

This situation is similar with regard to most other basic rights, including the freedoms of protest, press, speech, and religion. For example, there were more than 87,000 mass incidents (most of which were social protests) in 2005. The state tolerated most of them, and many of the protesters were rewarded by economic compensations (Su and He 2010: 157–84). As dinner-table freedom of speech has become commonplace, the number of journals and books published in the reform period has skyrocketed (Wang 1995: 149–72).

At the same time, the regime has brutally repressed some activities, and most of this repression clearly violated the laws. The repression of Falungong (Cheung

2004: 1–30), the recent crackdown on the Jasmine gatherings in some cities, and the persecution and even disappearing of *weiquan* (rights protection) lawyers (Fu and Cullen 2008: 111–28; Pils 2009: 243–60, 2011) and human rights advocates, including the high-profile artist Ai Weiwei (Cohen 2011), are just a few examples. The pattern of such repression is clear: once the regime finds such activities or persons threatening, it will strike them down and shrug off the objections from the international community. There is no doubt that this repression is well coordinated and systemic. As mentioned, the political-legal affairs leadership group, composed of the heads of the police, the national security department, the SPC, the SPP, and the military, is the ultimate decision maker. Its decisions on cracking down on certain activities or citizens have been carried out most effectively.

The contrast between the general expansion of basic rights in most areas and the severe repression in some areas has prompted scholars to wonder about the nature of law in China (Clarke 2011). The situation is reminiscent of the sovereign described by Austin that requires only that others obey its orders but does not limit itself through law or feel bound by its own orders (Hart 1961). A way to reconcile this discrepancy, nevertheless, is how the party leads. The contrast exposes "the contradiction between the PRC Constitution's new commitment to constitutional rights, and its old commitment to party rule and democratic centralism" (Pils 2009: 244). To allow most people to enjoy more basic rights conforms to the party's interest because the party has learned that, given little breathing time and space, people are likely to become dispirited. To achieve economic development and social transformation, the party cannot afford to continue the monopolization and politicization of people's scraps of freedom (Wang 1995: 149–72). But it does not mean that the party will take a laissez-faire attitude toward the ways in which people enjoy their rights. Although the party's "indifference zone" has grown, it retains iron control over areas or activities that might damage its interest, not to mention its very survival. Whether the basic rights shall be a constitutional principle may still be debatable, but one thing is clear: the realization of such basic rights will not be understood without understanding the operation of the party's leadership.

CONCLUSIONS AND IMPLICATIONS

How the CCP leads and how democratic centralism operates are crucial in Chinese constitutional studies. This is not just because it defines what power that other state apparatuses may enjoy (content). It is also because the CCP, as the ultimate decision maker, decides which questions shall be decided by it (jurisdiction) and when it intervenes (timing). It can also review its own previous decisions and make changes without clear constitutional constraints. When it comes to the CCP's relationship with other state apparatuses, the question is the extent to which the party has allowed them to share part of the mission, but this allocation is a matter of policy rather than law: the party can review and reallocate power as the situation demands. While the party allows and indeed must delegate work to other state apparatuses in such a vast country, it retains the final power and remains the final arbiter to all problems that arise and all disputes that it deems important. This shall hold true for various state apparatuses; the division of labor is simply related to the specific nature of the state apparatuses, be it congress or court.

That said, there is a dynamic between the party and other state apparatuses. Because there is no clear line of division of labor, there must be constant assertions of power, and very likely they would be launched under the banner of the party. In addition, because there is no constant or permanent dispute resolution institution or procedure, it is unrealistic to expect the party to solve all the disputes in a timely manner. Of course, once the party finds that some developments have gone too far, it will step in firmly. Nonetheless, there is ample room for other state apparatuses to develop, and the changing nature of this space defines the pattern of constitutional development in reform-era China. The same rationale is also applied in the development of basic rights.

We see here three patterns. First, the party's leadership is absolute; there may be a division of labor but no division of power. Second, absolute leadership does not mean absolute control; instead, there remains room for innovation, development, and power advancement for other state apparatuses and citizens' rights. This occurs because either the party's own interests so require, or it lacks capacity for effective control as a result of the difficulties inherent in principal-agent relationships. Third, the party retains the final say on issues that it regards as crucial and can always rectify some developments. These patterns allow us to understand the dynamic and even contradictory developments in these areas. On the one hand, there is significant development of the power of the state apparatuses and expansion of citizens' basic rights. On the other hand, the brutal repression and strict restriction of certain activists and behaviors in certain areas has persisted. From the perspective of the party's leadership, China's continued persecution of political dissidents and recent judicial innovation and the increasing political status of the people's congresses are reconcilable; they are just the different sides of China's constitutional development.

In fact, the issues discussed in this chapter are just examples of these broader patterns. The framework is helpful in understanding other constitutional issues, such as the relationships between the party and the military; between the party and the state administration, that is, the State Council,[8] and between the party and business or capitalism (McGregor 2011). It may also be illuminating to help understand the future trajectories of China's constitutional development and even the relationship between the center and Hong Kong, a specialized administrative region that the party vows to govern under the principle "one country two systems."

[8] Cf. Zheng (1997: 191–254).

For example, the local politics surrounding the competition for the position of chief executive officer in 2012 were overshadowed by the intentions of Beijing, or the party. Given how deeply and pervasively the party's leadership has permeated into all these important constitutional areas, it is an understatement to claim that it is first and foremost the foundation of the living constitution in China.

Using democratic centralism to deal with the relationship between the party and state apparatuses, among various state apparatuses, and between the central and the local has left them in an unstable situation. The current arrangement, with highly centralized power, entails tremendous costs in terms of governance, which could be dangerous or disastrous. Scholars have already suggested some ways to limit the power of the party, such as empowering the NPC, invigorating elections, expanding constitutional supervision, and strengthening judicial independence (Nathan 1996: 43–57). From the perspective of a living constitution, this chapter suggests a similar but significantly different option: A major way to improve China's constitutionalism lies in the juridification of the party's leadership.[9] The limit of the party's leadership should be legally delineated and implemented, and the current division of labor between the party and other state apparatuses should be transformed into division of power in a constitutional sense. Of course, this will not happen until the party realizes that it is in its own best interests, in this changing socioeconomic and political environment, to introduce or reluctantly "accept" such a constitutional reform. But it will enhance the possibility of effective commitment on the part of the party (North and Weingast 1989: 803–32).

REFERENCES

Backer, Larry. 2012. "A Constitutional Court for China within the Chinese Communist Party: Scientific Development and the Institutional Role of the CCP." Available at http://papers.ssrn.com/sol3/papers.cfm?abstract_id=1308598. Accessed March 12, 2012.

Cai Hongbin and Daniel Treisman. 2006. "Did Government Decentralization Cause China's Economic Miracle?" *World Politics* 58: 505–35.

Central Committee of the CPC. 1986. *Zhonggong zhongyang guanyu quandang bixu jianjue weihu shehuizhiyi fazhi de tongzhi (The Notice on that the Party must Firmly Support the Socialist Rule by Law)*. Available at http://news.rednet.cn/c/2008/04/19/1488274.htm?COLLCC=2428976617 and accessed January 30, 2012.

Chen Duanhong. 2008. "On China's Constitution as the Higher Law and Fundamental Law of China." *Zhongwai faxue (Peking University Law Journal)* 20(4): 485–511.

Cheng Li and Lynn White. 2006. "The Sixteenth Central Committee of the Chinese Communist Party: Emerging Patterns of Power Sharing," in Lowell Dittmer and Liu Guoli, eds., *China's Deep Reform*. Lanham, MD: Rowman and Littlefield, 2006, pp. 81–118.

Cheung, Anne S. Y. 2004. "In Search of a Theory of Cult and Freedom of Religion in China: The Case of Falun Gong." *Pacific Rim Law and Policy Journal* 13: 1–30.

Cho, Young Nam. 2008. *Local People's Congresses in China: Development and Transition*. New York: Cambridge University Press.

[9] See e.g., Larry Backer (2012).

Clarke, Donald C. 2010. "New Approaches to the Study of Political Order in China." *Modern China* 36: 87–99.
Clarke, Donald C. 2011. China's Jasmine Crackdown and the Legal System. *East Asia Forum* (26 May 2011). Available at http://www.eastasiaforum.org/2011/05/26/china-s-jasmine-crackdown-and-the-legal-system/. Accessed January 30, 2012.
Cohen, Jerome A. 1978. "China's Changing Constitution." *The China Quarterly* 76: 839.
Cohen, Jerome A. 2011. "Absolute Power: Ai Weiwei's Detention Shows Yet Again the Ills of a Police Authority Unchecked by the Law." *South China Morning Post*, April 12, 2011. Available at http://www.cfr.org/china/absolute-power/p24648 (visited 14 August 2013).
Deng Xiaoping. 1994. *Deng Xiaoping wenxuan (Selected works of Deng Xiaoping)*, vol. 2. Beijing: Renmin chubanshe.
Dowdle, Michael W. 1997. "The Constitutional Development and Operations of the National People's Congress." *Columbia Journal of Asian Law* 11: 1–125.
Dowdle, Michael W. 2002. "Of Parliaments, Pragmatism, and the Dynamics of Constitutional Development: The Curious Case of China." *New York University Journal of International Law and Politics* 25: 2.
Fu Hualing and Richard Cullen. 2008. "Weiquan (rights protection) Lawyering in an Authoritarian State: Building a Culture of Public-Interest Lawyering." *The China Journal* 59: 111–28.
Fu Yulin and Randall Peerenboom. 2010. "A New Analytic Framework for Understanding and Promoting Judicial Independence in China," in Randall Peerenboom, ed., *Judicial Independence in China*. New York: Cambridge University Press, 95–133.
Ginsburg, Tom and Tamir Moustafa (eds.). 2008. *Rule by Law: The Politics of Courts in Authoritarian Regimes*. Cambridge: Cambridge University Press.
Hamrin, Carol L. 1992. "The Party Leadership System," in *Bureaucracy, Politics, and Decision Making in Post-Mao China*. Kenneth G. Lieberthal and David M. Lampton, eds., Berkeley: University of California Press, 97–101.
Hand, Keith J. 2009. "Citizens Engage the Constitution: The Sun Zhigang Incident and Constitutional Review Proposals in the People's Republic of China," in Stephanie Balme and Michael Dowdle, eds., *Building Constitutionalism in China*. New York: Palgrave Macmillan, pp. 221–42.
Hart, H. L. A. 1961. *The Concept of Law*. Oxford: Clarendon Press.
He Xin. 2007. "Why Do They Not Take the Disputes? Law, Power, Politics in the Decision-Making of Chinese Courts." *International Journal of Law in Context* 3: 203–25.
He Xin. 2009. "Administrative Law as a Mechanism for Political Control in Contemporary China," in Stephanie Balme and Michael Dowdle, eds., *Building Constitutionalism in China*. New York: Palgrave Macmillan, pp. 143–62.
He Xin. 2009. "Enforcing Commercial Judgments in the Pearl River Delta of China." *American Journal of Comparative Law* 59: 419–56.
He Xin. 2011. "Debt Collection in Less Developed Areas of China: An Empirical Study from Shaanxi Province." *The China Quarterly* 206: 253–75.
He Xin. 2012. "Blackhole of Responsibility: The Role of the Adjudication Committee in a Chinese Court." *Law & Society Review* 46: 681–712.
He Xin. 2013. "Judicial Innovation and Local Politics." *The China Journal* 69: 1–23.
Jiang Shigon. 2010. "Written and Unwritten Constitutions: A New Approach to the Study Constitutional Government in China." *Modern China* 36: 12–46.
Jones, William C. 1985. "The Constitution of the People's Republic of China." *Washington University Law Quarterly* 63: 710.
Kellogg, Thomas E. 2007. " 'Courageous Explorers'?: Education Litigation and Judicial Innovation in China." *Harvard Human Rights Journal* 20: 141–88.

Kellogg, Thomas E. 2009. "Constitutionalism with Chinese Characteristics? Constitutional Development and Civil Litigation in China." *International Journal of Constitutional Law* 7: 215–46.

Lin Feng. 2000. *Constitutional Law of the PRC*. Hong Kong: Sweet and Maxwell.

Mao Tse-Tung. 1977. *Selected Works of Mao Tse-tung*, vol. 5. Beijing: Foreign Languages Press.

McGregor, Richard. 2011. *The Party*. New York and London: Penguin Books.

Mingpao News. 2011. "Bo Xilai: Liu changwei chen Chongqing changhong" (Bo Xilai said six politburo standing committee members support the revolutionary ideology." *Mingpao News* 23 Dec 2011.

Nathan, Andrew J. 1996. "China's Constitutional Option." *Journal of Democracy* 7: 43–57.

North, Douglass C. and Barry R. Weingast. 1989. "Constitutions and Commitment: The Evolution of Institutional Governing Public Choice in Seventeenth-Century England." *The Journal of Economic History* 49: 803–32.

O'Brien, Kevin J. 1990. *Reform without Liberalization: China's National People's Congress and the Politics of Institutional Change*. Cambridge: Cambridge University Press.

O'Brien, Kevin J. 2010. "How Authoritarian Rule Works." *Modern China* 36: 84.

Oliver, Blanchard and Andrew Shleifer. 2001. "Federalism with and without Political Centralization: China vs. Russia." *IMF Staff Papers* 48: 171–9.

Peerenboom, Randall. 2009. "More Law, Less Courts: Legalized Governance, Judicialization, and Dejudicialization in China," in T. Ginsburg and A. Chen, eds., *Administrative Law and Governance in Asia*. New York: Routledge, p. 197.

Peerenboom, Randall. 2010. "Introduction," in Randall Peerenboom, ed., *Judicial Independence in China*. New York: Cambridge University Press, p. 15.

Peerenboom, Randall and He Xin. 2009. "Dispute Resolution in China: Patterns, Causes and Prognosis." *East Asia Law Review* 4: 1–61.

Peng Zhen. 1982. "Bujin yao kao dang de zhengce, erqie yao yi fa ban shi" ("Not Only Follow Party Principles, Also Work According to the Law"). Available at http://cpc.people.com.cn/GB/69112/99985/100003/9812391.html. Accessed January 30, 2012.

Peng Zhen. 1983. "Zai zhongyang zhengfa weiyuanhui kuoda huiyi shang de jianghua." Speech given at the Enlarged Meeting of the CCP Politburo, February 26, 1983.

Pils, Eva. 2009. "Rights Activism in China: The Case of Lawyer Gao Zhisheng," in Stephanie Balme and Michael Dowdle, eds., *Building Constitutionalism in China*. New York: Palgrave Macmillan, pp. 243–60.

Pils, Eva. 2011. *Disappearing Lawyers in China*. Presented at the Conference on China's Criminal Justice System, Chinese University of Hong Kong, May 2011.

Qian Yingyi and Barry R. Weingast. 1997. "Federalism as a Commitment to Market Incentives." *Journal of Economic Perspectives* 11: 83–92.

Sharlet, Robert. 1977. "Stalinism and Soviet Legal Culture," in Robert C. Tucker, ed., *Stalinism: Essays in Historical Interpretation*. New York: Norton, pp. 155–79.

Shen Kui. 2003. "Is It the Beginning of the Era of the Rule of the Constitution? Reinterpreting China's 'First Constitutional Case'." *Pacific Rim Law and Policy Journal* 12: 199–231.

Shirk, Susan L. 1992. "The Chinese Political System and the Political Strategy of Economic Reform," in Kenneth G. Lieberthal and David M. Lampton, eds., *Bureaucracy, Politics, and Decision Making in Post-Mao China*. Berkeley: University of California Press, pp. 59–94.

Shirk, Susan L. 1993. *The Political Logic of Economic Reform in China*. Berkeley: University of California Press.

Shue, Vivienne. 1988. *The Reach of the State*. Stanford, CA: Stanford University Press.

Su Yang and He Xin. 2010. "Street as Courtroom: State Accommodation of Social Conflicts in South China." *Law and Society Review* 44: 157–84.

Tanner, Murray S. 1994. "Organizations and Politics in China's Post-Mao Law-Making System," in 5. Pittman B. Potter, ed., *Domestic Law Reforms in Post-Mao China*. Armonk, NY: M. E. Sharpe, p. 74.

Vogel, Ezra F. 2011. *Deng Xiaoping and the Transformation of China*. Cambridge, MA: Belknap Press of Harvard University Press.

Wang Shaoguang. 1995. "The Politics of Private Time Changing Leisure Patters in Urban China," in Deborah S. Davis, Richard Kraus, Barry Naughton, and Elizabeth J. Perry, eds., *Urban Spaces in Contemporary China: The Potential for Autonomy and Community in Post-Mao China*. New York: Cambridge University Press, pp. 149–72.

Wang Shaoguang. 2008. "Changing Models of China's Policy Agenda Setting." *Modern China* 34: 56–87.

Xia Ming. 2008. *The People's Congresses and Governance in China: Toward a Network Mode of Governance*. London: Routledge.

Xie Qingkui et al. 1998. *Zhongguo difang zhengfu tizhi gailun (General Outline of Chinese Local Government Structure)*. Beijing: Zhongguo guangbo dianshi chubanshe.

Yu Xiaohong. 2009. *Rise of Local Courts in China: Judicial Hierarchy, Institutional Adaptation and Regime Resilience*. Conference paper presented at China's Changing Courts, Columbia University Law School.

Zhang Liang (comp.) and Andrew J. Nathan and Perry Link (eds.). 2001. *The Tiananmen Papers*. London: Little, Brown and Co.

Zheng Shiping. 1997. *Party vs. State in Post 1949 China*. New York: Cambridge University Press.

Zheng Yongnian. 2007. "China's De Facto Federalism," in He Baogang, Brian Galligan, and Takashi Inoguchi, eds., *Federalism in Asia*. London: Cheltenham, pp. 213–41.

Zhou Li'an. 2008. *Zhuanxing zhong de difang zhengfu (Local Governments in Transition)*. Shanghai: Shanghai renmin chubanshe.

Zhou Xueguang. 2010. "The Institutional Logic of Collusion among Local Governments in China." *Modern China* 36: 47–78.

Zhu Suli. 2004. "The Relationship Between the Center and the Locality: Rereading 'On the Ten Major Relationships'," in Zhu Suli, ed., *Daolu tongxiang chengshi: zhuanxing Zhongguo de fazhi (Roads to the City: the Legal System in Transition China)*. Beijing: Falü chubanshe, pp. 45–83.

Index

Made in the USA
Coppell, TX
15 December 2019

13037400R00155